Piano & Keyboard
ALL-IN-ONE

FOR DUMMIES®
A Wiley Brand

by Holly Day, Jerry Kovarsky, Blake Neely,
David Pearl, and Michael Pilhofer

Piano & Keyboard All-In-One For Dummies®

Published by:
John Wiley & Sons, Inc.,
111 River Street,
Hoboken, NJ 07030-5774,
www.wiley.com

For general information on our other products and services, please contact our Customer Care Department within the U.S. at 877-762-2974, outside the U.S. at 317-572-3993, or fax 317-572-4002. For technical support, please visit www.wiley.com/techsupport.

Wiley publishes in a variety of print and electronic formats and by print-on-demand. Some material included with standard print versions of this book may not be included in e-books or in print-on-demand. If this book refers to media such as a CD or DVD that is not included in the version you purchased, you may download this material at http://booksupport.wiley.com. For more information about Wiley products, visit www.wiley.com.

Library of Congress Control Number: 2013956854

ISBN 978-1-118-83742-9 (pbk); ISBN 978-1-118-83756-6 (ePub); ISBN 978-1-118-83744-3 (ePDF)

Manufactured in the United States of America

10 9 8 7 6 5 4 3 2 1

Contents at a Glance

Introduction *1*

Book I: Piano & Keyboard 101 .... *5*

Chapter 1: Warming Up to the Piano and Keyboard 7
Chapter 2: Looking at the Different Keyboard Options 21
Chapter 3: Choosing and Buying Your Keyboard 41
Chapter 4: The Setup and Care of Your Instrument 63
Chapter 5: Getting Comfy at the Keyboard 81

Book II: Understanding Theory and the Language of Music *97*

Chapter 1: Looking at Notes and Beats 99
Chapter 2: Stopping for a Rest 109
Chapter 3: Tempo, Measures, and Time Signatures 115
Chapter 4: Navigating Sheet Music 125
Chapter 5: Varying Beats and Rhythms 137

Book III: Beginning to Play *153*

Chapter 1: Playing a Melody 155
Chapter 2: Working with Scales 171
Chapter 3: Adding the Left Hand 187
Chapter 4: Examining Form: Melody, Harmony, and Song Form 209
Chapter 5: Keys, Key Signatures, and the Circle of Fifths 235
Chapter 6: Building Chords to Accompany Melodies 257

Book IV: Refining Your Technique and Exploring Styles *281*

Chapter 1: Adding Effects and Flair to Your Piano Playing 283
Chapter 2: Getting into the Groove 305
Chapter 3: Going Classical 325
Chapter 4: Perusing Popular Genres and Forms 337

Book V: Exercises: Practice, Practice, Practice 357

Chapter 1: Developing Hand Technique 359
Chapter 2: Extending Your Scales...387
Chapter 3: Improving Finger Coordination and Footwork 409
Chapter 4: Jumping Across the Keyboard..429
Chapter 5: Exercising with Arpeggios and Alternating Hands..............443
Chapter 6: Stepping Up to Octaves and Chord Progressions 463

Book VI: Exploring Electronic Keyboard Technology 479

Chapter 1: Choosing Sounds and Effects...481
Chapter 2: Adding Accompaniment, Rhythm Patterns, and Arpeggiation............499
Chapter 3: Recording and Editing Your Sounds 525
Chapter 4: Using Onboard Learning Systems 551
Chapter 5: Playing Along with Recordings and Using Music Software 565

Appendix: Accessing the Audio Tracks 593

Index 601

Table of Contents

Introduction 1

About This Book 1
Foolish Assumptions 2
Icons Used in This Book 3
Beyond the Book 3
Where to Go from Here 4

Book I: Piano & Keyboard 101 5

Chapter 1: Warming Up to the Piano and Keyboard 7

What's So Special About the Piano? 7
    Advantages to playing the piano 8
    Advantages to learning music at the piano 8
    A skill and an art 9
Why People Learn to Play the Piano (and Why They Often Quit) 9
Getting to Know the Piano as an Instrument 11
Understanding the Language of Music 12
    Developing an ear for horizontal and vertical music 13
    Getting to know musical forms and styles 13
The Best Way to Play 14
What You Already Know About Playing the Piano 14
Electronic Keyboards and other Keyboard Instruments 15
    Examining keyboard designs throughout the years 15
    Touching on key weight 16
    Join the family: Grouping keyboards 16
Making the Most of Your Keyboard's Basic Features 17
    Working with sounds 17
    Exploring effects 18
    Getting into automatic playing features 18
Delving into More Advanced Digital Features 19
    Stepping into the virtual recording studio 19
    Shaping the sounds you play 19
    Checking out the computer connection 19
Practicing with and without Help 20

Chapter 2: Looking at the Different Keyboard Options 21

    Acoustic Pianos 22
        Lids 24
        String layout 24
        Keys, hammers, and strings 24
    Electro-Mechanical Keyboards 25
    Electronic Keyboards..28
        Combo organs 28
        Synthesizers 29
        Portable keyboards 31
        Workstations 32
        Arrangers 32
        Controller keyboards 33
    Appreciating How Digital Keyboards Make So Many Sounds..................34
    Considering Key Feel and Response 35
        Touch sensitivity 35
        Key weight 37
    Paying Attention to Polyphony...38

Chapter 3: Choosing and Buying Your Keyboard 41

    First Things First: Acoustic or Electric (or Both)? 42
        Pros and cons of acoustic keyboards 42
        Pros and cons of digital keyboards 43
    Looking At What's Important for the Beginner...................................45
    Playing Well With Others and Alone 46
        Going solo 47
        Accompanying vocalists 47
        Performing classical music with others...........................48
        Jamming in a pop, rock, or jazz band 48
    Picking the Perfect Acoustic Piano 49
        Taking location into account..49
        Getting all the pedals you deserve 50
        Finding good buys and avoiding scams 50
        If you've heard one, you haven't heard them all 51
        Looking at specific piano brands....................................51
    Selecting a Digital Keyboard That Lasts 52
        Digital pianos and organs 53
        Arrangers 53
        Stage pianos..53
        Workstations 54
        Synthesizers 54
        Avoiding obsolescence 54
        Knowing the digital features you want............................55
        Browsing some specific keyboard brands........................56
    Before You Drive It Off the Lot: Sealing the Deal...............................57
        Take it for a spin 57
        Love it and leave it...58

Never pay the sticker price 58
Shopping online 59
The MIDI Places You Can Go.. 59
A mini MIDI primer 60
Keyboard to computer.. 60
Keyboard to keyboard 61
MIDI and music notation.. 61

Chapter 4: The Setup and Care of Your Instrument **63**
Unboxing Your New Keyboard 63
Providing a Good Place to Put It.. 65
Making It Shine.. 66
Calling In a Pro for Tuning, Check-Ups, and Serious Repairs 67
Tuning pianos: Leave it to the experts............................... 68
Keeping digital keyboards happy 69
Dealing with serious problems 69
Setting Up Your Keyboard.. 71
Hook Me Up: Keyboard Connections 71
Making the electrical connection..................................... 72
Firing up your keyboard 72
Working with headphones.. 73
Connecting to external speakers and amps 74
Protecting Your Investment: Care and Upkeep 77
Avoiding temperature extremes 77
Combating dust with a keyboard cover............................. 77
Cleaning the keys and case... 78
Moving from place to place 78
Solving Minor Technical Problems 79

Chapter 5: Getting Comfy at the Keyboard **81**
Blake's E-Z Key Finder... 81
The white keys 82
The black keys — sharps and flats 84
What Your Parents Never Told You About Posture 85
To sit or not to sit... 85
Chairs versus benches 86
Stands and racks 89
It's All in the Hands 90
Arch those hands and fingers 90
Fingering 91
When to give your hands and fingers a rest....................... 92
Pedal Power: Getting Your Feet in on the Action 93
Piano pedals 93
Digital keyboard pedals 94

Book II: Understanding Theory and the Language of Music........ 97

Chapter 1: Looking at Notes and Beats 99

Meeting the Beat.. 100
Recognizing Notes and Note Values....................................... 101
Examining the notes and their components 101
Looking at note values 103
Whole notes... 103
Half notes 104
Quarter notes 104
Eighth notes and beyond 105
Extending Notes with Dots and Ties 106
Using dots to increase a note's value............................. 106
Adding notes together with ties...................................... 107
Mixing All the Note Values Together 107

Chapter 2: Stopping for a Rest 109

Getting to Know the Rests... 109
Whole and half rests 110
Quarter and eighth rests and beyond 111
Dotted rests 113
Practicing Beats with Notes and Rests 113

Chapter 3: Tempo, Measures, and Time Signatures 115

Playing Fast and Slow: Tempo 115
Grouping Beats into Measures... 116
Counting Out Common Time Signatures 118
Common time: 4/4 meter 119
Waltz time: 3/4 meter 120
March time: 2/4 meter 121
6/8 time... 122

Chapter 4: Navigating Sheet Music 125

Meeting the Staff, Clefs, and Notes.. 125
The treble clef 126
The bass clef.. 127
The grand staff and ledger lines 127
Climbing beyond the staff.. 129
An octave above, an octave below 129
Identifying Half Steps, Whole Steps, and Accidentals on the Staff........ 130
Working with half steps 131
Taking whole steps 132
Changing pitch with accidentals 133
Musical Punctuation: Bar Lines 136

Chapter 5: Varying Beats and Rhythms **137**

Getting a Jump on the Start: Pickup Beats and Measures..................137
Adding Time to Your Notes with Ties and Dots...................................138
Linking notes using ties...139
Extending notes using dots 139
Playing Offbeat Rhythms 142
Triplets love chocolate...142
Swing and shuffle time 143
Syncopation...145
Playing Songs with Challenging Rhythms 146

Book III: Beginning to Play.. *153*

Chapter 1: Playing a Melody **155**

Let Your Fingers Do the Walking...155
Positions, Everyone!..156
C position...157
G position...161
Shifting your hand position as you play 163
Cross Your Fingers and Hope It Works..163
Crossing over your thumb...164
Passing your thumb under 165
Playing Melodies in the Right Hand 166

Chapter 2: Working with Scales **171**

Building a Scale, Step-by-Step 172
Introducing Major Scales..173
Understanding major scales..173
Why sharps and flats are involved 174
Major scale degrees..176
Trying a major scale exercise..177
Introducing Minor Scales..177
Natural minor scales 178
Harmonic minor scales 180
Melodic minor scales 180
Trying minor scale exercises 181
Checking Out Blues Scales 182
Playing Songs Made of Scales 184

Chapter 3: Adding the Left Hand **187**

Exploring the Keyboard's West Side..187
Moving into position 188
Getting used to the new neighborhood 188
Left-Hand Melodies...190

South-Paw Scales 192
    C, G, and F major... 192
    A, E, and D natural minor.. 193
    A harmonic and melodic minor 193
Accompaniment Patterns 194
    Three-note patterns.. 194
    Four-note patterns.. 196
Adding the Left Hand to the Right Hand.. 198
    Sharing the melody in both hands.. 199
    Melody plus one note.. 200
    Melody plus three-note accompaniment pattern.............................. 200
    Melody in unison octaves... 201
Playing Songs with Both Hands 203

Chapter 4: Examining Form: Melody, Harmony, and Song Form 209

Shaping the Melody... 210
Measuring Melodic Intervals.. 212
    Interval shorthand.. 213
    Seconds.. 214
    Thirds... 215
    Fourths and fifths... 217
    Sixths and sevenths.. 219
    Octaves... 220
Combining Notes for Harmonic Intervals.. 220
    Playing two notes together... 221
    Adding intervals to the melody.. 221
    Harmonizing with the left hand... 223
Working with Musical Phrases and Periods... 225
Linking Musical Parts to Create Forms... 226
    One-part form (A) 227
    Binary form (AB).. 227
    Three-part form (ABA) 227
    Arch form (ABCBA) 228
Playing Songs with More Harmony 228

Chapter 5: Keys, Key Signatures, and the Circle of Fifths. 235

Home Sweet Home Key.. 235
    A whole ring of keys 236
    Using keys to play music 238
    Reading key signatures 238
The Circle of Fifths 240
    Key signatures with sharps 241
    Key signatures with flats.. 242
    Leaving and returning to the home key... 243
    Finding minor key signatures and relative minors 244

Reviewing All the Key Signatures 245
    C major and A natural minor 246
    G major and E natural minor 246
    D major and B natural minor 247
    A major and F sharp natural minor 248
    E major and C sharp natural minor 248
    B/C flat major and G sharp/A flat natural minor 249
    F sharp/G flat major and D sharp/E flat natural minor 250
    C sharp major/D flat and A sharp/B flat natural minor 251
    A flat major and F natural minor 251
    E flat major and C natural minor 252
    B flat major and G natural minor 252
    F major and D natural minor 253
Playing Songs with Key Signatures..253

Chapter 6: Building Chords to Accompany Melodies 257
The Anatomy of a Triad...258
Starting Out with Major Chords..259
Branching Out with Minor Chords 260
Exploring Other Types of Chords..260
    Tweaking the fifth: Augmented and diminished chords..............261
    Waiting for resolution: Suspended chords 262
Adding the Seventh for Four-Note Chords 264
Reading Chord Symbols...265
Relating Chords to a Scale or Key Signature.............................268
    Recognizing the major scale chord tones.............................268
    Trying a few common chord progressions............................269
Rearranging the Order of the Notes: Chord Inversions.............270
    The three triad inversions 270
    Three-note chords in your left hand 272
    Two-handed chords in a pianistic style................................273
Playing Songs with Chords 274

Book IV: Refining Your Technique and Exploring Styles.. 281

Chapter 1: Adding Effects and Flair to Your Piano Playing 283
Dynamically Speaking 283
    Starting with basic volume changes.....................................284
    Widening the range..284
    Making gradual shifts in volume 285
Articulate the Positive 286
    Interpreting articulation symbols...286
    The power of articulation 288

Control the Tempo 288
Pedal Power.. 289
Using the damper pedal.................................. 290
Hard facts on soft-pedaling............................. 291
The pedal in the middle 292
Touching on Grace Notes 292
Just Trillin'... 294
Don't Miss the Gliss 295
Trembling Tremolos 297
Dressing Up Your Songs 299

Chapter 2: Getting into the Groove 305

Great Left-Hand Accompaniment Patterns 305
Fixed and broken chords 306
Chord picking 308
Octave hammering... 308
Bouncy rock patterns 310
Melodic bass lines 313
Applying Great Intros and Finales 315
The big entrance 317
Exit, stage left 320
Playing Songs with Left-Hand Grooves 322

Chapter 3: Going Classical 325

Counterpoint as a Classical Revelation 327
Sussing Out the Sonata 328
Starting with the exposition 328
Moving on to something new: Development 329
Taking a rest with recapitulation..................... 330
Rounding Up the Rondo... 331
Figuring Out the Fugue... 332
Combining Forms into a Symphony 333
Observing Other Classical Forms 334
Concerto.. 334
Duet 335
Etude... 335
Fantasia 335

Chapter 4: Perusing Popular Genres and Forms............. 337

Feeling the Blues... 337
12-bar blues 338
8-bar blues 339
16-bar blues 339
24-bar blues 340
32-bar blues ballads and country 340

Playing the blues 341

12-bar ditties 342

Changing it up 343

Having Fun with Rock and Pop 344

Playing rock and pop songs 346

Pop! Goes the Piano 347

Popular picks 347

Topping the charts 347

A Little Bit Country 348

Country-style cooking 348

Finger-pickin' good 349

Improvising with Jazz 350

Jazzing it up 350

It's up to you 351

Substituting chords 352

Soul Searching 353

Saving your soul 354

Motown sounds 354

Funky sounds goin' round 356

Book V: Exercises: Practice, Practice, Practice 357

Chapter 1: Developing Hand Technique 359

Passing Over and Crossing Under 359

One under two, two over one 360

One under three, three over one 361

One under four, four over one 362

Extending scales with crossovers and pass-unders 363

Performance piece: Aria from La Cenerentola 366

Playing Intervals 367

Playing seconds with different finger combinations 367

Playing thirds with different finger combinations 372

Playing fourths with finger combinations 376

Playing fifths, sixths, and sevenths 378

Performance piece: "Take Me Out to the Ballgame" 381

Playing Chords Without Tension 382

Chord relaxation 382

Voicing chords 384

Chapter 2: Extending Your Scales 387

The 12 Major, Harmonic Minor, and Melodic Minor Scales 387

C major, harmonic minor, melodic minor 388

G major, harmonic minor, melodic minor 389

D major, harmonic minor, melodic minor 390

A major, harmonic minor, melodic minor 391
E major, harmonic minor, melodic minor...................................... 392
B major, harmonic minor, melodic minor 393
F♯ major, harmonic minor, melodic minor.................................... 394
D♭ major, C♯ harmonic minor, C♯ melodic minor 395
A♭ major, harmonic minor, melodic minor.................................... 396
E♭ major, harmonic minor, melodic minor..................................... 397
B♭ major, harmonic minor, melodic minor..................................... 398
F major, harmonic minor, melodic minor 399
The Three Diminished Scales 399
Starting on C 400
Starting on D♭ 400
Starting on D 401
The Chromatic Scale 401
The 12 Blues Scales 402
C blues 402
G blues.. 402
D blues.. 402
A blues 403
E blues 403
B blues 403
F♯ blues 404
D♭ blues 404
A♭ blues 404
E♭ blues 405
B♭ blues 405
F blues 405
Gaining Greater Command of Scales... 406
Varied articulation.. 406
Varied rhythmic groupings... 407
Performance Piece: "Variations on 'Twinkle, Twinkle,
Little Star'" 408

Chapter 3: Improving Finger Coordination and Footwork.........409

Parallel Movement at the Octave 409
Parallel octave exercise #1 410
Parallel octave exercise #2 411
Parallel Movement at the Interval 412
Parallel sixths 412
Parallel tenths 413
Contrary Motion Away from the Center 414
Scalewise motion away from the center 414
Chromatic motion away from the center.. 415
Contrary Motion Toward the Center 416
Scalewise motion toward the center... 416
Patterns toward the center.. 417

Combination Movement Exercise..418
Performance Piece: "Turkey in the Straw".............................419
Using the Damper Pedal 420
Pedaling Chords...420
    Broken-chord pedaling..422
    Block-chord pedaling 423
Uniform Pedal Changes on One Line..424
Varied Pedal Changes on One Line 425
Pedaling for Effect 426
Sustaining as the Hands Move 427
Performance Piece: "Simple Gifts" 428

Chapter 4: Jumping Across the Keyboard 429
Jumping and Landing Accuracy..429
    Note-to-note jumps 430
    Note-to-chord jumps...431
    Chord-to-chord jumps..432
    Accents on the downbeat 433
    Accents on the upbeat 434
Jumping with Both Hands Together 434
    Two-hand parallel motion jumps...................................435
    Two-hand contrary motion jumps.................................436
Left-Hand Accompaniment Patterns 436
    Bass note-to-chord pattern in 4/4................................437
    Bass note-to-chord pattern in 3/4................................438
    Ragtime and stride pattern..439
    Waltz pattern..440
Performance Piece: "Lily Pad Rag" 441

Chapter 5: Exercising with Arpeggios and Alternating Hands 443
Finger Jumps 443
    Jumping thirds 444
    Jumping fourths 445
    Jumping fifths 446
The Arpeggiator..446
    Triad arpeggio exercise #1...447
    Triad arpeggio exercise #2...448
    Seventh-chord arpeggio exercise 449
Broken Chords 449
    Alberti bass exercise 450
    Guitar-style broken chord exercise..............................451
    Blues-style broken chord exercise...............................452
    Octave, extended broken chord exercise....................453
Performance Piece: "Harp Heaven"...454

Playing with Alternating Hands: Hand-to-Hand Scale Handoffs.............456
    Scale handoff exercise #1..456
    Scale handoff exercise #2..458
    Arpeggio handoff exercise #1..459
    Arpeggio handoff exercise #2..460
    Crossing over with the right hand......................................461
    Crossing over with the left hand.......................................462

Chapter 6: Stepping Up to Octaves and Chord Progressions.......463
    Opening Up to the Octave..463
        Octave scale exercise...464
        Octave interval exercise 465
    Octave Jumps..466
        Exercise with shorter jumps 466
        Exercise with longer jumps 467
        Broken octave exercise with wrist rotation 468
        Broken octave exercise with hand contraction
            and expansion...469
    Octave Chords 470
        Adding one inner note...470
        Adding two inner notes 471
    Performance Piece: "Schumann's Octave Workout".........................472
    Seventh Chord Progressions..473
        Seventh chord progressions exercise #1..............................473
        Seventh chord progressions exercise #2..............................474
    Chord Cadences, Familiar Patterns..475
    Extended Chord Progressions..477
        Extended major-key chord progression 477
        Extended minor-key chord progression 478

Book VI: Exploring Electronic Keyboard Technology..... 479

Chapter 1: Choosing Sounds and Effects.....................481
    First Things First: Understanding Some Important Terminology 482
        A sound by any other name: Recognizing the various terms 482
        MIDI: Defining GM/GM2 484
    Knowing and Using Effects:..485
    Meeting the Main Types of Effects 486
        Reverb 486
        Delay...488
        Chorus/flanging/phase shifting 488
        EQ..490
        Distortion..492
        Rotary speaker 493

Filter..493
Wah-wah and auto-wah 494
Choosing Effects for Each Type Of Sound..495
Piano-type and synth sounds 495
Guitar sounds 497
Other sounds..497

Chapter 2: Adding Accompaniment, Rhythm Patterns, and
Arpeggiation 499
Getting Your Groove On: Working with Onboard Drum Rhythms........500
Selecting a drum pattern...501
Starting the pattern playing...504
Digging into natural drum fills...505
Incorporating intros 506
Playing with Accompaniment 506
How auto-accompaniment works 507
Starting a pattern playing...507
Breaking down an accompaniment pattern 508
Feeding the band the chord changes: Chord triggering.............509
Mixing the sound of the band..512
Letting the Keyboard Make the Choices for You 514
Taking advantage of one-touch settings 514
Diving into the music database..515
Using Some Fancy Extras...516
Adding harmony to your melodies..516
Hitting the chord pads 517
Exploring Arpeggiation 517
Looking at some arp examples...518
Exploring More Arpeggiator Features...520
Extending the range..520
Changing the timing/speed..520
Getting into the swing of things 521
Making the notes shorter/longer 521
Hearing the notes being held along with the arp.....................521
Keeping the arp playing without holding the keys....................522
Adding variety with different patterns...................................522
Trying Out Some Different Sounds: Matching Sounds and Arp Patterns.......522
Adding Fun Sound and Effects Tweaks..523

Chapter 3: Recording and Editing Your Sounds 525
Audio Recording versus MIDI Recording 526
Recording with analog and digital audio 526
Making sense of MIDI recording...529
Capturing What You Hear As It Happens: One-Pass Recording 530
Tackling audio recording in one pass 531
Grabbing a one pass MIDI recording.....................................532

Recording Multitrack MIDI 533
Setting up your session..533
Recording the first track.....................................535
Adding more tracks 535
Refining Your MIDI Recordings...536
Fixing small mistakes..536
Mixing your MIDI song 540
Trying Some Common Sound Edits.....................................542
Varying the basic timbre (waveform) 543
Changing the brightness (filter)........................545
Adjusting the amp parameters (volume over time).....................546
Personalizing the touch response of a sound 547
Getting Your Song out of the Keyboard and into the World.................549

Chapter 4: Using Onboard Learning Systems **551**

Working with Built-In Songs 551
Selecting a song...552
Slowing down the tempo.....................................553
Turning off one of the parts (RH or LH)............554
Repeating small sections 554
Introducing Casio's Step-up Lesson System 555
Following the steps: Listen, watch, and remember.......................555
Getting started: Picking what to work on 556
Lesson 1: Listening and letting the teacher show you how 557
Lesson 2: Playing and watching the display for guidance............559
Lesson 3: Progressing from watch to remember 559
Turning off some of the helpers........................560
Playing the whole song yourself 562
Exploring Yamaha's Educational Suite Lesson System 562
Following the steps: Listening, waiting, your tempo,
and minus one 563
Starting off by deciding what to work on.........564

**Chapter 5: Playing Along with Recordings and Using
Music Software** **565**

Exploring the Advantages of Playing Along 566
Connecting an Audio Device to Your Keyboard to
Hear Both Together 567
Finding a line input and getting connected 567
No input? No worries: Moving forward with a mixer 569
Getting in Tune 570
Figuring Out a Song You Don't Know................................571
Training your ear by trial and error...................571
Listening to a phrase to learn it 572
Using your computer to help 573

The Computer Connection: Using Software to Enhance Your
Music-Making..575
How MIDI works: Explaining common MIDI messages..................575
Examining MIDI ports 577
Connecting Your Keyboard to Your Computer 578
Using a direct USB connection..579
Utilizing a MIDI interface...579
Working with drivers and plug-and-play..581
Hooking Up to Your iPad 584
Exploring Popular Types of Music Software 585
Sequencer/MIDI recorder 585
Educational/learning software 587
Music notation software 588
Digital sheet music 589
Additional instruments/sounds 589

Appendix: Accessing the Audio Tracks..........................*593*

Index..*601*

Introduction

Welcome to *Piano & Keyboard All-In-One For Dummies!* You hold in your hands a well-rounded compendium of tips and advice about playing piano and other keyboard instruments, including electronic keyboards.

If you've never seen or put your hands on a piano or keyboard, no problem. This book starts at the very beginning and walks you through everything you need to know to tame that beast and make it sing sweet music. You'll also have fun along the way. That's the whole idea.

Maybe you have a little experience — like, say, maybe you were "encouraged" to take piano lessons as a youngster but are just now actually becoming interested in playing as an adult. Or maybe you poke around on your grandma's upright, or you got a Casio keyboard for your last birthday, and you want to start taking your playing a little more seriously. You too are in the right place. Or perhaps you're not bad on piano but are thinking of digging in to your wallet to buy a fancy new synthesizer or arranger keyboard, but aren't sure you can deal with the complicated-looking technology. This book can help you, too.

Basically, there's a whole lot here for anyone interested in playing piano or keyboards or taking their playing to the next level.

About This Book

Piano & Keyboard All-In-One For Dummies covers a wide range of topics, ranging all the way from what a quarter note is and how to find middle C, to breaking down the 12-bar blues structure, to hooking your keyboard up to your music player so you can jam out to your favorite tunes on headphones.

The chapters in Book I focus on getting to know the instrument — how to find a good, affordable one, what to look for, how to maintain it, and basically how it works and the best ways to play it. Book II turns to the fundamentals of music itself, with chapters covering how music breaks down into notes and rests, how to read sheet music, and how to keep up with beats and rhythm. Book III brings all that together and introduces scales, melodies, harmonies, keys and key signatures, and chords.

Book IV starts getting into more fancy stuff, like how to add flair to your playing, how to turn your left hand into your favorite accompanist, and what defines different classical and pop music forms. It also offers great tips on playing all kinds of music on piano and keyboard. Book V is all about practice. As with anything, playing piano and keyboard do require dedication and repetition — it is, after all, the way to Carnegie Hall — but these chapters try to keep things as fun as possible while refining your skills. Book VI is all about electronic keyboards, how to choose one, how to find out what it can do and get the most out of it, and how to take advantage of its more complex features. The book finishes with a guide to the free online music tracks that are sprinkled throughout this book. Listening to these tracks can speed up your understanding and help sharpen your playing skills.

The book also contains an absolute ton of music. You'll have plenty — *plen-tee* — of songs and snippets to play and have fun with. And a lot of it is available for listening on the free online audio tracks.

Within this book, you may note that some web addresses break across two lines of text. If you're reading this book in print and want to visit one of these web pages, simply key in the web address exactly as it's noted in the text, pretending as though the line break doesn't exist. If you're reading this as an e-book, you've got it easy — just tap the web address to be taken directly to the web page.

Foolish Assumptions

This books makes a few assumptions about you, the reader:

- ✔ You like to listen to music and especially like the sound of piano and keyboard.

- ✔ When you hear someone play the piano, it sparks something in you. You say to yourself something like, "I wish I could play like that."

- ✔ You haven't had any piano lessons before, or you had some lessons at some point in your life, but you basically see yourself as a beginner. Either way, you'd like it all laid out and explained in a simple and easy-to-understand way.

- ✔ You have a piano or keyboard but aren't playing it as much as you want to and need some help getting to the music making.

- ✔ You don't have a piano or keyboard but are considering a purchase and would welcome help with the whole process. Most likely, your keyboard will have at least 25 black and white keys, may or may not plug into the wall, and will cost you as much as you're willing to part with.

- ✔ You like to discover things for yourself.

If any of these assumptions is true for you, you're reading the right book.

Icons Used in This Book

As you go through the chapters of this book, you'll find the following friendly icons scattered here and there. They're designed to draw your attention to different kinds of information, from helpful guidance to pleasant diversions.

Be sure to pay attention to anything that has this icon attached. As you may guess, it's something important that you shouldn't forget.

When you see this icon, you know that some handy-dandy information follows that can save you time, money, energy, and more.

There's an occasional step into the swamp of technical jargon or complex discussion, and this icon gives you fair warning. It's not essential stuff. Feel free to flip past it if you just don't care.

Pay attention to text featuring this icon. It can help you avoid mistakes and problems.

The audio examples that appear throughout the text bring a lot of the music in this book to life. When you see this icon, it means you can find an online audio track related to what you're reading about. You can find these tracks and clips at www.dummies.com/go/pianokeyboardaio.

Beyond the Book

In addition to the book content, you can find a free online Cheat Sheet that includes advice on building scales, modulating to a new key, achieving the right posture for playing, and getting to know the different types of electronic keyboards. Go to www.dummies.com/cheatsheet/pianokeyboardaio to access this handy reference material, and then print it out and keep it handy.

You can also access additional free articles that cover information that simply couldn't fit into the book. You'll find information on using fake books to expand your repertoire, gigging with others, implementing syncopation, and checking out practice exercises by some great composers. Check them out at www.dummies.com/extras/pianokeyboardaio.

Finally, www.dummies.com/go/pianokeyboardaio is home to the more than 150 audio tracks that accompany this book. Head there to listen to notes, scales, chords, songs, exercises, demonstrations of the sounds of instruments and various keyboard features, and much more.

Where to Go from Here

The book is organized into parts containing chapters that are grouped according to broad, related topics. But you sure don't have to read it from front to back — or in any particular order. The idea is that you can skim through the table of contents and pick and choose whatever's interesting to you, based on where you are currently in your musical journey. Then go directly to that section and get cracking.

Still, if you really want some tips about where to begin, here are a few: If you've never touched a piano before, definitely start with Book I. If looking at printed music gives you heart palpitations, you really should think about heading to Book II. If you're okay on the very basics, try Book III, where you gain knowledge of important piano-playing fundamentals and techniques. If you're not too bad at playing but would like to dig deeper into some particular styles, like rock, country, or jazz, head to Book IV. If you're pretty good but could use some terrific warmups to get your fingers even more limber (limberer?), try Book V. And if you've got your hot little hands on a smokin' new keyboard or synthesizer and want to delve into its possibilities, head on over to Book VI.

Bottom line: Every person's musical journey is unique. Wherever you start — or end up — the important thing is to have fun (and keep playing!).

Book I
Piano & Keyboard 101

getting started
with

piano & keyboard

Contents at a Glance

Chapter 1: Warming Up to the Piano and Keyboard. 7

What's So Special About the Piano?..7

Why People Learn to Play the Piano (and Why They Often Quit)...................9

Getting to Know the Piano as an Instrument 11

Understanding the Language of Music..12

The Best Way to Play..14

What You Already Know About Playing the Piano..14

Electronic Keyboards and other Keyboard Instruments..................................15

Making the Most of Your Keyboard's Basic Features.......................................17

Delving into More Advanced Digital Features...19

Practicing with and without Help...20

Chapter 2: Looking at the Different Keyboard Options 21

Acoustic Pianos..22

Electro-Mechanical Keyboards 25

Electronic Keyboards...28

Appreciating How Digital Keyboards Make So Many Sounds 34

Considering Key Feel and Response 35

Paying Attention to Polyphony 38

Chapter 3: Choosing and Buying Your Keyboard 41

First Things First: Acoustic or Electric (or Both)?...42

Looking At What's Important for the Beginner 45

Playing Well With Others and Alone 46

Picking the Perfect Acoustic Piano..49

Selecting a Digital Keyboard That Lasts 52

Before You Drive It Off the Lot: Sealing the Deal 57

The MIDI Places You Can Go...59

Chapter 4: The Setup and Care of Your Instrument 63

Unboxing Your New Keyboard 63

Providing a Good Place to Put It 65

Making It Shine 66

Calling In a Pro for Tuning, Check-Ups, and Serious Repairs.........................67

Setting Up Your Keyboard 71

Hook Me Up: Keyboard Connections 71

Protecting Your Investment: Care and Upkeep 77

Solving Minor Technical Problems...79

Chapter 5: Getting Comfy at the Keyboard 81

Blake's E-Z Key Finder 81

What Your Parents Never Told You About Posture 85

It's All in the Hands...90

Pedal Power: Getting Your Feet in on the Action..93

Chapter 1

Warming Up to the Piano and Keyboard

In This Chapter

▶ Getting acquainted with the piano and music

▶ Discovering what you may already know about playing piano

▶ Grasping the basic attributes of a keyboard

▶ Understanding the benefits of reading music

▶ Access the audio track at www.dummies.com/go/pianokeyboardaio/

The piano remains a very popular instrument, with the number of people who love the piano growing and its popularity spreading throughout the world. Even as the piano is treasured for its quality as an instrument, it also adapts itself to the changing times through technological advances.

The first half of this chapter helps you understand what makes the piano so unique and what's involved in learning to play it. You may find out that you know a lot more about music than you thought you did, even if you're a beginner. Beyond the familiar black and white keys, though, keyboards can be wildly different instruments, and looking at the front panels may not give you much of a clue as to what's inside. The second half of this chapter gives you an overview of what keyboards are and just what you can do with them.

What's So Special About the Piano?

Playing the piano involves the following fundamental musical tasks:

✔ Playing different pitches and melodies

✔ Controlling the attack and release of a note

✔ Playing different dynamics (relative loudness and softness)

But playing the piano is different from playing other instruments in some important respects, and the piano has several attributes that make it an ideal tool for learning and understanding music.

Advantages to playing the piano

The piano occupies a central position in the world of music. It's the gold standard of musical instruments, utilized by composers and arrangers and featured routinely in nearly all musical styles, in chamber groups, rock bands, and jazz trios. (Okay, not marching bands.) The following characteristics make the piano a unique instrument — in a great way:

- **You can play many different notes at the same time.** The fancy word for this is *polyphonic.*

- **It's a complete solo instrument.** You can play a complete song or other musical work without additional accompaniment or other help from your musical friends. That makes the piano satisfying and self-sufficient.

- **It's the perfect accompaniment.** You can accompany a singer, a choir, a dance class, a silent movie, your own opera, or your own soap opera, not to mention any other instrument.

- **You can play almost anything on the piano.** The piano has an unmatched repertoire of music. You name it, there's piano music for it.

Advantages to learning music at the piano

The piano is an ideal instrument for learning all about music, starting with the design of the keyboard. The notes are laid out before your very eyes in a clear, organized, and orderly way. Understanding and playing musical pitches is quite easy because the keyboard presents a clear visual image for your brain to process the way musical notes go up (higher pitch), down (lower pitch), or stay the same.

Each key on the keyboard produces a single, distinct pitch, and you can't beat that for simplicity. Not much skill is required to make a nice, musical sound. Compared with some other instruments (cello, violin, clarinet, trombone, trumpet, bassoon, oboe, and tuba), playing any key on the keyboard, no matter how high or low the pitch, is as easy as playing any other key.

Another advantage of the piano is that you can play chords and layer sounds. The keyboard makes it easy to play harmonies and immediately hear how a combination of notes sounds.

A skill and an art

After all is said and done, the reason playing piano is so special may be that it's an activity that invites your full participation and rewards you just as completely. It has its mental side and its physical side. It requires both creativity and discipline, and engaging your mind and body is deeply satisfying.

As you learn to read music and play the notes on the piano (or keyboard, for that matter), you create information loops from your brain throughout your body. The first loop is from your eyes to your brain, as you take in the notes on the page and process the information. In the second loop, your brain sends signals to your hands and fingers, telling them how and where to move. Your fingers start to develop a sense of what it feels like to move around the keyboard and use different kinds of touch to produce different results from the piano. A third loop is made as your ears hear the sound from the instrument and send information back to your brain for it to process: Did I play the right notes and rhythms? Did I play a note too loudly or softy? Does what I play sound musical, overall? All this information helps you to modify the signals you send throughout your body to improve the results.

This full-sensory experience is paired with an interpretive element, as your inner artist is at work. The notes and directions on the page can only go so far in describing how the music should sound, which is why two pianists playing the same piece will create noticeably different performances. Even two performances by the same pianist will come out differently. Playing the piano lets you be the decider when you make music: how fast, how slow, how much more, how much less, how many encores to give your audience.

The combination of executing skills and interpreting the music is something that happens each time you play. Even when you simply play what's written, your personal interpretation comes through. With the piano, you're a musician from day one.

Why People Learn to Play the Piano (and Why They Often Quit)

Many people start taking piano lessons as kids, when they don't have much say in the matter. But adults come to the piano for many reasons, including wanting to take it up again because it didn't stick the first time around, when they were kids. Following are some reasons you may want to learn or relearn to play piano:

✔ **You want to re-create your favorite songs and compositions.** When you play a piece of music on the piano, you bring that music to life. Written music is like a blueprint — a set of directions that tell you what notes to play and when and how to play them. It takes a performer to complete the process that starts in the composer's mind but is unfulfilled until the music reaches the listener's ear.

✔ **You like a challenge.** There's no doubt that getting to the intermediate and advanced levels of piano takes time, patience, and practice. Some people relish this challenge. Whatever your ambition, learning to play piano is a never-ending challenge given the wealth of material at all levels. Some people set goals for themselves — to learn a certain piece they want to be able to play, or to be able to play piano for others at a party or family gathering. There are plenty of rewards to be had along the way, and sticking with it pays off when you start playing your favorite songs or when you get the chance to play music with others. There's nothing like being able to say, "I'm with the band."

✔ **You want to be able to play music in almost any style.** Playing a pop song or a classical sonata on piano doesn't require a different set of notes; when you know how to read and play piano music, you can play classical, jazz, rock, country, folk, cabaret, Broadway show tunes, and more. If you can play piano, you can speak the universal language of music.

Unfortunately, failure to quickly reach any of these goals leads some to throw in the towel. It's important to be realistic with your timetable and your expectations as you begin learning piano. Here are some top reasons why people give up playing the piano; don't let yourself fall victim to them, too:

✔ **Frustration:** Learning to play the piano takes patience. Coordinating hands and fingers, reading music, and committing to practice, practice, practice are the refrain of musicians everywhere, but making it all fun is the goal of this book.

✔ **No time:** Getting yourself to a basic beginner level of piano doesn't require hours and hours of keyboard work every day. Regular practice sessions in which you can focus and learn comfortably do wonders for improvement.

✔ **Self-criticism:** No doubt you're your own worst critic, and nobody likes playing wrong notes. Short-circuit your inner critic by celebrating small achievements and show off to your friends and family along the way so they can support you.

Getting to Know the Piano as an Instrument

The first step in learning to play the piano is familiarizing yourself with your instrument. The piano is a complex and fascinating contraption, and the modern piano reflects hundreds of years of developments and improvements in design and sound.

A prospective buyer has plenty of options when approaching the piano market today. The two styles of acoustic piano, grand and upright, come in a variety of sizes and prices, and both produce sound in a similar way. Their hammer action design allows you to control the volume and tone quality through the speed and nuance of your touch as you press down a key and send a felt-covered wooden hammer to strike a string, or set of strings, inside the piano. The resonance of the string vibrating is amplified by the wooden soundboard, which is parallel to the strings.

The wide range of digital keyboards available today offers some attractive alternatives to acoustic pianos, even if they fall short of capturing the sound and feel of the real thing. Digital pianos use sampled sounds — of pianos, electric pianos, harpsichords, and organs, as well as other instruments and sound effects — that are stored as digital information. You play these sounds by pressing a key and hearing the sound amplified electronically. Digital keyboards (covered later in this chapter) put a greatly expanded library of sound at your fingertips. Other advantages of digital pianos and keyboards include greater portability and "silent" practicing with headphones.

The hybrid piano combines acoustic and digital technology and is another enticing option available today. Though expensive, these pianos are well on their way to fulfilling their promise to combine the best of both worlds.

Check out the rest of the chapters in Book I to find out more about all the keyboard instruments, compare styles and designs, prepare yourself to go piano or keyboard shopping, and find out how to care for your instrument at home.

The piano did not grow obsolete with the development of electronic instruments in the last 50 years. The piano is popular in both its old-fashioned acoustic version and all the newer versions that feature digital sound; automatic playing features; and recording, editing, and web-integration technology. In other words, pianos are the best of both worlds these days, and no one needs to compromise if they don't want to. The piano has adapted and changed with the times, yet it's still treasured for the fundamental things that haven't changed. It's still an ideal solo instrument to have at home, it's ready to be played whenever the mood strikes you, and its intuitive design satisfies both your fingers and your ears.

Understanding the Language of Music

Playing the piano or keyboard means reading music. The best thing to keep in mind is that, in a way, you already know the language. You've heard it, sung it, danced to it, and gone to beddy-bye to it your whole life. If you haven't read music before, think of it as assigning new names and concepts to things you already know and making connections from the new language to the language you've already learned aurally.

Reading music means reading pitches, rhythms, and other notational symbols invented to communicate music from composer to performer. See the table of contents to find the chapters in this book that cover these topics.

When you know how to read music, you can play most any song or other musical composition written at the beginner level, no matter the style of music.

Perhaps you can pick up simple melodies by ear and hunt and peck with a few fingers to play the notes, but eventually you're going to want to develop your skills more. Learning to read musical notation opens up a way to communicate so much about playing any type of keyboard. It allows you to read the examples in this book and others; to buy sheet music and songbooks of your favorite piano pieces, artists, and songs; and to tackle instructional courses.

Some forms of print music use what are called *chord symbols* to indicate notes that can be played beneath a melody. They're usually intended for guitar players to strum along, but the keyboardist can also use them to enhance playing. A form of print music called a *fake book* provides only a melody and chord symbols, so you need to know your chords to follow along with those.

Coordinating mind and body

At the heart of playing the piano is movement. The subtle movements required to play piano or keyboard may not be as big as those required of ballet or swimming, but they're numerous. As a result, playing piano involves lots of coordination, which is where practice comes into the picture.

Playing while you read involves counting, reading, and responding. You achieve a smooth choreography as you coordinate your mind and body and continually isolate and integrate your hands and fingers and the melody and the harmony. You may start by playing a melody in your right hand, adding a left-hand part when your right hand is secure, and adding facility as you go. Keep in mind that it's normal and necessary to progress by taking one step back and two steps forward.

Developing an ear for horizontal and vertical music

Among the challenges and rewards of learning piano are understanding and combining the melodic and harmonic elements of music. In a way, a music score is a kind of sound map in which proceeding from left to right represents the horizontal flow of music through time, and any one freeze-frame of the score shows the vertical combination of notes sounding together at that moment, from low to high. A piano player, like the conductor of an orchestra, controls these vertical and horizontal elements and the total content in the music, and expresses the complete musical picture, not just a single component. Melodies and scales represent the horizontal parts, and harmony represents the vertical part.

Getting to know musical forms and styles

Even the simplest melody, say a lullaby or a folk song, carries with it a musical form and a musical style. To describe its qualities is to define the form and style. For example, "Frere Jacques," a song you play in Book III Chapter 1, gets its form from the way each of its four phrases is repeated, doubling the length of the song. The simplicity of the melody and the repetition define the song's style as a nursery rhyme — perfect for teaching a child.

As you play the other songs in this book, you come to understand that form and style describe how the musical material is used. For example, when you play "Worried Man Blues" in Book III Chapter 5, you see that its opening phrase is repeated with different notes but the same rhythms in its second phrase. The third phrase is the same as the opening phrase, but it leads into a new phrase, the fourth and last one. These four phrases make up the melody to the song and have a form that can be expressed as ABAC, with each letter representing each phrase.

Rhythm plays a powerful role in defining musical style. Both the Mozart sonata and the country riff use musical ornaments (covered in Book IV Chapter 1), but the songs use them in completely different ways. The most noticeable difference is in the way the ornaments affect the rhythm. Popular music grew increasingly rhythmic in the 20th century and continues to grow and develop rhythmically more than harmonically or melodically. Jazz developed its own rhythmic language that was completely different from anything else that came before it.

The Best Way to Play

You get the best results when you're comfortable and enjoying yourself, so keep the following tips in mind:

- ✔ **Be comfortable.** Comfort starts with freedom of movement. Make sure you're physically and mentally at ease when you practice, and watch out for signs of fatigue and tension. Take a break when you need it.

- ✔ **Play what interests you.** Find the songs and sections that use material you find interesting and useful for meeting your piano goals.

- ✔ **Appreciate the small steps.** Remind yourself that your rewards will come at all levels but may not come every day.

- ✔ **A beginner can play good music.** There's plenty of good music published for piano players of all levels, including beginners.

What You Already Know About Playing the Piano

Even if you've never even touched a piano before, you'll be surprised at how many things you can do right away. You also may already know a few pertinent musical facts — and if you don't, you can master them right now.

- ✔ **You can play a pentatonic scale.**

  Go to your piano or keyboard and play a sequence of black keys, up, down, or both. You've just played a five-note scale with a fancy name: *pentatonic.* The next time your friends ask what you've been up to, tell them you've been practicing some pentatonic scales.

- ✔ **You know the note names used in music.**

  The seven note names used in music follow the letters of the alphabet from A through G. When you play the white keys, you play notes like C, F, A, and D. And as you'll find out in later chapters, you add either "sharp" or "flat" to those letters to name the black keys.

- ✔ **You can name the two clefs used in reading piano music.**

  You read music for piano using the treble clef and the bass clef. Most of the time, your right hand plays notes in the treble clef, and your left hand plays notes in the bass clef.

Book I

Piano &
Keyboard
101

✔ **You know the total number of keys on a standard piano.**

They don't call 'em the old 88s for nothin'. You can count all the keys to see for yourself. Or check out the black and white keys: There's a pattern of 12 consecutive black and white keys from the right end of the keyboard to the left. Look for seven of these groups and the first four keys that begin another group before you run out of keys to count.

✔ **You can identify different musical styles.**

Listen to Track 1 on this book's online audio site. You'll hear short examples of four different piano pieces. Match each excerpt with one of the following music styles:

Composer	*Style*
Scott Joplin	Ragtime
J.S. Bach	Baroque
Erik Satie	Slow, post-Impressionist waltz
W.C. Handy	Blues

Electronic Keyboards and other Keyboard Instruments

The first thing to realize is that all keyboards aren't the same. They may make different types of sounds by different methods of sound production and are meant to do different things for the needs of different players. The following sections help you navigate this potentially confusing terrain.

Examining keyboard designs throughout the years

Keyboard instruments can be divvied up into the following categories, based on how they produce their sound:

✔ **Acoustic instruments:** These instruments require no power to make their sound. But they include the acoustic piano, the harpsichord, and old pump pipe organs and such. Each produces its sound in different ways and sounds distinctly different from the others. And their sounds are certainly reproduced in an electronic keyboard.

✔ **Electro-mechanical instruments:** These options produce their sounds mechanically or acoustically and then have amplifiers and electronics to make the sound louder. The classic Rhodes and Wurlitzer electric pianos fall into this group, as well as the funky Clavinet (clav) and the mighty Hammond organ. These sounds are important to know because they're included in almost every keyboard you try out today.

✔ **Electronic instruments:** Keyboards in this group produce their sounds by electronic means, either analog or digital, and are what this book covers most in-depth. Electronic keyboards use a variety of technologies to produce their sounds. Brochures and websites throw around terms like *sampling, analog synthesis, DSP,* and *modeling,* along with hundreds of seemingly meaningless acronyms.

Touching on key weight

Those black and whites may look the same at first glance, but keys (or the key mechanism) can vary greatly from instrument to instrument. The first main distinction is whether the keys are weighted. *Weighted* keys give the feel of playing an acoustic piano. These keys may seem harder to play, but they offer you much more control over your *dynamics,* or ability to play more softly and loudly.

Non-weighted keys are often called *synth-action;* they're lighter to the touch and can be faster to play. The next step up is *semi-weighted* keys, which are firmer, more solid light-touch keys. The quality can vary from model to model and brand to brand, so it's an important aspect to consider when buying a keyboard.

Join the family: Grouping keyboards

Electronic keyboards fall into well-established families or categories of instruments. Each has a relatively standard set of features and is meant to be used for specific musical needs and playing situations. Within each family, you encounter entry-level models that are more basic and then step-up models that add to the quality and number of sounds, the number of features, the size and quality of the keyboard feel, and so on. The main keyboard "food groups" are as follows:

✔ **Digital pianos:** Acoustic piano wannabes or replacements.

✔ **Stage pianos:** Digital pianos intended for the performing musician, with additional sounds and pro features.

- **Portable keyboards:** Fun, lightweight, and full of features to help you sound better.

- **Arrangers:** Keyboards with sophisticated backing features to produce the sound of a full band from your simple chord input.

- **Organs:** Instruments dedicated to reproducing the sound, features, and feel of the legendary Hammond B3. They may include some additional sounds such as pipe organ, combo organs, and even other keyboard and synth sounds.

- **Synthesizers:** Keyboards that allow you to make your own sounds and adjust the sounds provided. They can sound the most electronic and imaginative but now often include imitative and natural sounds as well.

- **Workstations:** Basically, synthesizers with onboard recording systems to allow you to create complete works of original music. Very advanced and feature-rich.

- **Controllers:** Keyboards that don't make sound themselves but are used to trigger sounds from your computer and other keyboards. These options use the MIDI standard to communicate with the sound-producing devices.

Book I Chapters 2 and 3 are your keys (pun intended) to getting more info on all these families of instruments.

Making the Most of Your Keyboard's Basic Features

You can just turn on your keyboard and start playing, and you'll have a great time. But electronic keyboards can do soooo much more than that. Your keyboard is brimming with features and cool capabilities, like any self-respecting tech product these days is. It doesn't offer video games or let you video chat with your friends — yet.

Working with sounds

Some keyboards offer a small grouping of sounds; simple digital pianos may have 16 or so. But most keyboards offer at least 100 and sometimes thousands of sounds. Finding them, selecting them, and understanding whether they're simple single sounds or complex combinations of instruments stacked on top of each other or split between your hands takes some study. Book VI Chapter 1 breaks that all down and provides step-by-step instructions.

Exploring effects

What you hear coming out of a keyboard is actually more than just a sound; it almost always has some extra sonic treatment called *effects* added to it. Effects are audio treatments such as reverb, chorus, EQ, and delay, and they add to the spaciousness, color, and tonality of each sound. Even in simple keyboards, you have the choice whether to use them, and many keyboards allow you to vary the settings of their effects to produce different results, sometimes completely changing what effect a sound uses. Book VI Chapter 2 has the details.

Getting into automatic playing features

Many of today's keyboards have some functions that can do some playing on their own (with your guidance, of course). You can sit back and let the keyboard do some of the work. Here are the most common features (Book VI Chapter 2 talks more about these):

- **Drum rhythms:** All portables and arrangers and many high-end digital pianos offer an on-demand drummer to add some groove to your performance. You can select the choices from the front panel, add fancy transitions called *fills,* and sometimes select progressively busier variations. Some stage pianos, synths, and workstations also offer these grooves, although they may be lurking within the arpeggiator feature.

- **Auto-accompaniment:** How about having a full backing band ready to play whatever style of music, song, or chords you think of? Portables, arrangers, and some high-end digital pianos can do that and more. If you haven't been around keyboards and music for some time, you may not realize just how good the backing bands on today's keyboards have become. In a word: amazing!

- **Arpeggiation:** With *arpeggiation,* you hold a few notes or a chord, and the keyboard repeats them over and over in a dizzying array of possible patterns — from simple up and down repetitions to pulsing grooves to complex rhythmic patterns. An arpeggiator is often what produces the fancy riffs you hear in pop and dance music. Many of the more advanced options can also produce realistic guitar strumming, harp flourishes, and even drum grooves.

Delving into More Advanced Digital Features

Many keyboards have pretty advanced features — some that you would've thought you needed a computer to do. The following sections dive deeper into these digital waters. The chapters in Book VI cover these things in more detail.

Stepping into the virtual recording studio

Keyboards now commonly include some form of recording so that you can play and then listen back to yourself. Two forms of recording are available:

✔ **Audio recording:** This method is the recording of the actual sound you produced. It's what you listen to from a CD, an MP3 player, or your favorite online music streaming service.

✔ **MIDI recording:** *MIDI* is the *Musical Instrument Digital Interface* standard, a fancy name for a digital way that musical products can talk to each other. It's not the sound you hear but rather a way of communicating the gestures, moves, and settings of your electronic device as you play it.

Each format has its own terms, capabilities, and benefits, and musicians at every level use each of them.

Shaping the sounds you play

So many of today's keyboards offer control over the sounds that are included, whether that's adjusting them a little bit or completely changing them, warping them, or building them from the ground up. For many musicians, creating the sound is as important as the music they play with it. The art of making sounds is usually called *programming* a keyboard, or *sound design.* If you've heard the terms *waveform, oscillator, filter, envelope generator,* or *LFO,* you know that they're the building blocks of this creative art.

Checking out the computer connection

Thanks to the development of MIDI, all keyboards can connect to computers and tablets for a broad array of activities and enjoyment, from recording and sound editing to playing additional sounds that are running on your computer to working with virtual teachers. This exciting world is the cutting edge of music making and study.

Practicing with and without Help

Lurking inside many portable keyboards and digital pianos are patient music teachers, waiting to help you learn a few tunes and build your musical skills. They never yell, won't slap your wrists with a ruler, and are willing to go over things as slowly and as many times as you need. Book VI Chapter 4 explains and demonstrates both the Casio and Yamaha ways of giving you virtual keyboard lessons and provides practical advice on how to get the most out of them.

But sometimes you hear a song and you just want to sit down and play it right away at your keyboard. Why wait until you can buy the music or go to your next piano lesson? Learning to play by ear and to figure out songs from recordings is a great skill to develop. Some can do it naturally, but for most people, it takes some work. Check out Book VI Chapter 5 for help.

Chapter 2

Looking at the Different Keyboard Options

In This Chapter

▶ Discovering what happens when you press a key

▶ Comparing acoustic and digital keyboards

▶ Meeting the many types of electronic keyboards available

▶ Describing key feel and polyphony

▶ Access the audio tracks at www.dummies.com/go/pianokeyboardaio/

*B*e it a piano, organ, or digital keyboard, keyboards come in all shapes and sizes. They can have many keys or just a few; they can be huge pieces of furniture or little boxes.

Yet at first glance, keyboards seem like they must all be the same. After all, each offers the familiar groupings of black and white keys, right? In truth, other than the fact that you place your fingers on the same keys to produce the same notes, the world of keyboards is vast, and each instrument is played somewhat differently from the others. They feel different, they're different sizes and weights, and they can vary significantly in cost. Some keyboards produce one sound, others offer a few sounds, and others may produce thousands of different sounds.

This chapter pulls back the curtain on the wide variety of keyboards out there. It aims to help you understand the basic technology of how they make their sound(s), what makes each one special, and what each is best for. I explain how digital pianos reproduce the acoustic for far lower cost, smaller size, and less required upkeep. You discover what touch sensitivity is and how that dynamic control over volume behaves differently on the various types of keyboards. And you learn to recognize when only the real acoustic instrument will do.

If you haven't yet purchased a keyboard, read this chapter to get a feel for your options, decide what kind of keyboard interests you, and then turn to Book I Chapter 3 for tips on buying your instrument.

Acoustic Pianos

Acoustic means "not electric." So, acoustic pianos are great for starving musicians because they work even when you can't pay the electric bill.

Pianos are the most popular acoustic keyboards hands down (there are also harpsichords and pump organs, but they are beyond the scope of this book). Pianos have a 300-year track record, an incomparable tone, and a sound-producing mechanism that has been refined to respond to every subtle variation in your touch. They come in two appropriately named designs:

✔ **Grand piano:** You may need a living room the size of a grand ballroom to house the 9-foot concert grand. You may want to consider other sizes, from a baby grand (measuring in at about 5 feet) to other sizes up to 7 feet. You can see a grand piano in Figure 2-1.

Figure 2-1:
Owning one
is so grand.

Photo courtesy of jgroup/iStockphoto.com

✔ **Upright piano:** These relatively small instruments, also called *verticals,* sit upright against a wall and can vary in height from the spinet up to full-size uprights. Figure 2-2 shows an upright piano.

Figure 2-2:
Upright, not
uptight.

Photo courtesy of klikk/iStockphoto.com

TIP

For a sampling of various piano styles, try the following recordings:

✔ *A to Z of Pianists* (Naxos)

✔ *Now Playing: Movie Themes — Solo Piano,* Dave Grusin (GRP Records)

✔ *Alfred Brendel Plays Schubert* (Philips)

✔ *Piano Starts Here,* Art Tatum (Sony)

Lids

The grand piano has an enormous lid that you prop open with a stick that comes with the piano. By propping open the lid, you can see the metal strings and other mechanical components . . . and maybe even those car keys that you misplaced last month. Because the sound of a piano starts with the strings inside the instrument, you get a louder and more resonant sound when you leave the lid open, allowing the sound to project off the wooden soundboard.

The upright piano also has a lid — and may even have a stick to prop it open — but only piano tuners actually use the stick to help them keep the lid open while they tune the strings. The slightly muffled sound of an upright isn't dramatically increased by opening the lid, but you can try pulling the piano away from the wall to get a bigger sound.

String layout

In the grand piano, the strings are horizontal; in the upright, the strings are vertical and set diagonally — with the treble strings crossing the bass strings — to fit in the smaller upright case.

The difference in the string layout affects the resulting sound of the two pianos. The strings in an upright are vertical, so the sound travels sideways, close to the ground. In contrast, the strings in a grand piano are horizontal — the sound travels up and fills the room.

Keys, hammers, and strings

Most acoustic pianos today have a row of 88 black and white keys. If you have 87, 89, or 32, you may have been cheated! Each of the 88 keys is connected to a small, felt-covered *hammer* (see Figure 2-3). When you press a key, its hammer strikes a string, or set of strings, tuned to the appropriate musical note. The string begins to vibrate, your ear picks up these vibrations, and you hear music. The entire vibration process occurs in a split second.

To stop the strings from vibrating, another mechanism called a *damper* sits over the strings inside the keyboard. Dampers are made of cloth or felt that mutes the strings by preventing any vibration. When you press a key, in addition to triggering the mechanism that vibrates the string, a piano key also lifts the damper. When you release the key (provided you're not holding down a pedal), the damper returns to mute the string.

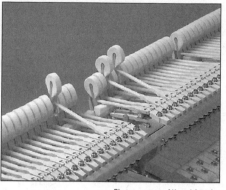

Figure 2-3:
Hammers
vibrate
piano
strings to
produce
music to
your ears.

Photo courtesy of Kawai America

Electro-Mechanical Keyboards

An *electro-mechanical* instrument is one that combines an acoustic/mechanical sound generator with some additional electronics, usually to help amplify or increase the volume of the sound produced. So the initial sound, both the tone and pitch, is determined by an acoustic mechanism (usually a string or metal object being plucked or struck in some fashion). All these instruments include a *pickup per string/tone* (a device that translates sound vibrations into an electrical signal) and an amplification system for you to hear their sound, which means they require electricity to operate. And without the sounds being fed into an onboard or external speaker, you wouldn't be able to hear them.

These instruments are so popular that they remain the core group of sounds (along with the acoustic piano) reproduced in all electronic keyboards to this day. So getting more familiar with their features and sound is an important part of your keyboard education.

The most common of these instruments include the following:

- Rhodes electric piano, sometimes called the Fender Rhodes and often alluded to as a *tine* piano (Figure 2-4)
- Wurlitzer electric piano, often referred to as a *reed* piano (Figure 2-5)
- Hohner Clavinet, commonly called *clav* for short (Figure 2-6)
- The Hammond organ, producing its sound through a tonewheel method (Figure 2-7)
- Hohner Pianet electric grand piano
- Yamaha CP-70/80 electric grand piano

Figure 2-4:
Rhodes MK1
suitcase
electric
piano.

Photograph courtesy of Ken Rich/Ken Rich Sound Services

Figure 2-5:
Wurlitzer
electric
piano,
model 200A.

Photograph courtesy of Ken Rich/Ken Rich Sound Services

Figure 2-6:
Hohner D6
Clavinet.

Photograph courtesy of Ken Rich/Ken Rich Sound Services

Figure 2-7:
Hammond
B-3 with
Leslie
speaker.

Photograph courtesy of Hammond Suzuki USA

Electronic Keyboards

Electronic keyboards produce their sounds completely by some electronic or digital means. They may contain tubes or resistors, chips, and circuit boards inside — but no vibrating strings or spinning elements are involved.

Combo organs

The early combo organs from the 1960s, such as the Vox Continental (Figure 2-8) and the Farfisa Compact, are common examples of electronic keyboards used in pop and rock music of that day. Throughout the 1950s and 1960s, electronic console and theatre organs were the main home keyboards other than an acoustic piano.

Figure 2-8:
Vox
Continental
combo
organ.

Photograph courtesy of Korg USA, Inc., and David Jacques

Synthesizers

All too often, electronic keyboards are called *synthesizers* (or *synths* for short). A synthesizer is an electronic instrument with the primary purpose of creating and shaping sound and the parameters to do so. So a digital piano that has some simple sound tweaking settings isn't a synth. A synth goes beyond the emulation of acoustic instruments and electro-mechanical keyboards; it's an instrument for people who enjoy the imaginative and creative possibilities of new and fresh sounds.

Sound can be created from analog, digital, sample-playback, or modeled technologies, and sometimes these technologies are combined in a single instrument. The earliest analog synthesizers had various modules of electronics.

Synthesizers today come in many shapes and sizes; some have mini keys and are relatively inexpensive, whereas others have full-sized keys but are only monophonic and have shorter key ranges (sometimes only 25 or 37 keys). Still others offer more polyphony and 49- and 61-key ranges. Some synths even offer 88-key weighted keys.

In the late 1960s/early 1970s, the Moog synthesizer started to be used in rock, pop, and other types of music. Figure 2-9 shows the Moog modular system that Keith Emerson used for the classic solo on Emerson, Lake & Palmer's "Lucky Man." Other brands soon followed, such as ARP, Sequential Circuits, Oberheim, EML, EMS, and Korg. These instruments are all examples of *analog electronics,* where electronic voltages move between components and are manipulated to produce the desired sound. Many of these famous analog synthesizers are still sought after and used today because each has its own characteristic sound and features. Analog synthesizers remain so popular that a number of companies are making new models today, from the simple to the highly complex. Examples include the Moog Sub Phatty, Dave Smith Instruments' Mopho, and the Arturia MicroBrute.

To help create sounds, the front panel and overall interface of a synthesizer have dedicated controls for the most important parameters for sound creation: Knobs and sliders are most common, although switches, buttons, ribbons, pads, and other controls may be available. Here are some typical controls:

Figure 2-9:
Keith
Emerson's
mighty
Moog mod-
ular system.

Photograph courtesy of Tony Ortiz, Archivist for Emerson, Lake & Palmer

✔ An *oscillator* produces the basic waveform or sound. A special type of oscillator called a *low frequency oscillator* (LFO) modulates another parameter to create *vibrato* (pitch fluctuation), *wah-wah* types of sound (filter fluctuation), and *tremolo* (volume fluctuation).

✔ A *filter* shapes the tonal character of the oscillator by blocking certain frequencies from passing or by accentuating them.

✔ An *amplifier* or *amp* adjusts the level of the sound.

✔ An *envelope generator* modifies the levels of a signal over time. This function is commonly applied to both the filter and the amp, but you can also use it to change pitch over time and other characteristics.

Check out Tracks 2 through 4 for examples of the Vox and Farfisa organs as well as a Moog synthesizer.

The mid-1980s saw the development of the digital keyboard and synthesizer that has continued through today. These products are really dedicated computers running software designed to do a specialized task: Make musical sounds. Most use custom chips and circuits and won't run your favorite shoot-'em-up games or connect to the Internet, but some can repurpose a computer to become a complete music studio. Some of the most famous digital keyboards/synths are the Yamaha DX7, the Korg M1 music workstation, the E-mu Emulator sampling keyboard, and the Casio SK-1. All the keyboards discussed in the next section are electronic, and they're by far the most common type you find today. Figure 2-10 shows a modern-day electronic keyboard.

Book I

Piano & Keyboard 101

Figure 2-10: The Korg Krome, a modern digital synthesizer/ workstation.

Photograph courtesy of Korg USA, Inc.

Portable keyboards

Portable keyboards usually fall in to the range of entry-level to slightly more advanced instruments that combine basic sounds with some fun and/or simple learning features and onboard accompaniment. They're geared more toward beginners and are very affordable. Portable electronic keyboards first came to prominence in the 1980s and were pioneered by Casio and Yamaha, as they still are today. This category of keyboards has really developed in recent years and now offers a surprising amount of features and value for the money.

Most portable keyboards use regular sized, non-weighted synth action keys, not weighted keys like a piano does. Key ranges come in 49- and 61-key lengths, sometimes offering up to 88 semi-weighted keys.

The sounds are produced by sample-playback technology and tend to be decent but pretty basic. Portable keyboards don't have a lot of memory for the samples, so don't expect pro quality; however, the sounds are surprisingly good for the money. What they may lack in quality they certainly make up for in quantity; these keyboards usually offer between 400 and 800 sounds! Along with real instrument sounds and some general-purpose synth sounds, these keyboards often have some fun sound effects and other noises that can be fun for kids (and kids at heart) to play with.

Workstations

A *workstation* is a synthesizer that has some form of onboard recording included. So a workstation is always a synthesizer (because it allows you to create new sounds), but a synthesizer isn't necessarily a workstation (because it doesn't necessarily have an onboard *sequencer,* or recording function).

Synthesizer workstations use digital forms of sound production, be they sample-playback, digital synthesis, modeling technology, or combinations of all these. User-sampling is sometimes included, so you can record your own sounds, sound effects, or load in sounds that others make.

The workstation tends to be a jack-of-all trades because it combines sound creation, music recording, and live performance features in one box. Many musicians buy one for the sound, regardless of whether they need all the other features, because often a manufacturer's best-in-class model is a workstation. Workstations usually come in 61-key synth action and 88-key weighted action key lengths, and the upper-end models usually offer after-touch. Some brands offer 73 or 76-key versions.

The workstation gets a bad rap as a recording platform in some circles because computer audio/MIDI recording systems have far outclassed its capabilities. But sometimes just turning on one dedicated system is easier and more intuitive for capturing a quick idea. And a workstation is an all-in-one, so it's far easier to take around with you. Thanks to the universality of MIDI, you don't have to make an either/or choice; you can use the workstation by itself or connect it to your computer and use those tools as well.

Arrangers

An *arranger* keyboard is an instrument that combines a wide variety of sounds with an automatic accompaniment system, which produces the sound of a full backing band from simple chords you play.

Many portable keyboards also have this feature, so what makes a product an arranger is the quality of the sounds, the inclusion of other pro features, and the general build quality of the case and onboard speakers. Really, the dividing line between portables and arrangers typically comes down to price. Anything higher than $500 or so is probably being called an arranger. Arranger keyboards usually use sample-playback technology to produce their sound, although some also offer a form of organ modeling as well.

The concept of automatic accompaniment was first introduced in home and theatre organs from the1950s and 1960s and moved into digital keyboards in the early 1980s. The basic idea is that by playing only minimal parts with your left hand (to feed the automatic accompaniment system) you can sound like you're playing with a complete band of musicians who know every song you do!

An arranger keyboard is considered *the* professional keyboard across much of Europe and throughout the Middle East, so it has many advanced features for live performance including mic input, vocal effects, and even onscreen lyric display so you'll never forget the words to a song again.

Controller keyboards

With the advent of MIDI in 1983, the concept of the sound module was born. Because MIDI allowed you to connect multiple keyboards and trigger them all from one master keyboard, you didn't need every other sound source to always have keys on it. You just needed a box that had the sounds you wanted. This setup saved you space and cost. Over time, a new class of keyboard arose out of this situation: the *controller* keyboard — a MIDI keyboard that usually produces no sound by itself but rather is designed to control other keyboards, modules, and (increasingly) music software instruments and applications.

A controller keyboard may come in any length. A whole class of mini- and micro-sized controllers has developed to serve the mobile musician looking to carry her whole music studio with her wherever she goes.

Besides keys for triggering notes, controller keyboards need to be able to send various types of MIDI messages to the receiving device. Selecting sounds is of course essential, as are some wheels, knobs, sliders, and/or switches to add some expression or variations to the sound, much like the knobs on a synthesizer. Velocity-sensitive drum pads have become common on most mid- and upper-end controllers.

Controller keyboards are often used not only to play sounds but also to operate the MIDI and audio recording software used on computers so that the controls also serve to mix track levels, position sounds in the stereo field, solo and mute tracks, and other recording console functions.

Appreciating How Digital Keyboards Make So Many Sounds

Today's keyboards are pretty amazing; press a button and any sound can come out. Acoustic piano, electric piano, and organs? Check. Saxes, flute, trumpet, trombone, violin, and cello? Check. Rock guitar, bass, drums, and even crowd applause? Check. Soaring synth leads, burbling electronic blips and bleeps, and swooshing and sweeping sound effects? All that and more.

Did you ever wonder how they make all these different sounds? Digital keyboards aren't all the same; they produce their sounds many different ways. Here are the major methods they use (check out Book VI Chapter 3 for how to use these methods to shape sounds):

- ✔ **Digital synthesis:** *Digital synthesis* is a broad category indicating that the manufacturer has designed a special method of making sound, using a computer chip to produce artificial tones that can be varied and manipulated into many different sounds. *Frequency modulation* (FM) is a form of *algorithmic synthesis* that Yamaha used to produce many highly successful synths like the DX7, and it's still used today in some products. Casio had what they called *phase distortion* (PD) in its CZ range of synths, and Kawai used a digital technology called *additive synthesis* in its K-series synths, to name just a few.

- ✔ **Sample-playback:** *Sampling* is the process of digitally recording the sound of a real-world object and being able to play it back and further manipulate the recording. *Sample-playback* can sound much more realistic than other forms of synthesis because it's using the real sound as opposed to a re-creation or imitation of an instrument's sound. Sampling first appeared in keyboards in the 1980s, and instruments like the E-mu Emulator, the Ensoniq Mirage, the Fairlight CMI, and Akai samplers became very popular. Because digital memory was very expensive in those days, the sounds were good but not yet great. Costs have come down over the years, and today sampling keyboards (and computer software) produce highly nuanced and very realistic sounds.

- ✔ **Physical modeling:** *Physical modeling* is another form of digital synthesis, but it specifically focuses on studying how a real-world instrument creates its sound and then re-creates each piece or component of the original device down to its materials, behaviors, and responses. For example, to replicate a drum's sound, you'd look to the materials the head and body are made from, the size of the body or shell, and so on, and how that part of the instrument would change over time after being activated or react depending on how it was struck. Stringed, woodwind, and brass instruments, drums, and mallet instruments are all areas that have been explored using this approach.

In the world of keyboards, the most common instruments modeled in this fashion are the clav, the Rhodes and Wurlitzer electric pianos, and especially the Hammond organ. This form of synthesis gives you very detailed control over all aspects of the sound and in some instruments lets you create new designs that don't exist in real life. Roland has done some very interesting things in this regard for the acoustic piano (in V-Piano), allowing you to imitate changing the strings' material and length, the hammer's size and material, and other futuristic manipulations. In software, a company called Modartt is doing similar things with its Pianoteq line of titles.

✔ **Virtual analog:** *Virtual analog* is similar to physical modeling but has grown into a category of its own; the initial goal was to re-create the complete layout and character of an existing (usually analog) synthesizer. Virtual analog is a very popular segment, and models exist in both hardware and computer software forms. The designer studies and often re-creates each element at the component level and attempts to re-create the sound, response, and complete feature set of a given classic synthesizer. From there, the designer often adds new features and expands the capabilities of the synth to bring it into the modern age. Many companies make new, imaginative synths with this method, creating an instrument with the types of parameters and capabilities of the classics along with their own ideas, often bringing together forms of digital synthesis along with the modeled analog synthesis. Examples include the Nord Lead 4, Access Virus TI2, Korg KingKORG, and Roland GAIA SH-01.

Considering Key Feel and Response

The design, feel, and touch of the key mechanism (commonly called the *key action*) used on modern keyboards can vary a great deal. Understanding how key actions work and what each offers can help you differentiate among the various types of keyboards and models offered. The following sections introduce a couple of important key action characteristics.

Touch sensitivity

Key actions come in two main classes: dynamic (touch-sensitive or velocity-sensitive) and non-dynamic. The term *dynamics* in music refers to changes in loudness or volume.

A *velocity-sensitive* key action responds to how firmly or softly you play the key, transferring that energy to the sound-producing mechanism to allow you to play many different volume levels from soft to loud. *Non-dynamic keyboards* have keys that are simple on/off switches that cause the sound to play. You create dynamics by using a foot pedal, not by varying the touch of your fingers on the keys.

The acoustic piano is velocity-sensitive and can produce an incredibly wide range of dynamics. The Rhodes and Wurlitzer electric pianos and the clav are also velocity-sensitive, although they have narrower ranges of dynamics. The pipe organ, all combo/console/theatre organs, and the harpsichord, on the other hand, aren't velocity-sensitive. For example, the harpsichord's quill always plucks the string the same way, so the dynamics don't change. Early analog synthesizers used organ keyboards, so they too were non-dynamic.

Later high-end analog synthesizer models added touch sensitivity; examples include the Yamaha CS-80, Sequential Circuits Prophet T8, and Moog Polymoog. But the advent of digital synthesis and MIDI made velocity-sensitive synthesizers and keyboards much more common.

Velocity-sensitive synthesizers have two sensors, as shown in Figure 2-11; the first is at the top of the key, where the key sits when at rest. The other is at the bottom of the key action, where the key reaches when pressed down fully. The system uses these sensors to measure how quickly the key moves from the top to the bottom and then translates that speed or value into a dynamic level. The idea is that the harder you press a key, the faster it actually moves downward. So soft touch is actually a slow depression of the key, and hard touch is a faster movement.

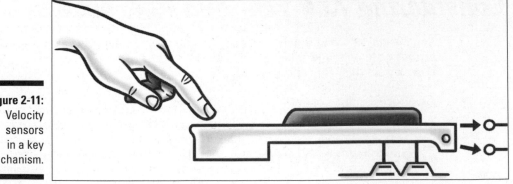

Figure 2-11: Velocity sensors in a key mechanism.

Illustration by Lisa Reed

The terms *velocity-sensitive* and *touch-sensitive* are often used interchangeably, but *velocity sensitivity* is the truly correct term for today's electronic keyboards because it's how MIDI translates the playing force into different values.

Key weight

A few types of keys are available on keyboards, some lighter and others heavier to the touch.

Key weight has nothing to do with the dynamics of the key mechanism discussed in the preceding section. Any type of key can be velocity-sensitive, regardless of which of the following weight classes it falls into:

- ✔ **(Fully) weighted:** A *weighted* or *fully weighted* key imitates the mass of the piano key action. Both acoustic piano keys and high-end digital piano keys are made of wood with a coating or veneer on top. The keys have a certain amount of weight to them, so your finger exerts more energy to make them move. This resistance gives you more feedback when you're trying to play dynamically, and that allows for more nuanced control of soft dynamics. (That control is why serious pianists prefer weighted keys). The key has a slightly protruding top front lip and is enclosed on the front surface.

- ✔ **Semi-weighted:** *Semi-weighted* keys provide a middle ground between weighted and non-weighted key mechanisms for synth actions. Some manufacturers add some weight to the non-weighted synth key or plastic piano-shaped key (usually by gluing a metal bar to the underside of the key) to increase its mass and make it feel a bit more solid to the touch. It usually has a spring in the mechanism to provide resistance to your touch.

- ✔ **Non-weighted:** *Non-weighted* or *synth-action* keys are the lightest, simplest action. They often have some spring in the mechanism to add some slight resistance — just enough to keep them from feeling loose and uncontrollable. Simpler plastic keys used on combo organs and synthesizers have little mass, or resistance, to them, so they can be played very easily and often more quickly. This key is made entirely of plastic and looks more like a diving board with no front edge. Non-weighted keys are preferred by non-pianists and for playing organ, clav, and synth sounds, which aren't called upon to reproduce wide dynamics.

Paying Attention to Polyphony

After you start to explore electronic keyboards, you need to understand and consider polyphony. *Polyphony* means "many voices," and in music it means having multiple tones or parts playing at the same time. In an instrument, it's the ability to play more than one note at a time. A trumpet, a flute, a saxophone, and even the human voice can sound only one note at a time, so they're *monophonic*.

The guitar has six strings, so it's considered six-note polyphonic. The acoustic bass has four strings, so it's — yup — four-note polyphonic. Acoustic and electro-mechanical keyboards have as much polyphony as they have keys. So the piano is considered 88-note polyphonic!

However, this one-to-one key-to-polyphony ratio isn't true of electronic keyboards because the key isn't attached directly to the sound-producing mechanism (for example, a string). Rather, a chip or circuitry inside the keyboard produces the sound, and the power of those electronics is what determines how many notes you can play.

In keyboards, some analog synthesizers are monophonic because in the early days, building a polyphonic synthesizer was very expensive. With the advent of digital technology, today's electronic keyboards generally seem to have big numbers for their polyphony; you see specs that state 32, 64, 100, 128, and up to 256 voices or notes of polyphony. However, various factors can quickly reduce the amount of polyphony truly available:

✔ Playing a piano sound for a couple of bars with the *damper* (or *sustain*) pedal down uses up a *lot* of notes in a short time.

✔ Some instruments use two voices to produce a stereo sound, so you cut the polyphony in half when playing one of them. The same issue applies when playing a *layered* sound (two sounds at the same time, such as piano and strings). At minimum, you're using two voices for each note played, and this number can double or quadruple depending on how the sounds are designed.

✔ If your keyboard is playing a drum rhythm or producing auto-accompaniment patterns as you play, they too require notes of polyphony to sound.

What happens when you run out of polyphony? The designers of electronic keyboards are very smart; what they usually do is "rob" or stop sounding the oldest sustaining note. So as you keep playing piano with the sustain pedal down, your earliest-played notes start to shut off, one by one, until you let off the pedal and start again. This way, you always hear the most recent notes as you play them, and only the notes that are already fading away are robbed. If a lot of voices are required to play a single layered or complex sound, this stealing of voices happens more quickly, and is more noticeable.

So when you're checking out a keyboard, reading the specs may not be enough. Yes, more polyphony is always better, but you have to figure out whether what a keyboard offers is enough for you depending on what features you plan to use regularly. Try playing your favorite songs, go for the layered sounds, or turn on any rhythms or accompaniment offered. Listen as you play for any noticeable note-stealing. Remember that this effect is most noticeable in solo, exposed playing. If you'll be playing in a band, you may not notice it as much, and that's a good thing.

Chapter 3

Choosing and Buying
Your Keyboard

. . . .

In This Chapter

▶ Choosing between acoustic and digital keyboards

▶ Shopping around and exploring your digital options

▶ Asking the right questions before you buy

▶ Understanding the needs of each skill level

▶ Considering what type of music you'll play and with whom

. . . .

Grandma's old upright piano may satisfy your urges to play the keyboard for a while. However, at some point you may experience the undeniable urge to purchase or rent a piano or keyboard of your own. Probably right around the time that Grandma gets tired of hearing you play "Yankee Doodle" for the hundredth time.

When the urge to acquire a piano or keyboard strikes, don't pull out that checkbook or debit card just yet. Spend the time to research, shop around, and choose exactly the kind of piano or keyboard you want.

If you're just starting out playing or have put in very little time studying so far, you don't need the top-of-the-line model. Likewise, if you're pretty accomplished, you may be tempted to just go for the most keyboard your budget can afford — but price shouldn't be the only criteria for your choice.

This chapter guides you through the various considerations you should evaluate to decide what's the right choice. Reflecting honestly about your skill level and where you think you want to go with your playing is a good first step. Making sure your choice offers you the sounds and features for your favorite styles of music is a must.

First Things First: Acoustic or Electric (or Both)?

The first thing you need to decide when selecting a keyboard is whether you want an acoustic one or not. (See Book I Chapter 2 for an explanation of acoustic and digital keyboards.) Don't just flip a coin. Make a list of pros and cons to help you decide which type of keyboard is best for you.

The following sections can help you get started with lists of some pros and cons for both acoustic and digital keyboards. Then personalize the lists, adding your own perceptions, factors, and concerns. It's *your* keyboard, after all. Base your buying or renting decision on the pros and cons that *you* come up with and that are the most important to you.

Pros and cons of acoustic keyboards

Psalteries, virginals, clavichords, and harmoniums are acoustic keyboards. Honestly, you don't need a list of pros and cons for these very rare instruments. If you find one and can't live without it, go ahead and purchase it.

Pianos, harpsichords, and pipe organs are also acoustic keyboards. The pros and cons in this section focus on acoustic pianos because they're the most commonly purchased acoustic keyboards.

Pros

The following characteristics are real selling points for an acoustic piano:

- **Sound quality:** No matter how good a digital keyboard is, it doesn't match the sound and feel of a grand piano — or even an upright piano.

- **Value:** Good-quality acoustic pianos appreciate in value over the years if kept in good condition. You can think of your purchase as an investment.

- **Aesthetics:** There's nothing like playing an acoustic piano. It feels real, it looks great, and you can imagine yourself on a concert stage.

Cons

Here are valid concerns about acoustic pianos:

- **Cost:** Plain and simple, new and even used pianos are generally more expensive than new digital keyboards.

- **Size and space:** Get practical and think about whether you have room to house the piano and play it. You should also measure the doorway while you're at it to make sure you can even get the piano where you want it.

✔ **Maintenance:** Annual or semiannual tuning at a cost of around $75 to $150 per tuning isn't cheap, but it's essential. (Book I Chapter 4 tells you more about maintaining your acoustic keyboard.)

Pros and cons of digital keyboards

You can *rent* some digital keyboards, but not all. Some of the fancier models are mostly for sale only, although you may find a used one in good condition. On the other hand, plenty of stores offer a rental option on larger digital pianos or digital organs. Many online stores will ship a keyboard to you and provide knowledgeable staff available by phone.

Looking for used keyboards online can yield lots of options, but you really need to be able to see and play a keyboard before you buy. (See the section "Shopping online" later in this chapter for online buying tips.)

Pros

Digital keyboards have the following positive points going for them:

✔ **Cost:** Unless you're talking about very high-end models, most digital keyboards are more affordable than pianos.

✔ **Size:** No matter where you live, you can find a spot for your digital keyboard. Plus, they are much, much easier to move.

✔ **Versatility:** Most digital keyboards come loaded with different sounds, so you can be a one-person band or make almost any sounds you want.

✔ **Maintenance:** Digital keyboards require no tuning and no tweaking — you just plug and play. (And dust — check out Book IV Chapter 4.)

✔ **Silence:** If you have grouchy neighbors, young children, or other house-mates who demand quiet, headphones really help. You can turn off the sound to the outside world and still hear yourself practice.

Cons

Consider the following before making a purchase:

✔ **Complexity:** Some digital keyboards come with a baffling number of sampled sounds, sequencing tools, effects, levers, and knobs. Figuring out how to utilize these features requires a steep learning curve. Additionally, knobs and levers can break, circuitry can go haywire, and any number of other things can go wrong over the years.

✔ **Power:** You must have electricity, or at least a whole bunch of D-size batteries, in order to play your digital keyboard.

✔ **Sound quality:** Some digital sounds are out-of-this-world fantastic, but others can be unconvincing when mimicking an acoustic instrument.

- **Keyboard action:** Many digital keyboards aren't *touch-sensitive,* meaning that whether you play the key hard or soft, you hear the same volume. Models with "weighted action" try to give you the feel of an acoustic piano; some succeed, and some fail.

- **Obsolescence:** Like most electronic devices and computers, today's keyboards probably won't be tomorrow's desire. Eventually you'll want to upgrade to the latest and greatest model, and very few digital keyboards retain their value.

- **Addiction:** If you buy one, pretty soon you'll want another, and another, and another. Or you'll want more sound samples, a better amp, a better speaker, a new stand, or a new case. The common mantra among keyboard players in the digital world is, "I need more gear!"

Going hybrid

They combine the best of both worlds! They offer unmatched versatility! They cost a million dollars! Well, not that much, but hybrid acoustic/digital keyboards are expensive. If the idea of a hybrid interests you, there are two ways to go: Buy an acoustic/digital hybrid piano, or have your acoustic piano retrofitted with a digital player system.

Among the growing list of things these hybrid pianos and player piano systems can do are

- Record, play back, and mute (muting stops the hammers from hitting the strings — but you can hear yourself by plugging in headphones).

- Connect with other MIDI instruments and MIDI files (see the section "The MIDI Places You Can Go" later in this chapter for more on MIDI).

- Access sound libraries and karaoke libraries, play along with pre-recorded tracks,

and play along with MIDI feeds available over the Internet through a USB or wireless connection. These options open the door to a wide range of instructional and entertainment possibilities.

Yamaha Disklavier leads the field of digital and acoustic technology with its hybrid pianos. PianoDisc, QRS, and Bösendorfer also make player piano systems that can be installed on your acoustic piano.

Be careful if you're thinking about retrofitting your piano with a player piano system. This can involve some significant physical alteration of your piano, and you won't be able to go back after it's done! Consult with a piano technician before signing on the dotted line. Ask how your piano would be affected by an installation, including the sound, the feel, and the value of the instrument.

Looking At What's Important for the Beginner

There's nothing wrong with recognizing that you're a beginner. Perhaps you took a few lessons many years ago and have now decided you want to get back to the joy of making music for fun and relaxation. That's great! You're likely a beginner and should be proud of that. (Sorry, being able to play The Kingsmen's "Louie Louie" or Harold Faltermeyer's "Axel F" [the theme from *Beverley Hills Cop*] doesn't make you an accomplished player. And it just may get you kicked out of your local music store if you keep coming in and playing them for hours on end.)

Maybe you never took a lesson or even touched a keyboard except for using the one on your computer to send a few e-mails and post pictures of your cat. Now you want to start to play the musical keyboard for fun or to get involved with your church or school. Wonderful! Playing music is a great way to let off a little steam, express yourself, and experience the joy of artistic creation.

Perhaps you've bought (or inherited) a rather old, beat-up acoustic piano and have only been taking lessons for a little while. You're doing okay with your lessons, but your piano sounds bad, won't hold a tuning, or takes up too much room in your home, so you're considering moving into the electronic realm.

Whatever your beginner story, here's a small list of things to consider when choosing an electronic keyboard:

- **Piano features:** The first fork in the road that you must consider when selecting a keyboard is whether you want to play primarily acoustic piano sound and styles of music. If so, you need to be sure that whatever you're looking at offers that sound; most keyboards today do, and you'll be surprised to see that even some organs and programmable synthesizers do. The basic piano features you need in this situation are

  - **A weighted key mechanism:** Only a weighted key action gives you the true piano feel experience.

  - **At least 61 keys (5 octaves):** Remember that an acoustic piano has 88 keys (a little more than 7 octaves). For beginner lessons, you play in only one to three octaves, but you'll be expanding your reach farther in no time.

  - **At least one pedal to help you sustain your notes:** This feature is called a *damper pedal* on an acoustic piano but may be called a *sustain pedal* or just a *momentary pedal* depending on your model.

✔ **A variety of sounds:** Every beginner should get a keyboard that offers more than one type of sound regardless of whether she has a piano-centric musical taste or goal. Being able to hear what you play with different tones keeps your playing and practicing experience interesting and fresh. You should have some variety.

✔ **A metronome or drum rhythms:** To develop your playing, you need a steady timekeeper to help get your rhythm solid. A *metronome* is the device students use for this purpose. Back in the day, it was a wooden, wind-up box that had a metal wand that swung back and forth, clicking as it went, but metronomes migrated to being electronic years ago. In your keyboard it can be as simple as a steady click or beep that you can set the speed of; you can also use built-in drum rhythms to not only keep your time steady but also make your practice and performance more polished-sounding and fun. You can buy these features separately, but getting a keyboard that already includes them is much simpler.

✔ **Other aids for study or learning:** If you're planning to study or take lessons or you want some help in learning to play, you should consider having a simple onboard recorder, which allows you to record and then listen back to your playing. Evaluating what you're doing is so much easier as an observer than as a participant.

✔ **Accompaniment features:** Some keyboards can provide extra band members to play along with you. You can simply add an extra hand for your piano playing or go all the way up to the sound of a full group of players: drums, bass, other chord parts, and fancy extras. Taking advantage of these features can deliver a very full sound without a lot of playing technique or effort. Accompaniment can make your practice time more interesting by letting you hear your pieces in different settings and giving you the experience of playing along with other musicians.

Playing Well With Others and Alone

Some features can become more important based on the situation(s) you'll be playing your keyboard in — features that are helpful for solo work may not mean much for a band member. This section contains some tips and observations to help you make the best choice for your needs.

An onboard music rack or stand can be helpful in lots of performance situations because most require you to read some music. Playing classical music in particular often involves reading from large scores, so you need to consider whether the supplied rack will hold the size and bulk of the music you'll be using. Forward-thinking musicians are starting to use tablet computers as their music readers, and those are more likely than huge paper scores to fit on the average supplied keyboard music rack.

Going solo

You can find two main schools of solo keyboard performance: the solo pianist and the one-man band.

As a *solo pianist,* you basically play piano, piano layered with strings or a warm synth sound, and perhaps some electric piano. So the best-quality sounds with all possible nuances work well. Your sound is very exposed so even subtle aspects like damper resonance and key-off samples can be heard and enjoyed. Having some backing rhythms is nice because they add to your performance while still allowing the solo piano approach to shine. You will be playing in small rooms or as background music a lot, so onboard speakers can usually carry your performance, making your setup much easier. If you're a singer-songwriter and will be playing in clubs with sound systems, you don't need much beyond your keyboard, a stand, and your pedal(s), plus maybe a microphone input with some dedicated reverb for your voice. A number of stage pianos and arranger keyboards offer this feature.

The one-man band is more of an outgoing entertainer; you're playing a wide variety of music, talking, and likely singing, and you need to come off like a complete band. The professional arranger is the best choice of keyboard for this work, for sure. You can put together this type of show with a workstation keyboard, but doing so requires much more time and effort developing the backing tracks to play all the songs you'll need to cover. Only the fussiest and most advanced keyboardists are likely to go that route. Choosing the right arranger keyboard for you comes down to quality and variety of sounds, accompaniment patterns, mic input, keyboard feel, and perhaps vocal harmony features.

Accompanying vocalists

Having a transpose function can be very helpful if you are playing in a duo or small group with a vocalist. A singer often needs to change the key of a song to stay in the most comfortable range. And because males and females have different vocal ranges, they almost never sing a given song in the same key as each other.

Learning how to play a song in more than one key is a more advanced musical skill, so why not let technology help you out? A *transpose* function shifts the tuning of the keyboard so you can keep playing in the key of C on the keys, but the notes that come out will be moved up or down by an amount you specify. So by simply selecting a transpose value, you can now play in any key you require with no change in your playing. Thank you, technology!

If this option is important to you, check out your potential keyboard candidates to see how easily you can access this feature; is it right on the front panel, or do you have to go wading through a lot of menu pages? Can you easily turn off the function so you're back to normal tuning/operation? Does the feature show or tell you that you're currently transposed? Pianists have told me stories about starting a song and getting angry or confused stares from a singer, only to realize that they were still transposed from the last song and had forgotten about it. Having to stop and start again because "it's the keyboard player's fault" can be very embarrassing.

Performing classical music with others

A great piano sound and perhaps pipe organ and harpsichord are obviously your main sound choices when playing classical music with others. But many musicians have stories of how they had to help augment a given classical or church ensemble to cover the parts of a missing or sick member and were the hero of the day when their keyboards could reproduce the solo string, woodwind, or even percussion instrument that was required. This benefit is certainly something to consider if your music choices will include all these instrument types.

Onboard speakers are another good feature because you don't need to be very loud when playing classical, and the sight of an electronic keyboard in this type of ensemble can already be a cause of some concern. Carry in an instrument amplifier or speaker system, and who knows what the reaction will be.

Jamming in a pop, rock, or jazz band

Playing in a band usually means you have to cover many more sounds than just typical keyboard sounds. Be sure to evaluate the synth, string, brass, and vocal sounds carefully so you ensure that you can cover all the styles of music needed.

You often have to cover more than one part, so split and layer features are important. You should be able to store these multisound parts and recall them easily. Having a special live mode where you can arrange sounds in order so you can change them easily during a song is also very helpful. This way, you can mix and match single sounds and multipart sounds in an easy list to select from. Many performers like to use a foot pedal to advance through these lists so their hands can stay on the keyboard at all times.

Having the ability to keep one sound sustaining while you change to your next sound is becoming more common, or at least more in demand from players. With this feature, current notes keep sounding while the new sound loads in the background; only when you play new notes do you hear the new sound, so you can get a seamless (not choppy) transition between sounds. This function, called names such as *patch remain, smooth sound transition, seamless sound change,* and so on, is certainly worth asking about.

Band work is the most common place where you see players using more than one keyboard. The most common reason for this arrangement is the feel of the keys. Playing piano on an unweighted synth action isn't very satisfying; trying to play tonewheel organ on a weighted keyboard is equally difficult and can be downright painful when you attempt to do the palm slides up and down the keys that are common in organ playing. Likewise, playing rhythmic clav and fast synth parts is much easier on the unweighted keys. (I discuss key weight earlier in the chapter.)

A second issue is that a single keyboard may not be able to provide enough key range per part for the split and/or layered parts you need to cover. A two-keyboard approach becomes the right answer. How to choose what type of keyboards depends on whether you are primarily a pianist who needs extra sounds, an organist who needs extra sounds, or perhaps an electronic music performer who needs a variety of instruments. Here are some of the most common approaches/combinations:

✔ Piano/stage piano on the bottom with an all-purpose synth/workstation on top

✔ Piano/stage piano on the bottom with an organ on top

✔ Weighted action workstation on the bottom with synth action synth/ workstation on top

✔ Weighted action workstation on the bottom with organ on top

✔ Organ on the bottom (sometimes dual manual organ) with stage piano on top

✔ Organ on the bottom (sometimes dual manual organ) with all-purpose synth/workstation on top

Picking the Perfect Acoustic Piano

If your pro and con list reveals that an acoustic piano suits your needs best, use this section to help select the right model piano for you.

Taking location into account

Most older pianos were produced with a particular climate in mind. The wood used to make them was weathered for the finished product's climate. Japan, for example, has a wetter climate than many locations in the United States. Therefore, the wood in many pianos manufactured for use in Japan has been dried out more than the wood used to make pianos for use in the U.S. If you live in the U.S. and you buy a piano made for use in Japan, you may face some serious problems with the wood parts of your piano drying out.

Many manufacturer websites allow you to trace the serial number of your piano, so you can check the vintage and country of birth for a piano you're looking at.

Getting all the pedals you deserve

Some underhanded dealers claim that they can save you money by offering you a piano with no middle pedal. Baloney! You may never use the middle pedal, but just in case Lang Lang comes over for lunch, you need to have one.

Getting a middle pedal isn't like adding a sunroof to a new car. Three piano pedals shouldn't be optional or part of a special package that costs more; three pedals are part of the overall purchase. If you want three pedals, ask to see piano models with three pedals.

Many upright pianos just don't have a middle pedal. So, if the piano you want is an upright with only two pedals, it's probably perfectly fine. Just ask about the third pedal to be on the safe side.

Finding good buys and avoiding scams

If you shop around and find a piano for a ridiculously low price — far lower than the same model anywhere else in town — it's either used, broken, or a Memorial Day sale to really remember.

If you decide to shop for a used acoustic piano, be patient and take a look at a variety of instruments. There are many very good pianos out there, and sometimes people need to sell them because they don't play them anymore, they're moving, or they need to make room for a new 70-inch HDTV setup. And if you've found your dream piano at a garage sale, the low, low price is not necessarily an indication of anything wrong. It's a *garage sale!* You may just find a perfectly good piano with many glorious years left in it for a fraction of the cost of a new one.

Be smart about any deal that seems too good to be true. If most stores offer a certain model for $20,000 and suddenly you're staring at the same model at PianoMax for $5,000, something's wrong. The soundboard may be cracked. It may be missing strings. Who knows? Hire a professional to look the piano over before you purchase it. (See Book I Chapter 4 for more information on finding piano technicians.)

Demo models are also good buys. Stores frequently loan pianos to local universities or concert halls for use by students, competitions, and guest artists. Even if it has been used only one time, the piano can no longer be sold as new. Of course, pianos don't have odometers, so you have to take the dealer's word for just how used a piano really is, but most dealers will be honest about this point.

If you've heard one, you haven't heard them all

Not only do different brands sound completely different, but the sound of two pianos made by the *same company* can sound and feel different, too. This is why you must, must, must put your hands and ears on every piano you consider. Play every darn key, and play at all volumes. Many pianos sound beautiful except for one key. If you don't play every key at the store, you'll notice the bad key after you get the piano home.

Play and listen to those keys again and again. Trust your instincts. Don't be rushed. Only you know what you like. Some people don't like the sound of a Steinway; some don't like a Baldwin. You're entitled to your own taste.

Looking at specific piano brands

The following are some good brands of pianos from around the world. Contact these companies directly and ask where to find their pianos in your area.

- ✔ **Baldwin Piano & Organ Company:** Makes Baldwin, Wurlitzer, Chickering, and Concertmaster pianos. www.gibson.com/en-us/divisions/baldwin.

- ✔ **Kawai America Corporation:** Offers every Kawai under the sun. www.kawaius.com.

- ✔ **L. Bösendorfer Klavier:** Carries all Bösendorfer models. www.boesendorfer.com.

- ✔ **Mason & Hamlin World Headquarters:** Makes grands and uprights. www.masonhamlin.com.

- ✔ **Pearl River Piano Group America Ltd.:** Makes Pearl River and Ritmüller pianos. www.pearlriverusa.com.

- ✔ **Steinway & Sons:** Has been making Steinway pianos since 1853; also offers Boston and Essex pianos. www.steinway.com.

- ✔ **Story & Clark:** Now makes hybrid pianos, with an optical sensor, USB ports, and MIDI ports standard on all models www.qrsmusic.com.

- ✔ **Yamaha Corporation of America:** Makes all types of Yamaha pianos. www.yamaha.com.

Selecting a Digital Keyboard That Lasts

After much deliberation, and for whatever reasons, you decide to buy a digital keyboard over an acoustic one. Think your job is done? Not so fast, pal. Now you must decide what *type* of digital keyboard you want:

✓ Digital pianos and organs

✓ Arrangers

✓ Stage pianos

✓ Workstations

✓ Synthesizers

Don't assume that you've necessarily gone the cheaper route by selecting a digital keyboard as your instrument of choice. These instruments can be quite expensive, sometimes costing more than an acoustic piano. But they're also very versatile. Instead of being limited to the sound of a piano, you can have literally hundreds or even thousands of different sounds at your fingertips.

The number of sounds you can use depends on the type of keyboard you select. Just like computers, digital keyboards have memory, storage space, and performance limitations. Some you can add memory and sounds to, but some are what they are and no more.

Sorting out all the different keyboard types and styles can leave your mind numb. But here are a few things you can count on:

✓ All digital keyboards today use sampled sounds, which vary in quality.

✓ You can choose from a variety of keyboard actions, or touch sensitivity — everything from nonresponsive action to weighted-action keyboards designed to mimic the touch and feel of an acoustic piano.

✓ The three common keyboard sizes are standard 61-key, 76-key, and 88-key.

✓ Digital keyboards have varying degrees of portability.

✓ Nearly all models come with a music rack, a plug-in sustain pedal, and MIDI (see the later section "The MIDI Places You Can Go") and/or USB connection capability.

Although the lines between digital keyboard categories are increasingly blurred, you can still find clear differences when it comes to sequencing capabilities, built-in speakers, sound effects, metronomes, auto-accompaniment features, recording features, extra pedals, and other plug-in devices. The following sections get more in-depth about the differences of these digital keyboards.

Digital pianos and organs

The two types of digital piano or organ for home use are

- ✔ Portable models.
- ✔ Upright and grand models.

Not surprisingly, the portables are more portable than the uprights and grands, which are designed after their acoustic sisters and are meant to occupy a relatively permanent spot in your home, not unlike an upright or grand piano. Both come with built-in speakers, although the speakers are smaller on the portable models. Both usually offer a few sound options like acoustic piano, electric piano, organ, and maybe vibes. They come with a music rack, a stand (if it's not part of the keyboard), and a plug-in pedal.

If you're looking exclusively for a digital organ, some very attractive models come with dual manuals and multiple organ effects like draw bars and rotary sound.

Arrangers

If you're looking to have lots of fun with different sounds and accompaniment features and you're not concerned with finding the best acoustic piano samples, an arranger is the digital keyboard for you. This type is loaded with "one-man band" features, like scads of sounds (500 or more); automatic drum, bass, and chord accompaniment; and recording and playback. Lower-end models are quite inexpensive and very portable.

Stage pianos

These keyboards, made for onstage performing, offer more professional keyboard sounds. If you're going to be the keyboard player in a band, or even a solo act, and will be gigging around town, the stage piano may be the choice for you. It doesn't have built-in speakers, so you need to have an external amplifier and speaker to hear yourself play, but you can plug in headphones. Also, a stage piano doesn't have as many functions as an arranger. Stage pianos come with a music rack and sustain pedal, but you need to purchase a keyboard stand and other accessories separately.

Workstations

Essentially a computer built into a keyboard, a workstation has everything: top-of-the-line sound samples, sequencing, recording and editing, and computer integration. These babies can be quite expensive, but if you've got big musical dreams, you may want to try one out.

Synthesizers

You can still buy a good ol' synthesizer and manipulate waveforms and filters, and work with both analog and digital sounds. Today's synthesizers come with more sounds to work with than older models, letting you go to town with some good preset sounds.

Avoiding obsolescence

As with computers, keyboards become outdated as quickly as they reach the stores. But keyboard manufacturers are constantly trying to make products that won't become obsolete by creating keyboards that can be upgraded or added to as technology advances.

Ask the manufacturer or a salesperson the following questions:

- **Can I add memory?** Adding memory to keyboards is quite common these days. More memory means the ability to accommodate new sounds, software, and hardware at a later date. Also ask what the memory limitations are.

- **Is the unit upgradeable?** Workstations offer operating system and software upgrades, making it easy to keep up with the latest improvements.

- **Can I purchase extra sound cards or libraries?** Many workstations have vast libraries of sounds. Whether they're developed by the original manufacturer or other sound developers, you can add extra sound cards and libraries to make old keyboards sound new again.

- **Is the company still making this model or series?** If not, the keyboard is already headed toward the land of obsolescence. But if it meets all the other criteria on this list and you can get it for a good price, just add memory, upgrades, and sounds over the years.

Knowing the digital features you want

Make a list of the digital keyboard features that are important to you before you even start shopping. This list can be different for each user. As technology expands, more and more keyboards feature all kinds of nice little bells and whistles. This list runs through digital keyboard features and tells you which keyboards to turn to for them:

- **Realistic piano sound:** Look at the home digital pianos with the best piano samples.

- **Realistic piano action:** Look at the home digital pianos with the best touch-sensitive keyboards and the best weighted-key action.

- **Built-in speakers:** Home digital pianos, for sure.

- **To perform onstage:** Look at stage pianos, and keep in mind that you also need amplification.

- **Portability:** Look at stage pianos and arrangers.

- **Multi-note polyphony:** Look at home digital pianos, stage pianos, and workstations. The bigger the number, the more notes you can play at once, so try for at least 32-note polyphony. Sure, you don't have 32 fingers, but if you use MIDI, 32-note polyphony comes in handy. Some models even have 128-note polyphony, which is excellent.

- **Multi-timbral:** Look at arrangers and workstations for this ability to play more than one sound at the same time. For example, you can play sounds from a piano, a violin, a banjo, and a bagpipe together on "Danny Boy."

- **MIDI capability:** Nowadays, they all have this. Read more about MIDI later in this chapter in the section "The MIDI Places You Can Go."

- **Pitch bend and modulation:** Look at arrangers, synthesizers, and workstations to make your sounds say "wah wah" and "woob woob."

- **Sound editing:** Look at workstations if you want to change the sounds, making the piano brighter, the horns brassier, and the goose calls goosier, for example.

- **Internal recording, editing, and sequencing:** Want to record what you play without using external recorders or a computer? You need a sequencer, which most digital keyboards have, but only workstations have the most advanced editing and sequencing features.

- **Automatic rhythm, harmony, and bass accompaniment:** Look at arrangers.

✔ **Strange sound effects:** Look at synthesizers if you want to program your own sounds. Be aware that some synthesizers are *monophonic,* meaning they can play only one note at a time.

✔ **Other mumbo-jumbo:** Flash ROM, DSP plug-ins, BIAS Peak, sub-oscillators, vocoders, modeling filters, arpeggiators — all this is very cool, but what does it have to do with you playing music? Not much. It simply indicates that your model is on the cutting edge of current keyboard features.

Whichever way you go, ask yourself this important question before you buy: Do you like the keyboard as an instrument? Take your time and make sure it sounds good to your ears. If the in-store keyboard is hooked up to an external amplifier and speaker, ask the salesperson if you can listen to the keyboard through an amp and speaker similar to what you'll be using — or headphones. Also consider whether the keyboard looks good, and whether you'll enjoy having it in your home where you'll feel comfortable and free to practice and play. And does the keyboard do what you want it to do, whether that's sound like an organ, a string section, or an alien band from a distant galaxy?

Browsing some specific keyboard brands

When you have a good idea of which type of digital keyboard fits your needs, you're ready for some recommendations. This section recommends several top brands and models to help you narrow the search for your keyboard.

Recommendations for digital pianos and organs

If you're having trouble finding any of these brands in stores in your area, contact the companies directly; they'll be happy to help sell you a keyboard.

✔ **Kawai America Corporation:** Recommended models are CE220 Digital Piano and ES7 Portable Digital Piano. www.kawaius.com.

✔ **Korg USA, Inc.:** Recommended models are SP-280 digital piano and LP-380 digital home piano. www.korg.com.

✔ **Nord Keyboards:** Recommended models are Nord C2D Combo Organ and Nord Electro 4. www.nordkeyboards.com.

✔ **Roland Corporation U.S.:** Recommended models are RG-1F Digital Mini-Grand Piano, RP-301: SuperNATURAL Piano, and AT-75 Atelier Organ. www.rolandus.com.

✔ **Yamaha Corporation of America:** Recommended models are AvantGrand, P105 Stage Digital Piano, and P95 Digital Piano. www.yamaha.com.

Recommendations for arrangers, workstations, and synthesizers

The following list points you toward some quality manufacturers of arrangers, workstations, and synthesizers. This isn't an exhaustive list of models by any means. Each company makes models with different features and price points (although none is really inexpensive).

Book I

Piano &
Keyboard
101

- ✓ **Alesis Studio Electronics:** www.alesis.com.
- ✓ **Casio Incorporated:** www.casio.com.
- ✓ **Dave Smith Instruments:** www.davesmithinstruments.com.
- ✓ **E-Mu Systems Incorporated:** www.emu.com.
- ✓ **Korg USA, Inc.:** www.korg.com.
- ✓ **Kurzweil Music Systems:** www.kurzweilmusicsystems.com.
- ✓ **Moog Music Incorporated:** www.moogmusic.com.
- ✓ **Nord:** www.nordkeyboards.com.
- ✓ **Novation:** http://us.novationmusic.com.
- ✓ **Roland Corporation U.S.:** www.rolandus.com.
- ✓ **Yamaha Corporation of America:** www.yamaha.com.

Before You Drive It Off the Lot: Sealing the Deal

If you've ever bought a car, you know that looking at and test-driving different models is almost as much fun as taking one home. Buying a keyboard should be a similar experience.

Take it for a spin

No matter what kind of music store you walk into, the pianos and keyboards are there for you to try out. Go ahead — touch it, play it. Push the buttons and turn the volume up and down. If it's a piano, have a seat and play a while. It's just you and the keyboard . . . and perhaps a dozen other customers and salespeople standing around listening.

Keep in mind that many digital keyboards on display are routed through processors, effects, and other digital enhancements to make them sound better. Don't be fooled by this extra gear. Kindly ask the salesperson to turn off all effects so that you can hear the keyboard as is. Otherwise, you may be disappointed with the way it sounds after you get it home — unless, of course, you also buy all the effects and processors.

Notice the following about each piano or keyboard you try:

- ✔ Is the overall sound full or wimpy, bright or dull?
- ✔ Do long notes actually last as long as you play them?
- ✔ On an acoustic piano, do the top five keys sound good, not metallic? Do the lower five keys sound good, not thick and sloppy?
- ✔ Do you get a quick response when you play the keys? Is the keyboard too sensitive, or not sensitive enough?
- ✔ Do your fingers have enough room on the keys?

Love it and leave it

You found the perfect keyboard for you, and you're in love. This is the one. Now leave the store quickly with a tip of your hat and a polite "I'll think about it" to the hovering sales manager.

You're in trouble if you sit down and negotiate the first time you walk into the store. You're too emotionally attached to think clearly. This is love — true love. Your keyboard is your baby. Before negotiating a price, leave the store and spend the next few hours or days searching for that identical piano at a lower price. When you're 100 percent sure that you can't find it cheaper and still can't live without it, head back to the store and start negotiating.

Never pay the sticker price

Many people think that the art of negotiating a price is reserved for car buying. On the contrary, the wonderful world of instruments and accessories is open for price haggling. The sticker price is merely a starting point. If the price of that baby grand you want is $15,000, you could find yourself taking it home (in a very big truck) for as low as $10,000.

Generally, you can hope to get anywhere from 10 to 15 percent off the sticker price. The closer you pay to the dealer's asking price, the more likely the salesperson is to throw in freebies like delivery to your home — which can sometimes cost as much as $300 — or a free year of tuning, piano cleaner, or fuzzy dice. A deal can work the other way, too: If you're buying accessories like a keyboard stand, amplifier, some software, and some cables, the salesperson will be more receptive to making a deal.

Go in the store with an absolute maximum dollar amount in your head. When you're sure about a particular model, sit down with the salesperson and ask what's the best he can do on that model piano. If you get an answer equal to or less than the maximum figure in your head, shake hands and write the check. If the price is nowhere close to what you're comfortable paying, stand up and say, "Well, thank you very much. You have my number if you change your mind." Remember, there are more piano stores and more piano models in this world.

A piano store is a store like any other, complete with sales at key times during the year. For example, Memorial Day is always a big piano-buying time. Shop around, and then keep an eye out for sales and promotions.

Shopping online

Surfing the Internet can be great for comparing keyboards and getting a handle on digital lingo. Virtual showroom tours, product demonstrations, and used and new price quotes abound. You can certainly find some available models that your local dealer doesn't carry and preview some models and features that manufacturers are planning to introduce.

One good place to check out what other people think about particular models is YouTube (www.youtube.com). Go to the search box at the top of the page and enter the brand and model you want to check out and add the words "unboxing" or "review." You'll likely get several videos of people testing out and commenting on your model.

As you start to focus on a few keyboards that interest you, read the FAQ and product specifications on the manufacturer websites (refer to the contact listings earlier in this chapter). Look at what models are being sold as used, and why. Study up on the features that interest you so that, when you go to a dealer, you'll be treated as an informed customer and not a know-nothing who can be suckered into a bad deal. And read customer reviews.

You can buy online, and in some cases pay less doing so, but it's important to keep in mind the limitations. Only a dealer can give you product support, answer your questions, and offer you a store warranty so that you can bring your instrument back for repairs or problems.

Because you do want to try out any instrument before you buy it, consider shopping Craigslist (www.craigslist.org) to find used instruments near where you live. That way you can hop in the car and go check them out.

The MIDI Places You Can Go

Your new digital or hybrid keyboard is wonderful — exactly what you wanted. But now you want to experiment with all the cool things you've heard about. This section explains several other types of musical devices, including MIDI and other recording systems, that can hook up to your new keyboard and that help you go even farther in your pursuit of a musical career — or just your desire to get the most out of your keyboard.

After you start investing in recording software and equipment, two things happen: You spend far less time practicing music and far more time studying up on new technology, and your bank account shrinks. For now, it's nice to know these recording options exist, but consider playing music for a while before diving into a new career as a recording engineer.

A mini MIDI primer

MIDI stands for *Musical Instrument Digital Interface.* It's not nearly as boring as it sounds. In fact, MIDI (pronounced *mid*-ee) can change your musical life.

In a nutshell, MIDI enables you to connect and communicate with other keyboards, your computer, or other digital equipment from your digital or hybrid keyboard. Suppose you have three keyboards. You select the first one to be the *controller* and set it to sound like a piano. You connect the other two keyboards to the controller and set each of them to different sounds, perhaps a flute and a tuba. As you play the controller, the other two keyboards are sent MIDI *messages* (binary codes) telling them which notes to play, how long, how loud, and so on. But it sounds like three players are playing three separate instruments, instead of just you on a piano.

But that's not all MIDI can do. By connecting a MIDI cable to your computer, you can record, edit, and notate your music using software programs on your computer. You can buy MIDI-recorded CDs and hear the songs played with the sounds of your own keyboard. Hybrid pianos and player piano systems also use MIDI to communicate with other digital equipment. MIDI software and recordings have become quite popular teaching aids because you can follow along note for note as your keyboard plays the songs.

Keyboard to computer

Digital keyboards offer you a host of options that help you record your music. You can record directly on your keyboard, or you can record by connecting your keyboard to your computer using MIDI cables. If you use MIDI, you can record exactly what you play without any fancy recording equipment. The MIDI messages you send from your keyboard as you play can be recorded in a computer or *sequencer.* Later, all you do is push "play" on the sequencer and hear note for note, volume for volume, exactly what you played.

There are many types of recording and sequencing software programs for your computer that give you recording and editing options that may not be available on your keyboard.

Book I

Piano & Keyboard 101

Digital recording and sequencing programs allow you to record on several different tracks. So, you can record yourself playing the melody of a song with a piano sound on track 1, followed by the drum part on track 2, and then the guitar part on track 3. But you never use any instrument other than your keyboard and the sounds that came with it. Play back the recording, or sequence, and it plays all three tracks at once, which sounds like a four-member band. Want more? Just add some violins on track 4. Perhaps the sound of rain on track 5. Pretty soon you've got the entire London Philharmonic playing on tracks 6 through 16.

Software programs allow you to edit, transpose, speed up, or slow down what you've recorded. You can also alter the volume levels on each track and add sound effects, like reverb, to enhance what you've played. But wait! There's more! You can purchase or even download MIDI files that you can load into your recording software so you can play along with files and add new tracks on top.

Keyboard to keyboard

You can connect your MIDI keyboard with another MIDI keyboard, or build a chain of three or more. Set each keyboard with a different sound patch, and play all the keyboards at once from your main, *controller* keyboard. See what it sounds like to combine piano and string sounds, brass and electric guitar, you name it.

MIDI and music notation

Music notation programs are a great tool to help you learn and improve your music reading and writing skills. When you hook up your MIDI keyboard to a computer and open up notation software, you can write music, read music, and play back whatever you're working on. Plenty of educational programs are available to help you with the basics of music notation; some are interactive and make learning fun. And don't forget that you can use notation programs to write out your latest opus so you can share your music with other musicians.

Chapter 4

The Setup and Care of Your Instrument

In This Chapter

▶ Getting the keyboard (and its miscellany) out of the package and assembled

▶ Finding the right spot for your keyboard

▶ Cleaning your keyboard

▶ Realizing when you can't fix it yourself

▶ Making electrical and audio connections

▶ Maintaining your keyboard and fixing minor problems

So you've chosen the right instrument for your needs and have brought it home to start making music. Where will you be able to focus on playing, practicing, and enjoying making music without distraction (and without distracting others)?

This chapter discusses how to set up your piano or keyboard, how to safely move it around, and how to keep it in tip-top shape. You'll also find out about the various types of keyboard connections (and connectors) that allow you to hook up to other gear to hear your keyboard in open air. The chapter talks a little bit about electrical safety and some best practices when using powered electrical gear. And you'll find out how to get help when you have a problem.

Unboxing Your New Keyboard

In the excited rush of opening up your new instrument, you may actually miss some important in-box element of your purchase. And the last thing you want is to injure yourself before you even get a chance to play. This section offers a few pointers.

Your keyboard comes wrapped in some type of plastic bag or material and has molded foam end caps on both ends to protect it and hold it in place in the box. What many people often miss is that some important accessory may also be located in the end of the foam insert. So look carefully at both end pieces.

Besides the keyboard itself (including the stand assembly if it's a home digital piano), look for the following items (not all will apply to your chosen model; check the beginning of your owner's manual for more information):

- **Power cable or external power supply:** Some of these connectors are two-piece affairs, with the larger, rectangular piece plus a second cable that connects between it and the outlet (like you see with some laptops).

- **Owner's manual or operation guide:** Your keyboard package includes some sort of documentation (traditionally a printed hard copy) to help you operate it. These instructions may be a complete owner's manual or just a brief getting-started guide to help you with only the most basic tasks. These booklets commonly show up in a clear bag, which may also include a warranty card and perhaps a CD-ROM. This disc likely contains most of your needed documentation — the owner's manual, a deeper *parameter guide* (which explains each and every function and parameter of the product), a voice/sound name list, and other documents.

  Note: To keep costs down, many manufacturers are moving toward including fewer printed materials and providing lengthier documentation as an electronic PDF file. Go to www.adobe.com/reader to download the free Adobe Reader application if you don't have it.

  Products often change, adding new features and fixing mistakes in documentation. A newer version of your keyboard's document(s) may be available for download from the manufacturer's website.

- **Warranty card:** A *warranty card* registers your ownership of the product with the manufacturer, ensuring your coverage for repairs/problems during a set time period the company offers. You aren't actually required to fill in/return this type of card to be eligible for warranty coverage. Your proof of purchase (a store receipt is best) guarantees your coverage of whatever the manufacturer offers.

  Many manufacturers offer extended warranty time periods (usually double the regular time) if you go to their websites to fill out your warranty info. This extension is a great benefit, and it's free, so check into this possibility and take advantage if it's available.

- **Additional hardware:** If you've bought a home digital piano with an included stand assembly, the screws, wing nuts, and other hardware connectors are in a separate bag somewhere in the box. Look carefully for any such items in the foam inserts or taped to the inside of the box.

✔ **Included sustain/damper pedal:** If your keyboard is supposed to come with a pedal, that pedal will usually be in a white cardboard box within the shipping box. Sometimes these free pedals are only small flat switches, so the box can be small and easily overlooked.

✔ **Additional cables:** Some keyboards come with a USB cable for connecting the instrument to your computer for MIDI and/or audio functionality. Although you may not require that capability right away, if it was promised to you, be sure to locate the cord.

✔ **Bundled goods from the retailer:** Some retailers put together special bundle promotions, where they add other goods (such as headphones, a carrying case, a stand, music books or software, and so on) to your package price. These items are always packed in one or more separate packages and either are given to you at the time of purchase or shipped at the same time. Look carefully for markings such as "Box 1 of *x*," "Box 2 of *x*," and so on.

Providing a Good Place to Put It

Whether you bought an acoustic or digital keyboard, the first thing to do when you get your new baby home is find a spot for it. This doesn't have to be a permanent resting place. Your ideal spot will have these characteristics:

✔ **No direct sunlight:** Even through a window, overexposure to sunlight can damage your keyboard over time. Direct sunlight can cause the wood to warp or dry out, affecting both the sound and overall appearance.

✔ **Controlled climate:** Don't expose your keyboard to wide temperature swings. Don't leave it on a porch that gets hot in the summer and cold in the winter. Place your keyboard near an interior wall rather than an exterior wall. Wood responds to changes in humidity, so consider setting up a humidifier or dehumidifier if you and your acoustic piano live in a dry or wet climate. (Your piano tuner will be glad to advise you on humidifiers and dehumidifiers for this purpose.)

✔ **Good ventilation:** For acoustic pianos, good ventilation reduces the buildup of excess moisture, which can affect the wood. For digital keyboards, ventilation keeps the inner workings cooled when the power is on. But don't put your keyboard right under an air conditioning unit or right over a heating duct.

✔ **Safety:** Don't set your keyboard in a precarious position where it can get bumped, fall, or have something fall on it.

✔ **Elbow room:** When you feel cramped or uncomfortable, you're more likely to avoid practicing. Lack of practice leads to poor playing, so give yourself ample space for stretching out when you play.

✔ **Convenience:** Make sure your room has plenty of electrical outlets. Using miles of extension cords is expensive, irritating, and ugly.

✔ **Lighting:** Until you're in a dark, smoke-filled bar or in front of hundreds of adoring fans, you should always play with good lighting. Not only is it easier to see the keys with good light, but reading music is next to impossible in the dark. You can set a lamp on or near your keyboard, but not the clip-on kind, which can damage the keyboard's finish.

Also keep in mind how the location of your piano or keyboard may impact your relationship with your neighbors. For example, don't put your keyboard in the room right over your downstairs neighbor's bedroom. All those practice sessions late at night will soon be history.

Making It Shine

A clean instrument sounds and looks better longer than one that's neglected — both advantages that can affect its value if you ever need to sell it. You don't have to go overboard when it comes to cleaning your acoustic piano or digital keyboard, but keep it free of dust and dirt as much as possible.

Don't be afraid to lay down the law when it comes to keeping your instrument clean, insisting that no one (not even you) eats or drinks around your keyboard. A spilled drink in the back seat of your car is one thing; a spilled drink on your keyboard can be fatal (for the keyboard, that is). And do you really want to clean out cracker crumbs from between the keys once a month?

In addition to keeping food and drink away from your keyboard, don't allow dust to build up on your instrument. Dust buildup may eventually short out the circuitry or cause the keys or buttons to stick. Either result is bad news. Cover your digital keyboard when you aren't using it, either with a purchased dust cover or a homemade cover, like a sheet. Dust buildup in acoustic pianos isn't as critical, but you should still keep it in check.

The two most important cleaning tools to have near your instrument are a feather duster and a small, medium-bristle paintbrush. At least once a month, use the feather duster for an overall dusting, followed by a detailing with the paintbrush, where you get in all the grooves and between the keys. Simply press down each key and clean both sides before moving to the next one. If you're in a hurry, just run the brush in between the keys and give it a better, more thorough cleaning later. Digital keyboards have lots of little buttons, digital displays, knobs, sliders, and other gadgets; turn the power off and clean these with a dry, soft, lint-free rag every couple of months.

Secret revealed: Special piano cleaner

Your dealer may suggest you buy a special cleaner packaged in a very handy and attractive bottle. Having just written a very large check, you jump at the chance to protect your investment, never mind the added cost.

You get home and decipher the scientific ingredient names on the label only to discover that you just purchased some expensive soap and water. Save your money and make your own

by using the following: An empty spray bottle, a marker, liquid hand soap, and water.

Rinse out the spray bottle until it's free of residue from any previous products. Use your marker to write "Piano Cleaner" on the outside. Add four or five squirts of soap to the bottle, and then fill it up with clean water. Shake well before spraying your rag and then wiping down your instrument.

Be careful what cleaning solvents you use on your keyboard's finish. The wood finish on many grand pianos, for example, can be ruined by normal furniture polish. Ivory keys should be cleaned with a dry cloth or a cleaner made especially for them. (Products made for cleaning piano cases and keys are available online.) For most keyboards (acoustic or electric), use a cloth that's slightly damp with plain soap and water (see the sidebar "Secret revealed: Special piano cleaner"). Don't be embarrassed to ask the dealer what cleaning products are advised and exactly how to use them.

When using a liquid solution on the finish, whether soap and water or window cleaner (sometimes recommended, but ask first!), use an old T-shirt or lint-free rag instead of a paper towel. Fabric cloths don't leave those little white fuzz balls as you clean. Don't spray liquid cleaners directly on your instrument. Spray first onto your rag or cloth, and then wipe the instrument. Continue again and again until the instrument is clean, but make sure you wipe up any excess moisture.

Calling In a Pro for Tuning, Check-Ups, and Serious Repairs

Playing the keyboard is one thing. Knowing how to repair and maintain one is another. Leave such matters to a qualified professional. You have enough to worry about with playing, reading music, and touring around the world.

This section gives you tips on hiring piano tuners, piano technicians, keyboard technical support people, and others who can help you maintain and prolong your instrument's life.

Tuning pianos: Leave it to the experts

Okay, so your friend can tune his own guitar, violin, or clarinet. Keep in mind how much larger your piano is, how many parts are inside, and how much more you probably paid for it. Swallow your pride, pick up the phone, and call a piano technician when it's time to tune your piano.

Piano technicians are skilled professionals with years of education and experience. It may look like the technician's just playing keys and tightening screws, but you won't even know where to begin if you try to do it yourself.

Don't think that you'll suddenly hear your piano go out of tune one day. Loss of intonation is a gradual process. Your tuning will be much overdue if you get to the point where you actually say to yourself, "Wow! My piano's out of tune." Schedule a tuning at least once a year — preferably twice a year. Generally, the visit will take two to three hours and cost you between $75 and $150, which is well worth the cost. After you establish a relationship with a technician, he or she will probably contact you each year, so you don't even have to remember to schedule an appointment for a tuning.

Too many years of tuning neglect results in a piano that's permanently out of tune. Ever heard an old honky-tonk saloon piano? Sure, the sound is sort of fun, but not when it's coming from your $30,000 9-foot grand piano. Frequent tuning ensures that the pitch of your piano doesn't drop (a condition that's reparable but sometimes problematic) and that any problems with the tuning pins, which are tightened and loosened during tuning, or the pinblock, which holds the pins, can be fixed as they arise.

You can get recommendations for a good piano technician from friends, teachers, music stores, and music schools. Check recommendations against the member directory of the Piano Technicians Guild at www.ptg.org, which includes individuals who have earned the distinction of Registered Piano Technician (RPT). Don't just select at random from the phonebook; a bad technician can ruin a piano.

Ask the technician to have a look under the hood and make sure everything is functioning properly:

✔ Do the pedals work?

✔ Are the legs secure?

✔ Are there any problems with the action?

✔ Is the soundboard cracked?

Technical support lines

Each and every time you buy a new keyboard, fill out and send in the registration card that comes with it — or register online, if that's an option. Don't be afraid that you'll be put on some mailing list; you're simply telling the manufacturer, "Just letting you know that I bought your really cool product. Here's my name and here's where I live." That's all.

Then any time you have a problem with your instrument, you can call the manufacturer's technical support line and speak with a knowledgeable professional (maybe even someone who designed your keyboard) about the specific problem you're having and how to rectify it. The call to technical support is usually free — if you've filled out that little card and mailed it in.

Keeping digital keyboards happy

You don't need to tune your digital keyboard. However, it does need some occasional attention. If you keep it clean and dust-free, chances are it will work and sound just fine for quite some time.

Over time, through constant pushing and pulling, the little buttons, digital displays, knobs, sliders, and other gizmos on a digital keyboard experience normal wear and tear. If a button appears to be stuck, don't try to fix it yourself with one of your own tools. Call a professional — perhaps the dealer who sold you the instrument or the manufacturer — for a dealer reference. For a minimal fee, the dealer can assess the damage (if any) and fix it for you. If your warranty is still good (usually only for one year), it could be free.

Never, ever, under any circumstances unscrew or open the top of your keyboard. Sure, it looks cool inside with all the computer chips and circuit boards. Sure, you think you know what you're doing and want to save a buck by fixing a problem yourself. But opening up your keyboard voids your warranty automatically and could damage your keyboard irreparably.

Dealing with serious problems

Unfortunately, some keyboard problems can arise that require some serious time, effort, and money to fix. If you experience any of the following problems, you should get estimates from at least two separate technicians before deciding whether or not to salvage your instrument:

- ✔ **The soundboard on your acoustic piano cracks or breaks.** The soundboard is the large, polished board under the strings. The soundboard can break during a move performed by unqualified movers. It can also break due to constant changes in humidity that cause the wood to swell and contract. Have your piano technician check out the soundboard for you during each tune-up.

✔ **You hear only a thump when you press an acoustic piano key.** Either the hammer, damper, or both are not functioning properly. You may have to replace the mechanism for that one key or replace the entire set of keys and hammers. Hope for the first option. Of course, the culprit could also just be a broken string, which can be fixed for under $20.

✔ **Your digital keyboard won't power on.** Your keyboard should always power on when plugged in correctly. If not, it may be dead.

✔ **Your LCD display shows nothing legible.** If the words and program names on the front panel display of your digital keyboard are suddenly a bunch of meaningless letters, the brains of your board may be fried.

✔ **You spill liquid all over your digital keyboard.** You probably just shorted out the entire board. Few, if any, of your buttons and keys are going to work. This is why you should never have a drink on or near your keyboard. The first thing to do is to shut the power off. Let it dry out completely (for days) before turning the power on again.

✔ **You spill liquid on your acoustic piano.** Quickly get a towel and start sopping it up. The wood, strings, hammers, and even keys may be damaged, but at least there isn't anything electrical to bug out.

How to move a piano

You *must* hire a qualified piano mover to transfer your baby to its new home. Don't be cheap about hiring a mover. Inexperienced movers can ruin your piano. And don't *ever* try to move the piano by yourself or with friends.

Don't watch the move. You should definitely be present to watch the movers and make sure they take extreme care when moving your precious baby. But you're guaranteed to grimace when you see them flip that piano over on its side. Save yourself the emotional distress and just turn away.

Moving a grand piano involves its own specialized piece of equipment called a *piano board*.

This long, flat board has lots of padding and several handles. The movers lay the piano on its side on this board and strap it all to a dolly. The piano board holds your baby securely and cushions any jarring bumps. If your movers show up without a piano board, bid them farewell and call new movers. To move upright pianos, movers typically place the piano (upright!) on a flat dolly.

Your local piano dealer can recommend several good moving companies that specialize in piano moving. The good ones actually receive endorsements from piano manufacturers.

Setting Up Your Keyboard

Any stand you use with your keyboard probably requires some assembly. But if you're working with a home digital piano or very large arranger keyboard that comes with a custom stand as part of the package, it's a good idea to connect the instrument to a power source to make sure it's working okay before you assemble the stand and place the keyboard on it. You'd much rather find out you've got a bum keyboard before you put together the stand, especially a complicated one with lots of doodads.

You can easily look up the weight of your new keyboard to be sure the stand can hold it, but you also need to consider the amount of force and constant vibration that playing the keyboard is going to exert. A small child or delicate player isn't going to produce much extra pressure on the stand, but if you're planning to play some bangin' rock and roll, highly rhythmic funk, or dramatic classical pieces, you should seriously consider the sturdiness of your stand. The cheapest stands are an *X* design, with a simple cross brace underneath. These types are okay, but they're not as sturdy and solid as a design that has at least four actual legs underneath. Check to see whether the keyboard/stand combo easily rocks back and forth (which you don't want).

Stand height is another important consideration. Good piano technique requires that your arm is basically level from the elbow across to the hand, so position your stand accordingly (keeping in mind the height of the keyboard itself as well). Angling your hand downward or upward causes stress and can tire and even hurt your wrist muscles. When sitting, the chair, stool, or bench you use often determines stand height. However, you can adjust the height on fancier piano benches and many computer desk chairs.

When standing, the straight forearm rule applies, with the added issue that you're more likely to cause the keyboard to vibrate or even move with your forceful playing. Be sure your stand doesn't bounce too much or move around and that all connections are hand-tightened securely.

Hook Me Up: Keyboard Connections

Your keyboard is electronic, so you're going to have to hook up some things before you can play. Even with just a little portable, you need to insert batteries to get started. The following sections cover the most common connections you'll encounter.

Making the electrical connection

Most people know not to stick their fingers, their tongues, or pointy objects into an outlet, but not everyone thinks carefully when plugging in power cables or adapters.

Always plug the power cable or power adapter into the keyboard before you plug it into the outlet. Don't let your finger slip over to the prong or tip of the plug when pushing it in. Look to see whether the plug has one prong larger than the other (to ensure you're grounded properly) before plugging it in.

Plugging a lot of devices into one outlet can be a fire hazard. Consider distributing them around to other outlets or even parts of your room/house if possible. Or buy multioutlet plugs that attach to the normal dual-outlet boxes found in the wall, giving you four or even six outlets. If you want to use one of these, be sure to secure it to the wall outlet with the long screw provided.

Many people choose to use a multioutlet strip that sits on the floor instead of crowding the wall outlet. If you do this, invest in an outlet strip that offers *surge suppression* or *surge protection*. This feature protects your gear from sudden spikes in the power that may damage your electronic keyboard.

That said, a strip-based surge protector won't protect you if your house is struck by lightning; you need much more expensive and advanced gear for that level of safety. If a strong thunderstorm is reported in your area, unplug your valuable electronic devices (and appliances) until the storm passes.

Firing up your keyboard

This chapter can't hope to explain each and every electronic keyboard and how they work. There's no substitute for reading the manual that came with your product. Read through the opening section of your manual regarding connections and first-time use before officially starting up your keyboard.

Follow these steps to safely get your keyboard going:

1. **Plug in any pedals you have.**

   Look carefully on the back panel to be sure you're plugging the pedal into the right jack. Read more about this hookup in your product's owner's manual or getting started guide.

2. **Find the main volume control and turn it all the way down.**

   This control may be labeled just Volume or Output.

3. **Locate the power switch or button; turn it on and wait for the keyboard to fully boot up.**

   The on/off control may be on the front panel, around the back of the unit, or even on the side. Remember, some units take a few moments to fully wake up and be ready to play.

4. **Play a single note over and over while you raise the volume to your desired level.**

5. **If your keyboard has built-in demos or songs, play one, step back a bit from it, and listen while adjusting the volume.**

   This step is a good way to enjoy your first listen to your new instrument in your home surroundings. Set the volume too loud, and you may find you start rattling pictures on the wall or disturbing some other item. Either batten down the offending vibrating object or lower the volume.

Working with headphones

Perhaps your keyboard doesn't have onboard speakers, or you just want to enjoy some private practice time. Every electronic keyboard offers a head-phone output for that purpose. (Often, if a keyboard does have onboard speakers, plugging a headphone in will automatically turn off the speakers. Smart, huh?)

Headphones bring the sound very close to your ears (and in the case of in-the-ear varieties, right into the ear canal), so be careful about listening at high vol-umes. Your hearing is precious and can easily be damaged by loud sound/music. Try to set the volume as low as you can while still hearing and enjoying it rather than as loud as you can before causing pain/bleeding.

Headphones and headphone outputs use two types of connectors: 1/4-inch and 1/8-inch jacks (holes) and plugs (prongs). Here's the breakdown:

- ✔ The most common musical instrument/audio connector is called the 1/4-inch plug, or *phone plug*. It's the largest plug used and makes a great connection because of its long shaft. It's available in mono and stereo versions, so be sure you have the stereo version, indicated by dual black rings near the tip of the plug.

- ✔ The other common size is the 1/8-inch, also called a 3.5 mm or *mini-plug*. It's the most common plug size for mobile phones, media players, and most earbud headphones. It makes a good connection but can be a bit fragile. Don't tug on the cable or put pressure on this connection.

Your headphones may have a different-sized plug from your keyboard's headphone output. Don't worry. Adapters that convert between the two sizes are common. Find them at your local music or electronics store, or online.

Armed with the right headphones and cable/connector, you can now plug in the phones to your keyboard. Do so before you put them over your ears.

Connecting to external speakers and amps

If your keyboard doesn't have onboard speakers and you want to share your playing with others (or you just don't want to wear headphones), you can connect your instrument to a number of different devices or speakers. The main requirement is that the other device must have its own power source; your keyboard's output signal isn't strong enough to drive basic speakers. Luckily, almost every device you're likely to choose from (home theater/stereo, computer, or MP3 player's speakers, or amplifier) fits that bill.

Here's a general rule for turning electronics (such as your keyboard) and audio gear on and off when connected to a separate amplifier, powered speaker, or whatever: With both devices off, always turn on the sound-producing item first (the keyboard). Then turn on the amplifier/powered speakers. This order ensures that any pops or wake-up sounds the device makes don't go out your speakers, possibly harming them or your hearing. When shutting down, turn off the amplifier/powered speakers first, followed by the sound-producing item. Just remember, first on, last off.

Connecting to your home stereo

All home stereo systems include some form of additional input, usually labeled as an AUX or Auxiliary input and sometimes Tape input. Home stereo audio/video gear commonly uses a different type of connector called an *RCA plug,* which has a small, thin plug connector surrounded by a metal shield. These plugs are mono, which means you need two cables to connect to your home stereo/theater device if you want to hear your keyboard coming out of both speakers. This plug makes a great connection because of its metal shield, which fits securely over the jack on the device you're plugging into.

Here are the most common situations for connecting:

✔ If your keyboard has two 1/4-inch line outputs labeled L/Mono and R (left/mono and right), you need two cables that have male mono 1/4-inch plugs on one end and male RCA plugs on the other. (The terms *female* and *male* are used to describe jacks and plugs in the obvious way.) These are very common, easily found items.

✔ If your keyboard has a single stereo 1/8-inch jack (labeled as an output), you need a special type of Y cable that has a male stereo 1/8-inch plug on one end and splits out into two cables with male RCA plugs.

✔ If your keyboard offers no jack labeled as an output, you can use the headphone jack to connect to your stereo. If it's an 1/8-inch jack, follow the advice in the preceding bullet. If it's a 1/4-inch jack, you need a cable with a male stereo 1/4-inch plug on one end that breaks out into two male RCA plugs on the other. This Y cord is readily available in musical instrument stores and online.

TIP

Use a cable long enough to make the connection without requiring adapters or additional connectors. These items can weaken the signal and make noise. Brick-and-mortar stores may have limited selections of cable lengths, so if you can't find the right cable length in a store, go online. Many companies offer a much wider variety of cable types and lengths on their websites than any local store carries. And many of the familiar-name stores offer a wider online selection than they carry in the store.

When you're armed with the correct cables, here's how to connect them:

1. **Make sure both devices are turned off and their volumes set to 0.**

2. **Connect the L output of your keyboard to the L AUX In and the R output of your keyboard to the R AUX In.**

3. **Turn on the keyboard first, waiting until it has fully powered up before moving on.**

4. **Set your home stereo to AUX and then power it on.**

5. **Bring the keyboard's volume up to around 50 percent.**

6. **While playing some notes on the keyboard, slowly bring up the home stereo volume to around 10 to 25 percent.**

   If you need a little more volume, go back to your keyboard and raise its output slightly.

Using your computer speakers

Computer speaker systems can range from sounding okay to very good. These speakers usually accept a single stereo 1/8-inch plug. The easiest connection is if you have a stereo 1/8-inch output or headphone jack on your keyboard. Then you only need a long cable with a stereo 1/8-inch plug on each end. If that isn't available, here are the two other common scenarios:

✔ The next easiest connection is to use the stereo 1/4-inch headphone output. This option requires a male stereo 1/4-inch plug on one end with a male stereo 1/8-inch plug on the other.

✔ You can use the two 1/4-inch main outputs if you really want to, but this strategy is the least desirable of those presented here. To go this route requires a Y cable that joins two mono 1/4-inch plugs into a single male stereo 1/8-inch jack — more complicated than necessary.

After you've got everything connected, follow the instructions from the preceding section for powering on and setting volume.

Plugging into amps and other 1/4-inch jack devices

Musical instrument amplifiers, powered speakers, and mixers and speakers (PA systems) all use 1/4-inch jacks for their inputs. The main distinction for you is whether the device is stereo or mono. Many keyboard and guitar amplifiers you find in a musical instrument store are mono. If you have only one powered speaker, you'll be playing in mono.

Your keyboard always sounds better when connected in stereo, but if you have to, you *can* listen to it in mono. Some better keyboard amps are stereo devices; even if they have only one cabinet, they still have dual speakers inside. These amps are better for keyboards than a mono keyboard or guitar amplifier. In the case of powered speakers, you can always buy and use two separate speakers to fully reproduce the stereo image your keyboard delivers. And you could always plug the right channel into one guitar amp and the left into another.

To connect in mono, use the line output labeled L/Mono. This output treats the internal signal properly for listening in mono, so you don't lose any of the frequencies or information. This output is almost always a 1/4-inch jack, so use a common male 1/4-inch to male 1/4-inch instrument cable, sometimes referred to as *unbalanced* or *guitar cables*.

Some smaller portables and digital pianos with onboard speakers don't have line outputs, so your only choice is the headphone jack. In this case, you need a cable that has the matching connector to your headphone jack (male 1/4-inch or 1/8-inch) with the mono 1/4-inch plug on the other end. It doesn't really matter whether the headphone plug is stereo because you won't be reproducing that imaging anyway. You'll more commonly find a mono 1/4-inch or 1/8-inch plug to the mono 1/4-inch plug you need for the amp/powered speaker.

If you need to use a PA system (possibly in your church, school, coffeehouse, or bar), connect your 1/4-inch line outputs to two channels of the mixer, which always has 1/4-inch jacks. Two normal line/instrument cables will do. Locate a control called *pan* and set one channel all the way left and the other all the way right so your sound comes out of both speakers in true stereo. Some mixers have stereo channels, which simply means that one channel can accept two 1/4-inch inputs and doesn't need the individual pan control(s). It will have a knob called *balance,* which should be kept straight up.

Protecting Your Investment: Care and Upkeep

Your electronic keyboard doesn't require much maintenance; that's one of the major advantages of it over an acoustic or electro-mechanical instrument. That said, it's not indestructible.

Water and electronics don't mix! Don't douse your instrument with water while cleaning or keep any drinks, vases, or calming waterfalls near it. Be on the lookout for children and overly zealous house/party/club guests carrying beverages near your prized possession. If anything liquid does spill on the keyboard, turn the instrument off immediately, unplug it, and wipe up the spill with a soft cloth. If you fear any liquid got inside the case, don't use the keyboard again until a skilled technician can look inside and assess the possible damage.

Avoiding temperature extremes

A keyboard doesn't operate well in extreme temperature conditions, period. The most common scenario is leaving it in your car when you move it to bring it to a friend's house or to a place you're going to play. Closed cars can get very hot in the summer and very cold in the winter. Get to where you're going and take the keyboard out of the car right away. Never leave it in the car overnight; always bring it into the building.

Be especially careful about the display and other plastic parts, which can disfigure easily in extremely hot, direct sunlight. If you're playing outside, try to ensure that the stage area is under some shade.

If the keyboard has been exposed to very cold conditions, allow it to come back to room temperature before turning it on. Changes in temperature can cause condensation to build up. Be sure to wipe off any you see.

Combating dust with a keyboard cover

A little dust or dirt on the outside of the case looks sloppy, but the real problem occurs when that grime gets into the buttons, switches, and sliders; inside the case; or stuck between the keys. These items can all quit working reliably when blocked by these contaminants.

Acoustic pianos and some digital pianos have a folding or sliding lid to cover the keys. Always keep this cover closed to protect the keys when you aren't playing.

If you plan to leave your instrument in the open and it doesn't have a built-in cover, throw a cloth or towel over it. Or buy a dust cover for your model.

Cleaning the keys and case

From time to time, dust and fingerprints show up on your instrument. The case, the keys, and especially a touch display need to be cleaned periodically. If water is a no-go, what should you use?

Most manufacturers recommend a soft, dry cloth to begin with. Try disposable feather dusters to remove light dust or dirt. Start from the back of the key and wipe forward, so you're bringing any dust/dirt particles forward to the edge of the key where you can remove them. If dust has gotten into the knobs or sliders, you can use compressed air to blow them clean. Look for products that were designed for computers, cameras, and electronics.

You can graduate to a slightly dampened cloth if needed as long as you wring out most of the liquid. For tough stains, you can use a mild, nonabrasive cleanser in the cloth. Never use any form of benzene, thinner, alcohol, or solvent on the keys or case. These products can mar or disfigure the plastic.

A dry microfiber cloth, like you'd use for eyeglasses, is the best solution for touchscreens. Any good dry product for cleaning eyeglasses is going to be safe. Some of the well-known cleaning products companies make electronic wipes or electronic cleaning cloths that are safe for computer screens, keyboard displays, and the like.

Moving from place to place

If you plan to transport your keyboard often, you should invest in a case or padded carrying bag for it. These items protect the keyboard from scratches and worse while making it easier to lift and carry. A thickly padded bag is fine for most situations, but if you need to stack a lot of things in the car and want to put stuff on top of the keyboard, look for bags that offer a solid or reinforced wall design, or consider getting a hard-shell case.

You may think there's no harm in just setting your smaller portable on the backseat while you make the short trip to practice, but you never know when you may need to slam on the brakes. The jerk who cut you off probably won't care that your keyboard just went crashing onto the floor, but you will. Better to put it safely in the trunk for the trip.

For heavy keyboards, look into rolling bags or cases, which have sturdy wheels on one end so you don't have to carry the instrument when going along flat surfaces. If you need to carry more gear than just the keyboard, consider getting a folding rolling cart or convertible hand truck.

Whatever you choose, don't be afraid to ask someone for help when lifting a larger keyboard onto a stand, taking it down again, carrying a case, and taking it out/putting it into your car.

Book I

Piano & Keyboard 101

Solving Minor Technical Problems

As with any electronic device, sometimes things go wrong with a keyboard. It may show funny symbols in its display, lock up or freeze, or simply not make sound. Perhaps you're just not sure how to do something or whether your keyboard can even do what you're thinking of. Here are a few tips to help you figure out what's wrong and what to do:

- ✔ If you hear anything funny or the unit freezes, the first action you take should be to turn it off, wait a few moments, and then turn it back on again. (Don't forget to turn the volume down on all your speakers and such). Sometimes the device just needs a fresh reboot.

- ✔ If restarting doesn't resolve the issue, look to your manual. Most owner's manuals include a basic troubleshooting section toward the back that goes over the most common scenarios users face. It may show you how to *reinitialize* the instrument, which resets it to factory status.

- ✔ If you've spilled any liquid in your keyboard or think something (dust, dirt, bugs, small candy, or whatever) has gotten inside the case, *never* try to open the unit yourself to look inside. Even with the unit off and the power cable removed from the wall, the insides of any electronic device aren't a safe place. You can get shocked or hurt worse by touching the wrong thing, not to mention that you'll instantly void your warranty coverage. Leave this type of work to the professionals!

- ✔ Go online to the manufacturer's website and look in the support section for any frequently asked questions (FAQs) related to your product. As the name implies, these queries come up all the time, so the company writes good explanations to keep from answering the same questions over and over.

- ✔ Search the web for your problem using your favorite search engine. Make sure the most pertinent keywords are in your search text, including the brand name, model name and number, and main issue terms.

Many brands have growing online communities, often not run by or directly affiliated with the company itself. These outlets can be great places to not only find answers to your problems but also meet other owners and share the fun of your product and music in general. Be sure to search these sites for answers before asking a question; often, the issue has come up before and has already been addressed. You may also want to try searching the web for general keywords such as "digital piano," "synthesizer," or "arrangers."

✔ If you still can't find your answer, try contacting the manufacturer's product support or customer service department. These departments often post their hours of operation and methods of contact on the company website. You may be able to e-mail the company or fill out an online form, which can save you a lot of hold time waiting on the phone.

Know that these replies can often come hours, if not days, after you submit them, so if you absolutely need to get help right away, call and stay on the line. Be patient; expect that it's going to take some time to reach someone, so don't get frustrated right away.

Chapter 5

Getting Comfy at the Keyboard

· ·

In This Chapter

▶ Naming the ebonies and ivories

▶ Navigating the keys using Blake's E-Z Key Finder

▶ Achieving perfect posture and comfort at the keyboard

▶ Putting the pedals to the metal

· ·

*Y*ou're staring at all these keys, trying to make sense of the whole thing, and you're wondering why you didn't just buy a pair of cymbals and call it a day. It seems quite intimidating, but to paraphrase The Jackson Five: It's as easy as A-B-C, 1-2-3.

This chapter helps you get acquainted with all the finer features of your keyboard, including the keys and the pedals. It also advises you on equipment, such as chairs, benches, and racks, that aid you in achieving proper piano-playing posture, and explains just what that posture looks like. This is also where you'll first encounter notes and note names, and which keys play which notes. In the next book — Book II — you'll find out a whole lot more about that. Here the idea is to get your feet wet and absorb the very basics of how playing notes on the keyboard works.

Blake's E-Z Key Finder

The first thing you notice on your keyboard is the not-so-colorful use of black and white keys aligned from left to right. The black ones are raised and are set farther back than the white ones, as you can see in Figure 5-1. (If the black and white keys are reversed, you're either playing a very old keyboard or the manufacturer messed up and you got an enormous discount. Congratulations!)

Figure 5-1:
Your basic
set of black
and whites.

Each key on the keyboard represents a specific musical note. These notes use a very easy naming system — the first seven letters of the alphabet, A-B-C-D-E-F-G. The names of the keys correspond to the names of musical notes. (The chapters in Book II go into a lot more detail on this.) For now, just remember that a G key plays a G note, an A key plays an A note, and so on.

But if you're looking at 88 keys, and only have seven alphabet letters to name them, how do you name the other 81 keys? For all 88 keys, the basic set of seven letter names repeats over and over, in *octaves,* which are groups of eight.

When you name the sequence of seven white keys from A to G, the next (eighth) note is A as the series begins again. You can count seven octaves from the lowest A to the highest A on an 88-key piano.

The following sections show you how to use Blake's E-Z Key Finder technique to locate the different notes on the keyboard. It's an unforgettable way to find any key on the board.

The white keys

To make things really easy, the seven note names (A-B-C-D-E-F-G) are all on the white keys. The black keys have names of their own, covered in the next section, but for now you can use the black keys as landmarks to find the correct white keys . . . even in the dark! The raised black keys help you locate any white key quickly and precisely.

The black keys always appear in repeating groups of two and three. You'll never see two sets of two black keys or two sets of three black keys in a row. This distinction of twos and threes is important and makes the job of finding white keys even easier.

Use your imagination and think of any set of two black keys as a pair of chopsticks. Think of any set of three black keys as the tines on a fork. (Take a glance at Figure 5-2.) "Chopsticks" starts with the letter C, and "fork" starts with the letter F. This handy memory-device forms the basis of the E-Z Key Finder technique for finding the white keys on the keyboard. The main points are as follows:

✔ To the left of the chopsticks (two black keys) is the note C.

✔ To the left of the fork (three black keys) is the note F.

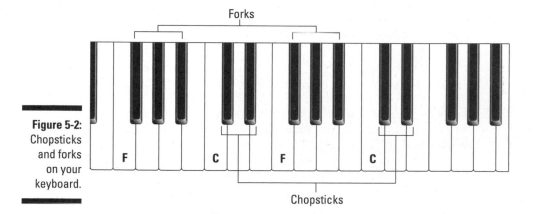

Figure 5-2: Chopsticks and forks on your keyboard.

Allow that to sink in while you look at your keyboard, and you won't forget it. But what about the other white keys, you ask? You know the alphabet fairly well, don't you? Look at the alphabet letters again: A-B-C-D-E-F-G.

Notice what letters surround C and what letters surround F. The same advanced logic applies to the white keys surrounding C and F. Moving up from C you have the notes D, E, F, G. When you get to G, think "Go" as in "go back to the beginning of the alphabet." The alphabet pattern repeats over and over again on the keyboard, as many times as you see chopsticks and forks.

To practice finding notes, play every C and F on the keyboard, from bottom to top. Then locate every D and G. Test yourself by playing all the other white keys while reciting the names of the keys. With the aid of the E-Z Key Finder, you'll never forget a key's name.

Now that you know the names of the white keys, you can play:

✔ The first nine notes of "Over the River and Through the Woods": D, D, D, D, B, C, D, D, D.

✔ The first six notes of "It's Raining, It's Pouring": B, D, B, E, D, B.

✔ The first seven notes of "The First Noel": E, D, C, D, E, F, G.

✔ The first eleven notes to the theme from Ravel's *Boléro:* C, B, C, D, C, B, A, C, C, A, C.

The black keys — sharps and flats

Play A, then B, then the black key in between A and B. You'll notice that it sounds like a different musical note. You're correct: Black keys represent separate musical notes from white keys. However, because no alphabet letter comes between the letters A and B, the black key between these two can't be given a logical alphabet name.

The black keys are assigned the same name as the closest white key but with one of the following suffixes added on:

✔ **Sharp** is used for a black key to the *right* of (or *higher* than) a white key.

✔ **Flat** is used for a black key to the *left* of (or *lower* than) a white key.

Here's another culinary metaphor to help you remember these suffixes. At your imaginary musical place setting, a white key represents a plate. Now imagine that

✔ A knife is *sharp* and lies on the *right* side of the plate.

✔ A napkin is *flat* and lies on the *left* side of the plate.

Put it to the test: Find the D plate (key). To the right is a sharp knife, D sharp. To the left is a flat napkin, D flat. Easy enough? Just remember chopsticks and forks, knives and napkins, and you'll never forget the names of the keys.

Because each of the black keys lies between two white keys, each black key has two names, depending on the white key you approach it from. For example, the black key to the right of C is C sharp, but it's also D flat. The split personality of each black key (note) seems odd at first, but after you get the hang of seeing each key from two different perspectives, it isn't that awkward.

You probably already noticed that no black keys reside between B and C or E and F. Before you demand a full refund from your local keyboard dealer, you should know that this is no mistake. Theoretically, C is also B sharp and, similarly, E is also F flat. But this is way too much needless music theory. Suffice it to say that there are no notes between B and C or E and F. You'll survive for now without knowing why.

Develop a clear mental image of the octave groupings on the keyboard, and then check your mental image against Figure 5-3. These groupings will help you navigate the 88s.

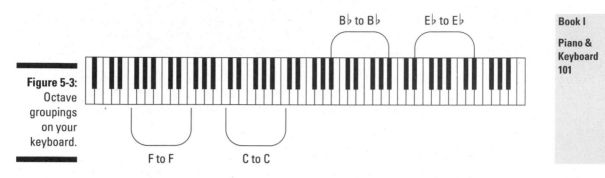

Figure 5-3:
Octave
groupings
on your
keyboard.

Now that you know the names of the white and black keys, you can play

✔ The theme from the movie *Jaws:* D sharp, E, D sharp, E, D sharp, E (keep repeating until someone screams).

✔ The first four notes of Beethoven's *Fifth Symphony:* G, G, G, E flat.

✔ The tune of "Shave and a Haircut, Five Cents": G, D, D, E, D, F sharp, G.

What Your Parents Never Told You About Posture

Good posture, including how you sit and how you hold your hands, keeps you comfortable at your keyboard for hours on end. Practicing good posture while you play also helps you avoid cramped hands, a tired back, and even more serious medical problems like carpal tunnel syndrome. After you're a famous concert pianist, you can look back fondly on this chapter and remember how it helped prepare you for a career with the keyboard.

To sit or not to sit

Depending on the type of keyboard — and sometimes the type of stage — that you're playing on, you can either sit or stand while you play.

As a general rule, most pianists sit at the piano, but many rock keyboardists stand behind their boards. Maybe they want the audience to have a better view of them playing. Or maybe they don't want to appear shorter than the guitarist and bass player.

It's probably a good idea to begin your musical endeavors in a seated position. No matter what kind of keyboard you play, sitting brings you closer to the keys and makes you more comfortable as you practice.

Whether sitting or standing, you should be comfortable at all times. Your feet should rest firmly on the floor. Your hands should have a nice relaxed arch to them. The keys should be at an appropriate height so that your hands and forearms are parallel to the ground, as shown in Figure 5-4.

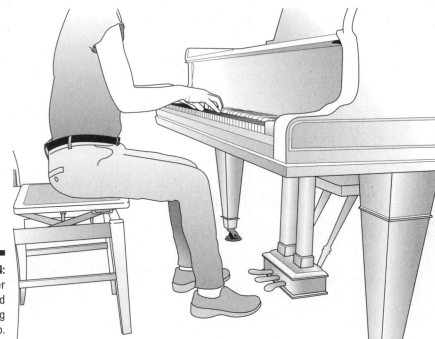

Figure 5-4:
Proper
posture and
positioning
at the piano.

Make sure your back is straight and that you aren't slumping, slouching, or hunching over. Not sitting up straight leads to backaches — the kind that discourage you from practicing.

Chairs versus benches

Both chairs and benches are acceptable options, and both are readily available at most piano stores and concert halls. Of course, both options have their pros and cons, and it's up to you to sort out what's the best fit for your playing.

Chairs

Your seat shouldn't be a recliner with flip-out footrest and side pockets for the TV remote. Piano chairs are usually plain, black chairs. Many have a padded seat, and some offer a useful mechanism to raise or lower the height just a bit, as shown in Figure 5-5.

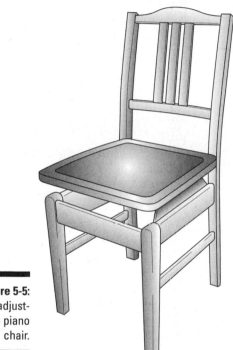

Figure 5-5:
An adjust-
able piano
chair.

The back on a chair provides some added support, but it also may cause you to slump more just because you can. As Mom and Dad always told you, slumping isn't attractive or good for your back. Also, the extra wood on chair backs often tends to creak, which isn't a pleasant sound during a performance of Debussy's *Clair de Lune*.

But paradoxically, the back on a chair is also its main advantage. The extra support is good for young, sometimes fidgety students because they feel more secure on a chair than on a backless bench. Heck, you can even strap on a booster seat for the young child prodigy. Plus, like it or not, everyone slumps occasionally. If you practice diligently into the wee hours of the night, at least you're practicing!

Maybe the biggest drawback of a chair is the inability to accommodate a duet partner. Many pianists enjoy playing duets with friends. You sit side-by-side and play the keyboard in two parts: one person playing the lower notes, and the other playing the upper notes. Sure, you can just pull up another chair, but where's the romance in that?

Benches

The standard piano bench, shown Figure 5-6a, measures approximately 2 feet high by 3 feet wide. The width allows ample room for shifting yourself to reach higher or lower notes while you play, and it also accommodates a duet partner.

Height is an important function of whatever you choose to sit on while playing. However, many piano benches aren't adjustable, forcing you to lean up into the keyboard or to sit atop a stack of phone books. The nicer benches come with knobs on the side that let you adjust the bench height for a more personal fit (shown in Figure 5-6b). The better benches also offer padding, which you begin to appreciate after a few hours of hard practice.

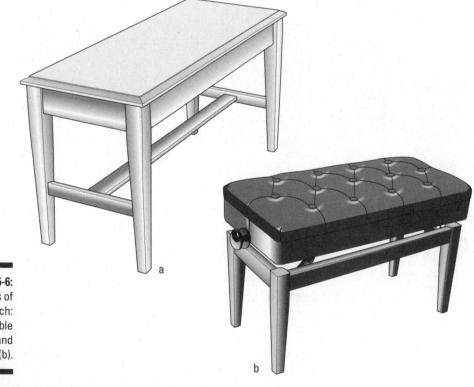

Figure 5-6:
Two types of
piano bench:
adjustable
(a) and
standard (b).

a

b

Book I

Piano &
Keyboard
101

Unlike a chair, a bench provides no back support, leaving you to keep a straight spine throughout the performance. On the plus side, a backless bench forces good posture during your playing. However, no back support also means no protection from falling backwards when you become too excited during the climax of a Bartók concerto or your jamming rock solo.

Some piano benches have hinged seats, allowing you to open the seat and store sheet music, books, or even a mid-concert snack. Just don't forget what you leave in there.

Stands and racks

Keyboard stands (see Figure 5-7) come in all shapes and sizes. Some are multi-tiered for adding more and more keyboards as your career or bank account grows. Keyboard stands also come in different colors. (If you don't like the colors, you can always buy a can of spray paint.)

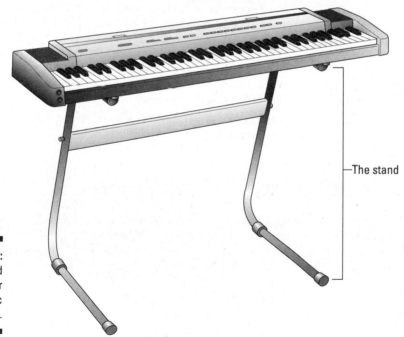

The stand

Figure 5-7:
Take a stand
for your
electric
keyboard.

Nearly every stand is adjustable because the manufacturer is never exactly sure just how tall its client base is. You can adjust the height of the keyboard so that you can sit or stand, depending on your mood. Just make sure that the keys are at the proper height (refer to Figure 5-4). The adjustability also allows you to spread multiple keyboards farther apart on the stand to allow easy access to the various buttons and knobs on each.

In addition to a stand, you may also need an *effects rack,* which is a wooden or metal box with holed brackets along the edge into which you can screw various components, samplers, effects processors, mixers, or even drawers. Racks can be stationary or on rollers, according to your personal needs and desires.

As always, make sure you have adequate lighting for your keyboard, music rack, and program/patch display.

It's All in the Hands

Comfortable hand position and comfortable posture while playing the piano or keyboard are of paramount importance. Poor hand position can cause your performance to suffer for two reasons:

- **Lack of dexterity:** If your hands are in tight, awkward positions, you can't access the keys quickly and efficiently. Your performance will sound clumsy and be full of wrong notes.
- **Potential for cramping:** If your hands cramp often, you won't practice often. If you don't practice often, you won't be a very good player.

Arch those hands and fingers

When you place your hands on the keys, you must keep your hands arched and your fingers slightly curled at all times. It feels weird at first, but you can't improve your playing technique until you get used to holding your hands this way. Arching your hands and fingers pays off with the following benefits:

- Your hands don't get tired as quickly.
- Your hands are less likely to cramp.
- You can quickly and easily access any key, black or white.

To get an idea of the hand shape you're after, find two tennis balls (or similarly sized balls) and hold one in each hand, as shown in Figure 5-8. This is how your hand should look when you play the piano . . . minus the ball, of course.

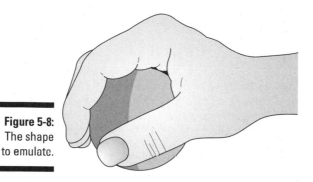

Figure 5-8:
The shape
to emulate.

Fingering

Fingering refers to using the best finger to play each note of a song, and correct fingering is always a very important part of piano playing. Some pieces, even the easy ones, have fingerings marked in the sheet music to help you plan which fingers to use to execute a particular musical passage most efficiently and comfortably. Somebody did the work of figuring that out for you, and you may as well take advantage of it.

The fingerings you see in music correspond to the left- and right-hand fingering you see in Figure 5-9. Number your fingers 1 through 5, beginning with the thumb as number 1 and moving toward the little finger, or pinkie.

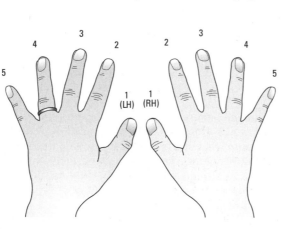

Figure 5-9:
Numbers
and digits.

While you get used to thinking of your fingers in terms of numbers, you may find it helpful to write these numbers on your hands before you sit down to practice. Use a washable marker or pen. Otherwise, you'll have to explain those numbered fingers to your date on Friday night, your boss on Monday morning, or your homeroom teacher.

When to give your hands and fingers a rest

Poor posture can lead to the beginning of serious and painful problems in your piano career. The sports claim "no pain, no gain" has no validity when applied to piano playing. Muscle tension and poor posture can cause pain. If you hurt, you won't play. If you don't play, you won't be very good.

Feeling cramped

Even if your posture is absolutely perfect, your hands will inevitably begin to cramp at some point. Cramps are your body's way of saying, "Hey, let's go do something else for a while." By all means, listen to your body.

Generally, you'll experience hand cramps long before you experience any other kind of body cramp during practice. Your back and neck may become sore from poor posture, but your hands will begin to cramp simply from too much use.

If your hands hurt, take a long break and do something that creates a completely opposite hand action. For example, throwing a ball to your dog is an opposite hand action; typing is not. If your whole body hurts, get a massage (including a hand massage) or take a luxurious cruise in the South Pacific. You deserve it.

Avoiding carpal tunnel syndrome

Much has been said about a career-oriented injury called *carpal tunnel syndrome* (CTS). CTS develops from overstraining the muscles and ligaments in your wrist through constant, repetitive action. And piano or keyboard playing is a constant, repetitive action.

As you can probably imagine, many a keyboardist and full-time blogger experience CTS during their careers. Unfortunately, many wait until it's too late for a simple remedy. They ignore what starts out as a dull pain in the forearms, wrists, and fingers until it becomes a severe pain whenever the hands are in motion. Severe CTS requires surgery to remedy, but the results aren't always 100 percent. As a piano player, you need 100 percent of your hand motion, so don't let any pain go unnoticed.

If you're bothered by pain in your wrists, no matter how minor, consult your physician for ways to reduce or prevent it. Of course, if you've already been diagnosed with CTS, talk with your physician about your piano-playing goals and ask what steps you can take to prevent any further damage or pain. (Your doctor will probably ask how you got interested in the piano, giving you an excellent opportunity to wholeheartedly endorse this book.)

Pedal Power: Getting Your Feet in on the Action

When you play the keyboard, your hands are busy on the keys, and your feet are called upon to work the *pedals* to control other aspects of the music.

Most pianos have two or three pedals, and synthesizers can have even more. Pipe organs often incorporate an entire keyboard of pedals to be played by the feet. This book doesn't go into the details of pipe organ pedals, but if you play a pipe organ, you can find a whole host of teachers at your disposal to help you figure out the pedals (see Book I Chapter 2 for a little more on pipe organs).

The various pedals on your instrument allow you to achieve different effects in your music. Most of the time, the composer indicates when to use which pedal, but you should feel free to experiment with the pedals and the interpretations they can bring to your music.

Piano pedals

Most pianos come equipped with three pedals, shown in Figure 5-10.

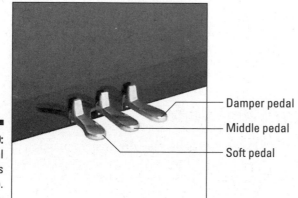

Figure 5-10: The typical three pedals on a piano.

Damper pedal

Middle pedal

Soft pedal

✔ **To the far right is the *damper pedal* (or *sustain pedal*).** When you hold this pedal down, the *dampers* — mechanisms that mute the strings — are moved away from the strings, allowing the strings to ring until you release the pedal, the sound gradually fades away, or you fall asleep and fall off the bench. You don't have to use the damper pedal every time you play a note because each key has its own damper. (For more on dampers, turn to Book I Chapter 2.)

Most musicians, and even nonmusicians who purport to know something about music, refer to the damper pedal as "the pedal" because it's the most popular and most frequently used pedal.

✔ **To the far left is the *soft pedal*.** This pedal works differently in uprights and grands, but you use it to make your piano sound softer.

The Italian name for the soft pedal is the *una corda*. On grand pianos, pressing down this pedal causes the entire set of hammers inside the piano to shift slightly to the side. When you play on any of the keys with the pedal down, the hammers hit only one string, or *una corda,* instead of the usual three.

✔ **In the middle is the *middle pedal*, or *sostenuto pedal*.** This pedal appears on many pianos, but not all. Unlike the damper pedal, which sustains all notes being played, the middle pedal allows you to sustain a specific note, or group of notes, while you continue playing other notes normally. Simultaneously hold down the middle pedal and play a key on the piano and the sound sustains. Now, quickly play other notes and you'll notice they don't sustain. Pretty cool, right? Well, pretty difficult, too — especially in the midst of playing Rachmaninoff's *Piano Concerto No. 3.* Many piano manufacturers now opt to save money and omit this pedal.

On some upright pianos, the middle pedal is called a *practice pedal* and has an entirely different function: It inserts a layer of felt between the hammers and strings to make the sound much softer and more muffled. This pedal allows you to practice late at night without disturbing others, so you might call it the good neighbor pedal.

Digital keyboard pedals

The most common digital keyboard pedals are the sustain pedal (which performs the same function as on an acoustic piano, explained in the previous section) and the volume pedal (which increases or decreases the volume). Nearly every keyboard comes with a plug-in sustain pedal; it doesn't move any dampers or shift any keys because there are no real strings inside a digital keyboard. Instead, the pedal sends an electronic signal to the brain of your keyboard, telling it to sustain the notes or increase or decrease the volume if you're using a volume pedal.

Other pedals you can add to your electric keyboard control such things as *vibrato,* which makes the note sound as if it's warbling; program changes; and special effects.

You can sample these various pedals and decide which ones are right for you at your local electric keyboard dealer. The salesperson should be more than happy to show you a whole line of different pedals, hoping that you want to spend even more money than you already are for the keyboard itself. If you're unsure about extra pedals, hold off on buying them. You can always buy and install them later, when you know that you'll use them. The plug for all pedals and most other accessories is a standard size, making additions a snap.

Book I

Piano & Keyboard 101

Book II

Understanding Theory and the Language of Music

Find out about using printed music to expand your repertoire in a free online article at www.dummies.com/extras/pianokeyboardaio.

Contents at a Glance

Chapter 1: Looking at Notes and Beats 99

Meeting the Beat...100
Recognizing Notes and Note Values...101
Extending Notes with Dots and Ties..106
Mixing All the Note Values Together 107

Chapter 2: Stopping for a Rest 109

Getting to Know the Rests..109
Practicing Beats with Notes and Rests.....................................113

Chapter 3: Tempo, Measures, and Time Signatures 115

Playing Fast and Slow: Tempo...115
Grouping Beats into Measures 116
Counting Out Common Time Signatures....................................118

Chapter 4: Navigating Sheet Music 125

Meeting the Staff, Clefs, and Notes...125
Identifying Half Steps, Whole Steps, and Accidentals on the Staff........130
Musical Punctuation: Bar Lines 136

Chapter 5: Varying Beats and Rhythms 137

Getting a Jump on the Start: Pickup Beats and Measures 137
Adding Time to Your Notes with Ties and Dots............................138
Playing Offbeat Rhythms 142
Playing Songs with Challenging Rhythms 146

Chapter 1

Looking at Notes and Beats

In This Chapter

▶ Understanding rhythm, beat, and tempo

▶ Reviewing notes and note values

▶ Counting (and clapping) out different notes and note values

*J*ust about everyone has taken some sort of music lessons, either formal paid lessons from a local piano teacher or at the very least the state-mandated rudimentary music classes offered in public school. Either way, you've been asked at some point to knock out a beat, if only by clapping your hands.

Maybe the music lesson seemed pretty pointless at the time or served only as a great excuse to bop your grade-school neighbor on the head. However, counting out a beat is exactly where you have to start with music. Without a discernible beat, you have nothing to dance or nod your head to. Although all the other parts of music (pitch, melody, harmony, and so on) are pretty darned important, without beat, you don't really have a song.

Everything around you has a rhythm to it, including you. In music, the *rhythm* is the pattern of regular or irregular pulses. The most basic thing you're striving to find in songs is the rhythm. Luckily, written music makes it easy to interpret other composers' works and produce the kind of rhythm they had in mind for their songs.

The first half of this chapter provides you with a solid introduction to the basics of counting notes and discovering a song's rhythm, beat, and tempo.

Note: The common U.S. name is quarter note, but in the U.K. they call it a crotchet. The U.K. names are also used in medieval music and in some classical circles. This book uses the U.S. common names for the notes, which are more universally standard.

The second half of this chapter shows you just how important the timing of your notes is when playing the piano. As they say, timing is everything, and every note in music has a starting point and an ending point. So notes need to have different values that can be counted. You'll also see how time in music can be measured in other ways: by measuring the rate of the beat to determine the tempo of a song, and by using a time signature to determine the beat pattern of a song.

You'll earn your place in the rhythm nation as you get to know the timely trio — note values, tempo indications, and time signatures — that creates rhythm. This chapter introduces you to these rhythm elements and gives you some practice tunes to play on your keyboard.

Meeting the Beat

A *beat* is a pulsation that divides time into equal lengths. A ticking clock is a good example. Every minute, the second hand ticks 60 times, and each one of those ticks is a beat. If you speed up or slow down the second hand, you're changing the *tempo* of the beat. *Notes* in music tell you what to play during each of those ticks. In other words, the notes tell you how long and how often to play a certain musical *pitch* — the low or high sound a specific note makes — within the beat.

When you think of the word *note* as associated with music, you may think of a sound. However, in music, one of the main uses for notes is to explain exactly how long a specific pitch should be held by the voice or an instrument. The *note value,* indicated by the size and shape of the note, determines this length. Together with the preceding three features, the note value determines what kind of rhythm the resulting piece of music will have. It determines whether the song will run along very quickly and cheerfully, will crawl along slowly and somberly, or will progress in some other way.

When figuring out how to follow the beat, *rhythm sticks* (fat, cylindrical, hard wood instruments) come in real handy. So do drum sticks. If you've got a pair, grab 'em. If you don't, clapping or smacking your hand against bongos or your desktop works just as well.

Eventually "hearing" a beat in your head (or "feeling" a beat in your body) is absolutely fundamental while you play music, whether you're reading a piece of sheet music or jamming with other musicians. The only way you can master this basic task is *practice, practice, practice.* Following along with the beat is something you need to pick up if you want progress in music.

Perhaps the easiest way to practice working with a steady beat is to buy a metronome. They're pretty cheap, and even a crummy one should last you for years. The beauty of a metronome is that you can set it to a wide range of tempos, from very, very slow to hummingbird fast. If you're using a metronome to practice — especially if you're reading from a piece of sheet music — you can set the beat to whatever speed you're comfortable with and gradually speed it up to the composer's intended speed when you've figured out the pacing of the song. You can also find metronome apps for your smartphone, which work just as well.

Recognizing Notes and Note Values

If you think of music as a language, then notes are like letters of the alphabet — they're that basic to the construction of a piece of music. Studying how note values fit against each other in a piece of sheet music is as important as knowing musical pitches because if you change the note values, you end up with completely different music. In fact, when musicians talk about performing a piece of music "in the style of" Bach, Beethoven, or Philip Glass, they're talking as much about using the rhythm structure and pace characteristics of that particular composer's music as much as any particular chord progressions or melodic choices.

Book II

Understanding Theory and the Language of Music

Examining the notes and their components

Notes are made of up to three specific components: note head, stem, and flag.

- **Head:** The *head* is the round part of a note. Every note has one. A whole note is just a head: 𝅝.
- **Stem:** The *stem* is the vertical line attached to the note head. Eighth notes, quarter notes, and half notes all have stems. Here is a half note: 𝅗𝅥.
- **Flag:** The *flag* is the little line that comes off the top or bottom of the note stem. Eighth notes and shorter notes have flags: 𝅘𝅥𝅮.

Stems can point either up or down, depending where on the *staff* they appear (you find out all about staves in Book II Chapters 3 and 4). Whether the stem points up or down makes no difference in the value of the note.

Instead of each note getting a flag, notes with flags can also be connected to each other with a *beam,* which is just a cleaner-looking incarnation of the flag. For example, Figure 1-1 shows how two eighth notes can be written as each having a flag or as connected by a beam.

Figure 1-1:
Eighth notes can have individual flags or connect with a beam.

Figure 1-2 shows four sixteenth notes with flags grouped three separate ways: individually, in two pairs connected by a double beam, and all connected by one double beam. It doesn't matter which way you write them; they sound the same when played.

Figure 1-2:
Sixteenth notes, written in different ways, all sound alike.

Likewise, you can write eight thirty-second notes in either of the ways shown in Figure 1-3. Notice that these notes get *three* flags (or three beams). Using beams instead of individual flags on notes is simply a case of trying to clean up an otherwise messy-looking piece of musical notation. Beams help musical performers by allowing them to see where the larger beats are. Instead of seeing sixteen disconnected sixteenth notes, it's helpful for a performer to see four groups of four sixteenths connected by a beam.

Figure 1-3:
Same deal with thirty-second notes.

Looking at note values

As you may remember from school or music lessons, each note has its own note *value*. Before we go into detail on each kind of note, have a look at Figure 1-4, which shows most of the kinds of notes you'll encounter in music arranged so their values add up the same in each row. At the top is the whole note, below that half notes, then quarter notes, eighth notes, and finally sixteenth notes on the bottom. Each level of the "tree of notes" is equal to the others. The value of a half note, for example, is half of a whole note, and the value of a quarter note is a quarter of a whole note.

Another way to think of notes is to imagine a whole note as a pie, which is easy because it's round. To divvy up the pie into quarter notes, cut it in quarters. Cutting the pie into eight pieces gives you eighth notes, and so on.

Depending on the time signature of the piece of music (see Chapter 4), the note value that's equal to one beat changes. In the most common time signature, 4/4 time, also called *common time,* a whole note is held for four beats, a half note is held for two, and a quarter note lasts one beat. An eighth note lasts half a beat, and a sixteenth note lasts just a quarter of a beat in 4/4 time.

Book II

Understanding Theory and the Language of Music

Figure 1-4:
Each level of this tree of notes lasts as many beats as every other level.

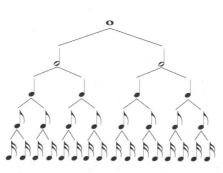

Often, the quarter note equals one beat. If you sing, "MA-RY HAD A LIT-TLE LA-MB," each syllable is one beat (you can clap along with it), and each beat gets one quarter note if the song is notated in 4/4 time. We talk more about time signatures and counting beats accordingly in Chapter 4.

Whole notes

The whole note lasts the longest of all the notes. It looks like this: ○.

In 4/4 time, a whole note lasts for an entire four beats (see Book II Chapter 4 for more on time signatures). For four whole beats you don't have to do anything with that one note except play and hold it. That's it.

Usually, when you count note values, you clap or tap on the note and say aloud the remaining beats. You count the beats of whole notes like this:

CLAP two three four CLAP two three four CLAP two three four

"CLAP" means you clap your hands, and "two three four" is what you say out loud as the note is held for four beats. When you see three whole notes in a row, for example, each one gets its own "four-count."

Half notes

It's simple logic what comes after whole notes in value — a half note, of course. You hold a half note for half as long as you would a whole note. Half notes look like this: ♩. When you count out three half notes, it sounds like this:

CLAP two CLAP two CLAP two

Because the highest-valued note in that sequence is a half note, you only count up to the number two.

You could have a whole note followed by two half notes. In that case, you count out the three notes as follows:

CLAP two three four CLAP two CLAP two

Quarter notes

Divide a whole note, which is worth four beats, by four, and you get a quarter note with a note value of one beat. Quarter notes look like half notes except that the note head is completely filled in: ♩. Four quarter notes are counted out like this:

CLAP CLAP CLAP CLAP

The laws of stem gravity

You may have noticed that sometimes a note's stem points up and sometimes it points down. Thanks to the laws of stem gravity, any notes on or above the middle line of a staff point downwards. This applies to all notes with stems. Also notice that up-stems start to the right side of a notehead, and down-stems start to the left of the notehead.

Because the highest-valued note there is a quarter note, you count up to one. Four quarter notes together last as long as one whole note.

Suppose you replace one of the quarter notes with a whole note and one with a half note, as shown in Figure 1-5.

Figure 1-5:
A mix of whole, half, and quarter notes.

In that case, you count out the notes like this:

CLAP two three four CLAP CLAP CLAP two

Eighth notes and beyond

When sheet music includes eighth notes and beyond, it starts to look a little intimidating. Usually, just one or two clusters of eighth notes in a piece of musical notation isn't enough to frighten the average beginning student, but when that same student opens to a page that's littered with eighth notes, sixteenth notes, or thirty-second notes, she just knows she has some work ahead of her. Why? Because usually these notes are *fast*.

An eighth note — ♪ — has a value of half of a quarter note. Eight eighth notes last as long as one whole note, which means an eighth note lasts half a beat (in 4/4, or common, time). You hold an eighth note for one-eighth as long as a whole note.

How can you have half a beat? Easy. Tap your toe for the beat and clap your hands twice for every toe tap.

CLAP-CLAP CLAP-CLAP CLAP-CLAP CLAP-CLAP

Or you can count it out as follows:

ONE-and TWO-and THREE-and FOUR-and

The numbers represent four beats, and the "ands" are the half beats.

Just think of each tick of a metronome as an eighth note instead of a quarter note. That means a quarter note is now two ticks, a half note is four ticks, and a whole note lasts eight ticks.

Similarly, if you have a piece of sheet music with sixteenth notes, each sixteenth note can equal one metronome tick, an eighth note two ticks, a quarter note four ticks, a half note eight ticks, and a whole note can equal sixteen ticks.

A sixteenth note has a note value of one quarter of a quarter note, which means it lasts one-sixteenth as long as a whole note. A sixteenth note looks like this: ♪.

If you have a piece of sheet music with thirty-second notes, which have, as you may have guessed, three flags or beams, remember that a thirty-second note equals one metronome tick, a sixteenth note equals two, an eighth note equals four, a quarter note equals eight, a half note equals sixteen, and a whole note equals thirty-two ticks.

You'll be glad to hear that you won't run into thirty-second notes very often.

Extending Notes with Dots and Ties

Sometimes you want to add to the value of a note. You have two main ways to extend a note's value in written music: *dots* and *ties*.

Using dots to increase a note's value

Occasionally, you'll come across a note followed by a small dot, called an *augmentation dot*. This dot indicates that the note's value is increased by one half of its original value. The most common use of the dotted note is when a half note is made to last three quarter note beats instead of two, as shown in Figure 1-6. Another way to think about dots is that they make a note equal to *three* of the next shorter value instead of two.

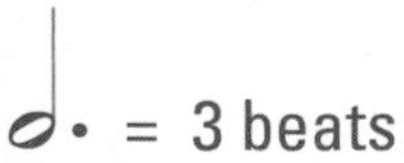

Figure 1-6:
A dotted
half note. ♩• = 3 beats

You may also see a dotted whole note. That means the whole note's value is increased from four beats to six beats.

Adding notes together with ties

Another way to increase the value of a note is by *tying* it to another note, as Figure 1-7 shows. Ties connect notes of the same pitch together to create one sustained note instead of two separate ones. When you see a tie, simply add the notes together. For example, a quarter note tied to another quarter note equals one note held for two beats:

CLAP-two!

Figure 1-7:
Two tied quarter notes equal a half note.

Don't confuse ties with *slurs*. A slur looks kind of like a tie, except that it connects two notes of *different pitches*.

Book II

Understanding Theory and the Language of Music

Mixing All the Note Values Together

You won't encounter many pieces of music that are composed entirely of one kind of note, so you need to practice working with a variety of note values.

The four exercises shown in Figures 1-8 through 1-11 can help make a beat stick in your head and make each kind of note automatically register its value in your brain. Each exercise contains five groups (or *measures*) of four beats each. The measures are notated with vertical lines, called *bar lines*.

In these exercises, you clap on the CLAPs and say the numbers aloud. Where you see a hyphenated CLAP-CLAP, do two claps per beat (in other words, two claps in the space of one normal clap).

Start out counting and then dive in after you count four.

Exercise 1

CLAP CLAP CLAP CLAP | CLAP two three CLAP | CLAP two three four |
CLAP two three four | CLAP CLAP CLAP four

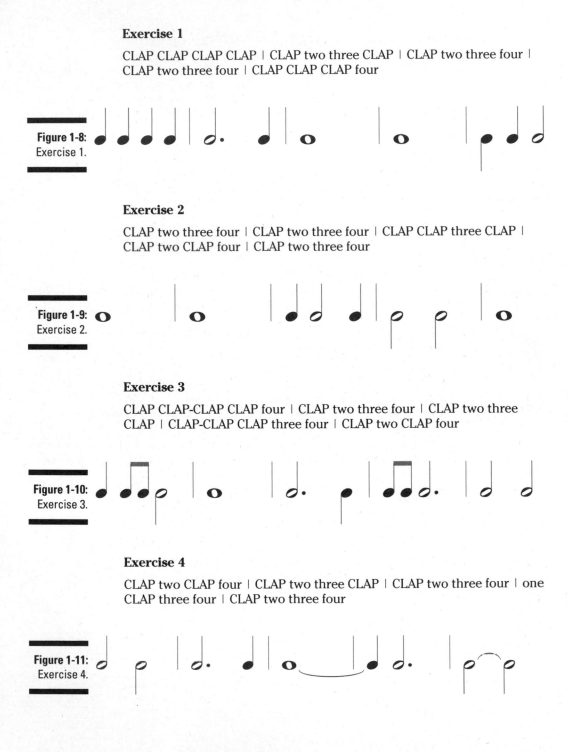

Figure 1-8:
Exercise 1.

Exercise 2

CLAP two three four | CLAP two three four | CLAP CLAP three CLAP |
CLAP two CLAP four | CLAP two three four

Figure 1-9:
Exercise 2.

Exercise 3

CLAP CLAP-CLAP CLAP four | CLAP two three four | CLAP two three
CLAP | CLAP-CLAP CLAP three four | CLAP two CLAP four

Figure 1-10:
Exercise 3.

Exercise 4

CLAP two CLAP four | CLAP two three CLAP | CLAP two three four | one
CLAP three four | CLAP two three four

Figure 1-11:
Exercise 4.

Chapter 2

Stopping for a Rest

. . . .

In This Chapter

▶ Counting out the values of rests

▶ Dotting rests to lengthen their breaks

▶ Mixing up notes and rests

. . . .

Sometimes the most important aspects of a conversation are the things that *aren't* said. Likewise, many times the notes you don't play make all the difference in a piece of music.

These silent "notes" are called, quite fittingly, *rests*. When you see a rest in a piece of music, you don't have to do anything but continue counting out the beats during it. Rests are especially important when writing down your music for other people to read — and in reading other composers' music — because rests make the rhythm of that piece of music even more precise than musical notes alone would.

Rests work particularly well with music for multiple instruments. Rests make it easy for a performer to count out the beats and keep time with the rest of the ensemble, even if the performer's instrument doesn't come into play until later in the performance. Likewise, in piano music, rests tell the left or right hand — or both — to stop playing in a piece.

Don't let the name fool you. A rest in a piece of music is anything but nap-time. If you don't continue to steadily count through the rests, just as you do when you're playing notes, your timing will be off and eventually the piece will fall apart.

Getting to Know the Rests

You might think of rests as the spaces between words in a written sentence. If those spaces weren't there, you'd just be stringing one long word together into gobbledygook.

Musical rests don't get claps (or notes from pianos or keyboards). You just count them out in your head. Just remember to stop playing while you're counting.

Figure 2-1 shows you the note values you know from Book II Chapter 1 and their matching rests.

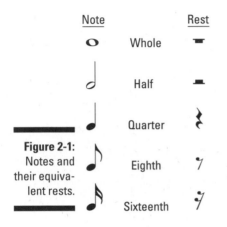

Figure 2-1: Notes and their equivalent rests.

Figure 2-2 shows the relative values of rests, ranging from a whole rest at the top to the sixteenth rests at the bottom. At the top is the whole rest, below it half rests, then quarter rests, eighth rests, and sixteenth rests. This section discusses each of these rests.

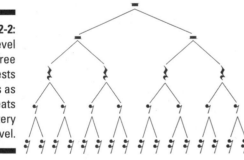

Figure 2-2: Each level of this tree of rests lasts as many beats as every other level.

Whole and half rests

When you see a whole note F, you play F and hold it for four beats. For a half note, you play and hold the note for two beats. So far, so good. Now, a *whole rest* (▬) asks you to *not* play anything for four beats. And a *half rest* (▬) asks you to not play anything for two beats.

Whole and half rests look like little hats — one hat off (⊤ = whole rest) and one hat on (⊥ = half rest). This hat analogy and the rules of etiquette make for a good way to remember these rests. Check it out:

- ✔ If you rest for the entire measure (four beats), take off your hat and stay for a while.

- ✔ If you rest for only half of the measure (two beats), the hat stays on.

These rests always look the same, making it easy for you to spot them in the music. A whole rest hangs from the fourth line up, and a half rest sits on the middle line, as shown in Figure 2-3.

Figure 2-3:
Whole and half rests on the staff.

Whole rest   Half rest

To see whole and half rests in action, take a peek at Figure 2-4. In the first measure, you play the two A quarter notes (use your 3rd finger) on beats 1 and 2, and then the half rest tells you not to play anything for beats 3 and 4. In the second measure, the whole rest tells you that you're off duty — you rest for four beats. In the third measure, you put down your donut and play two G quarter notes (2nd finger) and rest for two beats of rest. Finally, the whole show ends in the fourth measure with a whole note A.

Figure 2-4:
Practice your whole and half rests.

Count: 1, 2, 3, 4   1, 2, 3, 4   1, 2, 3, 4   1, 2, 3, 4

Quarter and eighth rests and beyond

Composers also use rests to tell you to stop playing for the equivalent of quarter notes and eighth notes.

I like to think of the *quarter rest* as an uncomfortable-looking chair. Have a look and see what you think: 𝄽. Because it's uncomfortable, you don't rest too long. In fact, you don't rest any longer than one beat in this chair.

The *eighth rest* — 𝄾 — and *sixteenth rest* — 𝄿 — are easy to recognize. They have the same number of flags as their note counterparts. An eighth note (♪) and eighth rest (𝄾) each has one flag, and a sixteenth note (♬) and sixteenth rest (𝄿) each has two flags.

Count all rests just like you count their kindred notes. Quarter rests are easy to count because they last only one beat. Eighth and sixteenth rests can be a bit harder to count simply because they happen faster. Don't be afraid to count out loud; doing so helps you place the eighth rests more precisely and may even cause others to sing along.

Figure 2-5 gives you a chance to count out some quarter and eighth rests. Try clapping the rhythms first, and then play them on your piano or keyboard using the suggested fingering above each note.

Figure 2-5: Counting quarter and eighth rests.

You'll read sixteenth note rests when you get into more advanced music. Until then, just remember what they look like (refer to Figure 2-1).

Using a metronome to count out notes and rests may help you figure out a piece of music. You can assign the ticks of the metronome to be any portion of the beat that you want. Having a quarter note equal one beat may seem natural much of the time, but instead of trying to think about half beats, you can also assign an eighth note to equal one tick. Then a quarter note would equal two ticks, a half note four, and a whole note eight ticks. The relation among the different notes and rests always stays the same no matter how many metronome ticks in a whole note.

Dotted rests

Unlike notes, rests are never tied together to make them longer. Rests are, however, sometimes dotted when the value of the rest needs to be extended. Just as with notes, when you see a rest followed by an *augmentation dot,* the rest's value is increased by one half of its original value.

Practicing Beats with Notes and Rests

The best way to really hear the way rests affect a piece of music is to mix them up with notes. The five exercises shown in Figures 2-6 through 2-10 are exactly what you need to practice making a beat stick in your head and making each kind of note and rest automatically register its value in your brain. Each exercise contains three groups of four beats each (and for the notes, only quarter notes, so your brain doesn't explode).

In these exercises, with four beats in every measure (4/4 time), you clap on the notes and count the rests aloud. Start out counting and then dive in after you count four.

Book II

Understanding Theory and the Language of Music

Exercise 1

CLAP CLAP CLAP CLAP | One two three four | CLAP two three CLAP

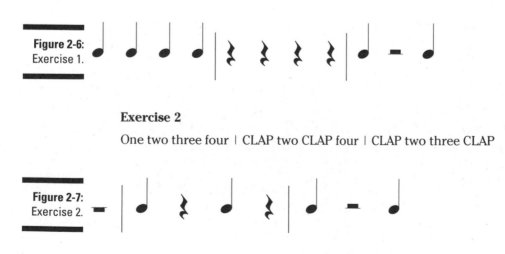

Figure 2-6: Exercise 1.

Exercise 2

One two three four | CLAP two CLAP four | CLAP two three CLAP

Figure 2-7: Exercise 2.

Exercise 3

One CLAP three CLAP | One two three four | CLAP two three CLAP

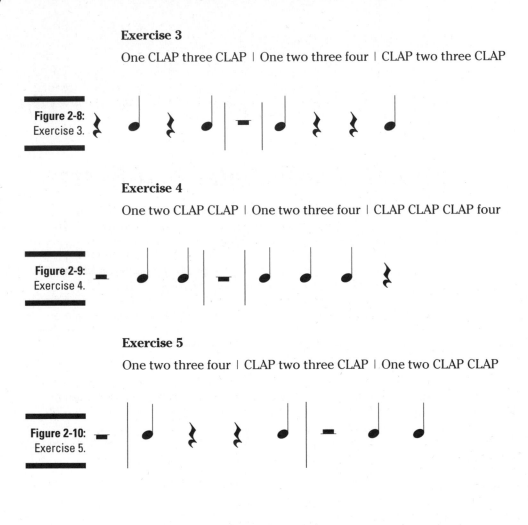

Figure 2-8:
Exercise 3.

Exercise 4

One two CLAP CLAP | One two three four | CLAP CLAP CLAP four

Figure 2-9:
Exercise 4.

Exercise 5

One two three four | CLAP two three CLAP | One two CLAP CLAP

Figure 2-10:
Exercise 5.

Chapter 3

Tempo, Measures, and Time Signatures

In This Chapter

▶ Understanding tempo

▶ Reviewing notes and note values

▶ Counting (and clapping) out different notes and note values

▶ Making some notes last longer than others

▶ Access the audio tracks at www.dummies.com/go/pianokeyboardaio/

A s you now know, the beat is what you tap your foot to; it's the steady pulse that provides the groovy groove of the music. A fast-paced dance song can get you pumping on the dance floor with a faster beat, and a slow love song can make you want to sway slowly to and fro with your honey in your arms. One of the first things to do when you play music is find out what the *tempo* is. How fast does the beat go?

Playing Fast and Slow: Tempo

Like heartbeats, musical beats are measured in beats per minute. A certain number of beats occur in music (and in your heart) every minute. When a doctor tells you how fast your heart is beating, you can think, "Who cares?" But when a composer or sheet music tells you how many musical beats occur in a specific length of musical time, you can't take such a whimsical attitude — not if you want the music to sound right.

Look at a clock or your watch and tap your foot once every second. You're tapping beats — one beat per second. Of course, beats can be faster or slower. Now tap your foot two times for every second.

How fast or how slow you tap these beats is called *tempo*. For example, when you tap one beat for every second, the tempo is 60 beats per minute (BPM) because there are 60 seconds in one minute. You're tapping a slow, steady tempo. When you tap your foot two times per second, you're tapping a moderately fast tempo at the rate of 120 BPM.

Composers use a tempo indication and sometimes a metronome marking to tell you how fast or slow the beat is. The *tempo indication*, shown above the treble staff at the beginning of the music, is a word or two that describes the beat in a simple way: fast, slow, moderately fast, and so on. A metronome marking tells you the exact rate of the beat, as measured in beats per minute. Table 3-1 lists tempo indications and their general parameters using common Italian and English directions.

As you learn to read and play music, keep in mind that tempo indications leave a good amount of discretion to the performer and can be followed in ways not limited to the exact rate of the beat.

Table 3-1	Tempos and Their Approximate Beats Per Minute (BPM)	
Tempo Indication	*Translation*	*BPM*
Largo	Very slowly (broad)	♩ = 40–60
Adagio	Slowly	♩ = 60–72
Andante	Moderately (walking tempo)	♩ = 72–96
Allegro	Fast, lively	♩ = 96–132
Vivace	Lively, brisk (faster than allegro)	♩ = 132–168
Presto	Very fast	♩ = 168–208

Don't forget to get a metronome or a metronome app. That way you don't have to spend all day wondering how to tap out 84 beats per minute.

Grouping Beats into Measures

Think of a music staff as a time line. (Book II Chapter 4 tells you all about the music staff.) In the same way that the face of a clock can be divided into minutes and seconds, the music staff can also be divided into smaller units of time. These smaller units of time help you count the beat and know where you are in the song at all times.

A short three-minute song may have 200 separate beats or more. To keep from getting lost in this myriad of beats, it helps to count the beats as you play the piano. But rather than ask you to count up into three-digit numbers and attempt to play at the same time, the composer groups the beats into nice small batches called *measures* (or *bars*).

Each measure has a specific number of beats. Most commonly, a measure has four beats. This smaller grouping of four beats is much easier to count: Just think "1, 2, 3, 4," and then begin again with "1" in each subsequent measure.

The composer decides how many beats to put in each measure and then marks each measure with a vertical line called a *bar line,* as shown in Figure 3-1 (clap to the rhythm slashes).

Book II

Understanding Theory and the Language of Music

Figure 3-1:
Bar lines group beats into measures.

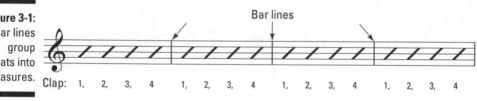

Why does it matter how many beats are in each measure? Measures help group beats into patterns. These patterns are made up of downbeats and upbeats, which are beats that are emphasized or de-emphasized, respectively. The repeating beat pattern determines a song's *time signature,* covered in the next section.

Now that you know how to count, play, and hold the three main note values, and what a bar is, try playing the music in Figure 3-2, which has a mix of different note lengths. Listen to Track 5 and follow along in the music one time before you play. It's true that the song's melody doesn't exactly bring a tear to the eye. The same note is used (good old G) throughout to help emphasize the rhythm created by combining the three note lengths.

A measure and a bar are the same thing. You'll hear them called by both terms.

Figure 3-2: Mixing up all the notes into measures.

Counting Out Common Time Signatures

In music, a *time signature* tells you the meter of the piece you're playing. Each measure of music receives a specified number of beats. Composers decide the number of beats per measure early on and convey such information with a time signature, or *meter*.

The two numbers in the time signature tell you how many beats are in each measure of music. In math, the fraction for a quarter is 1/4, so 4/4 means four quarters. Thus, each measure with a time signature of 4/4 has four quarter note beats; each measure with a 3/4 meter has three quarter note beats; and each measure of 2/4 time has two quarter note beats.

Figure 3-3 shows you three recognizable tunes that are written in each of these three time signatures. Notice how the syllable count and word emphasis fit the time signature.

Please keep in mind that 4/4 meter doesn't mean that each measure has only four quarter notes. It means each measure has only four *beats*. These beats may contain half notes, quarter notes, eighth notes, rests, whatever the composer wants — but all note and rest values must combine to equal the top number (or numerator) of the time signature.

Figure 3-3:
You can recognize the tunes of three common time signatures.

Old Mac - Don - ald   had   a   farm

Here we go round the mul - ber - ry bush

Yan - kee doo - dle went to town, a - rid - in' on a po - ny

Book II

Understanding Theory and the Language of Music

Common time: 4/4 meter

The most common meter in music is 4/4. It's so common that its other name is *common time* and the two numbers in the time signature are often replaced by the letter C.

In 4/4, the stacked numbers tell you that each measure contains four quarter note beats. So, to count 4/4 meter, each time you tap the beat, you're tapping the equivalent of one quarter note.

To hear an example of 4/4 meter, play Track 6, "A Hot Time in the Old Town Tonight." Notice how the beat pattern of 4/4 meter creates an emphasis on beats 1 and 3, which are downbeats (although beat 1 has the strongest emphasis). Beats 2 and 4 are upbeats. In many rock, R&B, and hip-hop songs, the upbeats are accented — this is commonly known as a *backbeat*. As you listen to the track, tap your foot on 1 and 3 (the downbeats), and clap on 2 and 4 (the upbeats).

Feel free to check out the sheet music as well, right here. Although you may not know the notes of the staff yet (don't worry — they're finally explained in the next chapter) — it can't hurt to look at the music as you listen, to get a feel for it if nothing else. It's also fine to simply tap your foot on the downbeats and clap on the upbeats.

A Hot Time in the Old Town Tonight

Waltz time: 3/4 meter

In the second most common meter, 3/4, each measure has three quarter note beats. Of course, this still doesn't mean that only quarter notes exist in this meter. You may have one half note and one quarter note, or you may have six eighth notes, but either way, the combination equals three quarter note beats.

In 3/4 meter, beat 1 of each measure is the downbeat, and beats 2 *and* 3 are the upbeats. It's quite common, though, to hear accents on the second or third beats, like in many country music songs.

Another name for 3/4 meter is *waltz time* because of the down-up-up beat pattern used for waltzing. Listen to Track 7, "The Beautiful Blue Danube." Notice the emphasis on beat 1 of each measure. Tap your foot on the down-beat, and clap on the upbeats. You could say that 3/4 was probably composer Johann "Waltz King" Strauss's favorite meter.

The Beautiful Blue Danube

Book II

Understanding
Theory and
the Language
of Music

March time: 2/4 meter

Chop a 4/4 meter in half and you're left with only two quarter note beats per measure. Not to worry, though, because two beats per measure is perfectly acceptable. In fact, you'll find 2/4 meter in most famous marches. The rhythm is similar to the rhythm of your feet when you march: "left-right, left-right, 1-2, 1-2." You start and stop marching on the downbeat — beat 1.

Track 8 is a good example of 2/4 meter. It's a famous dance by Jacques Offenbach called "Can Can." Feel free to march or "do the Can Can" as you listen. (For dancing tips, see www.youtube.com/watch?v=bRgWtRXhzUg.)

Can Can

6/8 time

If you notice that a time signature of 6/8 doesn't have a "4" in the bottom (denominator) position, you're no doubt already thinking that it can't be a meter based on quarter notes. If you're thinking that it might be a meter based on eighth notes, you're right. 6/8 meter is a grouping of six eighth notes per measure.

Sorting out the language of rhythm

Using words to describe the rhythmic qualities of music can get tricky. Time signature and tempo are different components that work together to create the rhythmic framework for music. A song in 4/4 and a different song in 3/4 can have the same tempo because tempo tells you the rate of the underlying beat: fast, slow, or exactly at the rate of 120 beats per minute, for example. A fast song and a slow song can share the same time signature — a fast waltz or a slow waltz, for example. The time signature tells you how the beats are organized into measures and how to count the measures. The rhythm of a melody is defined by its unique combination of note values and rests. All other accompanying rhythmic elements (the bass line, chords, drums, requisite tuba solo) combine with these elements and make up the rhythm of a song.

Book II

Understanding Theory and the Language of Music

Like the waltz, beats in 6/8 meter are grouped in threes, but there are two groups. 6/8 has an added down-up beat pattern on the first eighth note of each group — beats 1 and 4. Showing the emphasis using italics, you count a measure of 6/8 with one count for each eighth note beat, as follows: *One*, two, three, *four*, five, six. Beat 1 is a stronger downbeat than 4, so this beat pattern can feel like two broader beats (down-up), each with its own down-up-up pattern within.

Listen to Track 9 for an example of 6/8 meter. Tap your right foot on beat 1, tap your left foot on beat 4, and clap the upbeats (2, 3, 5, 6).

Chapter 4

Navigating Sheet Music

· ·

In This Chapter

▶ Getting to know the staff, clefs, and their notes

▶ Understanding half steps, whole steps, and accidentals

▶ Applying knowledge of the staves to the piano and guitar

▶ Memorizing notes with mnemonics

· ·

To play music, you have to know what note to play and when. A piano has 88 keys, each sounding a different musical note. With a bunch of lines and dots, a composer tells you which notes to play and how to play them — which of the 88 keys to press and how long to play each note. This chapter aims to help you understand how all that is written down and conveyed in printed music.

This chapter discusses the musical staves and where to find notes on them, as well as the concept of intervals. Mastering these concepts allows you to both navigate your way through a piece of sheet music and even begin to learn how to improvise.

Meeting the Staff, Clefs, and Notes

Notes and rests in music are written on what's called a *musical staff* (or *staves*, if you're talking about more than one). A staff is made of five parallel horizontal lines, containing four spaces between them, as shown in Figure 4-1.

Figure 4-1:
The treble
clef staff
(left) and the
bass clef
staff (right).

Notes and rests are written on the lines and spaces of the staff. The particular musical notes that are meant by each line and space depend on which *clef* is written at the beginning of the staff. You may run across any of the following clefs (though the first two are the most common):

- ✔ Treble clef
- ✔ Bass clef
- ✔ C clefs, including alto and tenor

Think of each clef as a graph of *pitches,* or *tones,* shown as notes plotted over time on five lines and four spaces. Each pitch or tone is named after one of the first seven letters of the alphabet: A, B, C, D, E, F, G, A, B, C . . . and it keeps on going that way indefinitely, repeating the note names as the pitches repeat in *octaves.* The pitch ascends as you go from A to G, with every eighth note — where you return to your starting letter — signifying the beginning of a new octave.

The treble clef

The *treble clef* is for higher-pitched notes. It contains the notes above middle C on the piano, which means all the notes you play with your right hand. The treble clef is also sometimes called the *G clef.* Note that the shape of the treble clef itself resembles a stylized G. The loop on the treble clef also circles the second line on the staff — which is the note G.

The notes are located in the treble clef on lines and spaces, in order of ascending pitch, as shown in Figure 4-2.

Figure 4-2:
The notes
of the
treble clef.

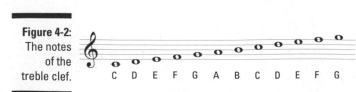

The bass clef

On the piano, the *bass clef* contains lower-pitched notes, the ones below middle C, including all the notes you play with your left hand. Another name for the bass clef is the *F clef*. The curly top of the clef partly encircles where the F note is on the staff, and it has two dots that surround the F note line. (It also looks a bit like a cursive letter F, if you use your imagination.)

The notes on the bass clef are also arranged in ascending order, as shown in Figure 4-3.

Figure 4-3: The notes of the bass clef.

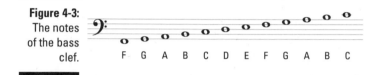

F   G   A   B   C   D   E   F   G   A   B   C

Book II

Understanding Theory and the Language of Music

The grand staff and ledger lines

Sooner or later, on either staff, you run out of lines and spaces for your notes. Surely the composer wants you to use more of the fabulous 88 keys at your disposal, right? Here's a solution: Because you play piano with both hands at the same time, why not show both *staves* (the plural form of *staff*) on the music page? Great idea!

Join both staves together with a brace at the start of the left side and you get one *grand staff* (it's really called that), as shown in Figure 4-4. This way, you can read notes for both hands at the same time.

Figure 4-4: Isn't this staff grand?

Why all the space between the two staves? Note that the bottom line of the treble clef staff is E, and the top line of the bass clef staff is A. That space is for the notes between those two notes.

That's where *ledger lines* come in. Ledger lines allow you to notate the notes above and below each staff. Middle C, for example, can be written below the treble staff or above the bass staff by using a small line through the notehead, as you can see in Figure 4-5. Either way, it's the same note on the piano keyboard.

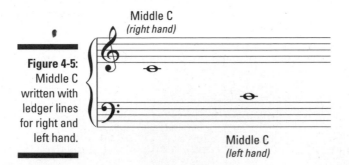

Figure 4-5:
Middle C
written with
ledger lines
for right and
left hand.

If middle C is written with a ledger line below the treble staff, you play it with your right hand; if it's written with a ledger line above the bass staff, you play it with your left hand.

If you're more of a visual learner, try thinking of it this way: The notes written in the middle of the grand staff, or between the two staves, represent notes in the middle of the piano keyboard.

The ledger line represents an imaginary line running above or below the staff, extending the five-line staff to six, seven, or more lines. A grand way to notate all the notes beyond the range of each staff, wouldn't you say? You can, of course, read notes in the spaces between the ledger lines just like you read notes in the spaces between the staff lines.

The notes B and D, surrounding middle C, can also be written by using ledger lines. That is, D can either be written below the bottom line of the treble staff, or it can sit on top of the middle C ledger line above the bass staff. Similarly, B can sit on top of the bass staff or below the middle C ledger line of the treble staff. Figure 4-6 illustrates these flexible note positions on the grand staff.

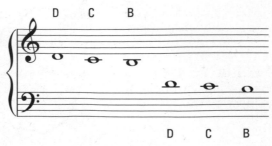

Figure 4-6:
Playing
the same
note with
different
hands.

Climbing beyond the staff

Middle C may be powerful, but it isn't the only note to receive the coveted ledger line award. Other ledger lines come into play when you get to notes that are above and below the grand staff. Notes written above the treble staff represent higher notes, to the right on your keyboard. Conversely, notes written below the bass staff represent lower notes, to the left on your keyboard.

For example, the top line of the treble staff is F. Just above this line, sits the note G. After G, a whole new set of ledger lines waits to bust out.

A similar situation occurs at the bottom of the bass staff. Ledger lines begin popping up below the low G line and low F that's hanging on to the staff for dear life. Figure 4-7 shows a generous range of notes on the grand staff and how they relate to the keyboard.

Book II

Understanding Theory and the Language of Music

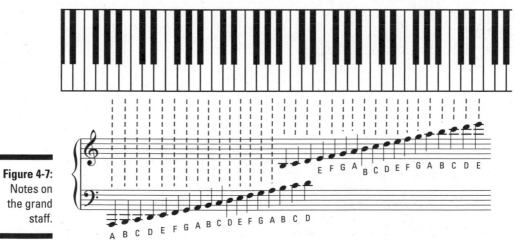

Figure 4-7: Notes on the grand staff.

An octave above, an octave below

Writing and reading ledger lines for notes farther up and down the keyboard can get a little ridiculous. After all, if you were to keep using ledger lines, you'd take up an impractical amount of space, and reading all those lines would become tedious. That's why composers invented the octave, or *ottava* line, which tells you to play the indicated note or notes an octave higher or lower than written. The abbreviation *8va* means play an octave above, and *8vb* means play an octave below. Figure 4-8 shows how these octave lines appear in written music.

Solving the mysteries that lurk between the clefs

The existence of middle C clears up some very big questions about the staves:

- ✔ If it's so important, then why isn't G on the middle line of the treble staff?

- ✔ Likewise, why isn't F on the middle line of the bass staff?

The answer to both of these mysteries is, of course, that the staff positions of G and F are determined by their distance from middle C. You might say middle C has some power in the musical world.

Figure 4-8: Octave lines.

Identifying Half Steps, Whole Steps, and Accidentals on the Staff

In Western music, an octave is broken up into 12 tones called *half steps,* or *semitones.* But a musical *scale* contains seven notes, meaning that some of the distance between notes in a scale spans one half step, and some spans at least two half steps. In other words, some half steps are skipped when building scales. (Check out Book III Chapter 2 for much more on scales.)

When musicians talk about the notes A, B, C, D, E, F, and G, they mean the *natural* notes — specifically, the notes that correspond to the white keys on a keyboard. The white keys of the keyboard were assigned the natural letter notes, which turn out to be the notes of the C major scale, beginning with C. However, because you're dealing with a musical vocabulary made up of 12 half steps (or semitones), the keyboard also has five black keys, repeated over and over, which represent the semitones that are skipped in the C scale. The black keys were added much later than the original white keys in order to help build more perfect musical scales on the piano.

Moving a whole step on the piano means you move two half steps from your starting position. Half steps and whole steps are called *intervals.* Knowing the difference between whole steps and half steps is important when working with the patterns used to build scales and chords.

You also employ half steps when you come across an *accidental,* a notation used to raise or lower a natural note pitch. So when a note is *sharped,* you add a half step to the note; when a note is *flatted,* you remove a half step from the note.

Working with half steps

In Western musical notation, the smallest difference between two pitches is the half step, or semitone. Using the piano keyboard as a reference, if you pick a key, play it, and then play the key that's right next to it (on the left or right) whether that key is black or white, you've moved one half step in pitch. See Figure 4-9 for an illustration of this principle.

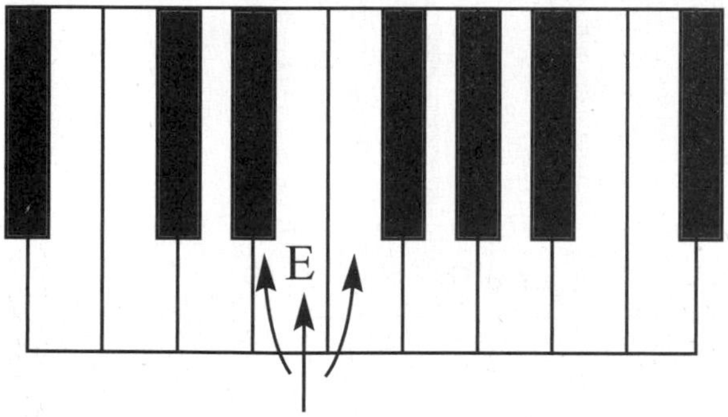

Book II

Understanding Theory and the Language of Music

Figure 4-9: Half steps to the left and right of the E key.

Because musical pitch is actually a continuous spectrum (think about a trombone sliding up the scale), many other *microtonal* sounds actually exist between consecutive half steps. But Western musical notation only recognizes the division of pitch into half steps. In contrast, many Eastern instruments, particularly sitars and fretless stringed instruments, use *quarter tones.* Quarter tones are pitches located halfway between each half step.

As you can see in Figure 4-9, if you start out playing an E on the piano, a half step to the left brings you to E♭ (E flat), which could also be called D♯ (D sharp). A half step to the right lands you on E♯, which is more commonly known as F, or F♮ (F natural).

When a musician refers to a note being *flatted,* you know you need to move one half step to the left of that natural note; if it's being *sharped,* you know to move one half step to the right. Every black key on a piano has two names: It can be referred to as the flat of the white key on its right or the sharp of the white key on its left. It doesn't matter which way it's named. For example, E flat and D sharp may be written as different notes, but they have the same pitch, or sound. Notes with the same pitch are referred to as *enharmonic.*

Taking whole steps

Following the logic that a half step on the piano is one key away from the starting point, it only makes sense that a whole step would be two keys or frets away from the starting point.

Say, for example, that you start on E on the keyboard. One whole step to the left of E would be D, as shown in Figure 4-10.

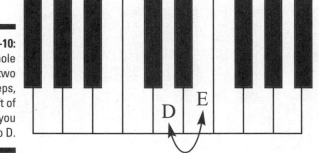

Figure 4-10: One whole step, or two half steps, to the left of E brings you to D.

Meanwhile, one whole step to the *right* of E would be F sharp, as shown in Figure 4-11.

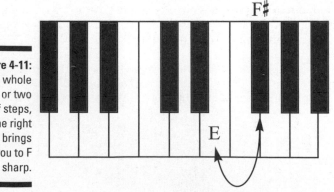

Figure 4-11: One whole step, or two half steps, to the right of E brings you to F sharp.

The distance between the consecutive white piano keys E and F, and B and C, equals a half step, whereas the distance between the remaining white keys (G-A, A-B, C-D, D-E, F-G) is a whole step. That's because the piano is designed around the *C scale*.

Changing pitch with accidentals

Accidentals are notations used to raise or lower a natural note pitch on the staff by a half step. They apply to the note throughout a measure until you see another accidental. You can use these different types of accidentals:

- ✔ Sharp (♯)
- ✔ Flat (♭)
- ✔ Double sharp (𝄪)
- ✔ Double flat (𝄫)
- ✔ Natural (♮)

Book II

Understanding Theory and the Language of Music

Sharps

A sharp is placed before a note to indicate that the note is a half step higher, as shown in Figure 4-12.

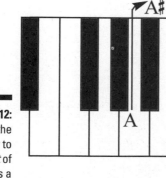

Figure 4-12: A sharp, the black key to the *right* of the A, is a half step up from A.

Figure 4-13 shows a sharped E (the enharmonic of F natural). E sharp is one half step up in pitch from E.

Figure 4-13:
E to E sharp.

Flats

A flat does just the opposite of a sharp: It lowers the note by a half step, as shown in Figure 4-14.

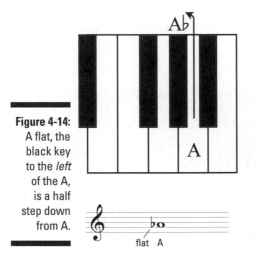

Figure 4-14:
A flat, the black key to the *left* of the A, is a half step down from A.

Figure 4-15 shows a flatted E. E flat is one half step down in pitch from E.

Figure 4-15:
E to E flat.

Every once in a while, you'll run into a *double sharp* or a *double flat.* The double sharp raises the natural note two half steps — or one whole step — whereas the double flat lowers the note two half steps, or one whole step.

Naturals: Cancelling sharps and flats

Last but not least is the *natural,* which you can see in Figure 4-16.

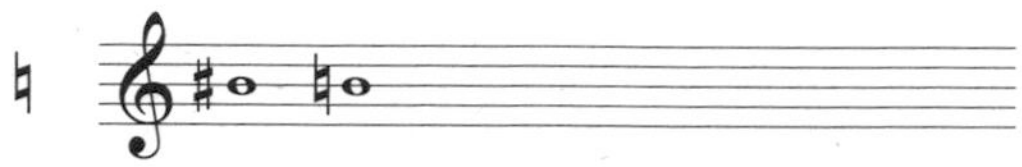

Figure 4-16:
A natural
cancels an
established
sharp or flat.

REMEMBER

When you see a natural sign next to a note, it means that any sharp or flat that's already in effect (either given in the key signature or in the same measure; see Book III Chapter 5 for information on key signatures) is cancelled for the rest of the measure. In other words, you're supposed to play the "natural" version of the note instead of whatever sharp or flat was in effect, even if it was a double sharp or double flat.

Mnemonics help you remember the notes

Having trouble remembering the names of the lines and spaces for each staff (and, consequently, the notes they represent)? Use a *mnemonic,* a word or phrase created from the letter names of these lines and spaces, to help you remember.

Try the following mnemonics, but feel free to make up your own. Unless otherwise noted, these mnemonics start on the bottom line of each staff and go up:

Treble clef lines (E-G-B-D-F):

✔ **Traditional:** **E**very **G**ood **B**oy **D**oes **F**ine

✔ **Musical:** **E**very **G**ood **B**and **D**raws **F**ans

✔ **Pianistic:** **E**ven **G**ershwin **B**egan (as a) **D**ummy **F**irst

✔ **Culinary:** **E**ating **G**reen **B**ananas **D**isgusts **F**riends

Treble clef spaces (F-A-C-E):

Bass clef lines (G-B-D-F-A):

✔ **Traditional:** **G**ood **B**oys **D**o **F**ine **A**lways

✔ **Recreational:** **G**ood **B**ikes **D**on't **F**all **A**part

✔ **Animal:** **G**reat **B**ig **D**ogs **F**ight **A**nimals

✔ **Musical:** **G**reat **B**eethoven's **D**eafness **F**rustrated **A**ll

✔ **Musical:** **G**randpa **B**ach **D**id **F**ugues **A** lot

✔ **Painful:** **G**iving **B**lood **D**oesn't **F**eel **A**greeable

Bass clef spaces (A-C-E-G):

✔ **Musical:** **A**merican **C**omposers **E**nvy **G**ershwin

✔ **Animal:** **A**ll **C**ows **E**at **G**rass

Read enough of these mnemonics and you'll be hard-pressed to forget them. Of course, if you do happen to forget these helpful tools, simply find the line encircled by the clef and move up or down the alphabet from there.

Musical Punctuation: Bar Lines

In addition to horizontal staff lines, music employs some vertical lines to help you keep track of where you are in the music, sort of like punctuation in a written sentence. Bar lines were introduced in Book II Chapter 3, but this section goes into more detail.

A *bar line* divides music into measures or bars, breaking up the musical paragraph into smaller, measurable groups of notes and rests. Measures help organize both the writing and reading of music for the composer *and* the performer. Figure 4-17 shows you how bar lines are written.

Figure 4-17: Bar lines divide music into measures.

Be prepared to see a few other types of bar lines in piano music. They give you directions on how the music is structured, when and where to repeat, and when to stop. Following are the names of the five types of bar lines and details on what they tell you to do:

- **Single:** Go on to the next measure.
- **Double:** Proceed to the next section (because you've reached the end of this one).
- **Start repeat:** Repeat back to this measure.
- **End repeat:** Repeat back to the measure that begins with a start repeat (or to the beginning if you don't see a start repeat).
- **Final:** You've reached the end! Stop playing!

Figure 4-18 shows you what each one looks like.

Figure 4-18: The five types of bar lines.

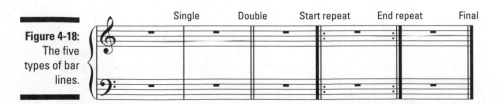

Single   Double   Start repeat   End repeat   Final

Chapter 5

Varying Beats and Rhythms

In This Chapter

▶ Starting a little early with pickups

▶ Tying and dotting your notes to make them last longer

▶ Getting offbeat with triplets, syncopation, and more

▶ Access the audio tracks at www.dummies.com/go/pianokeyboardaio/

*A*s soon as the music starts, you hear *beats* as a constant, ever-present force. But you can do a lot more than playing a note on every darn one of those beats.

This chapter shows you some ways to play around with the way rhythms interact with the beat, whether that means holding notes longer, playing off or around the beat, or even not playing at all. (For a review of the basics of rhythm and beats, check out Book II Chapters 2 and 3.)

Getting a Jump on the Start: Pickup Beats and Measures

You've probably heard the old adage, "Everything starts from nothing." Well, some songs actually begin with rests. That's right: The performer walks out on stage, sits at the piano, and rests for a few beats before hitting a single note. You may like a long and boring explanation of why some music starts with rests, but you'd probably prefer a clear explanation of pickup beats and measures.

Here's an easy example: The first two notes of the song "She'll Be Coming Round the Mountain" actually fall on beats 3 and 4 of a measure of 4/4 time. (Book II Chapter 3 tells you about time signatures.) These two melody notes are called *pickup notes,* because they pick up in the middle of the beat and start the song. How nice of them! To play "She'll Be Coming Round the Mountain," you start with a half rest and count "1, 2, She'll be . . ." as shown in Figure 5-1.

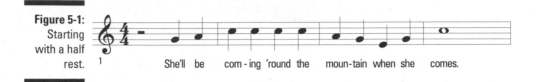

Figure 5-1:
Starting with a half rest.

Rather than note a bunch of rests at the beginning, the composer can opt to write a *pickup measure,* which contains only that part of the measure that's played or sung. In other words, the pickup measure simply eliminates any rests before picking up the tune. Figure 5-2 shows the notation in a song with a pickup measure.

Figure 5-2:
Starting with a pickup measure.

To play and count songs with pickup measures, follow three easy steps:

1. Note the meter.

2. Rest for the number of "missing" beats.

3. Play the pickup notes, and away you go.

Hundreds of songs begin with pickup measures, including "When the Saints Go Marching In" and "Oh, Susannah." Listen to Tracks 10 and 11 to get a feel for these great songs. If you're ready to play these songs with pickup measures, you can find the music for them at the end of the chapter.

Adding Time to Your Notes with Ties and Dots

Ties and dots are more than accessories and designs to spice up your wardrobe. In music, they're symbols that add more time or length to your notes. A quarter or half note doesn't quite cut it? Need to play the note a little bit longer? Just throw in some of these value-adding notations to extend the length of your notes.

Linking notes using ties

Let's review a minute: Half notes and whole notes last longer than one beat. But suppose you want to play a note that lasts longer than one measure or a note that lasts for two and a half beats? Music's solution is a curvy little line called the tie.

The *tie* does just what it sounds like: It ties two notes of the same pitch together, causing one continuous-sounding note. For example, a whole note tied to a quarter note lasts for five beats. Likewise, a quarter note tied to an eighth note is held for one and a half beats. Figure 5-3 shows you a few notes that are tied together, as well as how to count them.

Book II

Understanding Theory and the Language of Music

Figure 5-3: Ties that bind notes of the same pitch.

As mentioned earlier in this book, don't mistake a tie for a slur. They look similar because they're both curved lines, but a tie connects two notes that are the *same* pitch from notehead to notehead. In contrast, a *slur* connects notes of different pitches.

Listen to Track 12 and try to play along with Figure 5-3. When you see two notes tied together, play the first note and hold it for the combined value of both notes.

Extending notes using dots

Another way to extend the length of a note, and make it look a little fancier, is through the use of a *dot*. A dot on any size note or rest makes that note or rest last 50 percent longer.

Dotted half notes

A quarter note lasts one beat, a half note lasts two, and a whole note lasts four. You can see that you're in need of a note that lasts three beats. Probably the most common dotted note in music is the dotted half note, which gets a total of three beats, as shown in Figure 5-4.

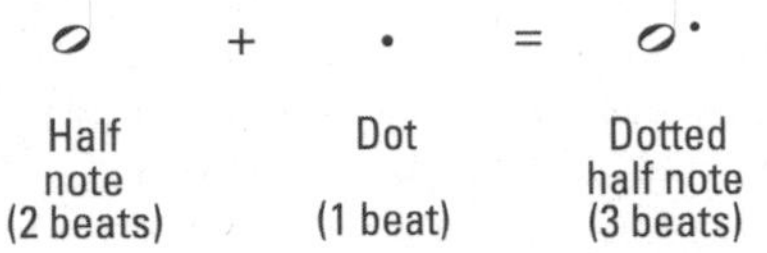

Figure 5-4:
The dotted half note.

Half
note
(2 beats)

Dot
(1 beat)

Dotted
half note
(3 beats)

This note gets a lot of use in 4/4. In 3/4 time, it takes up the entire measure. Figure 5-5 shows dotted half notes in action and tells you how to count them.

(To play a melody with dotted half notes, turn to the section "Playing Songs with Challenging Rhythms" at the end of the chapter for the music to *Scheherezade*.)

Figure 5-5:
Dotted half notes in 4/4 and 3/4 time.

Dotted quarter notes

When you add a dot to a quarter note, you get a great hybrid note that lasts for one and a half beats. Because of its length, the dotted quarter note is commonly paired with an eighth note in order to finish out the second beat (see Figure 5-6).

Figure 5-6:
A dotted quarter note paired with an eighth.

Count: 1 and 2 and   1 and 2 and   1 and 2 and   1 and 2 and   1 and 2 and

Dotted eighth notes

The dotted eighth note equals one and a half eighth notes, or three sixteenth notes. As you know from Book II Chapter 1, it takes four sixteenth notes to make one quarter note (or one beat). So, a dotted eighth note is often paired with a sixteenth note to make a full quarter note beat. In this combination, the normal eighth note beam connects the two notes, and the sixteenth note gets a shortened second beam (see Figure 5-7).

Figure 5-7:
A dotted eighth, a sixteenth, and their beams.

Book II

Understanding Theory and the Language of Music

Get some practice reading and playing some dotted notes with the exercise in Figure 5-8. Work on developing the kind of flexible counting system shown in the figure. You count only quarter notes in the first measure, then count out eighth and sixteenth notes for the measures that require that type of breakdown. When you're out of the rough in the last measure, you can go back to counting quarter notes. Just make sure you keep the beat steady!

Figure 5-8:
Practice with dotted notes.

"Swanee River" is a classic example of both dotted quarter notes and dotted eighth notes. Listen to it until you get the feel of the rhythm, and when you're ready to play the song, check out the later section "Playing Songs with Challenging Rhythms."

Playing Offbeat Rhythms

When you understand note values and ways to extend those values with ties and dots, you can expand your rhythmic range with some fancy ways to divide, delay, anticipate, and swing note values. After all, you live in a world filled with rhythm, and most of the music you hear day in and day out is surprisingly rhythmic, thanks to the influence of jazz, blues, and plenty of other folk and popular music from all around the world.

This section expands your musical knowledge with many of the fascinating rhythms you need to know to play your favorite music, whether it's jazz, classical, popular, or folk tunes. Start off with triplets and then move on to swing rhythms and syncopation.

As you read the following sections about dividing the beat and playing notes off the beat, tap your foot along to the examples. Even when you don't play a note right on the beat, you won't lose the beat.

Triplets love chocolate

Most notes divide a beat neatly by some factor of two. But every now and then, you may want to divide a beat into more than two eighth notes but less than four sixteenth notes. That means playing three notes per beat, aptly called a *triplet*.

The most common triplet pattern is the *eighth-note triplet,* which looks like three beamed eighth notes. To help you spot these triplets quickly, composers add a little number 3 above (or below) the beam. A popular variation on this triplet pattern is the quarter-eighth triplet, which looks like (get this) a quarter note and an eighth note but with a little bracket and a number 3. Figure 5-9 shows you both types of triplets.

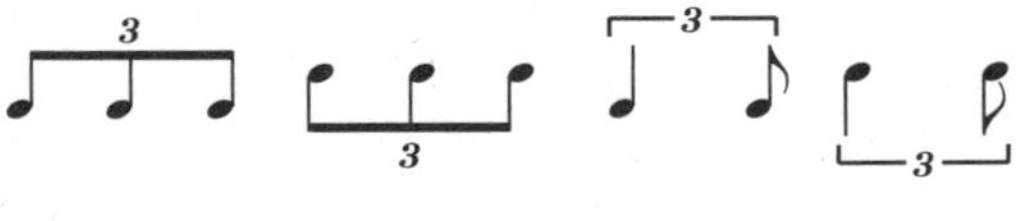

Figure 5-9:
Congrats!
You have
triplets.

You can hear an example of these triplets on Track 13 before you try to play them yourself in Figure 5-10.

TIP

To count these triplets, tap your foot and say "1 trip-let, 2 trip-let" or (if you like food metaphors) "choc-o-late" for every beat. The most important point is to divide the beat into three equal parts so each syllable gets its fair share.

Figure 5-10: Counting triplets.

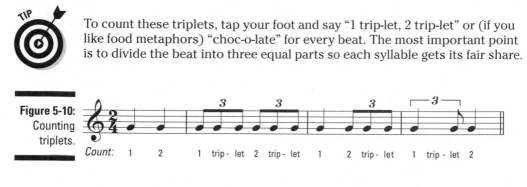

Now try playing the triplets in Figure 5-11. Keep thinking "choc-o-late" until you've gotta take a candy bar break.

Book II

Understanding Theory and the Language of Music

Figure 5-11: Practice with triplets.

REMEMBER

You can make triplets using other note values, too, but you probably won't have to play them for a while, at least not until you start jamming with your local drum circle. It's worth remembering, though, that with any triplet rhythm, 3 = 2: Three quarter-note triplets equal two quarter notes (two beats), and three sixteenth-note triplets equal two sixteenth notes (half a beat). You play three notes (equally) in the time you would normally play two notes of the same value.

Swing and shuffle time

The beat may go on and on, but music can be quite dull if every note you play is on the beat. By changing up the rhythm a bit and playing some notes off, around, or in between the main beats, your playing takes on a whole new life.

For example: The *swing beat.* Listen to Track 14 while you look at the four measures of music in Figure 5-12. The music track plays the eighth notes with a swing beat. The notes are the same, but the rhythm has a slightly different, swingin' feel. Instead of straight eighth notes played as "1-and, 2-and," you hear a long-short, long-short rhythm. The most accurate way to notate this swing rhythm is with a quarter-eighth triplet. (See the previous section for more on triplets.) But rather than write a ton of triplets, the composer gives you a big heads up along with the tempo indication above the first measure by telling you to "Swing," either in plain English or with a little symbol like the one in Figure 5-13.

Figure 5-12: Swing those eighths.

Figure 5-13: This notation says swing it.

When you see the swing notation, you should play all the eighth notes in the music as swing eighths. You can still count them as "1-and, 2-and, 3-and, 4-and," but the notes on the beats are longer and the notes off the beats are shorter.

The best way to understand the swing beat is to hear it. So popular is this classic American rhythm that it has its own type of bands and dance moves. Listen to some of the music of the big-band era, like the Duke Ellington Orchestra or the Tommy Dorsey Orchestra. They really had the whole world swingin'.

To play a song with swing eighths right now, skip to the song "By the Light of the Silvery Moon" in the section "Playing Songs with Challenging Rhythms" at the end of this chapter.

Shuffle feel has the same long-short swing eighths as swing time, but the shuffle beat is more readily associated with rock and blues-style music. A shuffle feel is characterized by a heavier beat than swing, which is lighter on its feet.

To play a song with a shuffle feel, skip to "I've Been Working On the Railroad" in the section "Playing Songs with Challenging Rhythms" at the end of this chapter.

Syncopation

One of the most common forms of playing off the beat is a little rhythmic concept called *syncopation*. To understand syncopation, you have to know about *downbeats* and *upbeats*. Start tapping your foot to a moderate 4/4 beat, and count eighth notes "1-and, 2-and, 3-and, 4-and." Your foot goes *down* on the downbeats and *up* on the upbeats.

Downbeats are the beats that are normally emphasized in a song. But through the miracle of syncopation, you emphasize some (or all) of the upbeats instead. You play those notes a little bit harder, or louder, than the others. For example, the note normally played on beat 3 is played on the upbeat before, and this anticipation naturally emphasizes the upbeat and creates syncopation.

Figure 5-14 shows a two-measure melodic phrase written first to emphasize the downbeat on beat 3, and then transformed into a syncopated rhythm, with the arrows showing the point of emphasis on the upbeat, on "and" before beat 3.

Book II

Understanding Theory and the Language of Music

Figure 5-14: Suddenly syncopation by emphasizing upbeats.

You can hear how syncopation works with a well-known melody. Listen to Track 15 while you follow along with the music in Figure 5-15. The track plays the opening four measures of the classic song "After You've Gone" first without any syncopation, and then with syncopation. Keep your foot tapping the beat throughout the entire eight measures and notice the emphasized notes on the upbeats (when your foot is up). The arrows mark the syncopated notes.

Figure 5-15: "After You've Gone," without (top) and with (bottom) syncopation.

If you're feeling the off-kilter groove of syncopation and are ready to play a syncopated song, try "Limehouse Blues" in the next section.

Playing Songs with Challenging Rhythms

The songs in this section give you a chance to play music featuring the rhythmic tricks covered in this chapter, from pickup measures to ties and dots to swing eighth notes and syncopation.

Here are a few tips on each of the songs to keep in mind:

- **"When the Saints Go Marching In" (Track 16):** This song has a pickup measure with a three-beat pickup. The last measure has only one beat in order to make a complete measure. Note that this song also has ties and dots.

- **"Oh, Susannah" (Track 17):** This song has two eighth-note pickups, which equal one beat and are counted "4-and." Notice how the last measure has only three beats; this is often done to complete the three missing beats in the pickup measure. Taken together, the pickup and last measure equal one complete measure.

- *Scheherazade* **(Track 18):** You find dotted half notes scattered throughout waltzes and other songs in 3/4 meter, like the theme from Rimsky-Korsakov's *Scheherazade*. Notice that this melody combines the use of ties and dots. The tie simply adds even more time to the dotted half note. For example, in the fourth measure, you hold the B note for four beats.

- **"Swanee River" (Track 19):** You hear dotted eighth notes in all types of music, but especially in dance tunes. Composer Stephen Foster made good use of dotted quarters as well as dotted eighths in his classic tune "Swanee River." You may want to listen to the track a couple of times before trying to play it yourself.

- **"By the Light of the Silvery Moon" (Track 20):** The swinging rhythm of the lyrics helps you get the hang of playing swing eighth notes in this tune.

- **"I've Been Working on the Railroad" (Track 21):** The chug-a-lug train rhythm of this song matches a shuffle feel quite naturally. The eighth notes are swing eighths, but the underlying triplet feel is a bit heavier than in a swing feel.

- **"Limehouse Blues" (Track 22):** The melody to "Limehouse Blues" has built-in syncopation, and you get lots of practice with this tune: Every other measure has a syncopated note held by a tie into the following measure.

Book II

Understanding Theory and the Language of Music

When the Saints Go Marching In

Scheherezade

Moderately fast

Book II

Understanding Theory and the Language of Music

Swanee River

By the Light of the Silvery Moon

By the light of the sil - ver - y moon,

I want to spoon to my hon- ey I'll croon love's

tune. Hon- ey- moon, keep a- shin- ing in June.

Your sil - v'ry beams will bring love dreams, we'll be cud- dl - ing

soon, by the light of the moon._____

Book II

Understanding Theory and the Language of Music

I've Been Working on the Railroad

Limehouse Blues

Book III
Beginning to Play

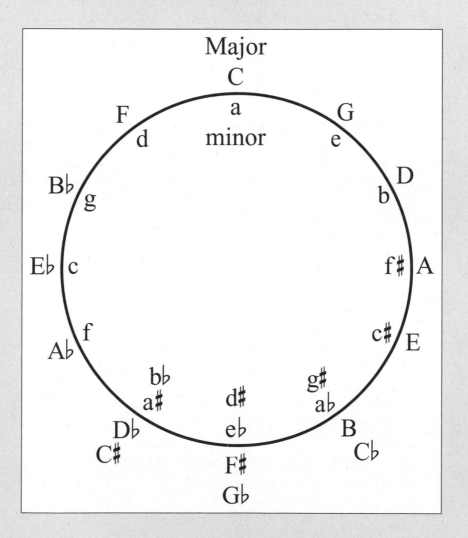

Contents at a Glance

Chapter 1: Playing a Melody **155**

Let Your Fingers Do the Walking...155
Positions, Everyone!...156
Cross Your Fingers and Hope It Works....................................163
Playing Melodies in the Right Hand..166

Chapter 2: Working with Scales **171**

Building a Scale, Step-by-Step...172
Introducing Major Scales...173
Introducing Minor Scales...177
Checking Out Blues Scales..182
Playing Songs Made of Scales...184

Chapter 3: Adding the Left Hand **187**

Exploring the Keyboard's West Side..187
Left-Hand Melodies..190
South-Paw Scales...192
Accompaniment Patterns...194
Adding the Left Hand to the Right Hand..................................198
Playing Songs with Both Hands...203

Chapter 4: Examining Form: Melody, Harmony, and Song Form **209**

Shaping the Melody..210
Measuring Melodic Intervals..212
Combining Notes for Harmonic Intervals.................................220
Working with Musical Phrases and Periods...............................225
Linking Musical Parts to Create Forms....................................226
Playing Songs with More Harmony...228

Chapter 5: Keys, Key Signatures, and the Circle of Fifths **235**

Home Sweet Home Key..235
The Circle of Fifths...240
Reviewing All the Key Signatures..245
Playing Songs with Key Signatures..253

Chapter 6: Building Chords to Accompany Melodies **257**

The Anatomy of a Triad...258
Starting Out with Major Chords..259
Branching Out with Minor Chords...260
Exploring Other Types of Chords...260
Adding the Seventh for Four-Note Chords................................264
Reading Chord Symbols...265
Relating Chords to a Scale or Key Signature.............................268
Rearranging the Order of the Notes: Chord Inversions.................270
Playing Songs with Chords...274

Chapter 1

Playing a Melody

. . . .

In This Chapter

▶ Putting your right hand in the proper position for a melody

▶ Extending positions to reach more keys

▶ Access the audio tracks at www.dummies.com/go/pianokeyboardaio/

. . . .

Melodies create a wonderful transformation in music: They turn a whole bunch of random notes into songs that entertain, please your ear, and sometimes get stuck in your head. It would be safe to say that you aren't really playing music unless you're playing a melody.

To really get the most out of this chapter about melodies, you should have a foundation of basic knowledge — in this case, that means you should first read the chapters in Books I and II. Without these fundamentals, attempting to play melodies and songs may lead to frustration.

This chapter helps you start playing melodies by talking about how your hands fall on the keyboard and then explaining two common positions: C and G. Because not all melodies stick to these original positions, the chapter also instructs you in shifting and extending positions. You put these techniques to use playing melodies in classical, folk, and Tin Pan Alley styles.

Let Your Fingers Do the Walking

To play a melody on the piano, you need to observe the way your hands make contact with the keyboard. If you don't develop comfortable moves, you'll find it hard to reach the notes you need to play — and your playing will look and sound more like Charlie Chaplin than Chopin.

As discussed in Book I Chapter 5 — think of your fingers as being numbered 1 through 5, with the thumbs being 1. This chapter refers to your fingers by number and to your hands by ultra-hip abbreviations: RH and LH. So, RH 1 means the thumb on your right hand.

In Figure 1-1, RH 2 plays D. Notice the relaxed but arched position of the hand and fingers. See, too, how the other four fingers are poised and ready to play the next note, whatever it may be.

Figure 1-1:
Playing
a key.

With correct hand position and fingering, your fingers literally walk along the keys. Practice enables them to walk with a fluid motion, with you guiding their movements.

As you play a melody, your fingers should travel gracefully up and down the keyboard. You aren't typing a letter or playing video games, so there's no need to punch or slap the keys.

Positions, Everyone!

So, you're at the keyboard, your back is supported and straight, the lights are on, and the music's waiting. Where does your right hand go? Good question. You need to get into position.

Position is a common term you hear regarding any musical instrument. Several positions exist for each musical instrument, giving the player points of reference all along the body of the instrument. The keyboard is no exception.

Using effective hand positions is vital to playing the keyboard well. From each designated position, you can easily access certain notes, groups of notes, and chords and then move to other positions.

When you sit down to play, survey the music to get a general idea of the hand positions the piece requires, and look for the hand position for the first notes.

C position

Many easy tunes start at middle C or close to it, so you often find yourself in C position at the beginning of a song. *C position* simply means placing your right-hand thumb on middle C and your other right-hand fingers on the four successive white keys, as shown in Figure 1-2. Put another way, RH 1 should be on C and RH 5 on G with the other three fingers in the middle. If the other three aren't in the middle, something very unusual is going on with your fingers.

Book III

Beginning to Play

Figure 1-2:
Getting into C position.

With your right hand in C position, which is sometimes also called *first position,* play the melody of "Frere Jacques" in Figure 1-3, playing one note at a time. It may be helpful to just imagine the moves your fingers will make as you listen to Track 23 a couple times before you attempt to play along.

Figure 1-3: "Frere Jacques" with right hand in C position.

Be sure to observe the numbers above the notes. These numbers, called *fingerings*, tell you which finger to use for each note. Most players appreciate fingerings because they indicate the best possible finger pattern for executing the notes. Of course, you may invent other custom fingerings. For now, though, try the helpful fingerings.

Try another song that uses C position. In "Ode to Joy," the melody begins on RH 3, travels up to RH 5, and then dips all the way down to RH 1. Beethoven, the composer of this piece, was a pianist, so no doubt he knew just how well this melody would play under the fingers. Figure 1-4 shows the opening melody to "Ode to Joy."

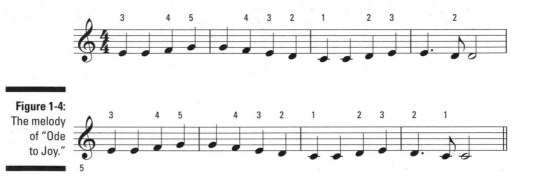

Figure 1-4: The melody of "Ode to Joy."

To play the full version of "Ode to Joy" right now, skip to the end of the chapter.

As you can probably imagine, not all melodies use only five notes. Eventually, you must come out of your safe little shell of five white keys, make a move, and extend certain fingers up or down. The following sections guide you through extensions from basic C position.

Thumbing a ride to B

From C position, your thumb can extend down to B. As you play B with your thumb, you simply leave your other fingers exactly where they are.

▶

To play "Skip to My Lou" (Track 24) in Figure 1-5, simply move your thumb one key to the left in measure 3 to play the B.

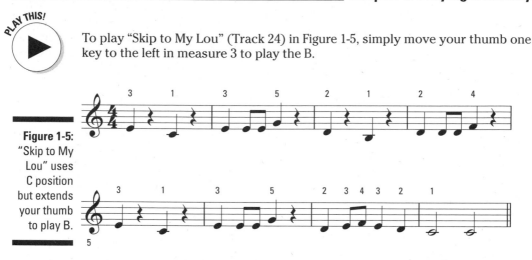

Figure 1-5: "Skip to My Lou" uses C position but extends your thumb to play B.

Good stretch, pinky!

From C position, RH 5 (right pinky) can reach up one key to the right to play A. In the campfire classic "Kumbaya," you anticipate the extension up to A by shifting fingers 2 through 5 to the right from the very start. Notice this shift in the fingerings above the notes in Figure 1-6: Instead of playing D with RH 2, you play E with RH 2, but keep your thumb on middle C. *Note:* "Kumbaya" begins with a two-beat pickup.

Figure 1-6: The melody of "Kumbaya" uses C position and stretches RH 5 to play A.

Don't take the word *stretch* too literally. I don't want you to injure yourself. It's quite alright to allow RH 1 through 4 to move toward RH 5 as you reach up to play A.

Stretching C position to the limits

In many songs that begin from C position, you shift your fingers or extend RH 5 and RH 1 to play all the melody notes. "Chiapanecas" is one such song. Using the music in Figure 1-7, try to play this Latin American song as it was meant to be heard: hot and spicy. You may want to listen to Track 25 before attempting it on your keyboard.

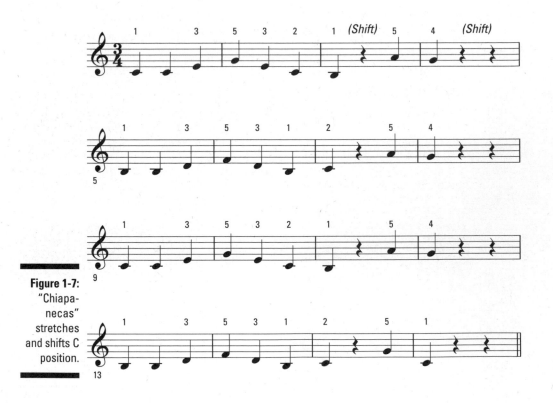

Figure 1-7: "Chiapanecas" stretches and shifts C position.

Check the time signature before you start playing. You don't want to be thinking "1, 2, 3, 4" if the song is in 3/4 time. And, by the way, "Chiapanecas" *is* in 3/4 time.

G position

To get into *G position,* move your right hand up the keyboard so that RH 1 rests on G. (This is the same G occupied by RH 5 in C position.) Figure 1-8 shows you this new position as well as the staff notes you play in it. Notice that RH 5 now rests all the way up on D.

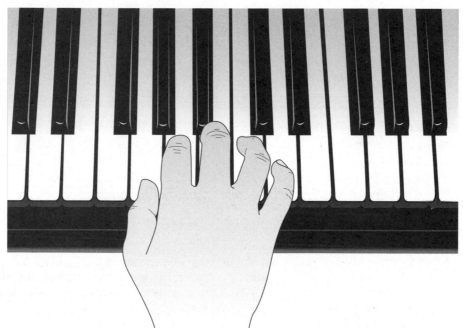

Figure 1-8:
Gee, I like G position!

The melody to "Little Bo-Peep" fits easily in G position. Give it a whirl by playing the music in Figure 1-9.

Figure 1-9: "Little Bo-Peep" is a breeze in G position.

Just like in C position, in G position you can extend RH 5 and RH 1 east and west to access E and F, respectively. Try out this extended G position by playing "This Old Man" in Figure 1-10. Watch the fingering in this song and shift your fingers where appropriate.

Figure 1-10: "This Old Man" uses G position with some stretching.

Shifting your hand position as you play

Knowing two positions, C and G, is great, but you really only get five or six notes in each position. Shifting your hand to different positions in the same song allows you to play a few more notes. To shift positions in the middle of a song, you just need a bit of planning and practice. One strategy is to simply make good use of a rest in the music to make a move while you have the chance. (The next section covers other methods for movement when the music doesn't provide rests in which to make the change.)

For example, in Figure 1-11 you play the first two measures in G position. During the rest on beat 4 of measure 2, you can move your hand down and get ready to play G in measure 3 with RH 5 — you've just shifted to C position.

Figure 1-11:
One song, two hand positions.

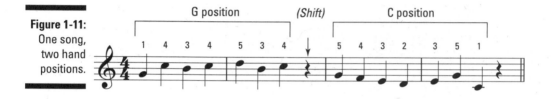

Cross Your Fingers and Hope It Works

Shifting positions can be smooth and easy when rests are involved, but when the melody doesn't stop, you must find alternative ways to move between positions. The best way is to use a little maneuver called *finger crossing*. Finger crossing is one of those techniques that can be awkward at first, but it has a whopping payoff once you get the hang of it.

Don't try to make your hand, wrist, fingers, or arm do something impossible. When you cross over or pass under, let your hand and arm follow your fingers with easy, fluid movements. Try to keep your forearm and hand more or less perpendicular to the keyboard without any excess twisting.

If you really want to make strides with your technique, feel the unbound freedom that comes with smooth finger crossings, and work on other smooth moves up and down the 88s, check out the exercises in the chapters in Book V.

Crossing over your thumb

Why cross over fingers when you can just move your hand? In C position, the thumb can sometimes extend to play B, but not always. For example, you may need to play B followed immediately by middle C. If you extend and contract your thumb back and forth between these two keys, it sounds clunky. Instead, you cross RH 2 over your thumb to play B, as shown in Figure 1-12.

Figure 1-12:
Crossing over your thumb to play more notes.

You can watch your hand on the keys when you cross over or under, but with practice you should easily feel where the keys are without looking. Whether you look or not, it's important to keep a relaxed arch in the hand and avoid twisting your hand as you cross a finger over your thumb.

The well-known "Minuet" from Bach's *Notebook for Anna Magdelena Bach* requires your RH 2 to cross over your thumb. As you can see in Figure 1-13, you shift positions briefly in measures 3 and 11, but the main focus is on the finger cross to B in measures 7 and 15.

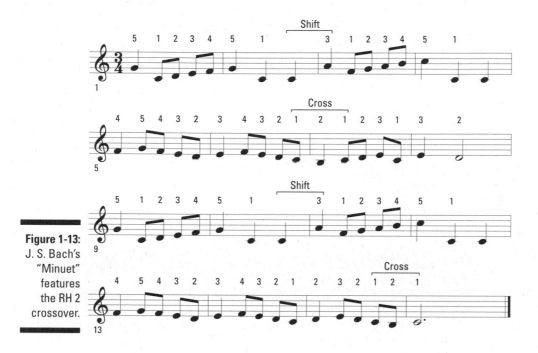

Figure 1-13:
J. S. Bach's
"Minuet"
features
the RH 2
crossover.

Passing your thumb under

You can pass your thumb under RH 2 to move to a new position. The song "Row, Row, Row Your Boat" gives you a chance to try out this little switch-o-rama between positions (see Figure 1-14). You start with your right hand in C position (middle C to G), but in measure 3 you pass your thumb under RH 3 to play F, and then you play the G at the beginning of measure 5 with RH 2. You've shifted your hand position with a pass under! You then continue with your hand in this new position. Your hand position will naturally shift downward from the high C in measure 5 as you follow the tune back to C position by measure 6, where you stay to finish the song.

Book III

**Beginning
to Play**

Figure 1-14: "Row, Row, Row Your Boat" requires the thumb to pass under.

Playing Melodies in the Right Hand

When you know the techniques for playing melodies in the right hand, you're guaranteed to want to put them to use playing more melodies. The following are four well-known melodies that let you apply the hand positions, position shifts, and finger crossings covered in this chapter:

- ✔ **"Ode to Joy" (Track 26):** You can stay in C position for almost the whole melody. In measure 12, you make a shift to reach with RH 1 and play the low G, which is the only note outside of C position.

- ✔ **"Autumn" (Track 27):** Your RH stays in G position for this melody from Vivaldi's *The Four Seasons.* Because of the many repetitions, this melody is a good one for practicing rhythm and counting.

- ✔ **"Oranges and Lemons" (Track 28):** This English folk song lets you practice shifting hand positions. Start in C position, move to G position in measure 8, and return to C position in measure 16 to repeat the opening phrase. Remember to make use of the rests to facilitate the position shifts.

- ✔ **"Simple Melody" (Track 29):** Irving Berlin's tune gives you the chance to practice passing RH 1 under RH 2. Not so simple? The song is so catchy you won't mind practicing until the movement feels natural.

Ode to Joy

Book III

**Beginning
to Play**

Autumn

Oranges and Lemons

Book III

Beginning
to Play

Simple Melody

Chapter 2

Working with Scales

In This Chapter

▶ Getting to know scale basics

▶ Building and listening to major and minor scales

▶ Playing melodies featuring scales

▶ Access the audio tracks at www.dummies.com/go/pianokeyboardaio/

*H*ave you ever heard the following from your musician friends?

✔ "Scales are boring!"

✔ "Scales are difficult!"

✔ "I never play scales!"

✔ "The scales in my bathroom read ten pounds more than I actually weigh!"

These statements are all lies, including the last one. For various selfish reasons, your friends don't want you to know the truth: Scales are easy, scales can be fun, every musician plays scales, and your friends actually put on a few pounds over Spring Break.

You can use scales to do some great things on the piano — like play entire songs. Okay, not all scales are songs. But it's true that all songs are created *from* scales, be it an entire scale or just a few notes from the scale. Remember the "Do-Re-Mi" song from *The Sound of Music?* The whole darn song is *about* scales, and those kids had fun.

This chapter shows you that it's well worth it to give scales a chance. Besides using scales to understand the notes in a song's melody, you can use scales to beef up your finger power on the piano. Plus, the more scales you know, the easier it becomes to play the piano.

You've probably heard this a thousand times before now, but it's true: Practice makes perfect. This chapter introduces you to several different types of scales. Pick the ones you like and play through them five to ten times a day. This practice warms up your fingers and builds finger dexterity. Think of shooting baskets every day before the big basketball game. You wouldn't go out on the court without a little practice, would you?

Building a Scale, Step-by-Step

Put simply, a musical *scale* is a series of notes in a specific, consecutive order. Major and minor scales are the two most common types, and they have the following attributes:

- ✔ They're eight notes long.
- ✔ The top and bottom notes are an octave apart, so they have the same name.
- ✔ The series follows a stepwise pattern up and down, and the name of each note in the scale follows the alphabet up and down.

Each scale gets its own wacky-sounding name, like *C major*. A scale derives its name from the following two things:

- ✔ The scale's bottom note, or the *tonic*. For example, a C major scale starts on C.
- ✔ The *stepwise pattern* used to create the scale. Music has two kinds of steps — *half steps* and *whole steps* — which are the building blocks of scales.

The "major" part of C major means the third note of the scale is a major third above the tonic. (You can find more on intervals in Book II Chapter 4.)

To review for a second, look at your keyboard or Figure 2-1. As you know by now, some white keys have a black key in between and some don't. On a piano keyboard

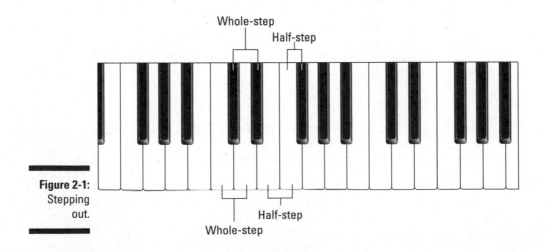

Figure 2-1:
Stepping
out.

✔ Two keys side by side (whether black or white) are one half step apart.

✔ Two keys separated by one other key (black or white) are a whole step apart.

✔ Two half steps equal one whole step.

Book II Chapter 4 explains how the suffixes *sharp* and *flat* are used to name the black keys. When you measure half steps up or down, you help define the black keys as sharps and flats. For example, find any D on your keyboard. Move one half step higher and play the black key to the right, D sharp. Now play one half step lower than D, or D flat.

Knowing these basic facts about scales, you can build any scale starting on any root note simply by applying the correct scale pattern (or combination of whole and half steps).

Introducing Major Scales

The two scales you most frequently use — and the most famous scales in Western music — are the *major* and the *minor* scales. You can make a major and a minor scale starting with any note on the piano. The difference between these two scales is the pattern of whole and half steps that you use to build them.

Major scales have a reputation for sounding happy, and minor scales get the sad rap, but it's really how they're used that counts.

Book III

Beginning to Play

Understanding major scales

Every major scale is built the same way. Don't let a scale salesman try to sell you a new and improved major scale — there's no such thing. (Actually, you should turn and run from anyone pretending to be a scale salesman.)

The ascending step pattern used by all major scales on the planet is

Whole-Whole-Half-Whole-Whole-Whole-Half (or WWHWWWH)

For example, you can form a C major scale by starting on C and applying this pattern. Play any C, and then play the major scale pattern of whole steps and half steps all the way to the next C. Figure 2-2 shows you the way. Starting with C, the layout of the white keys follows the scale pattern exactly, so you play the entire C major scale on white keys only.

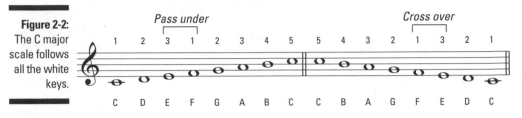

Figure 2-2:
The C major
scale follows
all the white
keys.

Pass your thumb under and cross over your thumb in the appropriate spots in order to successfully play up and down the scale. See Book III Chapter 1 for more on this finger-crossing business.

When playing most scales up and down, it's important to realize that the scale pattern is exactly reversed on the way down. All you have to do is remember which keys you played going up and then play the same ones in reverse order going down.

Why sharps and flats are involved

And now for something slightly different: Start on G and apply the major scale pattern. When you get to the sixth step, notice that a whole step up from E requires playing a black key, F sharp. Figure 2-3 shows you the G major scale in all its glory.

Figure 2-3:
The G
major scale
employs
one sharp:
F sharp.

The tonic note and scale pattern determine which notes will be sharps and which will be flats. G major uses one sharp. How about a major scale that uses one flat? Start on F and apply the pattern, as shown in Figure 2-4, and you've built yourself the F major scale, which uses B flat. (Note the new fingering for this scale pattern.)

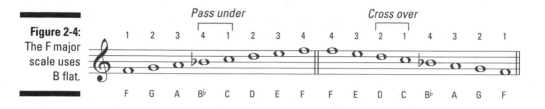

Figure 2-4:
The F major
scale uses
B flat.

How do you know it's B flat and not A sharp (its enharmonic)? Excellent question. The easy answer is that in a scale, every letter name has its turn. Because the third note, or *scale degree,* of the F major scale is A, the fourth note takes the next letter's name — B flat (one half step higher than A).

Take your newfound major scale knowledge and see how it applies to a portion of a song. "Joy to the World" (see Figure 2-5) opens with a complete descending C major scale and continues with an ascending pattern from the fifth degree of the scale up to the eighth to end the phrase.

Figure 2-5:
A joyful
melody
made from a
major scale.

Of course, the composer of a song isn't obligated to use every note from a scale in the melody. The scale is simply a menu to choose from. For example, "The Farmer in the Dell" (see Figure 2-6) is based on the F major scale, but it doesn't actually use the note B flat.

Figure 2-6:
A frugal
melody
needs only
five notes
of the major
scale.

Book III

**Beginning
to Play**

Major scale degrees

Each of the eight notes in a major scale is assigned a *scale degree* according to the order it appears in the scale:

- **1st note:** Tonic
- **2nd note:** Supertonic
- **3rd note:** Mediant
- **4th note:** Subdominant
- **5th note:** Dominant
- **6th note:** Submediant
- **7th note:** Leading tone (or leading note)
- **8th note:** Tonic

The 1st and 8th notes, the *tonics,* determine the name of the scale. (Scales that share the same starting notes are called *parallel scales.* For example, C major and C minor are parallel scales, because they both start on the same note: C.) Relative to the tonic note, the rest of the notes in the scale are usually attached to the numbers 2 through 7 (because 1 and 8 are already taken by the tonic). Each of these numbers represents a scale *degree,* and their pattern of whole steps and half steps determines the key of the scale.

The 1st and the 8th notes have the same name here because they're the exact same note — at the 8th note, the scale repeats itself. You won't hear a musician talk about the 8th degree of a scale — instead, she'll refer to the 1st note as the tonic.

So, for example, if you're playing a piece of music in the key of C major, which sequentially has the notes C, D, E, F, G, A, B, and C in it, and someone asks you to play the 4th and 2nd notes in the scale, you play an F and a D. And you do the same thing if that person asks you to play the subdominant and the supertonic.

Mastering scales is all about recognizing patterns. If you look at a piano keyboard, can you see where the 1, 2, 3, 4, 5, 6, 7, and 8 of each scale go? For the major scales, remember, the pattern is WWHWWWH. If you're given a scale and asked to play the sequence 5-3-2-1-6-4-5-8, do you know what notes you would play? Eventually, you want to be able to answer yes to these questions for all 12 major scales. Here's how:

- Picture each scale in your head and where it's located on the keyboard.
- Know the letter name and number of each note in each scale.
- Be able to play sequences of notes when given the key and number.

Only when you can do all three things for the 12 major scales can you stop practicing your scales.

Every single major scale you work with follows the WWHWWWH pattern, using different combinations of black and white keys on the piano, depending on the scale. To play each major scale on the piano, begin with the piano key that is the name of the scale. For the A major scale, for example, you begin with the A. Then play the major scale pattern: WWHWWWH. The scale ends on the same note it began with, only an octave higher.

To see the major scale for every key, refer to Chapter 8, which illustrates key signatures by showing the scale on the staff for each key. To hear all the major scales, listen to the tracks listed in the upcoming section "Listening to the major scales."

Trying a major scale exercise

Practice playing up and down the C major scale with the exercise in Figure 2-7. You can use it to reinforce the scale pattern mentally, perfect your fingering, and improve your finger crossing. Start out at a slower tempo and increase the speed as you become familiar with the notes and the moves.

Book III

Beginning to Play

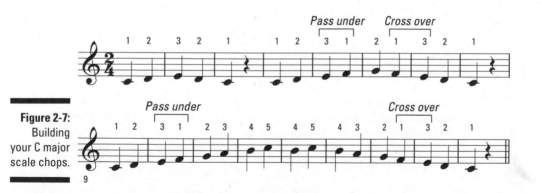

Figure 2-7: Building your C major scale chops.

Introducing Minor Scales

You need to understand something right away: Minor scales are no less important or smaller in size than major scales. They just have an unfortunate name. Minor scales come in a few varieties, each of which is covered in this section.

Like major scales, minor scales have eight notes, with the top and bottom (tonic) notes having the same name. But minor scales have their own, unique scale patterns: the natural minor, harmonic minor, and melodic minor patterns.

Each of the eight notes in a minor scale has a name:

- ✔ **1st note:** Tonic
- ✔ **2nd note:** Supertonic
- ✔ **3rd note:** Mediant
- ✔ **4th note:** Subdominant
- ✔ **5th note:** Dominant
- ✔ **6th note:** Submediant
- ✔ **7th note:** Subtonic
- ✔ **8th note:** Tonic

In the harmonic and melodic minor scales, the 7th degree is called the *leading tone*.

Natural minor scales

The *natural minor* scale uses the following ascending stepwise pattern:

Whole-Half-Whole-Whole-Half-Whole-Whole (or WHWWHWW)

Sure, it may look *similar* to the major scale pattern, but make no mistake, this slight rearrangement of half and whole steps makes all the difference in the world. The best way to understand the difference is to play and listen to a major and a minor scale side by side. Figure 2-8 shows the C major scale, followed immediately by the C minor scale.

Figure 2-8:
Major and
minor C
scales.

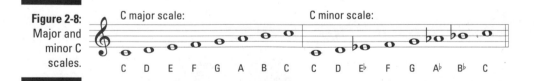

Hear the difference? Try something else: Play the melody in Figure 2-9, where the notes of a C minor scale are plugged into the same rhythms as the original "Joy to the World." Notice the difference in the sound.

Figure 2-9:
"Joy to the
World" in C
minor.

You can play a minor scale on only the white keys, too — just start with A instead of C. Apply the same scale pattern to the tonic note A, and you get the A natural minor scale. (That's because A is the *relative minor* of C. Book III Chapter 5 goes into more detail about that.) But apply the same pattern to other tonic notes and you encounter some minor scales with sharps (like E minor) and some with flats (like D minor), as you can see in Figure 2-10.

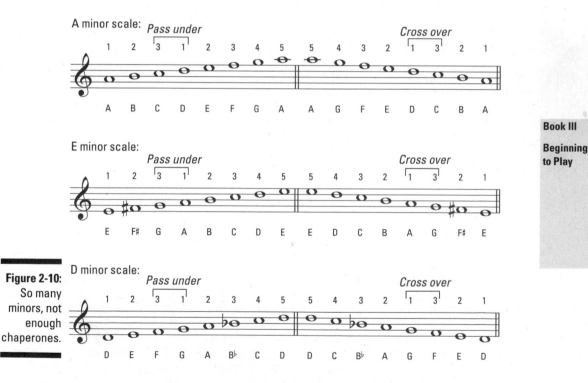

Figure 2-10:
So many
minors, not
enough
chaperones.

Book III

**Beginning
to Play**

The notes from minor scales make great, memorable melodies, too. Skip to the later section "Playing Songs Made of Scales" and try "House of the Rising Sun."

Harmonic minor scales

The *harmonic minor* scale differs from the natural minor scale (refer to the preceding section) by only one half step, but in making that slight change, you achieve a scale with a whole new sound. For example, to play the A harmonic minor scale, follow these steps:

1. **Start out playing the A natural minor scale.**

2. **When you get to the seventh note, G, raise it one half step to G sharp.**

   This change makes the distance from the sixth to the seventh scale degree one and a half steps and gives the harmonic minor scale its unique sound.

The complete pattern for an ascending harmonic minor scale is this:

Whole-Half-Whole-Whole-Half-1½-Half (WHWWH1½-H)

Play and compare the natural minor scale in Figure 2-11 with the harmonic minor scale next to it. Sounds rather exotic, doesn't it? You'll encounter this scale in lots of classical piano music.

Figure 2-11:
The A natural minor and A harmonic minor scales.

Melodic minor scales

Another variation on the minor scale is the *melodic minor* scale, which is notable (forgive the pun) because it has a different pattern depending on whether you're going up the scale or coming down. That's right — a chameleon-like scale that ascends one way and descends another. This flexibility is useful when you want the scale to sound, you guessed it, melodic. Try playing the A melodic minor scale in Figure 2-12, and you'll hear that the scale sounds pleasingly melodic going both up and down.

A melodic minor scale:

Figure 2-12: The A melodic minor scale.

Notice that the sixth and seventh degrees of the scale are raised a half step when ascending and are lowered a half step when descending. You probably recognized that the descending scale is identical to the natural minor scale, so only the ascending pattern is really new:

Whole-Half-Whole-Whole-Whole-Whole-Half (or WHWWWWH)

Composers sometimes combine scales for a song's melody just to spice things up a bit. In the section "Playing Songs Made of Scales" later in the chapter, play "Greensleeves" to hear a good example.

Trying minor scale exercises

Get some practice with the C natural, harmonic, and melodic minor scales by playing the following exercises (Figures 2-13a, 2-13b, and 2-13c). You can use these as a warm-up along with the C major scale exercise in the previous section.

Using scales any which way you like

Major and minor scales are definitely the most popular scales, but they aren't the only ones. Come on, admit it — you've experimented a little with these scale patterns. Curiosity begs you to insert a half step in place of a whole step sometimes to hear what happens.

Well, what happens is that you begin to form other scales, venturing into territory neither major nor minor. Some sound great, some sound not so great, and some sound sort of exotic.

Creating your own scales is not only acceptable, it's recommended. Fresh new scales inevitably give birth to fresh new melodies and harmonies.

People have experimented with scale patterns since the dawn of music, so go ahead and make up your own scales. Improvise a melody or a bass line using just a few notes of a scale. Write them down on staff paper, tape them to your walls, and decorate your life with scales!

Figure 2-13: Exercising the three C-minor scales: C natural (a), C harmonic (b), and C melodic minor (c).

Checking Out Blues Scales

Another very cool scale is the *blues scale*. You can hear it in rock, country, jazz, and of course . . . the blues.

This scale is a real rebel, practically throwing the rules of scale building out the window. Of course, there aren't really any hard-and-fast rules for scale building, but this scale is rebellious anyway. Here's how:

- ✔ It begins with one and a half steps.
- ✔ It has only seven notes.
- ✔ It has two half steps in a row.

Here's the step pattern for this seditious little scale:

1½-Whole-Half-Half-1½-Whole (1½WHH1½W)

To try it out, play the scale in Figure 2-14.

Figure 2-14:
Getting the blues.

Where else have you seen a scale with that much mojo? After you know the blues scale, playing it is as addictive as eating peanuts. You can use the notes in the blues scale, or *blue notes,* for all kinds of little riffs and melodies, like the one in Figure 2-15.

Book III

Beginning to Play

Figure 2-15:
Using the blues scale for a cool melody.

Playing Songs Made of Scales

In the age-old battle between theory and practice, there's no doubt that practice is more fun. Your efforts to grasp the theory behind scales throughout this chapter will be rewarded by putting them to good use playing the songs in this section.

Here are a few tips on the tunes:

- **"Danny Boy" (Track 30):** The classic "Danny Boy" uses all the notes from the F major scale, even good old B flat.

- **"House of the Rising Sun" (Track 31):** "House of the Rising Sun" is based on the E natural minor scale.

- **"Greensleeves" (Track 32):** "Greensleeves" uses the A natural minor scale (measures 1–5), the A melodic minor scale (measures 13–16), and the G major scale (measures 17–20). It's just a folk song, but they were some smart folk who wrote it!

Danny Boy

House of the Rising Sun

There is a house in New Or - leans they call the Ris - ing Sun _____ It's been the ru - in of man - y a poor girl, and Lord, I know____ I'm one. _____

Greensleeves

Chapter 3

Adding the Left Hand

In This Chapter

▶ Settling your left hand into position

▶ Playing melodies and scales with the left hand

▶ Exploring left-hand accompaniment patterns

▶ Playing songs hands-together

▶ Access the audio tracks at www.dummies.com/go/pianokeyboardaio/

*W*ant to know an industry secret? Many a keyboardist or pianist who plays with a band never even uses the left hand. Oh sure, you think the left hand is playing because it's moving up and down the left side of the keyboard and you're hearing lots of bass lines and chords. But au contraire, mon frére. The bass player fills in the bass notes; the guitarist covers the chords. The not-so-good keyboard player just fakes it.

Playing the piano with your left hand, or both hands together, is considerably more difficult than just right-hand playing. But you have no need to fake your way through a career. You can show those phonies how a real player does it! This chapter tells you how to get both hands jamming together.

This chapter numbers your fingers 1 through 5. Your right and left hands are abbreviated as "RH" and "LH."

Exploring the Keyboard's West Side

If you consider middle C the middle of the keyboard, you can think of the keys to the right of middle C as the East Side and the keys to the left of middle C as the West Side. It's time to head west.

To explore the lower keys, first reacquaint yourself with the bass clef. Book II Chapter 4 has some easy ways to remember the lines and spaces on this oft-neglected staff, but the best way to figure out this staff is to dig in and start playing. You'll soon recognize each line and space by sight, without even thinking about it.

Moving into position

Book III Chapter 1 shows you two positions for the right hand: the C and G positions. These positions are the same for the left hand except that C position has LH 5 (pinky) on the C below middle C, the second space up on the bass clef staff. In G position, LH 5 moves *down* to G, the bottom line of the staff. Figure 3-1 shows you the proper left-hand C position placement.

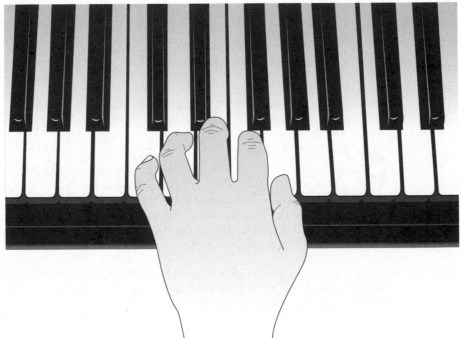

Figure 3-1:
Assume
C position
with the left
hand.

Getting used to the new neighborhood

You have several options for playing with your left hand: You can play scales, melodies, simple one-note harmonies, chords, or just plain cool-sounding accompaniment patterns. Single-note harmonies and chords are covered in Book III Chapters 4 and 6, respectively.

For a quick (and stimulating) drill, Figure 3-2 helps limber up the left-hand fingers in C position. Sing or say out loud the name of each note as you play it. Seeing, playing, saying, and hearing all at once go a long way toward helping you remember the notes on the staff.

Change your life by switching hands

If you aren't left-handed by nature, you can start training it to be more than useless. Start using your underappreciated left hand to perform everyday tasks you normally perform with your right hand, such as the following:

✔ Opening doors

✔ Flipping channels on the TV remote

✔ Steering your automobile (just be careful)

✔ Eating

✔ Brushing your teeth

✔ Opening tightly-sealed pickle jars (good luck)

By *consciously* switching hands for a couple of weeks, you *subconsciously* make your left hand stronger, more versatile, and more independent.

Figure 3-2: Reading and playing notes in the bass clef, starting from LH C position.

Book III

Beginning to Play

Figure 3-3 features a similar workout, but in G position. Again, remember to sing each note out loud. Never mind what those around you think of your ranting and raving — they're just jealous that you can play the piano.

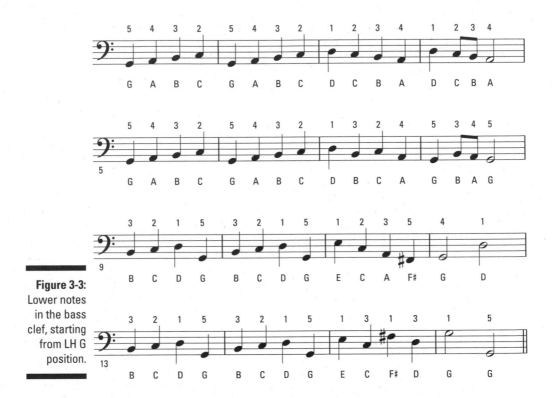

Figure 3-3:
Lower notes
in the bass
clef, starting
from LH G
position.

If you're ready to play songs with both hands, skip ahead to the section "Playing Songs with Both Hands" at the end of the chapter.

Left-Hand Melodies

Sometimes it's nice to play a melody with your left hand. You may tire of playing with your right hand, want to hear the melody lower, want to add a little variety to the song — or have an itch on the right side of your head.

Whatever the reason, playing melodies with the left hand helps familiarize you with the bass clef notes while strengthening your left-hand coordination.

Left-hand melodies are lots of fun, but remember to observe the correct fingerings as you play these classics, "Swing Low, Sweet Chariot" (Track 33, see Figure 3-4) and "Little Brown Jug" (Track 34, see Figure 3-5).

Figure 3-4:
Left-hand
melody:
"Swing
Low, Sweet
Chariot."

Figure 3-5:
Another
left-hand
melody:
"Little
Brown Jug."

South-Paw Scales

Scales may not be the most exciting things to play, but by playing left-hand scales you unwittingly master the following music essentials:

- ✔ Reading the bass clef
- ✔ Playing with the correct fingering
- ✔ Using nifty patterns and harmonies
- ✔ Realizing how much you miss playing with the right hand

Start with some major and minor scales by reading and playing the following scales left-handed. (Book III Chapter 2 tells you all about major and minor scales.) As with right-handed playing, remember to use the correct fingerings as indicated by the numbers above each note. How and when you cross your fingers is very important for obtaining a smooth sound and comfortable left-hand technique.

C, G, and F major

Figure 3-6 shows three major scales for the left hand. You can use the same fingering, both up and down the scale, for all of these. Applying the major scale pattern, you play a scale with no sharps or flats (C major scale), one sharp (G major scale), and one flat (F major scale).

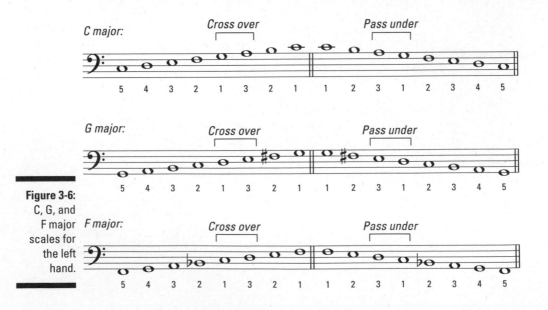

Figure 3-6: C, G, and F major scales for the left hand.

A, E, and D natural minor

You use the same fingering pattern in the three natural minor scales in Figure 3-7 as you do in the three major scales in Figure 3-6.

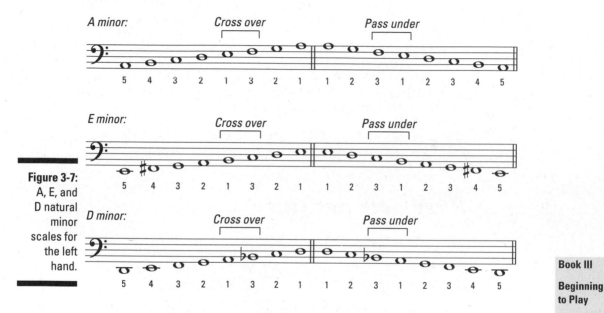

Figure 3-7: A, E, and D natural minor scales for the left hand.

A harmonic and melodic minor

The scales in Figure 3-8 offer a good opportunity to practice your crossovers and pass-unders in the left hand. The scale patterns change at the same point you shift your hand position. Listen for smooth transitions and an even touch throughout each scale.

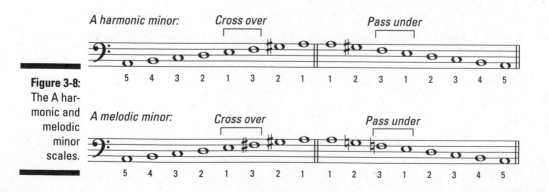

Figure 3-8: The A harmonic and melodic minor scales.

Book III

Beginning to Play

Accompaniment Patterns

Scales and melodies are fine material for the left hand, but they aren't Lefty's main gig. Rather, your left hand begs to be playing *accompaniment patterns* while your right hand noodles around with a melody or some chords. One of the most user-friendly left-hand patterns is the *arpeggio.*

Oh, no! More Italian? Yes, in addition to *pizza, rigatoni,* and *ciao,* the other Italian word that should be part of your everyday vocabulary is *arpeggio.* The word translates to "harp-like," which means absolutely nothing to piano players. However, after many years of bad translations, musicians have come to understand it to mean "a broken chord."

Well, nothing's really broken about an arpeggio — it works great. You simply play the notes of a chord one at a time, rather than all at once.

Three-note patterns

Three-note patterns are probably the easiest and most versatile left-hand accompaniment to play, and they fit the hand really nicely, too. For example, place your left hand on the keys in C position with LH 5 on C, LH 2 on G above that, and LH 1 on middle C. Fits like a glove, right?

The three notes you use for this pattern are the root, fifth, and top (octave) notes of the appropriate scale. (See Book III Chapter 2 for more on roots and scales.) Using the C major scale, for example, the notes are C, G, and C. Now comes the versatile part: The three-note pattern is the exact same in the C *minor* scale. So, you can apply the three-note pattern to major *or* minor harmonies by playing the root, fifth, and top notes of the scale, as shown in Figure 3-9.

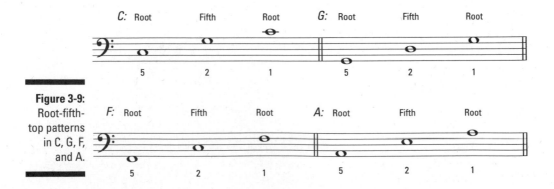

Figure 3-9: Root-fifth-top patterns in C, G, F, and A.

Playing the pattern in quarter notes

The easiest way to start playing this three-note pattern is with a quarter-note rhythm. In 4/4 meter, you play in an "up and back" motion — root, fifth, top, fifth — so that every measure begins with the root note of each arpeggio. In 3/4 meter, you play upwards — root, fifth, top — and then start again with the root for the next measure.

Figure 3-10 demonstrates these three-note patterns with a simple quarter-note rhythm in both meters. The first eight measures show how the pattern works in 4/4, and the next eight do it in 3/4. The letter names above the staff are chord symbols, which tell you the scale the pattern is derived from.

Figure 3-10:
Three-note
arpeggios in
quarter-note
patterns.

Cranking up the pattern in eighth notes

Play the three-note pattern using eighth notes for a more energetic, faster arpeggio. You play a full set of root-fifth-top-fifth for every two beats, so that beats 1 and 3 of every measure start again on the root note of the arpeggio. Gently rock your left hand back and forth over the keys until you feel this pattern is second nature to you. These eighth notes in 3/4 meter are slightly different: You can play all six eighth notes in a pattern or modify the pattern to give you time to move to other positions, as shown in Figure 3-11.

Figure 3-11:
Three-note
arpeggios in
eighth-note
patterns.

Four-note patterns

Adding another note to the three-note pattern gives you enough notes to make a major or minor chord. For this arpeggio, you add the third note of the scale. The four-note *major* arpeggio uses the root, third, fifth, and top notes of the scale. To form a four-note *minor* arpeggio, you simply lower the third note a half-step. For example, the notes of a C major arpeggio are C, E, G, and C. To make a C minor arpeggio, simply lower the third, E, to E flat, just like you do in the C minor scale (see Figure 3-12).

Figure 3-12:
Four-note
arpeggios.

Playing the pattern in quarter notes

As with the three-note arpeggios, different meters allow you some rhythmic options. Using quarter notes in 4/4 meter, you play up — root, third, fifth, top — once in each measure. Each subsequent measure begins again with the root note. For 3/4 meter, you play up in one measure — root, third, fifth — and hit the top note before coming down in the next measure — top, fifth, third.

Take a gander at the quarter-note patterns in Figure 3-13. Call out the name of each note as you play; hearing yourself helps you recognize the notes.

Book III

Beginning to Play

Figure 3-13: Up and down the four-note arpeggios.

Try the alternate fingerings in Figure 3-13, shown in parenthesis below the suggested fingerings. Every hand is different, and you may find one of these is more comfortable than the other.

Cranking up the pattern in eighth notes

With an eighth-note rhythm, you can have fun exploring different patterns for the four arpeggio notes. Just keep the correct four notes of each scale in mind — root, third, fifth, and top — and play two of them for every beat in the measure. Figure 3-14 gives you a few examples of different patterns.

Arpeggio, your friend in need

So, there you sit. It's late. The pianist finishes "My Funny Valentine" and heads off for an overdue coffee break. You decide to impress your friends and quickly steal up to the bench. The room is waiting. You open the songbook atop the piano and — egad! — all you see is a treble staff and chord symbols.

What you see is probably a *fake book*. This is a real songbook, but it only contains the melody and chord symbols, allowing a working pianist

to "fill in" the left hand as he or she feels best suits the situation. Of course, you *aren't* a working pianist, and *any* left hand would be suitable for this late-night situation.

First, take a deep breath. Next, open your bag of tricks and pull out some left-hand arpeggios. Use the chord symbols — the little alphabet letters above the staff — to locate the name of the lowest note (or root note) of the arpeggio and play away. Pretty soon you'll have new friends.

Figure 3-14: Four-note arpeggio patterns in eighths.

Adding the Left Hand to the Right Hand

No matter how much you enjoy playing melodies with the right and left hands separately, the time comes when you have to get them together.

You have several things to keep in mind when you attempt to play songs hands-together:

- ✔ When playing music from the grand staff, read the notes vertically (bottom to top) before moving on horizontally (left to right).

- ✔ Play the song a couple of times with the right hand by itself. Then play the song a few times with the left hand only. When you're confident with the notes for each hand, you can try playing the song hands-together.

- ✔ Play slowly at first and speed up the tempo as you become more comfortable with the song.

- ✔ Be patient and calm.

> ✔ Ask listeners to leave for a while and allow you a chance to practice. Invite them in for the concert after you feel good about your playing.

Sharing the melody in both hands

Start reading from the grand staff by passing a melody between your hands. In Figure 3-15 (Track 35) the melody to "When Johnny Comes Marching Home" starts in the left hand, and the right hand takes over as it climbs into a higher range. Go over the note names once or twice before you play in order to get comfortable recognizing all the notes and switching between the bass and treble clefs. Then you can make an easier transition to the keyboard.

Book III

Beginning to Play

Figure 3-15: RH and LH share a melody.

Melody plus one note

Mozart knew how to have a little fun with music, and it shows in his piece called "A Musical Joke" (Track 36). He takes a simple melody and tries it in a major scale, then in a minor one, and finally settles on the major version. In Figure 3-16, the left hand plays a single-note accompaniment to the melody, making it a good introduction to playing "hands-together," as the saying goes.

Figure 3-16:
A simple melody and accompaniment from Mozart.

Melody plus three-note accompaniment pattern

"On Top of Old Smoky" (Track 37, Figure 3-17) gets you working a melody with the right hand and some arpeggios with the left. After you get the hang of it, your left hand starts rocking back and forth effortlessly on the arpeggiated patterns.

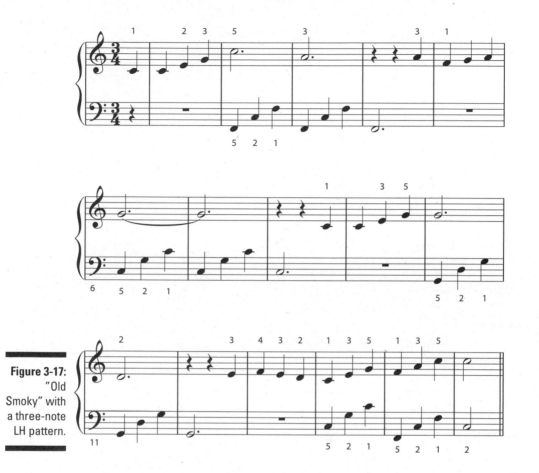

Figure 3-17: "Old Smoky" with a three-note LH pattern.

 If the bass clef gets too intimidating to read, hold your left hand in position for an arpeggio and move LH 5 to each new root note. From each root note you can easily find the appropriate arpeggio notes and go to town . . . or to the top of Old Smoky.

Melody in unison octaves

In the classic "Yankee Doodle" (see Figure 3-18), you can try another way of reading from both clefs at once with a double-handed melody. Although the melodies look completely different on the different staves, they're actually the same — you play the same named keys with both hands.

Book III

Beginning to Play

Figure 3-18: Double the melody.

Most people have faster note recognition reading the treble clef than reading the bass clef at this stage. For a challenge, look at the note in the bass clef *before* you look at the corresponding note in the treble clef to solidify your bass clef reading skills.

Playing Songs with Both Hands

You're ready for some two-handed music-making, and you're looking for some tunes that put it all together. Well, you've come to the right place — the songs in this section utilize both hands. Here are a few things you need to know in order to play them:

- ✔ **"The Sidewalks of New York" (Track 38):** For this song, you need to be able to read bass clef, play a (mostly) one-note accompaniment in the left hand, read sharps, and play in 3/4 time. Oh, and you should enjoy the swaying rhythm, too.

- ✔ **"Stars and Stripes Forever" (Track 39):** You need to know about pickup measures, playing in 2/4 time, and playing a left-hand accompaniment pattern with a melody.

Book III

Beginning to Play

The Sidewalks of New York

Book III

Beginning to Play

Stars and Stripes Forever

Bright March

Chapter 4

Examining Form: Melody, Harmony, and Song Form

In This Chapter

▶ Reviewing melody and harmony

▶ Hearing and playing intervals and harmonizing a melody

▶ Understanding musical phrases and periods

▶ Picking out and labeling the parts of a song

▶ Access the audio tracks at www.dummies.com/go/pianokeyboardaio/

*W*hen you listen to music, the melody is usually the first thing to grab your ear. You're less aware of the other notes being played along with the melody to form the harmony of the music.

Without harmony, you would hear one single note at a time. On your piano, you can play more than one note at a time, giving it the coveted distinction of being an instrument capable of *harmonizing*. Sure, other instruments in a band or orchestra can play collectively to form harmony, but you can harmonize all by yourself with a piano.

Playing many notes simultaneously is the essence of harmony. The notes you choose and how you arrange them around the melody determines the kind of harmony you produce, whether you use many notes or just one note with each hand. Go ahead and try it: Play two, three, four, even ten notes at once. Ah, sweet harmony . . . or a cluttered mess, depending on what notes you play.

Musical *form* means the structural blueprint used to create a specific type of music. For example, a sonata follows a specific song structure. Although style elements like the basic melody, theme, and key signature would be entirely up to you, the way the sonata as a whole fits together — the beginning, middle, and ending — is set right from the beginning by the constraints of the sonata form itself.

A lot of crossover exists between the definitions of form and genre, but they are two different concepts. *Genre* is more about how music sounds, regardless of its structure; examples are jazz, pop, country, and classical (although there are also certain forms unique to classical music).

The problem with identifying forms in modern music is that new music is still evolving. Students of music form in the 21st century may soon be studying anti-4/4 math-rock pioneers like Steve Albini alongside the composers Philip Glass and Beethoven.

Shaping the Melody

Most often, the melody is the part of the song you can't get out of your head. The *melody* is the lead line of a song — the part that the harmony is built around, and the part that gives as much glimpse into the emotion of a piece as the rhythm does. (Refer to the later section on harmony for more information.)

Much of melody's expressive power comes from the upward or downward flow of pitch. The pitch of a song goes up, and it can make the song sound like it's getting either more tense or more lively; the pitch of a song goes down, and it can give that part of the song an increased melancholic or dark feel. The shape of the pitch's travels is called its *contour*.

Here are the four common *melodic contours:*

- Arch
- Wave
- Inverted arch
- Pivotal

Contour simply means that the melody is shaped a certain way; the shape of a melody is especially easy to pick out when you have the sheet music right in front of you. The possibilities for building melodic phrases (that is, starting at the I chord, going up to the IV or V chord, and ending at the I chord; see Book III Chapter 6 for more information about chord progressions) with just four basic contours are virtually infinite.

Figure 4-1 shows a stretch of music that has an *arch contour*. Note how the melody line in the treble clef first goes up in pitch from a low point to a high point and how it then goes back down again, creating the arch. When music goes up in pitch gradually like this, it results in an increase in tension in that section of the composition. The lower the pitch gets in such a gradual arch, the more the level of tension decreases.

Figure 4-1: Arch contour.

Figure 4-2 shows music with a *wave contour*. Note how the melody line goes up, and down, and up again, and down again — just like a series of waves.

Figure 4-2: Wave contour.

Figure 4-3 shows music with an *inverted arch contour*. You may have noticed that the music in Figure 4-3 looks a lot like that in Figure 4-1. The only difference is that the melody line in Figure 4-3 goes down in pitch and then up to the end of the phrase. Therefore, the phrase starts out sounding relaxed and calm but contains an increase in tension as the arch rises toward the end of the phrase.

Figure 4-3: Inverted arch contour.

Figure 4-4 shows an example of music with a *pivotal contour*. A pivotal melody line essentially pivots around the central note of the piece — in the case of the music in Figure 4-4, the E. A pivotal contour is a lot like a wave contour, except that the movement above and below the central note is minimal and continuously returns to that central note. Traditional folk music uses this melodic pattern a lot.

Book III

Beginning to Play

Figure 4-4:
Pivotal
contour.

Any melody line in a piece of music generally falls into one of the preceding categories of contour. Try randomly picking up a piece of sheet music and tracing out the melody pattern yourself to see what we mean.

REMEMBER

The *range* of a melody is determined by the interval between the highest and lowest pitches of the song. The rise and fall of tension is often proportional to its range. Melodies with a narrow pitch range tend to have only a slight amount of musical tension in them, whereas melodies with a wide range of pitches are more likely to have a greater level of tension. As the range of pitches in a song is widened, the potential for greater tension increases.

Measuring Melodic Intervals

The distance between any two musical notes is called an *interval*. You need to understand the concept of intervals and the notes that make up each interval so that you can identify the right notes for harmonies. But you also use intervals to identify and build notes in a melody. As you play or sing the notes of a melody, the melody can do one of three things: It can stay on the same note, it can go up, or it can go down. When it goes up or down, the question of *how much* leads to the subject of *melodic intervals*.

You measure an interval by the number of half steps and whole steps in between the two notes. But because this method involves lots of counting, memorization, and complicated arithmetic, there is an easier solution: Use the major scale as a measuring tape.

Each major scale contains seven different notes plus the octave — that's eight notes that you can use to name intervals. For example, Figure 4-5 shows the ever-popular C major scale, with the notes numbered from 1 to 8.

Figure 4-5:
Numbering
the notes of
the C major
scale.

Pick two notes and count the scale notes (not the piano keys) in between to find the name of the interval. For example, if you play the first note of the C major scale (C) followed by the fifth note (G), you just played a *fifth* interval. If you count the scale notes in between C and G, you get five — C, D, E, F, G. From C to E (the *third* note in the scale) is a *third* interval, and so on. Not much originality in these names, but is this easy or what?

You don't have to start with the first note of the scale to make an interval of a fifth. This concept of intervals is all about distance. You can build a fifth on the note G by climbing up five scale notes to D. It's easy to check yourself by counting the scale notes in between.

Figure 4-6 shows you the C major scale and its intervals.

Figure 4-6:
A family of intervals on the C major scale.

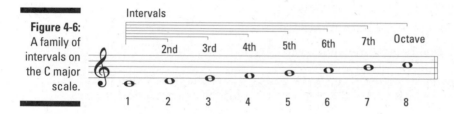

The C scale is the example because it's so easy, with no sharps or flats. However, this method of number-naming the intervals works for every single major scale. Simply write out the scale and number the notes from 1 to 8 — it works the same every time.

Interval shorthand

Like scales, intervals come in different varieties: *major, minor, perfect, diminished,* and *augmented.* Knowing these classifications helps you identify and build harmonies for the music you play. For example, if you want to build a minor chord to harmonize with a melody, you must use a minor interval. (Book III Chapter 6 tells you all about building chords.)

Here's your guide to making different types of intervals:

✔ **Major interval:** Measure a major second, third, sixth, or seventh by matching the second, third, sixth, or seventh notes of the major scale and counting the half steps from the root note.

✔ **Minor interval:** You can make a second, third, sixth, or seventh interval minor by lowering its major counterpart a half step.

Book III

Beginning to Play

- ✔ **Perfect interval:** This label applies only to fourths, fifths, and octaves.

- ✔ **Diminished interval:** You can make any interval diminished by lowering it a half step.

- ✔ **Augmented interval:** You can make any interval augmented by raising it a half step.

In an eternal attempt to be lazy, er, efficient, musicians use the following abbreviations when discussing intervals:

- ✔ *M* for major intervals

- ✔ *m* for minor intervals

- ✔ *P* for perfect intervals

- ✔ *dim* for diminished intervals

- ✔ *aug* for augmented intervals

- ✔ Numbers for the interval size, as in the number 5 for a fifth

So, when you see *P5,* you know it means a perfect fifth. When you see *M2,* it means a major second. When you see *m6,* it means a minor sixth.

Intervals can be measured upwards or downwards. That is, when you play a C-G fifth interval, you can say that G is a fifth above C or that C is a fifth below G. So, a *descending* interval is measured from the top note to the bottom note. Likewise, *ascending* means . . . oh, you can figure that out.

The rest of this section explains each interval on the scale and gives you an example of a well-known tune that uses the interval. You are strongly encouraged to play each example on your piano or keyboard. Nothing trains a musician more than playing and hearing at the same time. Put these intervals in your head along with the corresponding tunes, and you won't forget them.

Seconds

The first interval you sing in the celebratory song "Happy Birthday" is a *major second interval,* or *M2.* Go ahead and sing it. "Hap-py Birth-" Stop! On "Birth" you jump up a major second interval. Using the C scale, M2 is the distance from C to D.

Another song beginning with a M2 is "London Bridge," which you see in Figure 4-7. Every time you play the name of the bridge, you go up and back down a major second. Try it on your piano.

Figure 4-7: "London Bridge" uses major second intervals.

You create a *minor second,* or *m2,* simply by making the major second a half step smaller. In other words, play C to D flat. Think of m2 as the famous interval used in the *Jaws* theme by composer John Williams. Figure 4-8 shows you an m2 from Beethoven's ubiquitous "Für Elise." You'd recognize this melody anywhere, and now you can name the opening interval as an m2.

Figure 4-8: A minor second interval in action in Beethoven's "Für Elise."

Book III

Beginning to Play

Thirds

The first four notes of Beethoven's legendary *Fifth Symphony* employ a *major third,* or *M3.* If a composer could copyright an interval, Ludwig van Beethoven would have this one. And if that isn't enough, Ludwig tried to claim the *minor third,* or *m3,* too, by using it in the next four notes of the theme. Play Figure 4-9, a snippet of the *Fifth Symphony,* and you'll forever know major and minor thirds.

Figure 4-9:
Major
and minor
thirds from
Beethoven's
Fifth.

You also hear the M3 interval frequently in spirituals. Figure 4-10 demonstrates this interval in the songs "Amazing Grace" and "Swing Low, Sweet Chariot."

Figure 4-10:
The major
third interval
lifts the
spirits.

For some reason unknown even to Beethoven, an m3 seems to attract children. As you see in Figure 4-11, the opening notes of the children's favorites "This Old Man" and "It's Raining, It's Pouring" form an m3, which is smaller than an M3 by a half step.

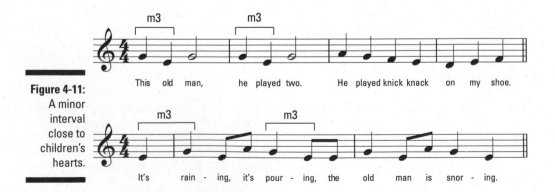

Figure 4-11:
A minor
interval
close to
children's
hearts.

Fourths and fifths

The fourth interval gets the hyperbolic classification of being perfect when it's five half steps above or below another note. From C up to F is a *perfect fourth,* or *P4.*

The sound of a P4 is perfect for conveying just about any kind of emotion. Composers use this interval to convey heroism, love, comedy, and even outer space in their melodies. It even crops up in folk songs! Play and sing the opening notes of "I've Been Working On The Railroad," and you jostle back and forth on a P4 until the lyric "the" ruins the fun, as shown in Figure 4-12.

Figure 4-12:
Perfect fourth interval in motion.

You can also remember the P4 interval going down and back up again in the theme of Schubert's *Unfinished Symphony* (see Figure 4-13).

Another perfect interval is the *perfect fifth,* or *P5.* Why is this one so perfect? Practically any song ever written has at least one P5 interval somewhere in it. And, hey, it fits the hand nicely: from C up to G is C position.

Book III

Beginning to Play

Figure 4-13:
Perfect fourth from Schubert's *Unfinished Symphony.*

As you play the first two notes of Figure 4-14, you may see stars. Both "Twinkle, Twinkle Little Star" and the theme to *Star Wars* begin with a P5.

Figure 4-14:
A shining
star, the
perfect fifth
interval.

Twin - kle, twin - kle, lit - tle star How I won - der what you are.

Play a descending P5 from G to C, and you may recognize the immortal classic "Feelings" and the theme from the *Flintstones* TV show. Speaking of classics, the romantic standard "Just the Way You Look Tonight" also begins with a descending P5 to the words "Some day." The Bach "Minuet" also opens with the descending P5, as you see in Figure 4-15.

Figure 4-15:
A fifth
interval
descending
perfectly.

 A handy way to remember perfect fourths *and* perfect fifths is by humming the opening bars of "Here Comes the Bride," in which one interval conveniently follows the other (see Figure 4-16). By the way, "Here Comes the Bride" originates in the "Bridal Chorus" sung in the opera *Lohengrin* by Richard Wagner.

Figure 4-16:
Perfect
fourth
and fifth
together.

Between a perfect fourth and a perfect fifth exists an interval that's exactly half of an octave (see Figure 4-17). From C, count up six half steps to F sharp, or G flat. If you call it F sharp, you call the interval an *augmented fourth* because it's larger than a fourth but not quite a fifth. If you call it G flat, the interval is a *diminished fifth* because it's a perfect fifth lowered by one half step. Many people remember this interval by singing "Maria" from *West Side Story* — the first two notes are an augmented fourth.

Figure 4-17: Augmented fourth/ diminished fifth.

The augmented fourth/diminished fifth interval sounds very strange and sometimes even scary. That is why it's sometimes called the *Devil's interval.*

Sixths and sevenths

A *major sixth,* or *M6,* interval is the opening interval of "My Bonnie Lies Over the Ocean." "My Bon-" is the M6 interval, from C to A. If you play C to A flat, you get a *minor sixth,* or *m6.* Figure 4-18 shows you both sixths.

Book III

Beginning to Play

Figure 4-18: Major and minor sixth intervals.

The *major seventh (M7)* and *minor seventh (m7)* are the last numbered intervals in the scale. You can call up a m7 by singing the first two notes of "Somewhere" from *West Side Story* (matching the first two words of the phrase, "There's a place for us"). Not many songwriters begin a melody with a major seventh interval; perhaps that's why there are few memorable examples.

In any case, it's an important interval to know because the seventh interval helps form the third most popular chord in all music. Get to know these two interval sizes and judge for yourself how melodic they are after you play the notes in Figure 4-19.

Figure 4-19:
Seventh (interval) heaven.

Octaves

You may think that the last interval in the scale would be called an eighth. You're partly right. For some reason, interval namers (another short-lived profession) grew tired of using numbers after the seventh and tried to liven things up with a fancy word. They came up with the prefix *octa,* which means "eight." An eighth interval is called an *octave (P8).* The interval-namers were so proud of their accomplishment that they classified it as a perfect interval.

Figure 4-20 shows you a perfect octave, an interval made memorable by Judy Garland singing "Over the Rainbow" in *The Wizard of Oz.* In the opening lyrics, from "some" to "where" is an octave leap. Another easy way to remember this interval is that both notes have the same name.

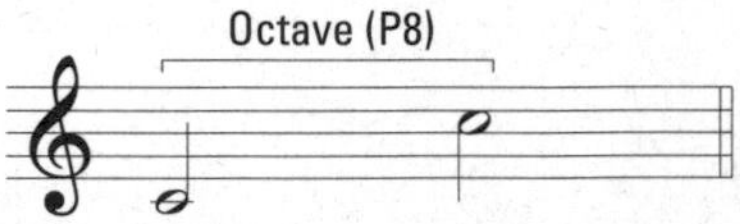

Figure 4-20:
Somewhere over the octave.

Combining Notes for Harmonic Intervals

In the preceding section, you play each interval as single notes to see and hear the distance between each. But that's not harmony. You have to play the intervals *together* to get harmony.

Playing two notes together

Figure 4-21 shows each interval — perfect, diminished, augmented, major, and minor — from seconds to an octave. Try playing the notes of each interval at the same time. Notice that the notes in each interval are stacked. When two notes appear stacked, or attached to the same stem, you play them at the same time. You know, in harmony.

They sound perfectly lovely, but how do you use these intervals to create harmony? You can

 ✔ Add intervals to the right hand under a melody line.

 ✔ Play intervals in the left hand while the right hand continues the melody.

 ✔ Do both.

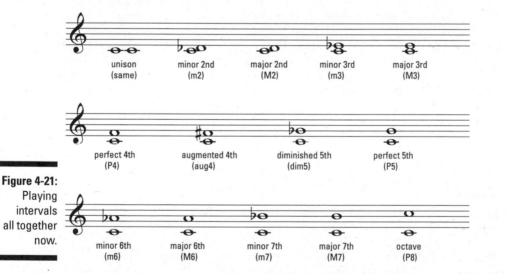

Figure 4-21:
Playing intervals all together now.

To start playing songs with harmonic intervals, skip ahead to the section "Playing Songs with More Harmony" at the end of the chapter.

Adding intervals to the melody

Adding harmonic intervals to the melody really fills out the sound. Figure 4-22 shows the melody of "Aura Lee" as a single-note melody in the opening phrase, followed by the same melody played with right-hand intervals added below the melody for the second phrase. As you play both phrases, listen to the difference this harmony makes.

Figure 4-22:
"Aura Lee" is a melody that begs for harmony.

It's not necessary for you to figure out how or when to add these intervals to a melody. The composer does that for you and notates these intervals in the printed music you play. But you should understand that all these intervals combine with the melody to make a very harmonic tune. Sure, you could just play the melody by playing only the top note of each group of notes, but your audience will appreciate the extra effort of playing the intervals. Besides, why do you think you have so many fingers?

Of course, if you want to add intervals to a melody yourself, try choosing the interval either a third below or a sixth below the melody note. Take a simple melody like "Yankee Doodle" and add an interval a sixth below each right-hand melody note. You can see how this is done in Figure 4-23.

A one-note melody. . .

Yan- kee Doo - dle went to town, rid - ing on a po - ny.

Figure 4-23:
Harmonizing "Yankee Doodle."

. . .becomes this with a 6th interval below

Yan- kee Doo - dle went to town, rid - ing on a po - ny.

If you've ever sung in a chorus or even made up a harmony to sing along to your favorite recording, you know that some notes sound good together and some don't. Certain intervals sound more stable, or resolved, than others. The intervals that sound resolved are thirds, fifths, and sixths; seconds, fourths, and sevenths can sound unresolved. (Octaves sound good, of course, because they match the same notes as the melody.) Generally, stable intervals are more *consonant* (harmonious and agreeable), whereas unstable intervals sound more *dissonant* (discordant and jarring, like the Devil's interval).

Harmonizing with the left hand

One of the easiest ways to add harmony to music is to play single notes with the left hand that form intervals when combined with the right-hand melody notes. Often, you simply play one note with the left hand and hold it for several measures as you continue with the melody.

In Figure 4-24, the right hand plays the opening phrase of "America, the Beautiful" while lefty plays single whole notes below. The harmonic intervals are simply moved an octave below, making use of the lower register of the piano and creating a nice, full sound.

Figure 4-24:
"America, the Beautiful" with single-note LH part.

You can fill out the sound even more by adding a harmonic interval to the left-hand part, as shown in Figure 4-25. When the left-hand part consists of whole- and half-note rhythms, adding this interval is easy enough.

Book III

Beginning to Play

Figure 4-25:
Adding more harmony to the LH part.

In Figure 4-25 the left hand plays stable, resolved intervals (thirds and fifths) except in one place: The unresolved interval of a seventh on beat 3 in measure 3 is resolved to an interval of a third to end the phrase on a more consonant harmony.

Another way to go is to add a harmonic interval below the melody in the right hand, plus add a bass note in the left hand, as shown in Figure 4-26.

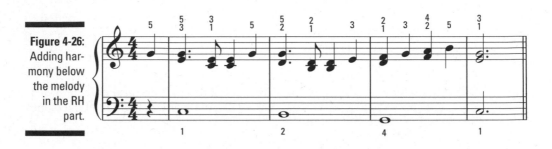

Figure 4-26: Adding harmony below the melody in the RH part.

To give a song a little more movement, you can play a harmony part in the left hand that matches the melody note-for-note (see Figure 4-27).

Figure 4-27: The LH harmony matches the rhythm of the melody.

And for the ultimate in harmony, make it a four-part style with simple intervals in both hands. Just a couple of notes create a nice, full sound, as shown in Figure 4-28.

Figure 4-28: A full, choir-like harmonic treatment.

Working with Musical Phrases and Periods

Two of the building blocks of musical form are phrases and periods. A *musical phrase* is the smallest unit of music with a defined beginning and end. Most musical phrases consist of a beginning I chord progressing to a IV or a V chord and ending again on the I chord. Theoretically, thousands of chord progressions may exist between that first I chord and the IV or V chord. However, you may lose your audience in that time.

Musical phrases are like sentences in a paragraph — just as most readers don't want to wade through a thousand lines of text to find out the point of a sentence, most music audiences are listening for the musical idea expressed in a phrase and get bored if it sounds like you're just meandering between chords and not coming to a resolution.

So how long is a musical phrase? It's really up to the composer, but generally, a phrase is usually two to four measures long. Within that space, a phrase begins, works through one or more chord progressions, and resolves itself back to the I chord.

When a composer *really* wants you to understand that a group of measures are to be linked together in a phrase and played as an important unit — kind of like a topic sentence in an essay — he or she links the phrase together with a curved line called a *phrase line,* as shown in Figure 4-29. Notice how the phrase both begins and ends on the I chord, or the G major chord.

Book III

Beginning to Play

Figure 4-29:
Note the phrase line in the bass clef.

Don't confuse phrase lines with ties and slurs. A phrase line ties an entire musical phrase together, whereas slurs and ties only tie together notes, or a small part of a phrase.

The next larger unit used in musical form is the period. Musical *periods* are created when two or three musical phrases are linked together.

Figure 4-30 shows an example of a musical period.

Linking Musical Parts to Create Forms

The division of music into *parts* occurs when you link two or more periods that sound like they belong together. (See the preceding section for a discussion of periods.) They share major harmonic focal points, similar melody lines, and similar rhythm structure. They may have other resemblances, too. Parts can be further linked together to create musical *forms*.

Composers conventionally give alphabetic labels to the musical parts within a composition: A, B, C, and so forth. If a part is repeated in a song, its letter also is repeated. For example, ABA is a familiar layout in classical music, where the opening *theme,* or the main musical idea that runs through a song (labeled A), after vanishing during part B, is repeated at the end of the song.

As the *contrast form,* where you have different musical sections that can differ widely from one another, AB forms come in a boundless array of possibilities. You may see recurring sections, unique ones, or any combination of both. For example, a *rondo* — a popular form in classical music — alternates between a recurring section and others that occur one time each. A rondo, then, would be labeled ABACADA . . . (and so on).

You may even encounter an *ongoing form,* which has no recurrence whatsoever: ABCDE. . . . This form creates what's known as a *through-composed* piece of music.

The following sections describe common forms you may encounter in music.

One-part form (A)

The *one-part form,* also known as *A form* or *unbroken form,* is the most primitive song structure and is also sometimes referred to as the *air form* or *ballad form.* In a one-part form, a simple melody is repeated with slight changes to accommodate different words, as in a *strophic* song like "Old McDonald Had a Farm." This song repeats the same musical line but changes the words with each verse.

The one-part form is mostly found in folk songs, carols, or other songs that are short and have a limited theme and movement. A forms come only in a single variety. They may be long or short, but they're always described as A (or AA, or even AAA).

Binary form (AB)

Binary form consists of two contrasting sections that function as statement and counterstatement. The pattern may be a simple AB, as in "My Country, 'Tis of Thee," or in simple minuets, where the form is usually AABB, with the second A and second B being variations of the first A and B.

In the binary form used in the Baroque period, the pattern can involve a change of key, usually to the key of the fifth of the original key if the piece is in a major key. Part A begins in one key and ends in the key of the fifth, while part B begins in the new key and ends in the original key. Each part is repeated, giving the pattern AABB.

Book III

Beginning to Play

Three-part form (ABA)

Songs frequently take the form ABA, known as *three-part form* or *ternary/ tertiary form.* This simple form is produced by varying and repeating the melody. For example, "Twinkle, Twinkle, Little Star" states a tune, varies it, and then restates it (which makes it ABA form). The B part here may be called the *bridge,* or the link, between the two A parts.

Here's how the three-part song form works:

- ✔ The first part, A, may be played once or repeated immediately.
- ✔ The middle part, B, is a contrasting section, meaning it's different than the first section.
- ✔ The last part is the same or very similar to the first part, A.

Three-part ABA form extends the idea of statement and departure by bringing back the first section. Both contrast and repetition are used in this form. Pop music is frequently a variation on ABA, called AABA, while blues is often AAB. AABA form is used in songs like "Over the Rainbow."

Arch form (ABCBA)

Music written in *arch form* is made up of three parts: A, B, and C. In arch form, the A, B, and C are played sequentially, and then part B is played a second time, directly following the C, and the song ends with the replaying of the A part.

Playing Songs with More Harmony

Feeling ready to play songs with more harmony? Each of the following songs explores different ways to use harmonic intervals.

- ✔ **"I'm Called Little Buttercup" (Track 40):** In this song the left hand plays single bass notes while the right hand plays the melody. The two parts move in different ways, so if you find it difficult to play at first, be patient and practice each hand separately until you feel comfortable with the notes. Then play hands-together.

- ✔ **"Marianne" (Track 41):** You can see and hear the harmonizing power of two-note harmony in this song. It may be helpful to play the melody, right hand only, along with the track a couple of times. Then try the left-hand part only. When you're relaxed and confident, put both hands together.

- ✔ **"Aura Lee" (Track 42):** Adding a melodic interval below the melody in your right hand and adding your left hand to the mix is simple to do, and oh so satisfying. If you get lost as you play, just slow down and try each hand separately until you feel like putting them together again. (You may recognize the melody as a song made famous by Elvis Presley. Elvis used different lyrics — something about loving him tender.)

- ✔ **"Shenandoah" (Track 43):** In this piece both hands play the same rhythm, with the left hand mirroring the melody with a soothing harmony line. Listen carefully as you play to match rhythms with both hands, just like two voices singing together.

- ✔ **"Auld Lang Syne" (Track 44):** Your left hand isn't limited to single notes or certain intervals. The composer may give you seconds, fourths, or anything else. Give both hands a shot at some four-part harmony with this song, which mixes up several types of intervals in both hands. Practice each hand separately before putting the two together.

I'm Called Little Buttercup

Moderately

Marianne

Moderately fast

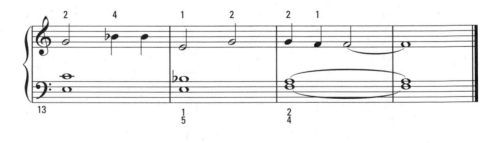

Aura Lee

Book III

Beginning to Play

Shenandoah

Slowly

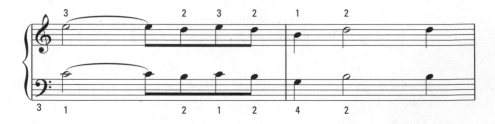

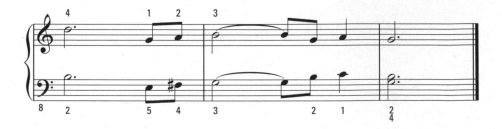

Auld Lang Syne

Chapter 5

Keys, Key Signatures, and the Circle of Fifths

In This Chapter

▶ Finding your music's home key

▶ Studying the Circle of Fifths

▶ Exploring the major and minor key signatures

▶ Playing songs with key signatures

▶ Access the audio tracks at www.dummies.com/go/pianokeyboardaio/

Keys allow you to drive a car, open doors, and even read maps. Some keys may be frustrating when you misplace them several times a week, but they're still handy and essential tools in life — and in music.

This chapter tells you about musical keys, and not the black and white ones you press when you play a keyboard. This is a completely, utterly, totally, wholly different type of key.

A *key* is a set of notes that corresponds to a certain scale (Book III Chapter 2 tells you all about scales). Keys and scales provide a foundation of compatible notes that composers and songwriters use to construct melodies and harmonies. Understanding them can go a long way toward deepening your understanding of the music you play.

Home Sweet Home Key

A musical key is a song's home. The key tells you several things about a song: which sharps and flats are used, which scale the song is based on, which of the scale notes is the song's home note — and much more.

A song has a single *home note,* and all the other notes used in a song have a relation to that home note based on how far away or near they are to home. So understanding a musical key means also understanding the relationships notes have to one another. A song can be thought of as a musical journey, and understanding where a song begins and where it goes on its journey is part of the joy of making music.

When a song is *in the key of C,* for example, it means that the song is primarily based on the C major scale, using mostly (or only) notes from that scale for the song's melody and harmony. Throughout the song, your ears get comfortable with notes from the C major scale. If the composer throws in a slew of other notes from another scale (such as F sharp, which is not in the C major scale), it's a bit unsettling to your ears. When the song returns to notes from the C major scale, your ears feel at home again.

The real definition of a song's key is not, of course, a song's home. As the musically minded will quickly point out, a song's key is its *tonal center,* meaning the tones of a scale that the melody and harmony of the song are centered around.

A whole ring of keys

Music uses many different keys that are named after the many different notes on your keyboard. In other words, you have a musical key for the notes A, B, C, D, E, F, and G, and yes, all the sharps and flats too.

Each key has its own unique character, look, feel, and sound. A composer uses a particular key to give his or her music the right sound and feeling. People have a lot of different and surprisingly passionate ideas about which keys sound best for which kinds of music. The best way to show you the difference keys can make to music is to have you play the same song written in two different keys. Play "Good Night, Ladies" (Track 45) as you see it in Figure 5-1, which is in the key of C.

You can also play "Good Night, Ladies" in any other key, such as the key of F (see Figure 5-2 and listen to Track 46). Although the *intervals* (the relationship of each note to the next) remain the same, the sound and character of the song change subtly simply by changing keys, in this case moving the song down to the key of F. (To read more about intervals, check out Book III Chapters 2 and 4.)

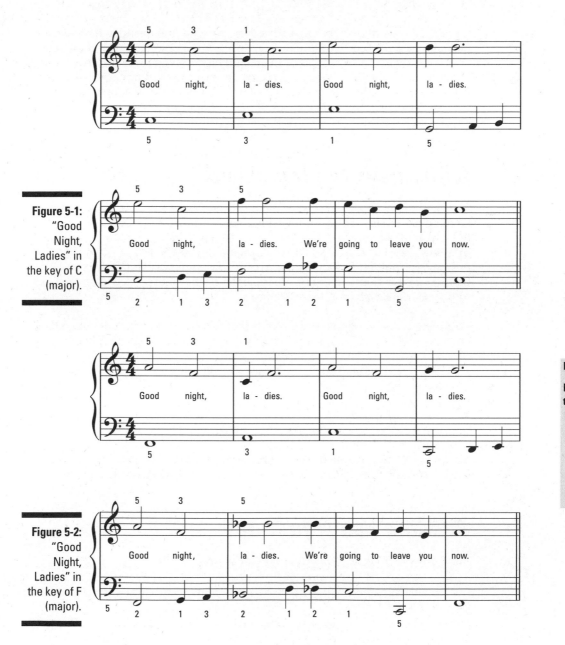

Figure 5-1: "Good Night, Ladies" in the key of C (major).

Figure 5-2: "Good Night, Ladies" in the key of F (major).

Book III

Beginning to Play

Composers and performers find keys very, very helpful because they allow music to be modified to fit different performers. For example, if a composer writes a song in the key of G, but the melody is too high for a particular singer to sing, the song can be *transposed* (changed) to a lower key (like F or E) to accommodate the singer's voice. The composer likes that the overall song isn't affected, only the *range,* which is the highness or lowness of the melody. Transposition is a frequent occurrence in music.

Using keys to play music

As a performer, recognizing and reading keys is an invaluable skill — more so than just knowing how high or low a song sounds. Understanding keys helps you play better because the key of a song tells you which notes to play or not to play. For example, if you play a melody in the key of G, you mostly play notes from the G major scale. Your knowledge of scales (see Book III Chapter 2) reminds you that G contains the note F sharp, so you can expect to play all the Fs in the song as F sharps.

To conserve ink, composers employ a tool called a *key signature.* Placed just after the clef on every line of music, a key signature allows the composer to

- ✔ Avoid writing all those little tic-tac-toe symbols next to every sharp in the song.
- ✔ Avoid writing flats next to every flat in the song.
- ✔ Instantly tell the performer what key the song is in.

As the music you play becomes more and more complex, you don't want to see sharps and flats cluttering the music you're trying to read.

Reading key signatures

What does reading key signatures do for you?

- ✔ It makes reading music easier because you know what notes to expect to play in each key.
- ✔ It makes playing music more fun because you can start to identify what makes one song different from another if you understand the idea of songs being in a key.
- ✔ It's a tool to help you remember the music, because you can identify a certain characteristic in the context of the key. For example, if the melody begins on the third note of the major scale and you know what key you're in, you can right away play the first note of the song.

Figure 5-3 shows you two key signatures: one for the key of G and one for the key of F. The first shows a sharp symbol on the top line of the staff, which tells you to play every F as F sharp. The G major scale contains one sharp, so this must be the key of G. The second key signature uses a flat on the middle line of the staff, telling you to play every B as B flat. This must be the key of F because the F major scale has one flat, and that's B flat.

Key of G:

Key of F:

Figure 5-3:
The sign on
the line.

You may think that only Fs on the top line are altered by the sharp in the key signature. Nope! The key signature applies to *every* F, not just the one on the top line. This, of course, is another time- and ink-saving decision.

The only time the same note is marked with a sharp or flat twice in a key signature is when you have two staves. In this case, you get one key signature on the treble staff and one on the bass staff, as shown in Figure 5-4.

Book III

**Beginning
to Play**

Figure 5-4:
A key sig-
nature for
each hand.

Playing a melody with a key signature is no more difficult than playing a song without one. You just have to remember (with a little help from your friendly key signature) which notes to make sharp or flat throughout. Figure 5-5 features the opening melody to a tune called "Worried Man Blues" in the key of G. When you play, keep in mind that all the Fs are actually F sharps.

Try the same song in the key of D, which has two sharps. Notice the key signature in Figure 5-6 and remember to play all the Fs as F sharps and all the Cs as C sharps.

Figure 5-5:
Playing a
melody in
the key of G.

Figure 5-6:
Trying
the same
melody in
the key of D.

To play the entire melody of "Worried Man Blues" with the left hand added, skip to the section "Playing Songs with Key Signatures" at the end of the chapter.

A key signature tells you instantly which key the song is in. You may be thinking, "Well, if I have to count all the sharps or flats and then figure out which scale they're in, that's not very instantaneous!" With a little experience, you'll start to recognize the most common key signatures. Without counting, without playing — without even thinking about it really — you'll simply glance at the key signature and know immediately which key the song is in. Most beginning piano music sticks to the key signatures with few sharps and flats or none at all.

The Circle of Fifths

Lucky for you, there's a method to the madness of key signatures, an order that starts with no sharps and flats and cycles the ring of keys to all twelve keys. Figure 5-7 shows the famous *Circle of Fifths* with the letter names for each possible home key, or tonal center. As you travel around the circle, you find each of the twelve keys in the Western tonal system. The numbers inside the circle tell you how many sharps or flats are in each key signature.

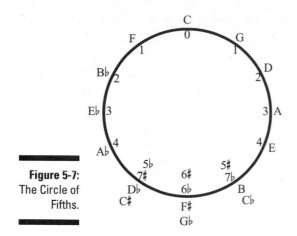

Figure 5-7:
The Circle of
Fifths.

As you check out the Circle of Fifths, note the following important points:

✔ Each key is a fifth up from the previous key, circling clockwise. (See Book III Chapter 4 for the scoop on fifths and other intervals.)

✔ The key of C, at the top, has no sharps or flats.

✔ The keys on the right half of the Circle are all sharp keys, gaining one sharp at each position traveling clockwise from the top.

✔ The keys on the left half of the Circle are all flat keys, gaining one flat at each position traveling counterclockwise from the top.

✔ The three keys at the bottom of the circle can be either sharp *or* flat keys; the composer gets to decide.

Among the marvels of this oracle of tonality, the Circle shows the relationship of the keys to each other. The keys that are neighbors have a lot in common, like seven of eight scale tones. Very often a song travels smoothly to a neighboring key during its musical journey. The keys that are farthest away from each other have little in common, and a musical journey from one side of the Circle directly to the opposite side sounds quite abrupt.

The order of sharps and flats as they're written on the grand staff follows the Circle of Fifths, adding a sharp or flat in the same order as the Circle.

Key signatures with sharps

Suppose you want to play a song on the piano that has two sharps in the key signature. If you look at the Circle of Fifths in Figure 5-7, you can quickly see that the key with two sharps is two positions away from C, so the song is in the key of D.

Eventually you want to be able to know what key a song is in without glancing at the Circle. Here's how.

To read a key signature that contains sharps:

> 1. **Locate the last sharp (the one farthest to the right) on either the treble or bass clef.**
>
> 2. **Move up one half step from the sharp to find the name of the key.**

For example, if you have two sharps, F sharp and C sharp, the last one on the clef is C sharp. Up a half step from C sharp is D. Therefore, the song is in the key of D.

Figure 5-8 shows you key signatures for all sharp keys.

Figure 5-8:
Sharp keys.

G   D   A   E   B   F♯   C♯

Naming keys with lots of sharps requires a bit of brain power because note spelling can get tricky. For example, on your piano keyboard the key one half step up from E is F. Technically, you can also spell F as E sharp. So, if the sixth sharp in the key signature is E sharp, you raise it one half step to determine the correct key, which is F sharp. You can't determine the key to be G flat because you would be skipping the letter name F in the sequence of note names.

Key signatures with flats

To read a key signature that contains flats:

> 1. **Locate the next-to-the-last flat (the one that's second from the right) in the key signature.**
>
> 2. **The name of that flat is the name of the key.**

For example, if you have three flats in a key signature — B flat, E flat, and A flat — the next-to-last one is E flat, and so the song is in the key of E flat. Figure 5-9 shows all the flat keys.

Figure 5-9:
Flat keys.

F   B♭   E♭   A♭   D♭   G♭   C♭

Give yourself a hand

An easy way to find the key signature for the most common keys uses mnemonics. All you need are five fingers and a decent memory.

The most common keys you're likely to play in are C, F, G, D, A, E, and B. The first two are a piece of cake to remember: C has no sharps or flats, and F has only B flat. For the other five common keys (which happen to all have sharps), follow these steps:

1. **Memorize the order G-D-A-E-B with a simple mnemonic of your choice:**

   Good **D**iamonds **A**re **E**xpensive to **B**uy

   Glass **D**oors **A**re **E**asily **B**roken

   Grand **D**ivas **A**ren't **E**ver **B**ashful

2. **Count out the keys in order on the fingers of one hand until you get to the key you need.**

   For the key of A, count G, D, A. How many fingers are you holding up? Three. The key of A has three sharps.

The sharps in a key signature always appear in ascending fifths, starting with F sharp. Thus, the three sharps in the key of A are F sharp, C sharp, and G sharp.

The one key for which this naming method doesn't work is the key of F. Because it has only one flat (B flat), there's no such thing as a "next-to-the-last" flat for you to read. But all you have to do is remember that one flat in the key signature means that a song is in the key of F. You can also remember that F is the key with one flat because it's one position before the key of C in the Circle of Fifths, or a fifth below C, so it must have one flat.

Book III

Beginning to Play

Leaving and returning to the home key

No matter what a home looks or sounds like, its basic purpose is to be the place you return to after you've been away. The same applies to keys.

Melodies and harmonies often venture outside a song's basic key. Particularly in jazz music, performers lift the music and give it a fresh sound by exploring notes and chords outside the original key. Composers as far back as you can imagine have used various keys to carry the music to new and unfamiliar places. After such an "out of key" experience, you feel a sense of coming home when the song returns to the original key.

To get a better grasp of this concept of musical travel, listen to a snippet of the song "After the Ball" on Track 47. It begins in the key of G and travels to the key of A for a few measures before returning home to G. Just by listening, see if you can tell when the song leaves the home key and when it returns home to its original key. Then listen to the piece again as you follow along with the music in Figure 5-10.

Figure 5-10:
Changing
keys
and then
returning
home.

Did you hear it? In measure 5, the music begins to venture outside of the original home key of G, and it starts to return safely and smoothly to the home key of G in measure 9.

To play "After the Ball" in its entirety and with the left hand added, skip to the section "Playing Songs with Key Signatures" at the end of the chapter.

Finding minor key signatures and relative minors

The Circle of Fifths works the same way for *minor* keys as it does for major keys. The minor keys are represented by the lowercase letters *inside* the Circle of Fifths shown in Figure 5-11.

The minor keys on the inside of the circle are the *relative minors* of the major keys on the outside of the circle. The relative minor and its major key have the same key signature. The only difference is that the relative minor's scale starts on a different tonic, or first note. The tonic, or starting point, of a relative minor is a minor third — or three half steps — lower than its relative major key. But there is no difference in the key signature between a major key and its relative minor.

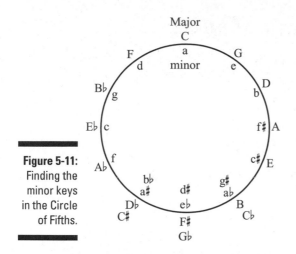

Figure 5-11:
Finding the
minor keys
in the Circle
of Fifths.

For example, C major's relative minor is A minor (refer to Figure 5-11). A minor's tonic note is A, which is three half steps to the left of C on the piano.

On sheet music, the relative minor is the note one full line or space below the major key note. C is in the third space on the treble clef, and A, its relative minor, is in the second space, below it.

On the piano, a major chord and its relative minor chord go together like bread and butter. Many, many songs use this chord progression because it just sounds good. (You can find more about chords and chord progressions in Book II Chapter 6.)

Reviewing All the Key Signatures

The following sections provide a rundown of the major and natural minor key signatures and a couple of octaves' worth of notes in those keys, arranged in a scale. (The key signatures are ordered following the Circle of Fifths instead of alphabetical order.)

Don't be thrown by the word *natural* when it's used to describe minor key signatures in this section. As Book III Chapter 2 explains, more than one kind of minor exists.

Book III

Beginning
to Play

C major and A natural minor

Figure 5-12 shows the C major key signature, and Figure 5-13 shows the A natural minor key signature, C's relative natural minor.

Figure 5-12:
The C major key signature and scale.

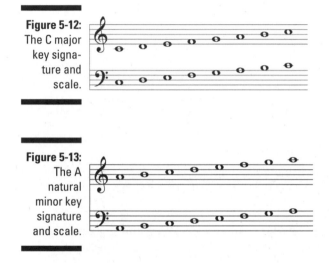

Figure 5-13:
The A natural minor key signature and scale.

As you can see, the C major and the A natural minor have the same key signature (that is, no sharps and no flats) and the same notes in the scale because A is the relative natural minor of C. The only difference is that the C major scale starts on C, whereas the A natural minor scale starts on A.

G major and E natural minor

Figure 5-14 shows the G major key signature, and Figure 5-15 shows the E natural minor key signature, G's relative natural minor.

Figure 5-14:
The G major key signature and scale.

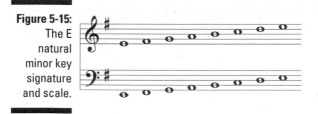

Figure 5-15:
The E natural minor key signature and scale.

You've now added one sharp (F) to the key signature. The next stop (D) has two, and you keep adding one more sharp until you get to the bottom of the Circle of Fifths.

D major and B natural minor

Figure 5-16 shows the D major key signature, and Figure 5-17 shows the B natural minor key signature, D's relative natural minor.

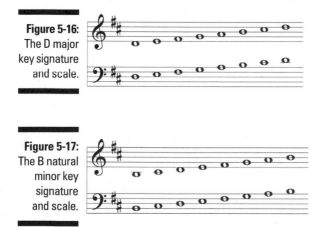

Figure 5-16:
The D major key signature and scale.

Figure 5-17:
The B natural minor key signature and scale.

Book III

Beginning to Play

A major and F sharp natural minor

Figure 5-18 shows the A major key signature, and Figure 5-19 shows the F sharp natural minor key signature, A's relative natural minor.

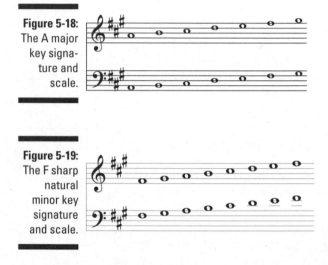

Figure 5-18: The A major key signature and scale.

Figure 5-19: The F sharp natural minor key signature and scale.

E major and C sharp natural minor

Figure 5-20 shows the E major key signature, and Figure 5-21 shows the C sharp natural minor key signature, E's relative natural minor.

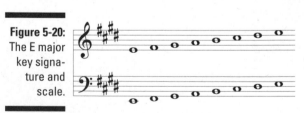

Figure 5-20: The E major key signature and scale.

Figure 5-21:
The C sharp natural minor key signature and scale.

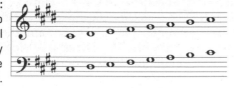

B/C flat major and G sharp/
A flat natural minor

Figure 5-22 shows the B major key signature and C flat major key signature. Figure 5-23 shows the G sharp natural minor key signature and the A flat natural minor key signature.

Figure 5-22:
The B major and C flat major key signatures and scales.

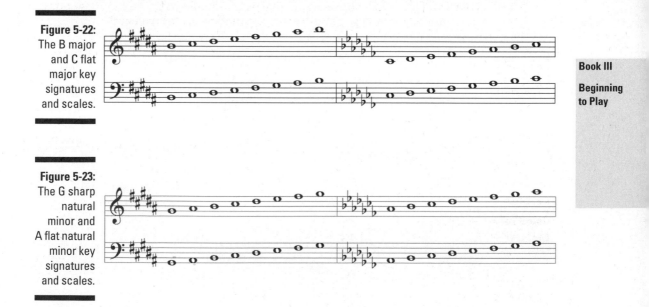

Figure 5-23:
The G sharp natural minor and A flat natural minor key signatures and scales.

Confused by the double naming here? Take a look at a keyboard, and you see that a black key doesn't exist for C flat. Instead, you see a white key: B. C flat and B are *enharmonic equivalents* of one another, meaning they're the same but with different names. All the notes in the key of B major and the key of C flat major sound exactly the same — they just use different musical notation. The same goes for G sharp natural minor and A flat natural minor — same notes, just different notation.

As the number of sharps has been going up by one at each stop on the Circle of Fifths, from this point on, the number of flats will be going down by one until returning to the 12 o'clock (C major/A natural minor) position.

F sharp/G flat major and D sharp/ E flat natural minor

Figure 5-24 shows the F sharp major key signature and the G flat major key signature. Figure 5-25 shows the D sharp natural minor key signature and the E flat natural minor key signature. More enharmonic equivalents!

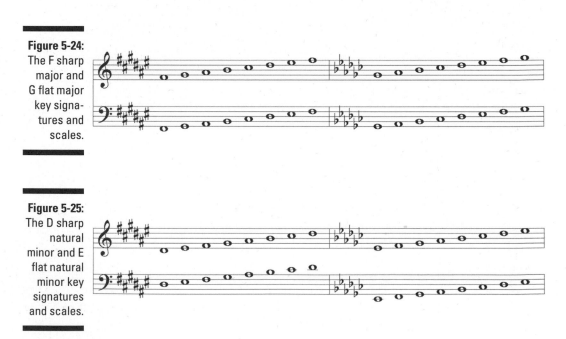

Figure 5-24: The F sharp major and G flat major key signatures and scales.

Figure 5-25: The D sharp natural minor and E flat natural minor key signatures and scales.

C sharp major/D flat and A sharp/ B flat natural minor

Figure 5-26 shows the C sharp major key signature and the D flat major key signature. Figure 5-27 shows the A sharp natural minor key signature and the B flat natural minor key signature.

Figure 5-26:
The C sharp major and D flat major key signatures and scales.

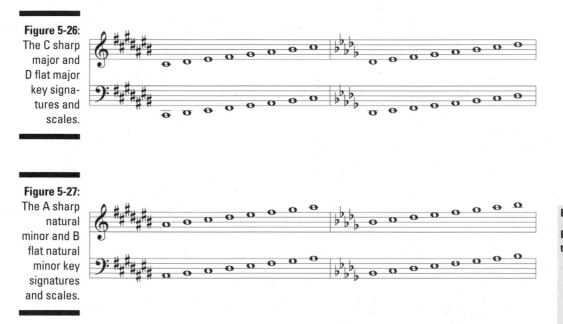

Figure 5-27:
The A sharp natural minor and B flat natural minor key signatures and scales.

Book III

Beginning to Play

These are the last of the enharmonic equivalent key signatures you have to remember. Also, these are the last of the keys with sharps in their signatures. From this point on, you're working with flats alone as you continue going up the left side of the Circle of Fifths.

A flat major and F natural minor

Figure 5-28 shows the A flat major key signature and the F natural minor key signature, which is A flat's relative natural minor.

Figure 5-28:
The A flat major and F natural minor key signatures and scales.

E flat major and C natural minor

Figure 5-29 shows the E flat major key signature and the C natural minor key signature, which is E flat's relative natural minor.

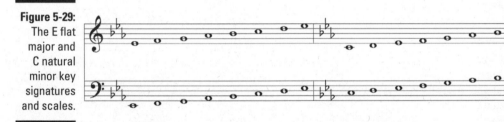

Figure 5-29:
The E flat major and C natural minor key signatures and scales.

B flat major and G natural minor

Figure 5-30 shows the B flat major key signature and the G natural minor key signature, which is B flat's relative natural minor.

Figure 5-30:
The B flat major and G natural minor key signatures and scales.

F major and D natural minor

Figure 5-31 shows the F major key signature and the D natural minor key signature, which is F major's relative natural minor.

Figure 5-31:
The F major and D natural minor key signatures and scales.

Playing Songs with Key Signatures

The songs in this section give you a chance to read and play music written with key signatures. Here are some pointers as you prepare to play each piece:

- ✔ **"Worried Man Blues" (Track 48):** This is the full version of the song that introduces key signatures earlier in the chapter. Written in the key of G, it has one sharp (F sharp) to keep in mind. The left-hand part is pretty simple, but you may want to go over the fingering and position changes in the last five measures before you try it hands-together.

- ✔ **"After the Ball" (Track 49):** This is also the full version of a song introduced earlier in the chapter. This one illustrates a melody in the key of G that makes a brief sojourn to another key before returning to the home key at the end. Check out the natural sign before the note C in the right hand, in measure 26. This helpful reminder cancels out the C sharp played two measures before.

Book III

Beginning to Play

Worried Man Blues

After the Ball

Book III

Beginning to Play

Chapter 6

Building Chords to Accompany Melodies

In This Chapter

▶ Building chords of all types

▶ Translating chord symbols

▶ Inverting the notes of a chord

▶ Seeing how chords and key signatures are connected

▶ Playing songs with major, minor, and seventh chords

▶ Access the audio tracks at www.dummies.com/go/pianokeyboardaio/

*P*laying melodies is nice and all, but harmony is the key to making your music sound fuller, better, cooler, and just downright great. Playing chords with your left hand is perhaps the easiest way to harmonize a melody. Playing chords with your right hand, too, is a great way to accompany a singer, guitarist, or other performer. This chapter shows you step-by-step how to build chords and use them to accompany any melody.

Three or more notes played at the same time form a *chord*. You can play chords with one or both hands. Chords have but one simple goal in life: to provide harmony. (Book III Chapter 4 tells you all about harmony.)

You may have encountered chords already in a number of situations, including the following:

- ✔ You see several musical notes stacked on top of each other in printed music.

- ✔ You notice strange symbols above the treble clef staff that make no sense when you read them, like F♯m7(-5), Csus4(add9).

- ✔ You hear a band or orchestra play.

- ✔ You honk a car horn.

Yes, the sound of a car horn is a chord, albeit a headache-inducing one. So are the sounds of a barbershop quartet, a church choir, and a sidewalk accordion player (monkey with tip jar is optional). Chances are, though, that you probably won't use car horns or barbers to accompany your melodies — chords on the piano and keyboard are much more practical.

The Anatomy of a Triad

Chords begin very simply. Like melodies, chords are based on scales. (Book III Chapter 2 gives you the skinny on scales.) To make a chord, you select any note and play other scale notes at the same time.

Generally, the lowest note of a chord is called the *root note.* The root note also gives the chord its name. For example, a chord with A as its root note is an A chord. The notes you use on top of the root note give the chord its *type,* explained later in this chapter, starting with major and minor chords.

Most chords begin as *triads,* or three *(tri)* notes added *(ad)* together. Okay, that's not the actual breakdown of the word, but it may help you remember what triad means. A triad consists of a root note and two other notes: for example, the root plus a third interval and a fifth interval. (Book III Chapters 2 and 4 tell you about all the fun and games involved in intervals.)

Figure 6-1 shows a typical triad played on the white keys C-E-G. C is the root note, E is a third interval from C, and G is a fifth interval from C.

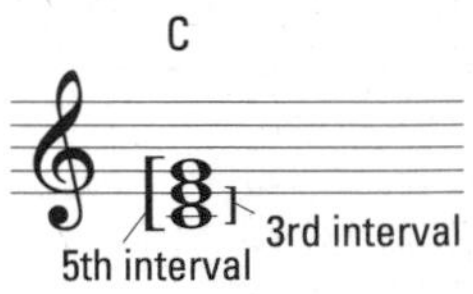

Figure 6-1:
This C chord is a simple triad.

You build new chords by altering this C triad in any of the following ways:

✔ Raising or lowering notes of the triad by a half step or whole-step

✔ Adding notes to the triad

✔ Both raising or lowering notes *and* adding notes

For example, Figure 6-2 shows you four different ways to change the C triad and make four new chords. Play each of these chords to hear how they sound. The note intervals are marked in each chord.

Figure 6-2:
Making new
chords from
the C triad.

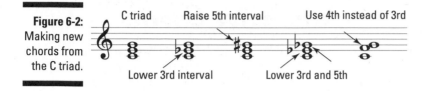

Starting Out with Major Chords

Major chords are the most frequently used, most familiar, and easiest triads to play. It's a good bet that most folk and popular songs you know have one or two major chords.

You make major chords with the notes and intervals of a major scale. (You may remember scales from Book III Chapter 2.) You build a major chord by starting out with a root note and then adding other notes from the desired chord's scale. For example, suppose you want to build a G major chord. Play the root note G and add the third and fifth notes (or third and fifth intervals) from the G major scale on top of the root note.

Major chords, such as the four in Figure 6-3, are so common that musicians treat them as the norm. These chords are named by just the root, and musicians rarely say "major." Instead, they just say the name of the chord and use a chord symbol written above the staff to indicate the name of the chord.

Figure 6-3:
Major
chords.

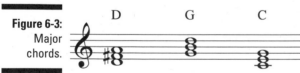

Use fingers 1, 3, and 5 to play major chords. If you're playing left-hand chords (see Figure 6-4), start with LH 5 on the root note. For right-hand chords, play the root note with RH 1.

Figure 6-4:
Major
chords for
lefty, too.

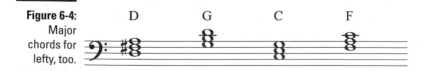

To play a song with left-hand major chords right now, skip to the section "Playing Songs with Chords" at the end of the chapter and play "Down by the Station."

Branching Out with Minor Chords

Like the major chord, a *minor chord* is a triad comprised of a root note, a third interval, and a fifth interval. Written as a chord symbol, minor chords get the suffix *m*, or sometimes *min*. Songs in minor keys give you lots of opportunities to play minor chords.

Don't be fooled by the name "minor." These chords are no smaller or any less important than major chords. They're simply built on minor scales, rather than on major scales.

You can make a minor chord two different ways:

- ✔ **Play the root note, and add the third and fifth notes of the minor scale on top.** For example, play A as the root note, and add the third note (C) and fifth note (E) of the A minor scale.

- ✔ **Play a major chord and lower the middle note, or third interval, by one half step.** For example, a C major chord has the notes C-E-G. To play a C minor chord, lower the E to E flat.

Figure 6-5 shows several minor chords. Play them to hear how they sound and then compare these chords to their major counterparts in Figure 6-3.

Just like playing major chords, use fingers 1, 3, and 5 for minor chords. For left-hand minor chords, play the root note with LH 5; for right-hand chords, play the root note with RH 1.

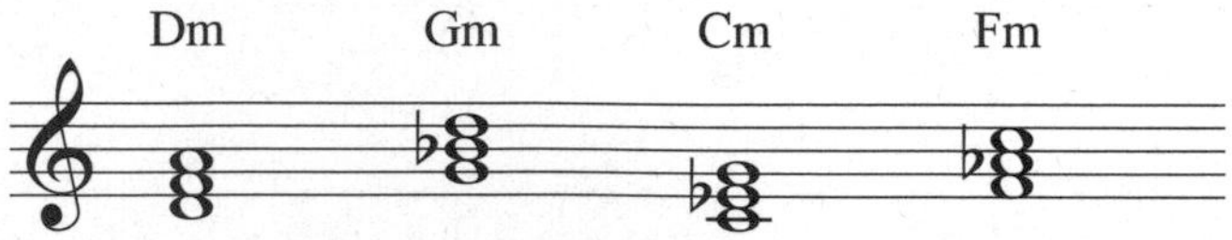

Figure 6-5:
Minor, but
not insig-
nificant,
chords.

Dm   Gm   Cm   Fm

To play "Sometimes I Feel Like a Motherless Child," a song in a minor key with lots of minor chords, go to the section "Playing Songs with Chords" at the end of the chapter.

Exploring Other Types of Chords

Major and minor chords are by far the most popular chords, but other types of chords also shine in music. You form these other chords by altering the notes of a major or minor chord and/or by adding notes to a major or minor chord.

Tweaking the fifth: Augmented and diminished chords

Major and minor chords differ from each other only in the third interval. The top note, the fifth interval, is the same for both types of chords. So, by altering the fifth interval of a major or minor chord, you can create two new chord types, both triads.

An *augmented chord* contains a root note, a major third (M3) interval, and an *augmented fifth* (aug5), which is a perfect fifth (P5) raised one half step. Think of an augmented chord as simply a major chord with the top note raised one half step. Figure 6-6 shows several augmented chords.

Figure 6-6: Augmented chords raise the fifth one half step.

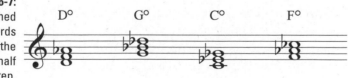

When writing the chord symbol, the suffixes for augmented chords include *+, aug,* and ♯5. One advantage of ♯5 is that it actually tells you what to do to change the chord — you sharp the fifth.

A *diminished chord* contains a root note, a minor third (m3) interval, and a *diminished fifth* (dim5), which is a perfect fifth (P5) interval lowered one half step. Figure 6-7 gives you a selection of diminished chords.

Book III

Beginning to Play

Figure 6-7: Diminished chords lower the fifth one half step.

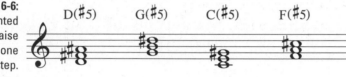

Note the suffix used to signal a diminished chord in the chord symbol: *dim*. You may also see the suffix *dim* in the chord symbol, as in *Fdim* (Table 6-1, later in this chapter, offers a helpful guide to chord symbols.)

TIP

You may find it easiest to use fingers 1, 2, and 4 for augmented and diminished chords played with the right hand. For the left, try 5, 3, and 2.

Figure 6-8 shows you an example of how you may encounter diminished and augmented chords in a song. The melody is the last phrase of Stephen Foster's "Old Folks at Home." Take these new chords for a spin and see how they subtly affect a song's harmony.

Figure 6-8:
Augmented and diminished chords in "Old Folks at Home."

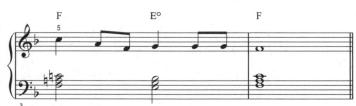

Waiting for resolution: Suspended chords

Another popular type of three-note chord, although it's technically not a triad, is the *suspended chord.* The name means "hanging," and the sound of a suspended chord always leaves you waiting for the next notes or chords.

The two types of suspended chords are the *suspended second* and the *suspended fourth.* Because of their abbreviated suffixes, these chords are often referred to as the *sus2* and *sus4* chords; you see them written as *Csus2* or *Asus4,* for example. Here's how you create them:

- ✔ **Asus2 chord** is comprised of a root note, a major second (M2) interval, and a perfect fifth (P5) interval.

- ✔ **Asus4 chord** has a root note, a perfect fourth (P4), and a perfect fifth (P5) interval.

The sus4 is so popular that musicians often just call it the *sus chord.* So, when the bandleader says to play "a sus chord on beat 1," that probably means to play a suspended fourth. But asking for clarification is a good idea.

Figure 6-9 shows you some of these suspenseful chords.

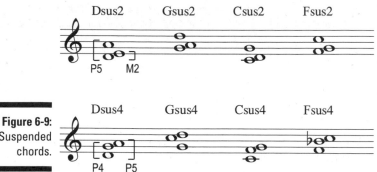

Figure 6-9:
Suspended
chords.

What's being suspended, exactly? The third. A suspended chord leaves you hanging, and its resolution comes when the second or fourth resolves to the third. This doesn't mean that all sus chords have to resolve to major or minor triads; actually, they sound pretty cool on their own.

Fingering suspended chords is easy. For the right hand, use fingers 1, 2, and 5 for sus2 chords; use fingers 1, 4, and 5 for sus4 chords. For the left hand, use fingers 5, 4, and 1 for sus2 chords; use fingers 5, 2, and 1 for sus4 chords.

Play along with Figure 6-10 (Track 50) and listen to how the chord that follows each sus chord sounds resolved.

Book III

Beginning
to Play

Figure 6-10:
A little
suspension
tension.

Adding the Seventh for Four-Note Chords

Adding a fourth note to a triad fills out the sound. Composers often use chords of four notes or more to create musical tension through an unresolved sound. Hearing this tension, the ear begs for resolution, usually found in a major or minor chord that follows. These tension-filled chords make you want to keep listening, and to a composer, that's always a good thing.

The most common four-note chord is the *seventh chord,* which you build by adding a seventh interval above the root note of a triad. Played on the piano by itself, the seventh interval may not sound very pretty, but it sounds good when you add it to a triad. In fact, the result is perhaps the third most popular chord in Western music. You'll be amazed at how many great songs use chords with seventh intervals.

Each of the four types of three-note chords introduced earlier in this chapter — major, minor, augmented, and diminished — can become a seventh chord. Simply adding a seventh interval (the seventh note of the scale) on top of any of these triads makes that chord a seventh chord.

The basic seventh chord uses the *minor seventh* interval, which is the seventh note up the scale from the chord's root but lowered one half step. For example, if the root note is C, the seventh note up the scale is B. Lower this note by a half step and you get a minor seventh above the C, which is B flat.

The four-note chords shown in Figure 6-11 are all seventh chords. The chord symbol is simple and easy: It's the numeral 7 placed after the triad symbol.

Figure 6-11: There's nothing plain about these seventh chords.

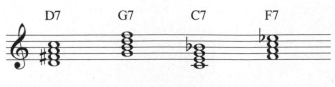

The suffixes used by seventh chords are placed *after* the triad type's suffix. For example, if you add a minor seventh to a minor triad, the suffix *7* comes after *m*, giving you *m7* as the full chord type suffix for a minor seventh chord.

To play seventh chords, use fingers 1, 2, 3, and 5 in the right hand. You may want to use RH 4 instead of RH 3 for certain chords, when the chord shape feels natural with RH 4. With the left hand, play the root note with LH 5 and the top note with LH 1.

To play Brahms's "Lullaby," featuring seventh chords in the left hand, skip to "Playing Songs with Chords" at the end of the chapter.

Reading Chord Symbols

When you encounter sheet music or songbooks containing just melodies and lyrics, you usually also get the little letters and symbols called *chord symbols* above the staff, as shown in many of the figures in this chapter. Knowing how to build chords from chord symbols is an extremely valuable skill. It equips you to make a G diminished chord, for example, when you see the chord symbol for it: *Gdim*.

A chord's symbol tells you two things about that chord: *root* and *type*.

- ✔ **Root:** The capital letter on the left tells you the chord root. As with scales, the root note gives the chord its name. For example, the root of a C chord is the note C.

- ✔ **Type:** Any letter and/or number suffix following the chord root tells you the chord type, like *m* for minor and *7* for seventh chords. Major chords have no suffix, just the letter name, so a capital letter by itself tells you to play a major triad.

Music written with chord symbols is your set of blueprints for what type of chord to construct to accompany the melody. For any chord types you may come across in your musical life (and there are plenty of chords out there), build the chord by placing the appropriate intervals or scale notes on top of the root note. For example, *C6* means play a C major chord and add the sixth interval (A); *Cm6* means to play a C minor chord and add the sixth interval.

Figure 6-12 shows the tune "Bingo" (Track 51) with its chord symbols written above it in the treble staff. The notes in the bass staff match the chord symbols and show you one way to play a simple chord accompaniment in your left hand.

Figure 6-12:
Transforming
chord
symbols into
notes on the
staff.

Play the chord with the melody note that's directly below the chord symbol. The chord lasts until you see a chord change at the next chord symbol. So if you see a C chord at the beginning of measure 1, like in "Bingo," play it on beat 1. If there isn't a chord change, like in measure 5, you can play the C chord again, or not — your choice.

To play a song with chord symbols right now, skip to the section "Playing Songs with Chords" at the end of the chapter and play "Scarborough Fair."

You may encounter many curious-looking chord symbols in the songs you play. Table 6-1 lists the most common and user-friendly chord symbols, the variety of ways they may be written, the chord type, and a recipe for building the chord.

Note: The examples in the table all use C as the root, but you can apply these recipes to any root note and make the chord you want.

Table 6-1	Recipes for Constructing Chords	
Chord Symbol	*Chord Type*	*Ingredients*
C	Major	1-3-5
Cmin; Cm	Minor	1-♭3-5
Caug; C(♯5); C+	Augmented	1-3-♯5

Chord Symbol	Chord Type	Ingredients
Cdim; C*dim.*	Diminished	1-♭3-♭5
Csus2	Suspended second	1-2-5
C(add2); C(add9)	Add second (or ninth)	1-2-3-5
Cm(add2); Cm(add9)	Minor, add second (or ninth)	1-2-♭3-5
Csus4	Suspended fourth	1-4-5
C(♭5)	Flat fifth	1-3-♭5
C6	Sixth	1-3-5-6
Cm6	Minor sixth	1-♭3-5-6
C7	Seventh	1-3-5-♭7
Cmaj7; CM7; C△7	Major seventh	1-3-5-7
Cmin7; Cm7; C-7	Minor seventh	1-♭3-5-♭7
C*dim.*7; Cdim7	Diminished seventh	1-♭3-♭5-6
C7sus4	Seventh, suspended fourth	1-4-5-♭7
Cm(maj7)	Minor, major seventh	1-♭3-5-7
C7♯5; C7+	Seventh, sharp fifth	1-3-♯5-♭7
C7♭5; C7-5	Seventh, flat fifth	1-3-♭5-♭7
Cm7♭5; CØ7	Minor seventh, flat fifth	1-♭3-♭5-♭7
Cmaj7♭5	Major seventh, flat fifth	1-3-♭5-7

Book III

Beginning to Play

Figure 6-13 shows you exactly how to make a chord from a recipe in Table 6-1. The number recipe 1-3-♯5-7 is applied to three different root notes — C, F, G — to illustrate how chord building works with different root notes and thus different scale notes. By the way, the resulting chord is called a Cmaj7♯5 because you add the seventh interval and sharp (raise one half step) the fifth interval.

Figure 6-13:
Building a chord from a chord symbol.

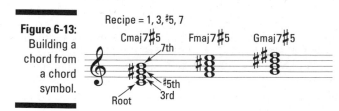

Relating Chords to a Scale or Key Signature

Chords didn't just pop up one day when some early musician tripped and fell over his lute, accidentally strumming the strings as he hit the ground. They have a logical relationship to scales and therefore to the concept of playing in a given key signature. (Flip back to Book III Chapter 5 for more on key signatures.) By understanding this relationship and memorizing it in all 12 keys, you give yourself a head start for anticipating what chords a song uses based on what key it's in.

The use and study of note relationships and chords is called *harmony*. A specific series of chords is referred to as a *harmonic progression* or *chord progression*. You can find many great books, such as *Music Theory For Dummies* by Michael Pilhofer and Holly Day (Wiley, 2011) as well as videos, teachers, and schools to study more about these relationships; look for the general term *music theory*.

Recognizing the major scale chord tones

If you build triads from a major scale using only the scale tones, you get Figure 6-14. (A *major scale* is comprised of a note, then up two whole steps, a half step, three more whole steps, and a final half step. You can read more about these scales in Book III Chapter 2.)

Figure 6-14:
The major
scale triads.

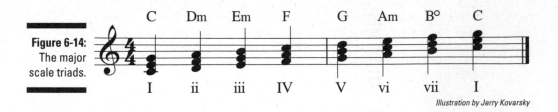

Illustration by Jerry Kovarsky

You can see that there are major triads for the C, F, and G notes in this example. Minor chords occur on the D, E, and A notes, and the B is a diminished chord. Music theory uses Roman numerals to indicate the numbers — capital numerals for major chords and lowercase for minor. The chords are usually referred to by their number in the scale, so the first chord is the I (1) chord, the second is the ii (2) chord, and so on.

So the I (1), IV (4), and V (5) chords are major. The ii (2), iii (3), and vi (6) chords are minor. And the vii (7) chord is diminished. Figure 6-15 shows the scale tone chords for a few other keys.

Listen to Track 52 to hear the scale tone triads played in a few keys.

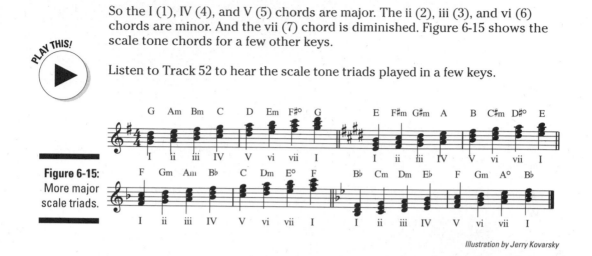

Figure 6-15: More major scale triads.

Illustration by Jerry Kovarsky

Trying a few common chord progressions

Some very common chord progressions have been used for countless hit songs over the years. The basic blues progression in Figure 6-16 has been used not only for blues songs but also for most of the '50s and '60s rock and roll songs. Think Chuck Berry, Elvis Presley, and B.B. King. It uses the I, IV, and V chords from a given key, played in the order pictured. You can find many fancier variations of this setup, but this progression is the basis of the blues and early rock and roll.

Book III

Beginning to Play

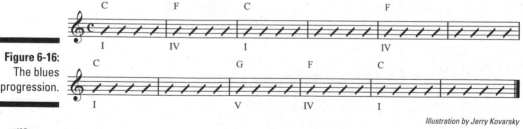

Figure 6-16: The blues progression.

Illustration by Jerry Kovarsky

Check out Track 53 to hear the blues progression chords.

The vertical slashes on the staff in Figure 6-16 are commonly used when writing a chord chart. They show you how many beats to play each chord and leave you free to play the chords however you want. Feel free to think of the chords and try to play these progressions in more than one key. Good luck!

Countless pop songs from the '40s, '50s, and '60s, as well as doo-wop vocal songs, are based on the four-chord sequence in Figure 6-17.

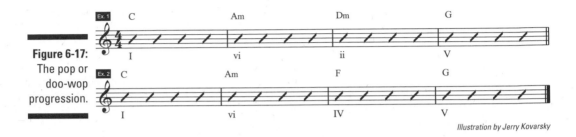

Figure 6-17: The pop or doo-wop progression.

Illustration by Jerry Kovarsky

The first example uses I, vi, ii, V; the second uses the common variation I, vi, IV, V.

Listen to Track 54 to hear both the doo-wop chord progressions.

Rearranging the Order of the Notes: Chord Inversions

Always playing chords with the root at the bottom means you have to jump your hand around the keyboard, which can result in difficult, choppy-sounding playing. By simply rearranging the order of the notes of a given chord, you can make much smoother transitions. These different groupings of the notes are called *inversions*. Rearranging the order of the notes doesn't affect whether a chord sounds major or minor.

The three triad inversions

You can play any three-note chord from three positions (Figure 6-18):

- **The root position:** The traditional note grouping (root, third, and fifth)
- **The first inversion:** The root note moved to the top of the chord (third, fifth, and then root)
- **The second inversion:** The third moved up on top of the root (fifth, root, and then third)

Figure 6-18:
The three possible inversions of each type of chord triad.

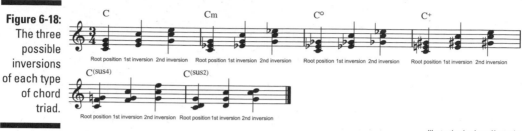

Illustration by Jerry Kovarsky

As you play the three inversions, you can hear that the chord quality sounds basically the same.

Listen to Track 55 to hear the chords and inversions shown in Figure 6-18.

Figure 6-19 shows you how to play the blues progression by always moving to the closest note to form the needed chord. Moving to the nearest note is called *voice leading* in music theory, where each note in the chord is considered a *voice*. Pay attention to the marked fingerings to play them as smoothly as possible.

Figure 6-19:
Using inversions to create smooth voice leading for the blues.

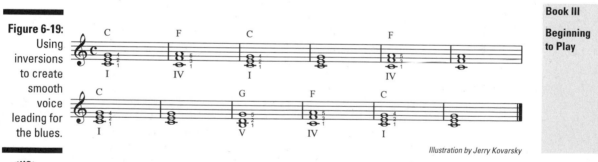

Illustration by Jerry Kovarsky

Book III

Beginning to Play

Listen to Track 56 to hear the blues progression using chord inversions.

You can apply the same concept to make the pop/doo-wop progression sound smoother as well, as shown in Figure 6-20; Example 1 uses the ii chord, or the Dm, and Example 2 uses the IV chord, the F major. Now it sounds like what you hear on recordings, right?

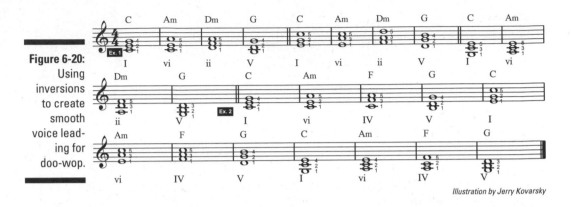

Figure 6-20: Using inversions to create smooth voice leading for doo-wop.

Illustration by Jerry Kovarsky

Three-note chords in your left hand

If you play an arranger keyboard or play in an ensemble with a bass player, you can use these types of inversions in your left hand for a smoother sound. Because the arranger style or the bass player always provides the root tone, you're free to use these close inversions. Figure 6-21 shows some possible ways to play the three-chord rock sound with some rhythm added. Each example starts on a different chord inversion and uses different rhythm patterns. If you have onboard drums, pick a simple rock pattern and play along with it. (Book VI Chapter 2 has the lowdown on playing with onboard rhythm patterns.) Repeat each two-bar phrase over and over.

Figure 6-21: Smooth left hand examples for I, IV, and V.

Illustration by Jerry Kovarsky

You can do the same thing for the doo-wop chords in Figure 6-22. You have two variations for each starting chord inversion, one always using the straight repeated rhythm with good use of close chord movement, and the other varying the rhythm a bit more. Repeat each two-bar phrase over and over.

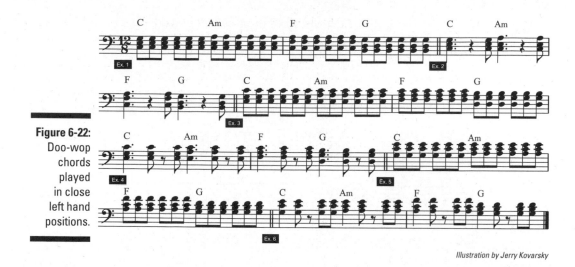

Figure 6-22:
Doo-wop
chords
played
in close
left hand
positions.

Illustration by Jerry Kovarsky

Figure 6-22 employs a time signature, 12/8, that you may not be familiar with. Each measure has 12 beats, and each group of three eighth notes forms a strong pulse. So it feels like each measure actually has four beats, with each beat getting three subdivided pulses: **1**-2-3, **2**-2-3, **3**-2-3, **4**-2-3.

Listen to Tracks 57 and 58 to hear the blues and doo-wop progressions played using left hand chord inversions (shown in Figures 6-21 and 6-22).

Book III

Beginning to Play

Two-handed chords in a pianistic style

When you're playing chords on an acoustic piano or an electric piano, you use the closest inversion chords possible in your right hand and play the root note in your left hand — either a single note or two notes an octave apart for more power (best on acoustic piano). Figures 6-23 and 6-24 show the basic voicings and fingerings, and then examples with rhythm added to each hand.

Figure 6-23:
I, IV, and V
chords
played in
a pianistic
style.

Illustration by Jerry Kovarsky

Check out Track 59 to hear the blues progression played in a two-handed, pianistic fashion.

Figure 6-24:
Doo-wop chords played in a pianistic style.

Illustration by Jerry Kovarsky

Listen to Track 60 to hear the doo-wop progression played in a two-handed, pianistic fashion.

Playing Songs with Chords

The songs in this section give you some experience adding chords to familiar songs. As you play the songs, try to identify the chords as you play them in the left hand and match them to the chord symbols written above the treble staff. First locate the chord root, then the third, fifth, and seventh (if included). If you notice any chord inversions, see how they affect the chord progression and melody.

✔ **"Down by the Station" (Track 61):** This song lets you play a few major chords with your left hand. If you play along with the audio track, you'll notice that it plays both the chords and the melody. You can play the left hand part by itself until you get comfortable with the shape of the chords in your hand. Then add the melody.

- ✔ **"Sometimes I Feel Like a Motherless Child" (Track 62):** This spiritual gives you practice playing minor chords and a couple of major chords, too. It also has some chord inversions, so if you need to brush up on inversions, review the previous section.

- ✔ **"Lullaby" (Track 63):** You'll find all kinds of seventh chords in all kinds of music, from classical to pop. Johannes Brahms's famous "Lullaby" is an example of how seventh chords can create a little harmonic variety. Just don't let it lull you to sleep.

- ✔ **"Scarborough Fair" (Track 64):** This song is in a minor key — D minor. It gives you a chance to play chords in your left hand based on the chord symbols. If you have trouble building the chords, review the sections on major and minor chords earlier in this chapter. The bass clef staff is left open for you to write in the notes of each chord.

- ✔ **"Red River Valley" (Track 65):** This song calls for lots of chord inversions. It has triads and seventh chords along with first, second, and third inversions and a few garden-variety root position chords. Notice how the left hand plays half-note chords, with a few quarter-note changes in important places. You can change the inversion of a chord when the chord symbols are infrequent, as in this folk song.

Down by the Station

Sometimes I Feel Like a Motherless Child

Book III

Beginning to Play

Lullaby

Scarborough Fair

Book IV

Refining Your Technique and Exploring Styles

a

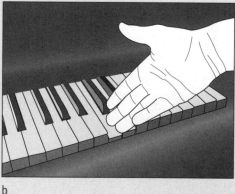

b

c

d

Contents at a Glance

Chapter 1: Adding Effects and Flair to Your Piano Playing 283

Dynamically Speaking...283
Articulate the Positive..286
Control the Tempo 288
Pedal Power 289
Touching on Grace Notes 292
Just Trillin'...294
Don't Miss the Gliss..295
Trembling Tremolos 297
Dressing Up Your Songs 299

Chapter 2: Getting into the Groove 305

Great Left-Hand Accompaniment Patterns..................................305
Applying Great Intros and Finales 315
Playing Songs with Left-Hand Grooves 322

Chapter 3: Going Classical 325

Counterpoint as a Classical Revelation 327
Sussing Out the Sonata 328
Rounding Up the Rondo 331
Figuring Out the Fugue 332
Combining Forms into a Symphony 333
Observing Other Classical Forms 334

Chapter 4: Perusing Popular Genres and Forms. 337

Feeling the Blues 337
Having Fun with Rock and Pop..344
Pop! Goes the Piano...347
A Little Bit Country..348
Improvising with Jazz..350
Soul Searching..353

Chapter 1

Adding Effects and Flair to Your Piano Playing

In This Chapter

▶ Experimenting with volume and emphasis

▶ Employing pedals for different effects

▶ Adding flair with grace notes, trills, and tremolos

▶ Access the audio tracks at www.dummies.com/go/pianokeyboardaio/

*P*laying the right notes and rhythms of a song is important, but how you play is even more important. Playing music with feeling, technique, and passion makes a performance worth listening to. Dressing up the music and making it your own takes more than just playing the notes. And throwing in a few special effects doesn't hurt, either.

Dazzling effects and techniques in your music keep the audience listening, sometimes even on the edges of their seats. With a little practice, all these effects are easy. And when you add them to the right spots in the music, your playing comes alive and you sound like a real pro.

Note: This chapter is mainly applicable to the piano, not to the electronic keyboard. Adding effects and flair to your keyboard playing is, to put it mildly, an entirely different ball game. Check out the chapters in Book VI for a whole lot more about that.

Dynamically Speaking

How loud you should play depends 5 percent on what the composer wants and 95 percent on how close your neighbors live. The composer usually requests that certain notes be played at certain volumes. Your neighbor usually requests that all notes be played in a sound-proofed box. These varying degrees of volume give the music a different dynamic. And that's exactly what volume levels are called in music: *dynamics*.

As with TVs, car stereos, and crying babies, the world of volume has a wide range: from very soft to very loud. Composers are quick to realize this and tell performers exactly where to play in the volume spectrum. Of course, to make things a bit fancier, all dynamics in music are Italian words.

Starting with basic volume changes

When you talk about volume, you say something is loud or soft. This kind of description is always a good starting point. From there you can explain *how* loud or *how* soft. Music uses the same principle: You start with two little Italian words, *piano* (soft) and *forte* (loud), to describe the volume of notes.

The piano itself, formally known as the *pianoforte,* derives its name from the ability to play soft and loud. Why the name has been shortened to "soft" probably has something to do with cranky landlords.

By writing *piano* or *forte* under a melody line (called a *dynamic marking*), a composer tells you to play certain notes soft or loud. Many years and inkwells later, abbreviations for these words are now the norm. You see soft and loud marked simply as *p* and *f,* written in fancy, stylized fonts.

When you see a dynamic marking, whatever the requested volume may be, you continue to play at this volume level until you see a new dynamic marking.

Try basic dynamics out with a tune. Figure 1-1 has two phrases from "Hickory Dickory Dock" marked *piano* and *forte.* Bring out the dynamic contrast as you play it.

Figure 1-1:
Dynamic contrasts of *piano* and *forte.*

Widening the range

If soft and loud were the only volume levels available, stereos and audio players would just have two volume buttons. But, as you know, anywhere you turn the volume knob or slider gives you a variety of volume levels: "kind of soft," "not very loud," you name it. Rather than keep track of some more highly descriptive but long Italian words, you need only remember one abbreviation for the in-between volumes: *m*, which stands for *mezzo* (medium). Place this word before *piano* or *forte*, and you get two more shades of volume.

For extreme volumes like "very soft" and "insanely loud," just throw a few more *p*s or *f*s together. The more you have, the more you play. That is, *pp* means "very soft." The written word isn't *piano-piano*, though. Instead, you use the Italian suffix *-issimo*, loosely translated as "very," and you end up with *pianissimo*. The symbol *ff* would be "very loud," or *fortissimo*.

Gather all these words, abbreviations, and suffixes together and you get the list of dynamic ranges shown in Table 1-1.

Table 1-1	Dynamic Markings	
Abbreviation	*Name*	*How the Note Sounds*
ppp	*Pianississimo*	Almost inaudible
pp	*Pianissimo*	Very quiet
p	*Piano*	Soft
mp	*Mezzo piano*	Not too soft
mf	*Mezzo forte*	Kinda loud
f	*Forte*	Loud
ff	*Fortissimo*	Very loud
fff	*Fortississimo*	Ridiculously loud

Making gradual shifts in volume

Two dynamic symbols that you encounter quite often are those that tell you to gradually play louder or gradually play softer. These symbols look like bird beaks. A bird gets louder as it opens its beak; softer as it closes its beak. So, with this marvelous Audubon analogy, check out Figure 1-2 and see if you can tell what the chicken scratchings mean.

Figure 1-2: Indications of gradual volume changes.

To gradually play louder is a *crescendo;* to gradually play softer is a *diminuendo.* Composers opposed to using the bird beak symbols in their music write out these Italian words or use the abbreviations *cres.* and *dim.*

Whether they appear as words, abbreviations, or symbols, these instructions are almost always preceded and followed by dynamic markings that tell you to play from volume A gradually to volume B. Maybe the composer wants you to gradually go from very soft *(pp)* to very loud *(ff)*, or perhaps the music indicates a subtle change from *mezzo piano (mp)* to *mezzo forte (mf)*. Whatever the case, it's up to you to decide how to play these volume changes.

Sometimes the composer asks you to increase and then decrease the volume in sort of an up-and-down effect. Many musicians call this dynamic marking, shown in Figure 1-3, a *hairpin* because of how it looks.

Figure 1-3:
Get loud, get soft, get dynamic.

To play more dynamics right now, skip to the "Dressing Up Your Songs" section at the end of the chapter and play "Polovtsian Dance."

Why even bother with volume changes? Why not just play everything really loudly so everyone can hear? That approach works fairly well for some heavy metal guitar anthems, but with piano music the subtle degrees of volume show off your ability to convey emotion in your playing.

Articulate the Positive

Articulating when you play refers to the way you play each note. The various ways to play a note are called *articulations,* or *attacks,* which may imply a little more force than necessary, so the less-combative word is used here.

Interpreting articulation symbols

Articulations come in all shapes. Each is represented by a symbol that tells you how to play the note: accented, long, short, and so on. You can change the entire sound and style of a song by changing even just a few articulations. Table 1-2 shows you the symbols that composers use to indicate the various articulations.

Table 1-2		Musical Articulations
Symbol	**Name**	**How to Play the Note**
•	Staccato	Short
—	Tenuto	Long
>	Accent	Hard
∧	Accent (Housetop)	Harder
>•	Accent with staccato	Hard and short
≥	Accent with tenuto	Hard and long

To add these articulations to music, the composer just places the appropriate symbol right underneath or right above the note.

In addition to the symbols in Table 1-2, which apply to only one note, composers use an articulation marking that applies to a group of notes. In music, a *slur* is a curved line over two or more notes of different pitches that indicates that the notes should be played *legato,* or connected in a smooth manner. Think of playing the notes within a slur as if they're being sung by someone with a beautiful voice.

Be careful not to mistake a *tie* for a *slur.* A slur is applied to notes of different pitch and often groups many notes in a melodic phrase. A tie is also a curved line, but it connects one notehead to another notehead of the same pitch. Slurs start and end near the notehead or the stem, as shown in Figure 1-4, a bit of "O Sole Mio."

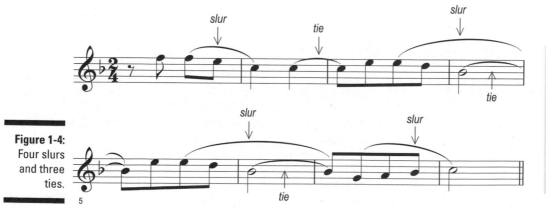

Figure 1-4: Four slurs and three ties.

Book IV

Refining Your Technique and Exploring Styles

The power of articulation

If you play music without articulations, you can forget about pleasing your audience. Listening to music without articulations is like suffering through a speech given in a monotone voice. Boring.

To understand the importance of articulation, try playing a bit of the melody of "Camptown Races" using articulation markings (see Figure 1-5). Then play it again without the articulations — just ignore them. You should be able to tell that it has more verve and personality with articulations than without.

Figure 1-5:
Giving a melody some individual character with articulations.

If a piece of music doesn't already have articulations, choose articulations that you think may fit the music and apply them. Pencil in your own articulations and see how the music sounds your way. It's not like you're changing the melody, just the style. Of course, following the composer's articulations (when they exist) is always your best bet for achieving the sound and style the composer intended — if that's your goal.

For a complete version of "Camptown Races" with more articulations right now, skip to the section "Dressing Up Your Songs" at the end of the chapter.

Control the Tempo

Just as you can shade your music with dynamics, you can make subtle variations to the tempo. The tempo marking at the beginning of a song tells you how fast to play the song. As a rule of thumb, your goal should always be to keep steady time without unintentionally slowing down or speeding up. But there are times when you *do* intend to slow down or speed up. Time in music is flexible in this way: You can change tempo very slightly or quite dramatically when the music calls for it.

Not surprisingly, musical words and symbols exist to tell you what to do and how much to do it. Of course the words are usually in Italian. Here are the three most important indications you need to know:

- **Accelerando:** When the composer wants you to put some speed on, you'll see this word or its abbreviation, *accel.* It means accelerate!

- **Ritardando:** When the composer wants you to slow down, you'll see this word or its abbreviation, *rit.*

- **Fermata:** The symbol ⌒ stands for *fermata.* When you see it, pause or hold the note(s) under the fermata and stop counting time. There's no rule governing how long you should hold a fermata — the composer intentionally leaves that to the performer's discretion. A good starting point is to hold the note(s) under the fermata for twice as long as its written value.

Figure 1-6 shows the melody to "For He's a Jolly Good Fellow," which illustrates these tempo changes. In a typically playful rendition of the song, you naturally slow down and hold the highest note, and maybe speed up for the final phrase.

Figure 1-6: Playing around with tempo.

Pedal Power

Book I Chapter 5 talks about the pedals that come with acoustic and digital pianos. This section tells you a bit more about how to use these to assist the dynamics and articulations when you play, adding to the ways you can dress up your music.

Book IV

Refining Your Technique and Exploring Styles

Using the damper pedal

When piano players talk about using the pedal, they usually mean using the *damper pedal,* which is the one on the right as you sit at a piano. Because the damper pedal allows the notes to sustain after your fingers release the keys, it's often called the *sustain pedal.*

There are a few different ways to indicate when to put the pedal down, when to lift it, and when to make a quick up-down pedal change. As Figure 1-7 shows, the abbreviation *Ped.* tells you when to put the pedal down. Keep the pedal down until the asterisk or the end bracket of the pedal line. A notch in the pedal line indicates a pedal change: Lift your foot enough to allow the pedal to clear, and then press the pedal down again.

Figure 1-7:
Pedaling
indications.

The best way to learn how to pedal is to just try it out as you play. Although all damper pedals have the same function, each instrument can have its own pedal personality, and just as you adjust to the accelerator and brake system of a car, you have to try out a damper pedal to get a good feel for it.

The most important thing about pedaling is simply not to overuse it. Things can get blurry in a hurry, and for the listener your song with too much pedal can become the aural equivalent of runny makeup. Listen carefully to the music as you play to hear it as others hear it.

At its most basic function, the damper pedal connects one melody note or chord to the next where there would be a break in the sound without using the pedal. Play Figure 1-8, and use the pedal to connect the first note of the melody to the second, and so on. Then play the excerpt again without the pedal. You'll hear that the two-note phrases don't sound nearly as smooth as the first version because you have to lift your hands to move to the next note, resulting in breaks between the notes within a slur.

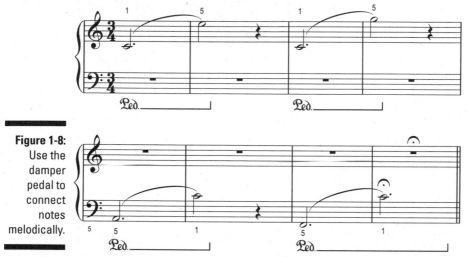

Figure 1-8:
Use the damper pedal to connect notes melodically.

Use the pedal to help your music sound smoother *(legato),* hold a note or a chord for a long time, or give your music a more resonant quality.

Hard facts on soft-pedaling

When the composer wants you to use the soft pedal, which is on the far left as you sit at the piano, you see the indication *una corda.* When you see the indication *tre corda,* you release the soft pedal.

You can use the soft pedal anytime you like, of course, to play quietly or to create a hushed atmosphere or an intimate feeling. Try it out on the lullaby "All Through the Night" in Figure 1-9.

Book IV

Refining Your Technique and Exploring Styles

Figure 1-9:
Create a
soft sound
with the soft
pedal.

The pedal in the middle

Depending on the kind of piano you're playing, the middle pedal can have two different functions.

✔ **The sostenuto pedal:** The traditional grand piano has a pedal that acts like a damper pedal *for only the note or notes your fingers are playing when you press the pedal down.* For example, you play a big bass note, put the middle pedal down, and then noodle some staccato upper-register filigree, with the bass note sounding throughout, thanks to the sostenuto pedal.

✔ **The practice pedal:** Many upright pianos have a practice pedal between the soft pedal and the damper pedal. This pedal mutes the strings, allowing you to hear what you play but softening the sound quite a bit. The practice pedal has a notch at the opening where you can lock the pedal into position with your foot as you play with the muted setting.

Touching on Grace Notes

The term *grace note* sounds pretty fancy, but grace notes are actually a very simple effect that can make your music sound more complex. A grace note is a note that you play just slightly before a real note. You might think of it as a *graze* note, because your finger just grazes the grace note before playing the real note.

Grace notes are written in different ways. Figure 1-10 shows the most common types of grace notes. A single grace note looks like a small eighth note with a slash through it. Think of the slash as meaning "cancel the rhythmic value." Multiple grace notes look like small sixteenth notes. You play them very quickly, so it sounds like you're rolling into the main note.

Figure 1-10:
Amazing grace notes, how sweet the sound.

You don't always have to play grace notes super-fast. The character and effect of a grace note is determined by the tempo and style of the music. The idea is to use a grace note to give its main note a little lift.

To hear some grace notes in action, listen to Track 66 as you follow along with the music to the rousing classic "Pop! Goes the Weasel," which is just bursting with grace notes (see Figure 1-11).

Figure 1-11:
This weasel pops with the help of some grace notes.

Book IV

Refining Your Technique and Exploring Styles

Grace notes are a common feature of blues, jazz, country, and classical piano music styles. Heck, you can use grace notes anywhere you like. The best grace notes are those that are a half step or whole step away from the full melodic note, but feel free to try ones that are even farther apart. Beginning a song's melody with a grace note is an excellent idea, especially if the song is in the jazz or blues style.

Just Trillin'

If you've ever heard the sound of a piccolo twittering high above the band in a John Phillip Sousa march, you've heard the effect of a *trill*. What sounds like a very elaborate trick for the piccolo player is actually a very simple procedure of alternating between two notes in rapid succession. The same holds true for trills in piano music.

What does a trill sound like? (You mean the piccolo metaphor isn't good enough for you?) A trill sounds like a bunch of 32nd or 64th notes, as shown in Figure 1-12. Trills add a certain classical finesse to your playing style.

Figure 1-12: What a trill sounds like.

To save the time and ink required to write all those darn beams, composers use a shorthand symbol for trills: They write a *tr* above the trilled note. You know — *tr* as in the first two letters of *trill*. Sometimes music isn't so complicated.

Generally speaking, a note is trilled upward to the note a whole step above the main note. However, sometimes a composer wants a downward trill or even a half-step trill, and writes the specific note to be used in the trill in one of several ways (see Figure 1-13).

Figure 1-13: Simon says, "Trill this note."

(Trill C to D)   (Trill C to C♯)   (Trill C to B)   (Trill C to D)   (Trill C to B♭)

In addition to the *tr* abbreviation, the composer can write a sharp or flat sign, which tells you to trill to the note's sharp or to the note's flat. Another way of notating the trill is to write the specific trilled note as a small, stemless notehead in parentheses next to the original note.

To play some trills yourself, skip to the section "Dressing Up Your Songs" at the end of this chapter and play "Trumpet Voluntary."

Don't wait for the composer to give you permission to trill — add trills yourself. Find a note you think would sound good played as a trill and write *tr* above it. Half notes and whole notes are usually the best ones to trill because they're long enough to allow you time to get those fingers fluttering. Experiment with half-step and whole-step trills in different directions.

Don't Miss the Gliss

A *glissando* (also known as a *gliss* in this lazy music industry) is a fast slide across several keys on the keyboard. There's nothing quite like starting and ending a song with this effect. It will dazzle any audience.

To try a right-hand gliss, put your thumb on a high C note and drag your thumbnail down across the keys very quickly all the way to the bottom of the keyboard. Cool, huh?

Figure 1-14 shows you how composers notate this effect, which is generally with a wavy line and the abbreviation *gliss* going from the starting note in the direction of the gliss. For example, if you see a wavy line going up from C, play the note C and slide up the keyboard. Sometimes the specific ending note is shown at the other end of the wavy line; other times, it's up to you to decide where to stop.

Figure 1-14:
Gliss me,
gliss me,
now you
gotta
kiss me.

(Slide quickly from F to F)

(Slide quickly from C to C)

(Slide from C to your choice)

Sometimes the composer specifies both the beginning *and* ending notes of the gliss — for that, just practice, practice, practice. Starting on a specific note is easy, but stopping on the right note is like trying to stop a car on a dime. Sometimes you can use your other hand to play the final note if it's not busy playing something else.

Depending on the direction of the gliss and the hand you use, different fingers do the job. Figure 1-15 shows you the correct hand positions for each glissando:

- ✔ **Downward with right hand:** Gliss with the nail of your thumb (RH 1), as shown in Figure 1-15a.

- ✔ **Upward with right hand:** Gliss with the nail of your middle finger (RH 3) and perhaps a little help from RH 4, as shown in Figure 1-15b.

Book IV

**Refining
Your
Technique
and
Exploring
Styles**

- **Downward with left hand:** Gliss with the nail of your middle finger (LH 3) and perhaps a little help from LH 4, as shown in Figure 1-15c.

- **Upward with left hand:** Gliss with the nail of your thumb (LH 1), as shown in Figure 1-15d.

After raking your fingers across the keys several times, your fingers may start hurting. If so, you're using the wrong part of your finger to gliss; when done properly, a glissando shouldn't hurt. Make sure you're using your *fingernail,* and above all, don't play a gliss with your fingertips. Not only can this cause a blister, but the squeaking sound is worse than nails on a chalkboard.

Try playing a downward and an upward gliss in Figure 1-16, a Jerry Lee Lewis-inspired number. The effect of a glissando is altogether powerful, energetic, and just plain rocking.

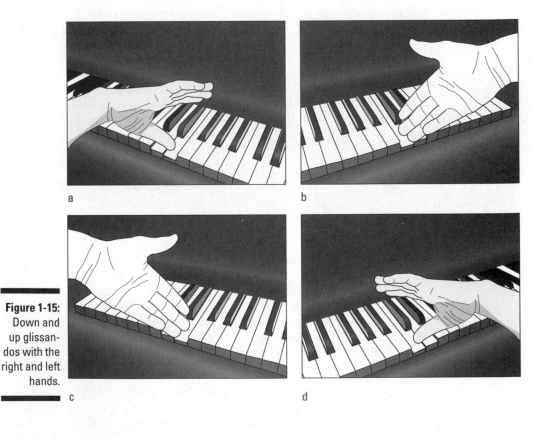

Figure 1-15:
Down and up glissandos with the right and left hands.

Figure 1-16: Use a RH gliss to begin and end a song.

Trembling Tremolos

As mentioned, a trill occurs when you flutter your fingers very quickly between two notes that are close together, either a half step or whole step apart. So, what do you call fluttering between two notes that are farther apart? You can call it whatever you want, but the music world calls it a *tremolo*.

To play a tremolo, pick an interval — anything larger than a whole step — and alternate playing the two notes as quickly as possible. Like a trill, a tremolo sounds as if you're playing a bunch of 32nd or 64th notes. But unlike the notation for a trill, which just puts *tr* above one note, the notation for a tremolo actually shows you both notes that your fingers rumble between.

In Figure 1-17, you see that the two notes of a tremolo have the same note length. At first glance, this notation looks like there are too many beats in

Book IV

Refining Your Technique and Exploring Styles

each measure, but the three diagonal lines between the notes signal that this is a tremolo and therefore the two notes share the note length. You only count the beats of the first note.

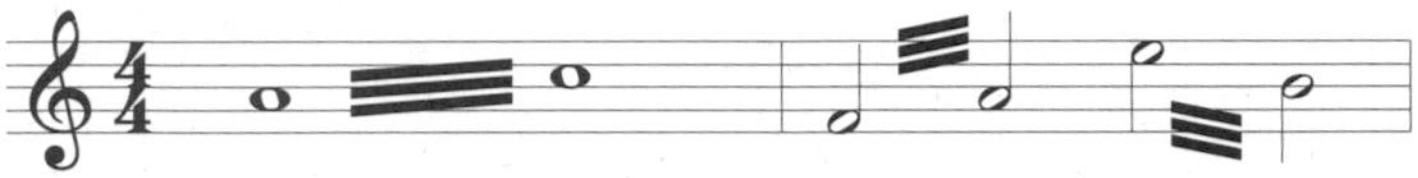

Figure 1-17:
Tremolo
notation.

You can also play tremolo chords. All you do is break the chord into two parts: a bottom note and the remaining top notes. Shake the chord into a tremolo by alternating between the two parts as quickly as possible. Tremolo chords may look intimidating, but if you can play the chord, you can play the tremolo.

Figure 1-18 gives you a chance to play a few tremolo chords. For the first measure, put your hand in position for a G major chord and rock between the top notes (B and D) and the bottom note (G) very quickly. Move to the next measure and do the same with a second inversion C chord, and so on.

Working under the hood

In the 20th century, many composers and pianists became bored with the normal sounds of a piano. No longer satisfied by the effects of trills, glissandi, and tremolos, these brave (and misunderstood) pioneers started tinkering around under the piano lid.

Try it yourself. Open your piano lid and pluck the strings with your fingernail. Now try a gliss across all the strings while holding down the sustain pedal. The sound is mysterious and a bit creepy.

Composers like Henry Cowell and John Cage didn't stop there. Oh, no. They began writing pieces that incorporated these sounds, asking the player to pluck certain notes on the inside of the piano. And you think playing the black and white keys is hard! Pushing the limits even further, a phenomenon called *prepared piano* became quite popular (and still is) with modern composers. A myriad of new sounds were

created by inserting various objects between the piano strings — screws, yarn, pillows, and so on.

Hardware between the strings can damage your expensive piano. If you really want to experience these sounds the right way, check out the following recordings:

✔ *The Banshee,* **Henry Cowell:** Among other things, you hear strumming or plucking of the piano strings.

✔ *Airplane Sonata,* **George Antheil:** A number of strange piano effects are evident in this eclectic piece.

✔ *Tabula rasa,* **Arvo Pärt:** The piano is prepared with screws between the strings.

✔ *The Firm Soundtrack,* **Dave Grusin:** This piece uses all types of things on the piano, including a violin bow playing across the strings.

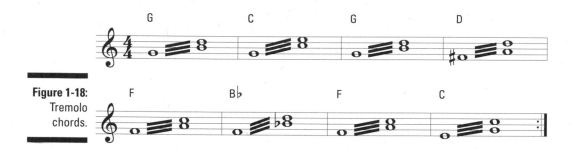

Figure 1-18:
Tremolo
chords.

Tremolo chords come in handy when playing rock and roll, especially as part of a band. A tremolo turns the otherwise dull task of playing straight chords into a sizzling rhythmic romp.

Dressing Up Your Songs

This section lets you cut loose with the dynamics, articulations, ornamentations, and other fancy techniques that let you dress up your music. For each song, a few tips and the techniques used are noted. Let 'er rip!

- ✔ **"Polovtsian Dance" (Track 67):** This haunting melody by Alexander Borodin is perfect for adding some dynamic shading. Follow the volume indications and hairpins and get as much as you can out of the *pianos* and *fortes*.

- ✔ **"Camptown Races" (Track 68):** Go hog-wild with the articulation markings on this song. Define each and every staccato, tenuto, and accent to give the song a strong shape.

- ✔ **"Trumpet Voluntary" (Track 69):** Listen to Jeremiah Clarke's famous "Trumpet Voluntary" on Track 64 to get an idea of how it should sound. Then try it yourself. Each trill starts on the note D, played with RH 2, and trills upward to E (the next highest scale tone), played with RH 3. Alternate very rapidly between these two notes while counting the number of beats required for the trill, a dotted quarter note. The squiggly line following the *tr* tells you how long to keep trillin'.

- ✔ **"Also Sprach Zarathustra" (Track 70):** Tremolos of any size sound great played by either hand. Probably the most popular left-hand tremolo is the octave tremolo. Stretch your hand over a C octave and let this interval rumble in a familiar melody. You may recognize this piece as the theme to the movie *2001: A Space Odyssey*.

- ✔ **"Quiet Sunset" (Track 71):** Follow the damper pedal indications when you play this piece to create smooth connections between melody notes and between successive chords. Practice pedaling from one note to the next during the melodic phrases and from one chord to the next during the chordal phrases, and listen for smooth, unbroken lines.

Book IV

Refining Your Technique and Exploring Styles

Polovtsian Dance

Camptown Races

Trumpet Voluntary

Also Sprach Zarathustra

Quiet Sunset

Chapter 2

Getting into the Groove

. . . .

In This Chapter

▶ Mastering accompaniment patterns for your left hand

▶ Finding new ways to begin and end a masterpiece

▶ Access the audio tracks at www.dummies.com/go/pianokeyboardaio/

. . . .

Want to make even a simple song like "Row, Row, Row Your Boat" into a showstopper? This is the chapter for you. This chapter helps you apply a handful of tricks and techniques to just about any song you encounter in your piano career. Whether it's an attention-grabbing intro or finale, a cool accompaniment pattern, or just a nice little riff thrown in, the tricks in this chapter help you to spice up your music.

Great Left-Hand Accompaniment Patterns

One of the most important tools for your bag of tricks is a good supply of left-hand accompaniment patterns. Any time you're faced with playing straight chords or even playing melodies from a fake book (which pretty much just gives the chord names), you're left to your own resources to supply an interesting-sounding bass line.

Fret not. Look no further. Put away the antacid tablets. This section gives you excellent and professional-sounding left-hand patterns that you can apply to just about any song you come across. Each of these patterns is versatile and user-friendly. This section shows you when you can apply the pattern to a 3/4 as well as a 4/4 meter.

TIP

It's important to practice these patterns again and again to master the right notes and the way each pattern feels under your fingers. After a while, though, you can ignore the printed music and just try to feel the pattern: the distance between the intervals, the shape of the chord, the rhythm, and so on. The more comfortable you are with the pattern, the more easily you can apply it to any key, any chord, and any scale.

Fixed and broken chords

The easiest left-hand accompaniment is chords, whether you play them as straight chords or arpeggios. Start with the basic chords and find inversions that work well for you without requiring your left hand to move all over the keyboard. (Turn to Book III Chapter 6 for more on chords, arpeggios, and inversions.) Also, you should experiment with various rhythmic patterns. For example, try playing quarter-note chords instead of whole-note chords. Or try a dotted quarter and eighth-note pattern.

PLAY THIS!

In Figure 2-1 (Track 72) the left hand plays a simple chord progression with several different rhythmic patterns. Play these a few times and decide which rhythmic pattern works, sounds, and feels best to you.

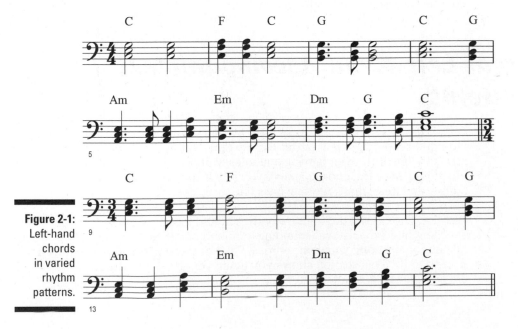

Figure 2-1:
Left-hand chords in varied rhythm patterns.

You can change the texture and add some variety with a constant arpeggiated pattern in the left hand. For every chord symbol in Figure 2-2 (Track 73), use the root, fifth, and octave notes of the chord's scale to form an up-and-down pattern throughout the song. This pattern works for fast or slow songs.

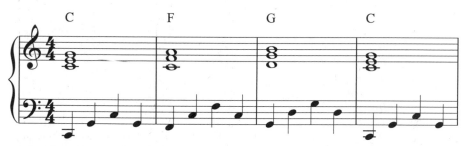

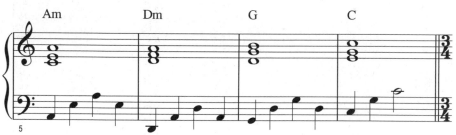

Figure 2-2: Root-fifth-octave patterns are easy to play and sound great.

Book IV

Refining Your Technique and Exploring Styles

To play a song using the left-hand accompaniment in Figure 2-2 right now, skip to the end of the chapter and play "Love Me Like You Used To."

Chord picking

Left-hand *chord picking* is a style well suited to country music. But even if you aren't a fan of that genre, you can apply this pattern to just about any song you like.

Most chords are made up of a root note, a third interval, and a fifth interval. You need to know these three elements to be a successful chord-picker.

To play this pattern, break a chord into two units: the root note and two top notes. Play the root note on beat 1 and the top two notes together on beat 2. To make it sound even more impressive, do something a little different on beat 3: Play the fifth of the chord by itself but one octave Lower.

Now try playing this pattern in the piece "Picking and Grinning" (see Figure 2-3, Track 74). After you get the feel of this bouncy rhythmic pattern, you won't even need to look at your hands. Your pinky will find the two alternating bass notes because they're always the same distance from the root.

Octave hammering

This easy (if tiring) left-handed groove is really fun and easy if your right hand is just playing chords. But if you're playing a melody or something more complicated than chords with your right hand, this pattern may not be a practical choice.

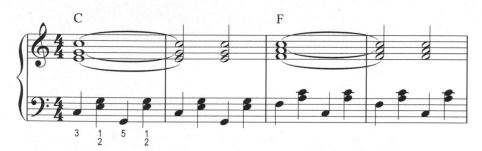

Figure 2-3:
Left-hand
chord
picking in
"Picking
and
Grinning."

Book IV

**Refining
Your
Technique
and
Exploring
Styles**

To hammer out some octaves, you simply prepare your left hand in an open *octave position,* with your pinky and thumb ready on the two notes, and make sure your wrist is loose enough to bounce a bit with the appropriate rhythm. When the chord changes, keep your hand in octave position as you move directly to the next set of octaves. You can play the octaves using any rhythm that sounds good to you — try whole notes, half notes, even eighth notes, depending on the rhythmic character of the song.

"Octaves in the Left" (see Figure 2-4, Track 75) lets you roll out some octaves.

Figure 2-4:
Hammer out
octaves in
"Octaves in
the Left."

As you become more familiar with harmony, you can add to these left-hand octave patterns with octaves built on the notes of the chord. For example, the octaves in "Jumping Octaves" (see Figure 2-5, Track 76) move from the root note to the third interval note to the fifth interval note for each right-hand chord.

Bouncy rock patterns

In addition to slamming octaves, a nice rock and roll-sounding bass pattern may use other intervals drawn from scale notes.

Figure 2-5:
Build
octaves on
different
chord notes
in "Jumping
Octaves."

You can create a great bass pattern using the octave, the fifth, and the sixth intervals of each chord. Try this rockin' accompaniment along with "Rockin' Intervals" (see Figure 2-6, Track 77). You can modify the pattern to fit a two- or one-measure pattern in 4/4 meter. After a few times through, your hands will know what to do, and you can apply the pattern to any major chord.

Book IV

**Refining
Your
Technique
and
Exploring
Styles**

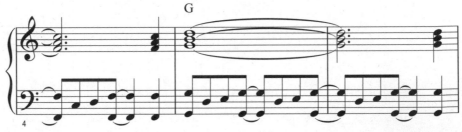

Figure 2-6:
A driving
left-hand
pattern
with the
octave, fifth,
and sixth
intervals
in "Rockin'
Intervals."

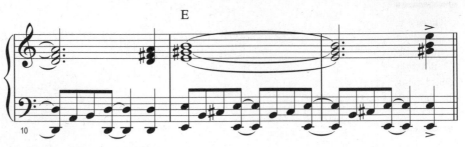

The great Chuck Berry made the locomotive-sounding pattern demonstrated in "Berry-Style Blues" (see Figure 2-7, Track 78) very popular on the guitar. It was only a matter of time before some trail-blazing pianist adapted this guitar pattern to the piano. All you have to do is alternate between playing an open fifth and an open sixth on every beat.

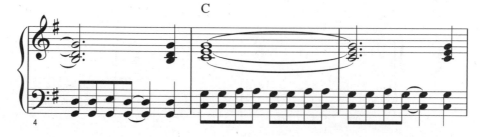

Book IV

Refining Your Technique and Exploring Styles

Figure 2-7: Open intervals that chug along in "Berry-Style Blues."

Melodic bass lines

Some left-hand patterns are so widely used that they're better known than the melodies they accompany. "Bum-ba-di-da" (see Figure 2-8, Track 79) is one such pattern that was made famous by Roy Rogers in his show-closing song, "Happy Trails." All you need are three notes from each chord's scale: the root, the fifth, and the sixth. Play them back and forth, over and over.

Figure 2-8:
Mosey
along with
the bum-ba-
di-da bass
pattern.

To play a song with the bum-ba-di-da bass line right now, jump to the later section "Playing Songs with Left-Hand Grooves" and play "Country Riffin'."

Another melodic left-hand pattern played by every pianist from novice to pro is the "boogie-woogie" bass line. It doesn't even need a melody. This bass line uses notes from a major scale but lowers the seventh note of the scale a half step (also called a *flatted seventh*) to give you that bluesy sound.

For each new chord in the boogie-woogie bass line (see Figure 2-9, Track 80), you play the following scale notes up the keys and then back down: root, third, fifth, sixth, flatted seventh.

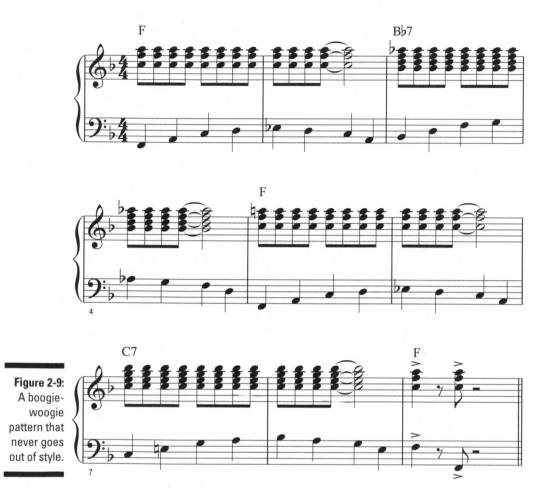

Figure 2-9:
A boogie-
woogie
pattern that
never goes
out of style.

Applying Great Intros and Finales

A good pianist should always be able to begin and end a piece in an interesting way. You can join the ranks of good pianists by filing away some stock intros and finales (sometimes called *outros*) you can apply to any piece of music at any given time. An intro or finale is your time to shine, so milk it for all it's worth.

Few things are more fun than playing a great intro or finale. Heck, some of them sound great alone, without a song attached.

Book IV

Refining
Your
Technique
and
Exploring
Styles

Most of the intros and finales in this section are geared toward popular music. When it comes to classical music, the composer usually gives you an appropriate beginning and ending. Of course, if you really want to fire up Chopin's *Minute Waltz,* you can always add one of these intros.

You can add the intros and finales in this section to virtually any piece of music. Just follow these steps:

1. **Check the song's style.**

   Each intro and finale has a different style or sound. Consider the style of the song you're playing and choose an intro that works best with it. For example, a rock and roll intro may not sound very good attached to a soft country ballad. But, then again, anything's possible in music.

2. **Check the song's key.**

   All the intros and finales you find in this book are written in the key of C. If the song you want to play is also in the key of C, you're ready to go. If not, adjust the notes and chords of the intro and finale you choose to correspond with the song's key by using the helpful hints shown with each intro and finale.

3. **Check the song's first chord.**

   All the intros I show you transition easily into the first chords or notes of a song, provided that the song begins with a chord built on the first tone of the scale. (Book III Chapter 6 explains these types of chords.) For example, if the song you're playing is in the key of C and begins with a C major chord, any of the intros here work perfectly because they're written in the key of C. If your song starts with a different chord, use the hints provided with each intro to adjust the chord accordingly.

4. **Check the song's last chord.**

   Like intros, you can tack the finales onto the end of a song if the song ends with a chord built on the first tone of the scale (and most songs do). For example, if the song you're playing is in the key of C and ends with a C major chord, you'll have no problem with one of these finales because they're written in the key of C. If your song ends with a different chord, you need to adjust the finale to the appropriate key.

Adjusting the intros and finales into different keys involves a lot of transposing work. If you're just starting out with the piano, only apply these intros and finales to songs in the key of C. (This book includes many such songs.) When you're ready to apply an intro or finale to a song of a different key, check out which note of the scale it starts on and try to match the interval patterns in the new key.

The big entrance

When the singer needs a good intro, who's going to play it? The drummer? Probably not. You are. And it can't be any old intro — it's gotta be good. The audience has a tendency to talk between songs, so it's your job to shut 'em up and announce the start of the new song. Playing a few bars of show-stopping, original material really gets things hopping and leaves them begging for more.

The "Get Ready, Here We Go" intro

The intro in Figure 2-10 (Track 81) is bound to grab the audience's attention. It has been used in just about every style of music, from vaudeville to ragtime to Broadway. Hear it once and you'll never forget it. Play it and you'll be hooked. Just keep repeating the measures between the repeat signs, or *vamp*, until you're ready to start the melody. (Book II Chapter 4 talks about repeat signs and what they do.)

Figure 2-10: Intro #1.

The "Rockin' Jam" intro

You can knock some socks off with a rock and roll intro like the one in Figure 2-11 (Track 82). The triplets are tricky, but you can play this one fast or slow. A slower-tempo version works well with a blues song, and a fast version is good for . . . well, a fast rockin' song. This intro also contains grace notes, which you can read about in Book IV Chapter 1.

The "Sweet Ballad" intro

When a slow ballad is next on the set list, the intro in Figure 2-12 (Track 83) works well. The left-hand part sets up a root-fifth-octave pattern introduced in the earlier section "Fixed and broken chords." The right-hand part makes use of parallel sixths, moving sweetly down the scale.

Book IV

Refining Your Technique and Exploring Styles

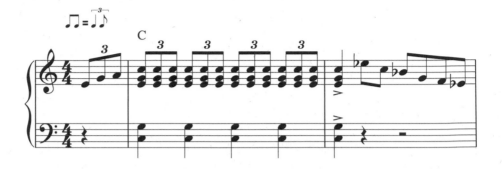

Figure 2-11:
Intro #2.

Figure 2-12:
Intro #3.

The "Killing Time" intro

Sometimes you need to repeat an intro over and over. Perhaps you've forgotten the melody. Perhaps you're waiting for divine inspiration. Or maybe you're waiting for the singer to decide to join you. Whatever the case, you can easily repeat an intro like the one in Figure 2-13 (Track 84) until the time comes to move on. Simply play the first four measures over and over until you're finally ready. You're simply vamping on a G7 chord, which leads you (and the preoccupied singer) into the key of C when you're both ready.

Figure 2-13:
Intro #4.

The "Saloon Salutations" intro

When you're just tinkering around in a piano lounge, perhaps all you need is a few bars of honky-tonk style piano, like the ones in Figure 2-14 (Track 85). Notice how effective the grace notes (measure 1) and tremolos (measure 2) are in this intro.

Figure 2-14:
Intro #5.

Book IV

Refining Your Technique and Exploring Styles

Exit, stage left

The band is building up to the final chord, and it's time for the big finish. The singer belts the last lyric, and it's up to you to drop the curtain. Quick! Grab a handful of these finales and you're sure to receive an encore request.

The "I Loved You, You Left Me" finale

The finale shown in Figure 2-15 (Track 86) is a simple but effective ending, perhaps even a tear-jerker when played with the right emotion. You certainly wouldn't want to use this as an end to a rocking song like "Burning Down the House," but it fits nicely with any major-key ballad (like the one you introduced with Intro #3 in Figure 2-13).

Figure 2-15: Finale #1.

The "Let's Load Up the Bus" finale

After a classic rock jam, something like the finale in Figure 2-16 (Track 87) finishes the song with the appropriate amount of flair. The triplets take you down the C blues scale. They should be played as smoothly as possible, so feel free to slow down the tempo until you conquer the correct fingering. And make sure to really punch that last chord!

Figure 2-16: Finale #2.

The "Last Call" finale

The triplets in the finale of Figure 2-17 (Track 88) give this closer a distinctive feel that works best with a blues or jazz piece. It has the sound of winding down to a halt.

In this finale, you play the notes of chords C, C diminished, Dm7, and C again. You can easily transpose and attach this finale to a song in any key by applying the correct chord types and breaking them up. For example, in the key of G, the chords are G, G diminished, Am7, and G.

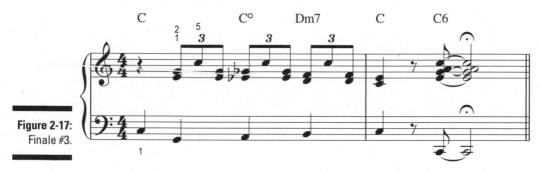

Figure 2-17: Finale #3.

The "Shave and a Haircut" finale

Everyone knows it. Everyone loves it. Very few know how to notate it. How could this section possibly not include the ever-famous "Shave and a Haircut" closer? Figure 2-18 (Track 89) shows you this all-time classic in all its glory. You can play this finale with unison octaves, so the name of each scale note is placed in the middle of the grand staff. With this information, you can buy a shave and a haircut in the key of your choice.

Figure 2-18: Finale #4.

Book IV

Refining Your Technique and Exploring Styles

Playing Songs with Left-Hand Grooves

The songs in this section put together the techniques introduced in this chapter: left-hand accompaniment patterns and intros and finales. You can enjoy the songs on their own and also use them as examples of how to apply these tools to your own songs.

- ✔ **"Country Riffin'" (Track 90):** This little ditty is easy on the fingers but even easier on the ears. The bum-ba-di-da bass line sets the groove and the "Last Call" finale brings the song home. With a sauntering feel that will lighten the mood, it's sure to be a crowd pleaser.

- ✔ **"Love Me Like You Used To" (Track 91):** This song combines a left-hand accompaniment pattern from earlier in this chapter with an intro and finale. The left-hand part sets the root-fifth-octave arpeggiated pattern to a slow-tempo groove that supports the entire song.

Country Riffin'

Book IV

Refining Your Technique and Exploring Styles

Love Me Like You Used To

Chapter 3

Going Classical

. . . .

In This Chapter

▶ Picking up on characteristics of classical piano and keyboard

▶ Understanding counterpoint and how it began

▶ Reviewing classical forms

. . . .

*T*his chapter is a brief introduction to the classical style, an important one for players of piano and keyboard. For a complete treatment on the topic, check out the oldie but goodie, *Classical Music For Dummies* by David Pogue and Scott Speck (Wiley, 1997).

Many people think of *classical* music as old, intellectual, sometimes boring music written by a bunch of dead guys who wore wigs. This may be true (except for the "boring" part), but the sound and feel of classical music is unique. You, too, can apply the sound and feel of classical music to your songs, even ones written in this century.

Figure 3-1 is an excerpt from a classical piano piece by Mozart called *Sonata in C*. Notice the use of arpeggios in the left hand and the trills scattered throughout in the right hand. Then, after introducing the cute little melody, what does he give you? Scales!

Composers like Liszt and Grieg wrote some very dramatic and loud piano music. For example, the opening bars of Grieg's monumental *Piano Concerto* begin with loud, descending octaves, as shown in Figure 3-2.

Figure 3-1: Excerpt from Mozart's *Sonata in C.*

(8va means to play these notes one octave higher than written)

Figure 3-2: Excerpt from Grieg's *Piano Concerto.*

But classical composers could also do soft and sweet, and one way they sweetened their sound was by *rolling their chords.* Liszt, for example, loved to end his odes with a beautiful, soft chord, rolled gently from the bottom note up to the top. The squiggly line next to the chords in Figure 3-3 gets you ready to roll.

Classical pianists to check out

Legends in the classical piano world: Vladimir Horowitz, Alicia de Larrocha, Artur Rubinstein

On today's classical piano playlist: Martha Argerich, Evgeny Kissin, Lang Lang

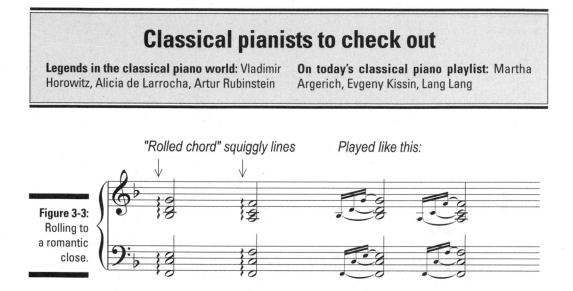

"Rolled chord" squiggly lines   *Played like this:*

Figure 3-3: Rolling to a romantic close.

Counterpoint as a Classical Revelation

During the Golden Age of classical music, from the late 1700s to the mid-1800s, composers were competing viciously with one another to create new and more vibrant types of music. With the adoption of the piano by classical artists, existing ways of playing music could be further developed, including *counterpoint,* which uses both hands to create melody and harmony.

Composers of the period began writing music for the left hand that was just as complicated as the music written for the right. The left-hand music they created often mirrored closely what the right hand had been playing.

Prior to the Classical period, the bass line in most music was limited to simple melodic accompaniment. This limited use of the bass line was a carryover from the music of the Catholic Church, where the organ provided simple bass lines (figured bass) to accompany vocalists.

The invention of counterpoint not only enhanced the melody of musical arrangements, but it also blurred exactly where the melody ended and the harmony began. Almost every classical composer, using all the forms discussed in this chapter, has used counterpoint in his or her own music — even the right-handed ones. Figure 3-4 shows an example of counterpoint.

Book IV

Refining Your Technique and Exploring Styles

Sussing Out the Sonata

The *sonata* was the most popular form used by instrumental composers from the mid-18th century until the beginning of the 20th century. This form is considered by many to be the first true break from the liturgical music that had made such an impact on Western music from the Medieval period on through the Baroque period.

Sonatas are based on the song (ternary) form, ABA, which means they have three defined parts: exposition, development, and recapitulation. (For more on common forms, check out Book III Chapter 4.) The true genius of the sonata is that not only does its structure allow many of the rules of basic music theory to be broken, but it also *encourages* such defiance. With a sonata, it's perfectly allowable to switch to a new key and time signature in the middle of the song. The following sections explain the three parts of a sonata.

Starting with the exposition

The first part of a sonata, called the *exposition,* presents the basic thematic material of the *movement,* or each self-contained part of a piece of music. This part is also often broken up into two thematic parts:

- **First part:** Generally, the first part of the exposition presents the main theme of the song, or the musical "thread" that ties the piece together. This first part usually is the line that sticks the most in your head.

- **Second part:** The second part of the exposition is a "reflection" of the first part, in that it sounds a lot like the first part but is slightly changed.

Put on Beethoven's Sonata in C Minor, Opus 13 to get a good example of these two defined parts, or look at the excerpts shown in Figures 3-5 and 3-6 from the same sonata.

Figure 3-5:
Excerpt from the opening theme, first part, of Beethoven's Sonata in C Minor, Opus 13.

Figure 3-6:
Excerpt from the second part of Sonata in C Minor, Opus 13, which is a reflective theme of the first.

Moving on to something new: Development

The second part of the sonata form, called the *development*, often sounds like it belongs to a completely different piece of music altogether. This part can move through different key signatures and explore musical ideas that are completely different from the original theme.

Book IV

Refining Your Technique and Exploring Styles

Often this part of the sonata is the most exciting. Here you'll find big chords and increased tension with the use of stronger rhythm and greater *interval content* (number of interval steps between each note).

Figure 3-7 shows an excerpt from the development of Sonata in C Minor, Opus 13.

Figure 3-7: Excerpt from the second part, or development, of Beethoven's Sonata in C Minor, Opus 13.

Taking a rest with recapitulation

After the excitement of a sonata's development, it feels natural to come to rest where you began. The third and final part of a sonata is the *recapitulation,* where the composition returns to the original key and the musical theme expressed in the first section and brings it all to a close. Figure 3-8 shows an excerpt of the final movement of Beethoven's Sonata No. 8 in C Minor, Opus 13.

Figure 3-8:
Excerpt
from the
third part of
Beethoven's
Sonata
No. 8 in
C Minor,
Opus 13.

Rounding Up the Rondo

Rondos expand on the freedom of expression inherent in the sonata form by allowing even more disparate sections of music to be joined together by a common musical section. The formula for a rondo is ABACA. Technically, with a rondo you can indefinitely continue adding brand new sections — featuring different keys or time signatures — to a particular piece so long as you keep linking them together with the opening (A) theme. The A section of Mozart's *Rondo Alla Turca* ties more than six different musical ideas together using this form. See Figure 3-9 for an excerpt.

Book IV

**Refining
Your
Technique
and
Exploring
Styles**

Figure 3-9:
Excerpt
from the A
section of
Mozart's
*Rondo Alla
Turca.*

Figuring Out the Fugue

Another major musical form to come out of the Classical period was the
fugue, the form fully developed by Bach in the Baroque era. A fugue is a
highly evolved form of imitative counterpoint, in which two (or more) musical lines use the same theme, either at the same pitch or transposed. Fugues
are defined by the way the notes in the treble clef and the notes in the bass
clef switch off carrying the main theme and driving the rhythm of the piece,
resulting in a call-and-response feel.

Note, for example, in Figure 3-10 how the eighth notes and sixteenth notes
appear first in one clef and then in the other, making both clefs alternately
responsible for carrying the harmony (eighth notes) and melody (sixteenth
notes) of the music.

Figure 3-10: Excerpt from Bach's Fugue in C Major.

Combining Forms into a Symphony

Literally, a *symphony* is a harmonious melding of elements. In music, a symphony is a piece of music that combines several different musical forms and is usually performed by an orchestra.

Traditionally, a symphony consists of four movements (self-contained sections inside a single musical piece):

- Sonata allegro, or fast sonata

- Slow movement (free choice)

- Minuet (a short, stately piece of dance music set in 3/4 time)

- Combination of sonata and rondo

The idea of a symphony is that it combines a multitude of musical forms harmoniously, so the aforementioned pattern is absolutely not set in stone.

The symphony form leaves the field for musical experimentation wide open. Some pieces that have come from this form are the most enduring and recognizable classical music pieces ever recorded. The most famous one, of course, is Beethoven's Symphony No. 5 (Opus 67), whose opening line, "Bu-bu-bu-BUM," is possibly the most universally known opening theme of any type of music. Figure 3-11 shows you the music for this legendary theme.

Figure 3-11:
Bu-bu-bu-
BUM. . . .

Observing Other Classical Forms

Other classical forms are also enduring and important, if slightly less popular. They're more determined by how many performers are involved in the performance than the official structure of the music performed or the role of the performers themselves.

Concerto

A *concerto* is a composition written for a solo instrument backed by an orchestra. The concerto often creates superstars of classical music, such as pianist Lang Lang and violinist Itzhak Perlman. The soloists often carry as much weight as the long-dead composers themselves do.

Duet

Anybody who's ever sat through a piano lesson has probably played a *duet,* which is a piece of music written for two people. A duet generally consists of two pianists or a pianist and a vocalist. When other instrumentation is used, such as a bass and a violin, or some other combination, the term *duo* is most commonly applied.

Piano duets are most often used as teaching devices, with the student handling the basic melody line and the more advanced pianist handling the trickier accompaniment.

Etude

An *etude* is a brief musical composition based on a particular technical aspect of music, such as building scales, designed to help instruct the performer through musical exercise.

Fantasia

Fantasias are freeform and try to convey the impression of being completely improvised and divinely inspired, and are most often written for a solo instrument or a small ensemble. The modern equivalent of the fantasia is free jazz.

Book IV

Refining Your Technique and Exploring Styles

Chapter 4

Perusing Popular Genres and Forms

In This Chapter

▶ Dealing with the blues

▶ Topping the charts with rock and pop

▶ Dancing away the heartache with country

▶ Kicking back with jazz and soul

▶ Access the audio tracks at www.dummies.com/go/pianokeyboardaio/

Discussing *form* when talking about popular music is tricky because the term is often misused. Think of form as being the specific way a piece of music is constructed, with governing rules to that type of music's construction (such as the classical forms discussed in Book IV Chapter 3). Genre, on the other hand, refers to a song's style, such as the instrumentation used, overall tone of the music, and so on.

However, some popular modern genres of music have been around long enough that specific patterns can be seen in their overall construction. These genres are the blues, rock/pop/folk, country, jazz, and soul.

Feeling the Blues

The blues is the first truly American folk music (aside from the unique music that the Native Americans had before the European invasion). The structure of the blues is the common ancestor of pretty much all other constructions of American popular music and has been influential around the world. Around the turn of the 20th century, field holler, church music, and African percussion had all melded into what is now known as the blues. By 1910, the word *blues* to describe this music was in widespread use.

Blues music uses *song,* or *ternary,* form in three parts that follows an AABA pattern of I, IV, and V chords in a given scale. (You can read about song form in Book III Chapter 4.) The B section is the *bridge,* a contrasting section that prepares the listener or performer for the return of the original A section. (Plenty of people complain that rock music only uses three chords: the I, IV, and V chords. Well, that all started with the blues!)

The blues is almost always played in 4/4 time, with the rhythm beat out either in regular quarter notes or in eighth notes and with strong accents given on both the first and third beats of each measure.

The most common types of blues songs are the 12-bar blues, the 8-bar blues, the 16-bar blues, the 24-bar blues, and the 32-bar blues. The "bar" refers to how many measures are used in each style of blues (see Book II Chapter 3 for more about measures).

12-bar blues

The name is pretty self-explanatory: In *12-bar blues,* you have 12 bars, or measures, of music to work with. In each verse of the 12-bar blues (you can have as many verses as you want, but usually a 12-bar blues composition has three or four), the third 4-bar segment works to resolve the previous 4 bars. The resolution, or conclusion, to the I7 chord at the end of the verse may signal the end of the song. Or, if the 12th bar is a V7 chord, the resolution to the I7 chord signals that you go back to the beginning of the song to repeat the progression for another verse. If the song continues on to a new verse, the V7 chord at the end of the song is called the *turnaround.*

The most commonly used pattern — from left to right, starting at the top and working down — for the 12-bar blues looks like this:

I7	I7	I7	I7
IV7	IV7	I7	I7
V7	IV7	I7	V7/I7 (turnaround)

So if you were playing a 12-bar blues song in the key of C, you would play it like this:

C7	C7	C7	C7
F7	F7	C7	C7
G7	F7	C7	G7/C7 (turnaround)

If you can hit those chords in that order, you have the bare bones for Muddy Waters's classic "You Can't Lose What You Ain't Never Had." Change the tonic (I) chord to an A (AAAA DDAA EDAE/A), and you have Robert Johnson's "Crossroads Blues."

You don't always have to use the seventh chords, but it sounds more bluesy when you do.

If you're playing the 12-bar blues in a *minor* key, here's the common pattern to use (here rendered without the sevenths):

i	iv	i	i
iv	iv	i	i
ii	V	i	v/i (turnaround)

Count Basie's famous and much-loved variation on the 12-bar blues took elements of both the major and minor keys, as shown here:

I	IV	I	v
IV	IV	I	VI
ii	V	I	v/I (turnaround)

8-bar blues

8-bar blues is similar to 12-bar blues — it just has shorter verses in it and a slightly different common use of chord progressions. Here's the standard pattern used for 8-bar blues:

I	IV	I	VI
ii	V	I	V/I (turnaround)

16-bar blues

Another variation on the basic 12-bar blues is the 16-bar blues. Where the 8-bar blues is four bars shorter than the 12-bar blues, the 16-bar blues, as you can probably guess, is that much longer.

The 16-bar blues uses the same basic chord pattern structure as the 12-bar blues, with the 9th and 10th measures stated twice, like so:

I	I	I	I
IV	IV	I	I
V	IV	V	IV
V	IV	I	V/I

24-bar blues

The 24-bar blues progression is similar to a 12-bar traditional blues progression except that each chord progression is doubled in duration, like so:

I	I	I	I
I	I	I	I
IV	IV	IV	IV
I	I	I	I
V	V	IV	IV
I	I	I	V/I (turnaround)

32-bar blues ballads and country

The 32-bar blues pattern is where you see the true roots of rock and jazz music. This extended version of the 12-bar blues pattern has the AABA structure, also called *song form,* that was adopted by rock bands in the 1960s. The pattern is also referred to as the SRDC Model: Statement (A1), Restatement (A2), Departure (B), and Conclusion (A3).

A typical 32-bar blues layout can look something like this:

(A1)	I	I	VI	VI
	ii	V	IV	V
(A2)	I	I	VI	VI
	ii	V	IV	I
(B)	I	I	I	I
	IV	IV	IV	IV
(A3)	I	I	VI	VI
	ii	V	IV	V/I

When it was first created, 32-bar blues wasn't nearly as popular with "true" blues performers as the 12-bar structure was, partly because it didn't work as well with the short call-and-response form of lyricism that earmarked the blues. It did work well for the country music genre, though, and Hank Williams (Sr.) used this construction in songs like "Your Cheating Heart" and "I'm So Lonesome (I Could Cry)." Freddy Fender used this structure in his hits "Wasted Days and Wasted Nights" and "Before the Next Teardrop Falls."

However, when this particular blues structure was picked up by people like Irving Berlin and George Gershwin, a lot — perhaps all — of the true heart of blues disappeared from the resulting music. The 32-bar blues transitioned into popular songs like "Frosty the Snowman" and "I Got Rhythm."

The 32-bar blues also was significantly altered by the intervention of other classically trained composers, who mixed the ideas of the sonata and the rondo (see Book IV Chapter 3) with the traditional American blues. The result was the eventual creation of non-bluesy-sounding songs that used such aspects of classical music as the ability to change keys during the bridge section of a song.

Playing the blues

The *blues* even has its own scale, remember (which you can read about in Book III Chapter 2). In this section, you don't apply the blues style to an existing song, but rather create your own blues from scratch. That's right: You get to be a composer.

You can play fast blues, slow blues, happy blues, and sad blues. Whether your dog left you or your woman (or man) has done you wrong, playing the blues is as easy as counting to 12.

Two important elements in blues music are form and rhythm. When you have these down, add a few more essential musicalities, like grace notes or tremolos. Then you can make any of your songs sing the blues.

To play the blues, you use the following elements:

- ✔ 12-bar form (there are others, as mentioned earlier)
- ✔ Swing or shuffle rhythm
- ✔ Seventh chords
- ✔ Tremolos
- ✔ Sad story to tell (everybody's got one)

Book IV

Refining Your Technique and Exploring Styles

12-bar ditties

Most blues music utilizes a widely recognized form called *12-bar form,* aptly named because each musical phrase of the song is 12 bars (measures) long. The 12-bar blues has a chord sequence that repeats over and over, usually with different lyrics and perhaps some melodic variation, until you genuinely feel sorry for the storyteller.

Melody notes, rhythms, and lyrics may differ from one 12-bar phrase to the next, but the chords usually stay the same. The chords most often used in the 12-bar form are all seventh chords; they are as follows:

- **The I7 chord:** Chord with the first scale note as its root note
- **The IV7 chord:** Chord with the fourth scale note as its root note
- **The V7 chord:** Chord with the fifth scale note as its root note

These three chords appear in the same order and for the same number of measures every time the 12-bar phrase is repeated. (Seventh chords are introduced in Book III Chapter 6.)

To play your own 12-bar blues, just follow these easy instructions, playing with either hand or both hands. When you have the chord progression memorized, try playing the chords with the left hand while your right hand plays a simple melody, riff, or blues scale.

1. **Play an I7 chord for four measures.**

2. **Play an IV7 chord for two measures.**

3. **Play an I7 chord for two measures.**

4. **Play a V7 chord for one measure.**

5. **Play an IV7 chord for one measure.**

6. **Play an I7 chord for two measures.**

7. **Repeat Steps 1 through 6 until you have your audience singing with you.**

Figure 4-1 (Track 92) shows an example of 12-bar blues that uses chords only. They may be just chords, but you should still play them with conviction.

Figure 4-1:
The 12-bar
blues.

Changing it up

All blues players realize that the same chords over and over can become
repetitive (to both audience and musician), so they substitute other chords
within the 12-bar form. For example, try a IV chord in measure 2 and play a
V7 chord in measure 12 as a turnaround, as shown in Figure 4-2.

Book IV

**Refining
Your
Technique
and
Exploring
Styles**

Figure 4-2:
Chord sub-
stitutions for
the blues.

Having Fun with Rock and Pop

Most early rock and pop songs follow the structure of either the 12-bar blues or the 32-bar blues. Chuck Berry's "Johnny B. Goode" is one variation of the 12-bar blues structure used in rock, as is the Rolling Stones's "19th Nervous Breakdown." The Beach Boys were masters of the 32-bar structure, using it in such songs as "Good Vibrations" and "Surfer Girl." The Beatles also used this structure in many of their songs, including "From Me to You" and "Hey Jude." Jerry Lee Lewis's "Great Balls of Fire," The Righteous Brothers's "You've Lost That Loving Feeling," and Led Zeppelin's "Whole Lotta Love" all also use the AABA 32-bar form.

In 32-bar pop music, the music is broken into four 8-bar sections. Songs like Fats Waller's "Ain't Misbehavin'" and Duke Ellington's "It Don't Mean a Thing" follow the AABA 32-bar structure, whereas Charlie Parker took the rondo approach (ABAC) to the 32-bar variation in songs like "Ornithology" and "Donna Lee."

Compound AABA form really should be called AABAB2 form (but it isn't), because in this form, after you play the first 32 bars, you move into a second bridge section (B2) that sends you right back to the beginning of the song to repeat the original 32 bars of the song. The Beatles's "I Want to Hold Your Hand," The Police's "Every Breath You Take," and Tom Petty and the Heartbreakers's "Refugee" all follow this pattern.

The *verse-chorus* structure (also called ABAB form) is the most widely used form in rock and pop music today. Verse-chorus form follows the structure of the lyrics attached to it. You can, of course, write an instrumental piece that follows the same pattern as a verse-chorus rock or pop song, but the structure itself gets its name from the way the words in a song fit together.

Verse-chorus songs are laid out like this:

- **Introduction (I):** The introduction sets the mood and is usually instrumental, although sometimes it may include a spoken recitation, like in Prince's "Let's Go Crazy."

- **Verse (V):** The verse begins the story of the song.

- **Chorus (C):** The chorus is the most memorable lyrical point of the song — the song's *hook*.

- **Verse (V):** Another verse continues the story.

- **Chorus (C):** The second chorus reinforces the hook.

- **Bridge (B):** The bridge, which may be instrumental or lyrical, usually occurs only once in the song and forms a contrast with the repetition of verses and choruses.

- **Chorus (C):** The final chorus repeats the original chorus to fade, or it just stops at the I chord.

The typical rock/pop song structure, as described here, is IVCVCBC. And just as in the 12-bar blues structure, the chords of choice are the I, IV, and V chords.

Thousands, perhaps even millions, of popular songs follow this structure. The Beatles's "Ob-La-Di, Ob-La-Da," Tom Jones's "Sex Bomb," Kenny Rogers's "The Gambler," Lady Gaga's "Poker Face," and Eminem's "Lose Yourself" are all examples of this structure used in contemporary pop music. The really amazing thing is how different from one another, either by virtue of lyrics or the music itself, one song can sound from the next.

Book IV

Refining Your Technique and Exploring Styles

Solid rock pianists to check out

Legends of rock piano: Jerry Lee Lewis, Billy Joel, Elton John, Rick Wakeman, Tony Banks

On today's rock piano playlist: Bruce Hornsby, Tori Amos, Ben Folds, Jordan Rudess, John Medeski

Playing rock and pop songs

Pull out your bag o' tricks and find the following musical ingredients to make any song rock:

- Rockin' intervals
- Glissandos (see Book IV Chapter 1)
- Chords
- Lots and lots of pyrotechnics for your elaborate stage show (plus lights, makeup, big hair, a smoke machine — all the necessities)

Jerry Lee Lewis practically invented the classic rock piano sound. For this style, all you need is an opening glissando, fast chords, and lots of energy.

Pour these elements into the 12-bar blues form and you're ready to roll. Figure 4-3 (Track 93) shows a rockin' bass line that follows a typical blues chord progression in the key of C. (See the earlier section "Playing the blues" for more on blues chords.)

Figure 4-3: Lefty provides the rockin' bass line.

Pop! Goes the Piano

Arguably, every song on the radio is a *popular* song because few radio stations play songs that listeners don't like. Country, rock, hip-hop, Latin, and many other styles of music are popular with one audience or another. But most people know the term *pop* (short for "popular") to be the category for Top 40 songs and superstar ballads and dance numbers by such artists as Beyoncé, Black Eyed Peas, Celine Dion, Justin Timberlake, Prince, and a multitude of others.

Pop music can be rhythmic, romantic, nostalgic, funky, sad, and about 13 other adjectives. This section concentrates on the one style of pop music perfectly suited to the piano: the slow and smooth-sounding pop ballad.

Popular picks

To play a pop ballad, you need a small arsenal of musical ornamentations, including the following:

- Right-hand intervals
- Chord arpeggios
- Damper pedal
- Dimmer switch (essential for setting the right mood)

Topping the charts

To add a little pop romance to any song, take a simple melody and add the ever-so-sweet sixth interval below each right-hand melodic note. The new melodic line should look like the one in Figure 4-4. For some reason unknown to many a trusted and frustrated musicologist, the sixth interval adds an element of romance to a melody.

Book IV

Refining Your Technique and Exploring Styles

Popular pop piano personalities to check out

Legends of pop piano: Billy Joel, Elton John, Laura Nyro, Carole King

On today's pop piano playlist: Vanessa Carlton, Enya, Norah Jones, Fiona Apple

Figure 4-4:
Romancing
the sixth
interval
tone.

TIP

This trick of adding the sixth may look difficult, but it's not. All you do is find the sixth interval below the first melody note and freeze your hand in that position. Your pinkie always plays the top note and your thumb always plays the bottom interval note. As you play up and down the melody, your hand lands on the correct interval every time.

A Little Bit Country

Before there was rock and roll, there was *country*. This style often sounds relaxed, lyrical, simple, and grassroots-ish, but it ain't afraid to rock, roll, and rumble. Artists like Keith Urban, Carrie Underwood, Shania Twain, and Brad Paisley put all kinds of musical influences in their country music, including elements of rock, blues, and even jazz. Influences aside, though, the folks in Nashville still call it country.

Country-style cooking

To enhance your musical dish with the tastes of country on the piano, add some of these stylistic flavorings:

- Intervals
- Grace notes
- Tremolos
- Bum-ba-di-da bass line
- A ten-gallon hat, a pair of boots, and maybe even a nice and shiny belt buckle (purchased from a local Western store)

Finger-pickin' good

Figure 4-5 shows a nice, relaxed-sounding slice of the country music style. The right-hand intervals are unique in that the melody notes are actually on the bottom while the top notes stay the same. Grace notes and tremolos peppered throughout give this example the feeling of an Old West saloon.

Figure 4-5: Good ole' country music.

Country keyboarders to check out

Country piano legends: Ray Charles, Floyd Cramer, Moon Mullican, Del Wood, Charlie Rich

On today's country piano playlist: Jimmy Nichols, Michael Rojas, Catherine Styron Marx

Book IV

Refining Your Technique and Exploring Styles

The left-hand accompaniment pattern is challenging, so practice each hand separately until you can confidently put them together. After this inspiring tune, you may find yourself adding a saddlebag to your piano bench.

Improvising with Jazz

If there's one particular music style that embraces all that the piano can do, it's *jazz*. Celebrated by many as America's greatest art form, jazz is king when it comes to interesting chord harmonies, changing rhythms, and improvisation. Legendary jazz pianists like Bill Evans, Art Tatum, Bud Powell, and many others have taken these elements and added them to classic songs to make them a little more jazzy.

The true spirit of jazz has always been improvisation, which makes identifying the actual construction of jazz most difficult. The goal in jazz is to create a new interpretation of an established piece (called a *standard*), or to build on an established piece of music by changing the melody, harmonies, or even the time signature. It's almost like the point of jazz is to break *away* from form.

The closest way to define how jazz is constructed is to take the basic idea behind blues vocalizations — the *call-and-response vocals* — and replace the voices with the various instruments that make up the jazz sound: brass, bass, percussion (including piano), and wind instruments, along with the more recent inclusion, the electric guitar. In Dixieland jazz, for example, musicians take turns playing the lead melody on their instruments while the others improvise *countermelodies,* or contrasting secondary melodies, that follow along in the background.

The one predictable element of music in the jazz genre — excluding *free jazz,* where no real discernible rules exist but jazz instrumentation is used — is the rhythm. All jazz music, with the exception of free jazz, uses clear, regular meter and strongly pulsed rhythms that can be heard throughout the music.

Jazzing it up

All the legendary jazz pianists use tried-and-true musical tricks from time to time to freshen things up. Borrow these tricks yourself:

- Chord substitutions (see the section "Substituting chords" later in this chapter)
- Swing rhythm
- Syncopation

✔ Knowledge of scales

✔ Knowledge of chords

✔ Nickname like Duke, Bird, or Cool Cat

It's up to you

It's time to be creative. Improvisation is perhaps the most important element of jazz music. It can be *literal improvisation,* where you (the performer) make up your own rhythms and riffs, or *implied improvisation,* where the music is originally written in a way that just sounds improvised.

The easiest way to improvise is by changing the rhythm of a melody. For example, take the simple quarter-note melody of "Yankee Doodle" and transform it into a swingin' jazz tune by adding swing eighth notes, syncopation, and a well-placed rest now and then to keep things cool (see Figure 4-6, Track 94).

Figure 4-6: "Yankee Doodle" swings.

Great jazz players to check out

Jazz piano legends: Bill Evans, Thelonius Monk, Art Tatum, Herbie Hancock, Duke Ellington

Jazz piano pioneers: Dave Brubeck, Chick Corea, Keith Jarrett

Unsung heroes of jazz piano: Ahmad Jamal, Marian McPartland, Billy Strayhorn

On today's jazz piano playlist: Gerri Allen, Brad Meldau, Marcus Roberts

Substituting chords

Few jazz compositions use the standard major and minor chords throughout. In fact, few jazz pianists play the original chords written in a song. Instead, they break the rules and substitute new chords to liven up otherwise simple melodies.

Figure 4-7 is the well-known children's song "Merrily We Roll Along." As you play it, notice the simple chord progression of C-G7-C.

Figure 4-7: "Merrily" with standard chords.

Even "Merrily We Roll Along" can sound not-so-childish with the use of *chord substitution.* The idea is to find a more interesting chord progression from I to V7 to I. Try the following options:

✔ **Use major scale tones for chord roots.** Move up the scale from C to G7, building triads on each successive scale note, as in Figure 4-8.

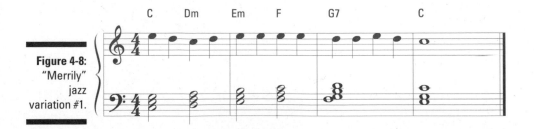

Figure 4-8: "Merrily" jazz variation #1.

✔ **Use black and white keys for new chord roots.** Move up in half-steps, building chords on each new root note, as in Figure 4-9.

Figure 4-9: "Merrily" jazz variation #2.

✔ **Move up in fourths.** Start a chord pattern in measure 2 by playing an Em7, then move up a fourth and build a seventh chord on each new root note, as shown in Figure 4-10.

Figure 4-10: "Merrily" jazz variation #3.

Soul Searching

Talk about a broad category of music! *Soul* can encompass anything from *R&B* ("rhythm and blues") to *gospel, hip-hop,* and *rap.* Such soulful styles have been made popular by artists like Stevie Wonder, Aretha Franklin, and Otis Redding, and can feature a lot of wonderful piano playing. It's also great for dancing, although not so much while sitting at the piano.

Saving your soul

Danceable soul music requires danceable rhythms, so have the following rhythmic concepts in your repertoire before strutting over to the keys:

- ✔ Syncopation
- ✔ Right-hand intervals
- ✔ Dotted eighth-sixteenth pattern
- ✔ Disco ball (rent from your local party supply outlet)

R&B ivory ticklers to check out

Soul legends at the piano: Herbie Hancock, Billy Preston, Stevie Wonder

On today's R&B piano playlist: Alicia Keys, John Legend, Brenda Russell

Motown sounds

In the 1960s, Motown Records had a stable of artists specializing in the R&B sound. So popular were these artists that their style became known as the *Motown sound.* But don't think the 1960s are gone; you can add the Motown sound to any of your favorite songs.

Using a left-hand pattern with a syncopated rhythm, play Figure 4-11 (Track 95). Pretty soon you'll be hearing the Temptations doo-wopping right along with you.

Figure 4-11: Motown syncopation.

Funky sounds goin' round

Soul and R&B styles often incorporate elements of *funk* — you know, like James Brown, Chaka Kahn, or George Clinton. Heavy syncopation coupled with dotted eighth-sixteenth rhythmic patterns provide the funky feel for this funky sound. Play Figure 4-12 with a little attitude.

Figure 4-12: Funky patterns.

Book V

Exercises: Practice, Practice, Practice

Contents at a Glance

Chapter 1: Developing Hand Technique......................359

Passing Over and Crossing Under 359
Playing Intervals 367
Playing Chords Without Tension 382

Chapter 2: Extending Your Scales...........................387

The 12 Major, Harmonic Minor, and Melodic Minor Scales...................387
The Three Diminished Scales...399
The Chromatic Scale..401
The 12 Blues Scales..402
Gaining Greater Command of Scales 406
Performance Piece: "Variations on 'Twinkle, Twinkle, Little Star'"........408

Chapter 3: Improving Finger Coordination and Footwork.........409

Parallel Movement at the Octave 409
Parallel Movement at the Interval 412
Contrary Motion Away from the Center..414
Contrary Motion Toward the Center..416
Combination Movement Exercise 418
Performance Piece: "Turkey in the Straw" 419
Using the Damper Pedal...420
Pedaling Chords...420
Performance Piece: "Simple Gifts" 428

Chapter 4: Jumping Across the Keyboard 429

Jumping and Landing Accuracy 429
Jumping with Both Hands Together...434
Left-Hand Accompaniment Patterns..436
Performance Piece: "Lily Pad Rag"..441

Chapter 5: Exercising with Arpeggios and Alternating Hands 443

Finger Jumps...443
The Arpeggiator..446
Broken Chords...449
Performance Piece: "Harp Heaven" 454
Playing with Alternating Hands: Hand-to-Hand Scale Handoffs............456

Chapter 6: Stepping Up to Octaves and Chord Progressions.......463

Opening Up to the Octave 463
Octave Jumps..466
Octave Chords...470
Performance Piece: "Schumann's Octave Workout"..........................472
Seventh Chord Progressions 473
Chord Cadences, Familiar Patterns...475
Extended Chord Progressions..477

Chapter 1

Developing Hand Technique

In This Chapter

▶ Smoothing your traversing technique and extending the scale beyond five-finger position

▶ Focusing on finger placement and timing

▶ Exercising finger combinations with greater control

▶ Playing chords solidly and releasing tension

▶ Practicing with chord progressions

▶ Access the audio tracks at www.dummies.com/go/pianokeyboardaio/

This chapter is all about teaching your hands to do what you want them to do. It covers the technique of passing under and crossing over, gives you plenty of practice playing different intervals, and ends with lots of pointers on playing smoothly and easily, without tension.

Passing Over and Crossing Under

One of the biggest challenges in developing good technique is smoothing out the transitions as you move your hands up and down the keyboard. Imagine playing fluid lines, shifting hand positions seamlessly, and covering the keyboard territory with flexible fingering. You often hear people say, "They make it look easy," when they watch great piano players. That's because great piano players have figured out how to make it easy for themselves.

Before Bach's time, keyboard players avoided using their thumbs, which must have resulted in some really awkward fingerwork. Adding the thumb means you can play more notes within one hand position, but the problem remains that the thumb has a very different size, shape, and angle when compared with the other fingers. If you run out of fingers when the melodic line continues up or down, you have to move your hand position, and do it without breaking the musical line. The two best options are to pass the thumb under or cross the other fingers over.

The keyboard terrain sets up different scenarios for these transitions, with possibilities available in the various white and black key combinations. Because the thumb is shorter, the easiest way to cross over it or pass it under is with a black-white combination, because you can use the key height and location to your advantage. With one of your long fingers on a black key you naturally elevate your hand, like a bridge, for your thumb to pass under. With your thumb on a white key, it's easier to cross a long finger over if it's reaching for a black key. It's more difficult to pass or cross from white key to white key because you have less room to pass under and farther to cross over. These more difficult transitions can cause you to twist your hand position, flare out your elbow, tuck in your elbow, or otherwise contort yourself as you move up or down the keyboard, and the extra movement can get in the way of playing smoothly and comfortably.

The answer is to keep your hand quiet and keep your arm perpendicular to the keyboard as you move out to the extremes or into the middle. This will make your scale runs sound smooth and feel more comfortable. But making these traverses seamless does take practice. The exercises in this section give you practice crossing over and passing under with different finger combinations, using a variety of scales. You also find out how to make these transitions more comfortable.

The performance piece at the end of the section showcases your smooth scale runs. It's an arrangement of an aria from the opera *La Cenerentola* (Cinderella) by Rossini.

One under two, two over one

You first want to find a hand shape that eases the transition from one hand position to the next. Start by making a rounded "O" shape with fingers one and two. It helps to keep the two fingertips relatively close together and the top of your hand raised high but still flat.

Now feel your fingertips on each key as you play the following exercise (Track 96). Make sure you're not flattening your thumb or hitting the key with the side of your thumb. Similarly, watch that you're not overextending your 2nd finger; you want to come down on the key with the center of your fingertip. You may find it easier to straighten your 2nd finger a bit as it crosses over your thumb to play a black key and curve it a bit when it plays a white key. You can apply this to your 3rd and 4th fingers in the following exercises.

One under three, three over one

Work on smoothing out your hand movements with this exercise (Track 97). Keep your hand position quiet and watch for twisting. Moving sideways smoothly, make sure not to collapse your wrist when your thumb passes under. Control the volume of a note by planning a hand shape that allows control of the attack speed. Guide fingers to perform a smooth movement.

One under four, four over one

This finger combination is more challenging because you need to contract your hand fully for the position shift and still make it sound smooth and effortless. Make sure the crossing/passing finger hits the nearest spot on the key to strike it comfortably. Watch your fingers carefully to see whether you're overreaching.

Book V

Exercises: Practice, Practice, Practice

Extending scales with crossovers and pass-unders

Now you can combine the crossing and passing practice you've done in the following two exercises with extended scale runs (the second one is Track 98). Exercise slower to focus on smooth transitions, and faster to focus on lightness and agility.

C and G major scale passages

B flat and F major scale passages

Book V

**Exercises:
Practice,
Practice,
Practice**

Performance piece: Aria from La Cenerentola

This aria is well suited to polishing your scale runs and light, staccato touch. Single out the sixteenth-note scale runs to practice the crossovers and pass-unders before you play. Make as much contrast as you can between the staccato and legato. You can listen to this on Track 99.

Playing Intervals

Playing piano can be like having a choir at your fingertips. You have a ten-member group, some are shorter and some are taller, some like to show off and some prefer to blend in, and one or two really don't take well to being singled out. As the conductor of the fingertip chorale, you have control over how each "voice" in your choir responds to your direction. You can bring up the bass, hush the choir while the soprano has a solo, or lift up every voice for the full-out finale.

This section gives you some exercises to gain command over each finger combination so that when you're playing two notes together you have the strength and control to balance and blend. These interval exercises also let you scrutinize the many combinations of fingers, intervals, and positions on the keyboard to get to know how each finger responds. Special attention is given to strengthening those fingers that need it the most.

Playing seconds with different finger combinations

Seconds are any interval combination on adjacent keys, white or black. Because of the keyboard layout, that means a variety of hand and finger positions to work on.

Each of the finger combination exercises in this section includes a study for the right hand and the left hand separately. Play through these exercises a few times slowly at first — concentrating on each hand — listening carefully to adjust the balance and timing of each finger combination. Curve your fingers and keep the finger joints firm to play the seconds evenly. Then gradually increase your speed each time you play the exercise. As you increase your speed and accuracy, play this section as a series, starting with the right and left hand in the first finger combination, moving on to the right and left hand in the next finger combination, and so on.

As you play the seconds with each finger combination, imagine the two fingers moving together as one unit. In the first combination, for example, finger two and finger three move together to strike each interval in a synchronized motion.

Finger combination: Two and three

Start your 2nd and 3rd fingers. Adjust your attack and your timing to play the seconds evenly while changing hand positions. Listen to it on Track 100.

Finger combination: Three and four

Try to eliminate excess movement by keeping your hand close to the keyboard.

Book V

**Exercises:
Practice,
Practice,
Practice**

Finger combination: One and two

You may find playing the seconds evenly difficult to do with this finger combination. Your first two fingers are such different lengths! Bring your fingertips close together, like you're forming an "O," before striking the keys.

Finger combination: Four and five

Work on building strength in your 4th and 5th fingers by keeping the joints firm to make the accents strong.

Book V

Exercises: Practice, Practice, Practice

Playing thirds with different finger combinations

These exercises improve your agility as you maneuver both major and minor thirds. The different finger combinations keep all your fingers nimble.

Finger combination: One and three

Make sure you have a nice, high arch to your hand, and let your fingers hang down and your fingertips lightly touch the keys.

Finger combination: Two and four

This next exercise is a good one to play with both staccato and legato articulation.

Book V

Exercises: Practice, Practice, Practice

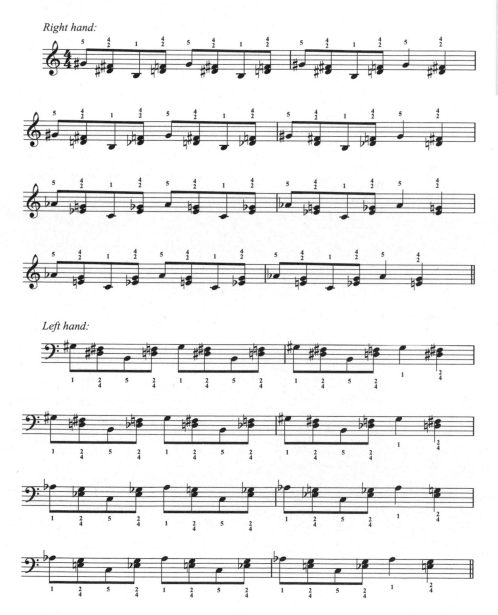

Right hand:

Left hand:

Finger combination: Three and five

Balance the thirds so the two notes are the same volume. Make sure your thumb stays relaxed and isn't playing louder than the other fingers.

Finger combinations: One and four, two and five, one and five

Here's your "Mt. Everest" exercise for the thirds (Track 101). Keep your wrists up high, and lift your fingers up like spider legs, bringing them down evenly in twos. And not too fast — stay relaxed and melt into the keys.

Book V

Exercises: Practice, Practice, Practice

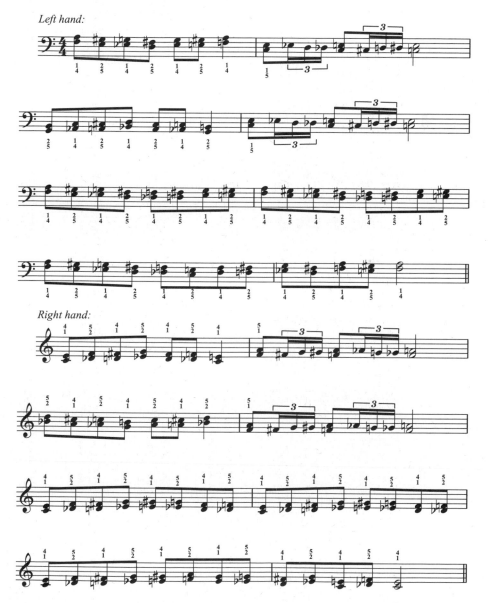

Playing fourths with finger combinations

Practicing fourths is really good for finger independence. The different finger combinations keep your muscle coordination sharp.

Finger combinations: One and four, two and five

This one is especially good for the 4th finger. Work on keeping it curved, and prepare it directly above the key that it's going to strike.

Finger combinations: One and three, one and two

You're stretching here. Maintain a good shape in your 5th finger; don't let it go flat as it reaches to play its note. Help your pinky by letting go of the fourth interval and moving your hand out, arched, toward the pinky.

Book V

Exercises: Practice, Practice, Practice

Playing fifths, sixths, and sevenths

Your hand is open wider, and you're moving your hand across the keyboard while maintaining a nice, rounded hand shape. Watch for twisting.

Exercise in fifths

12/8 time is counted as 12 eighth notes to a measure, with each eighth note getting one count. Each measure can have a rhythmic pattern of four strong beats, on one, four, seven, and ten, with three eighth notes inside each strong beat. Keep both fingers five and one pointing down into the keys.

Exercise in fifths and sixths

As you play this exercise, fingers four and five are round, but not stiff. Give these fingers some power and flexibility by bouncing your wrist lightly: "down-up, down-up" as you count "one-and, two-and . . ."

Book V

Exercises: Practice, Practice, Practice

Exercise in fifths, sixths, and sevenths

Give this exercise (Track 102) a bluesy, rhythmic feel with a fairly deep wrist bounce on the strong beats in 12/8 time. (That's one, four, seven, and ten.)

Performance piece: "Take Me Out to the Ballgame"

This familiar old ballpark favorite (Track 103) is arranged with — you guessed it — different interval combinations in each hand. Play each interval pair by using a single, confident hand move.

Playing Chords Without Tension

Chord playing is one of the greatest pleasures — and biggest advantages — of playing the piano. The piano sounds best when you make the most of its full harmonic potential.

To get your piano to really sing out, you need flexibility in the wrist to increase your attack speed when you play chords. To balance, or voice, the chord notes, you need control in your fingers to vary the quality of your touch. Naturally, you want to dig into the big chords and get your hands around the really fat harmonies, but keeping stiff fingers and awkward hand positions is tiring and can potentially cause some physical problems. Avoiding these problems and improving your chord voicing are the benefits of learning how to relieve the tension in your fingers, hands, and arms.

This section helps you learn to play chords with a relaxed approach, gain a better chord technique, and improve your sound. You can use the exercises to develop fluid motion and release muscle tension as part of a cycle to practice with each chord. The exercises start with single chords, move into a variety of chord progressions, and then combine melody with chords.

Chord relaxation

The most important thing to do is make sure you don't hold tension in your hands, arms, and body when you play chords. You do need a certain amount of muscle tone and firmness in the finger joints to play nice, solid chords, but you also want to build in the habit of releasing tension while you play. As you exercise, monitor your body for any area in which you may be holding tension — your arms, shoulders, neck, or even your face (in the form of a grimace or facial tic). Your aim is to breathe through your body as you play and to establish a cyclical pattern of tension and release.

A simple two-chord progression

Start with this simple two-chord progression, and put the following steps into a cycle for each chord.

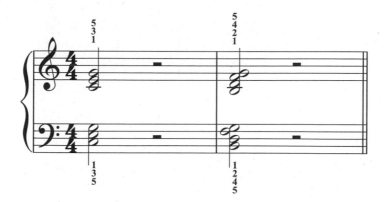

1. With your hands held slightly above the notes in the chord, imagine the shape of the chord in your mind and feel (but don't play yet!) that shape in your fingers.

2. Allow your arm weight to drop onto the keyboard as you comfortably play the chord and hold the shape in your fingers.

3. With a loose, flexible feeling in your wrists, let the weight travel and be absorbed in your wrists with a light bounce.

4. Keeping the chord notes held down, let the wrist float back up and release the notes under your fingers as you lift up from the keyboard, releasing any muscle tension in your fingers, hands, arms, and shoulders.

During the rest between the two chords, release any tension throughout your arms and torso, and prepare for the next chord shape as in step 1.

A longer progression

Now try practicing the cycle in a longer progression. Don't hold any stiffness — after playing a chord, let your wrist relax and absorb the weight you've put into the keys. Instead of channeling the weight to your fingertips and holding it there as you press down the keys, let it travel to your wrists where the weight is absorbed and released with a slight bounce. You need to maintain just enough muscle tone and shape in your hands and fingers to hold down each chord note.

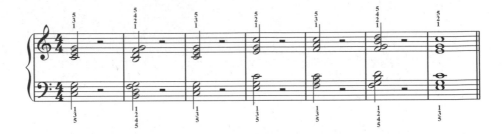

Finding the places to release muscle tension depends on the type of chordal passage you're playing. During a rest you have an obvious spot to relax your hands and release your muscles. On long-held chords you can release tension while holding down the notes, and you can find quick "breaths" as you release staccato chords. You'll have plenty of examples to practice these releases in the following exercises.

Voicing chords

Every time you strike a chord you get to be a sound engineer — you can set your own equalizer (EQ) levels with each chord. Maybe you want to hear more bass, more top note, or bring out the notes in the middle for the fullest sound possible. Most of the time you want the top note to sing out the strongest, with support from the bottom note next and the inner chord notes balanced next. When you play chords, you continually fine-tune your voicing to highlight melodic movement that takes place within a chordal setting.

You can custom-balance each chord tone with subtle differences in your attack speed. You achieve this with variations in the quality of touch for each finger. The piano is designed to transmit and, in effect, amplify these nuances from the key to the hammer to the strings and into sound. Any number of variations in your touch affect the attack speed of each chord tone. Experiment with voicing in the next exercise, bringing out the moving voice, which changes from the top, to the middle, to the bottom note of the chord.

When you want to bring out a certain note within a chord, try using a gentle touch on the other chord notes. A gentle touch should slow the attack speed, bringing down their volume.

Right hand:

Left hand:

Chapter 2

Extending Your Scales

In This Chapter

▶ Practicing major, harmonic minor, and melodic minor scales

▶ Working on chromatic, diminished, and blues scales

▶ Establishing solid fingering for all scales and varying your practice methods

▶ Playing a performance piece to showcase your scales

▶ Access the audio tracks at www.dummies.com/go/pianokeyboardaio/

*Y*ou've come to the chapter of scales, the heart of piano exercises. If you love them, you'll find lots to keep you happy here, and maybe some new scales to challenge your fingers. If you don't love them, well, hopefully you'll like them a little more after you try a few of them in a new presentation.

You can get a good workout here, with scales and fingering for all 12 major, harmonic minor, and melodic minor scales, plus diminished, chromatic, and blues scales. It's paradise if you seek speed and accuracy and if you love patterns. There's nothing like the feeling of flying up and down the keyboard as your scale-fingering starts clicking and you feel a lightness in your touch.

The 12 Major, Harmonic Minor, and Melodic Minor Scales

The major and minor scales are the backbone of piano technique. And for good reason — much of the music we love is based on these scales. Each scale is just two octaves up and down, grouped so you can play the major, harmonic minor, and melodic minor scales starting on the same note before moving on to the next key. You follow the Circle of Fifths, starting with C (Track 104). Follow the fingerings carefully, playing slowly or hands-alone to start.

C major, harmonic minor, melodic minor

G major, harmonic minor, melodic minor

Book V

**Exercises:
Practice,
Practice,
Practice**

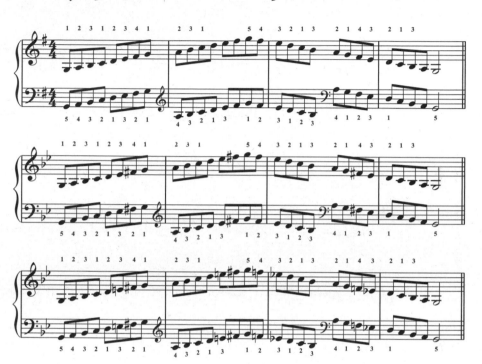

D major, harmonic minor, melodic minor

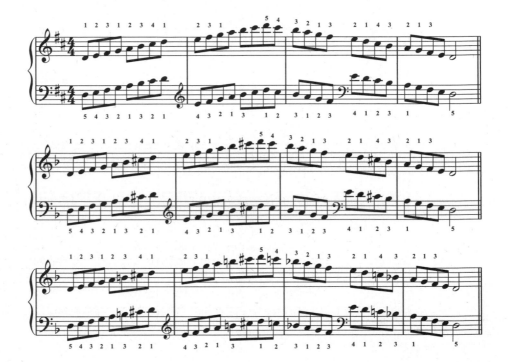

A major, harmonic minor, melodic minor

Book V

Exercises: Practice, Practice, Practice

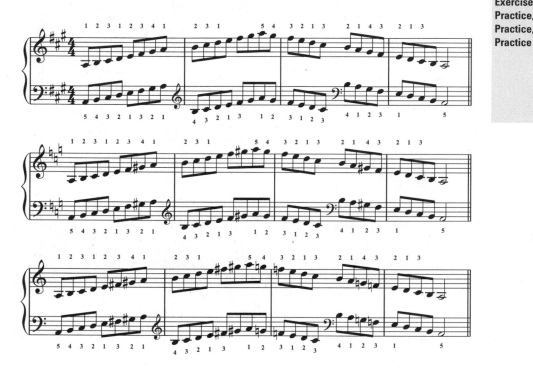

E major, harmonic minor, melodic minor

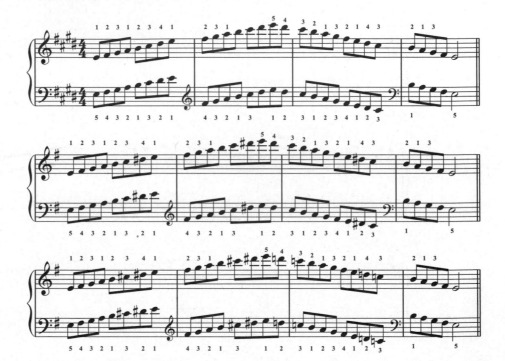

B major, harmonic minor, melodic minor

Book V

**Exercises:
Practice,
Practice,
Practice**

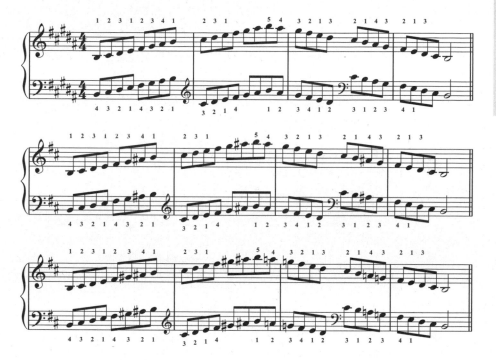

F♯ major, harmonic minor, melodic minor

D♭ major, C♯ harmonic minor, C♯ melodic minor

Book V

Exercises: Practice, Practice, Practice

A♭ major, harmonic minor, melodic minor

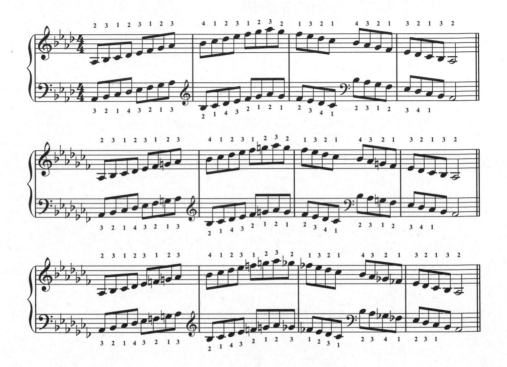

E♭ major, harmonic minor, melodic minor

Book V

Exercises: Practice, Practice, Practice

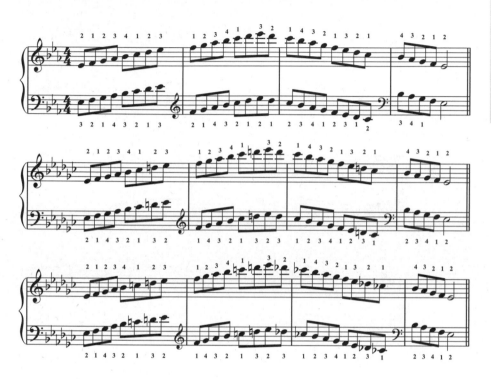

Bb major, harmonic minor, melodic minor

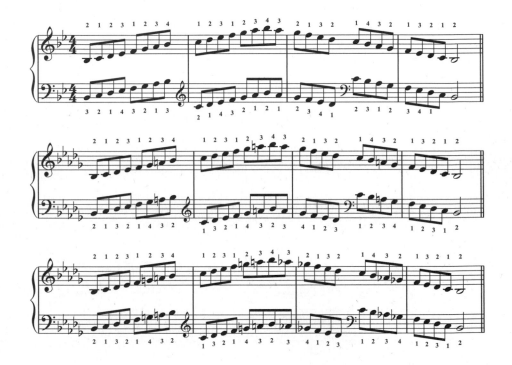

F major, harmonic minor, melodic minor

Book V

**Exercises:
Practice,
Practice,
Practice**

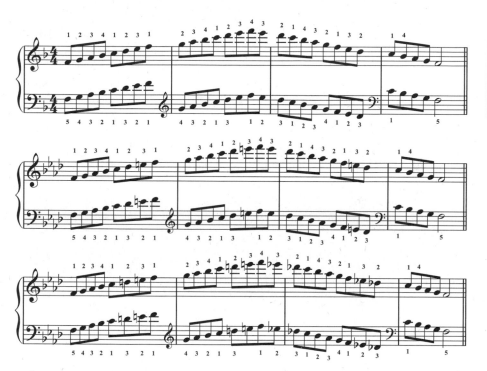

The Three Diminished Scales

The diminished, or octatonic, scale is unique and fun to practice because of its symmetrical pattern. The eight-note scale follows a whole-step/half-step/ whole-step/half-step pattern, which means you can think of every other note as the root of a diminished scale consisting of the same eight notes.

Starting on C

Starting on D♭

Starting on D

The Chromatic Scale

Try playing a two-octave scale starting on a different note, or in a different octave. Play all the black keys with your 3rd finger. Use your thumb to play all white keys except C and F in your right hand, and E and B in your left hand.

The 12 Blues Scales

The blues scale is made of the root, flat third, fourth, flat fifth, fifth, and flat seventh of any given key.

C blues

G blues

D blues

A blues

Book V

**Exercises:
Practice,
Practice,
Practice**

E blues

B blues

F# blues

Db blues

Ab blues

Eb blues

Book V

**Exercises:
Practice,
Practice,
Practice**

Bb blues

F blues

Gaining Greater Command of Scales

You gain greater command and improve finger flexibility with variations that take you out of the usual routine (Tracks 105 and 106). To invigorate your scales and reinforce fingering, change it up a bit by varying the articulation and rhythmic groupings.

Varied articulation

Varied rhythmic groupings

Book V

**Exercises:
Practice,
Practice,
Practice**

G harmonic minor

D harmonic minor

A harmonic minor

Performance Piece: "Variations on 'Twinkle, Twinkle, Little Star'"

Mozart applied the fundamentals of music in brilliant ways, using them to give balance, character, and proportion to even the smallest of forms, like this variation (Track 107).

Chapter 3

Improving Finger Coordination and Footwork

In This Chapter

▶ Exercising with hands in parallel and contrary motion to improve coordination

▶ Reviewing the basics of pedaling and practicing with chords and melody lines

▶ Enhancing your playing with fancy pedaling and playing performance pieces

▶ Access the audio tracks at www.dummies.com/go/pianokeyboardaio/

The first half of this chapter shows you how to continue practicing single-note lines in each hand, now with melodies that move in parallel and contrary motion. These exercises increase your hand and finger independence and improve your coordination. The key is to integrate the multiple movements into a single feeling. You're teaching your body to feel a combination of movements as one and adapting mentally to imagine the whole rather than all the parts. Put it all together in the performance piece, "Turkey in the Straw."

The second, piano-centric half of the chapter is all about your right foot and what it can do together with your hands. You'll find out how to use the sustain pedal to get a range of different sounds, blend tones, and bring off tricks that you can't do without it.

Parallel Movement at the Octave

These exercises are similar to scales but with more melodic flexibility in the movement of the lines. Normal scale fingering applies most of the time, but the music takes you away from these patterns. The key to good fingering is finding the most comfortable solution to fit the music (exercise #1 is Track 108).

Parallel octave exercise #1

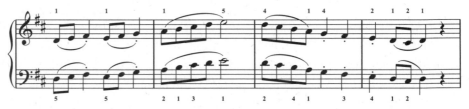

Parallel octave exercise #2

Book V

**Exercises:
Practice,
Practice,
Practice**

Parallel Movement at the Interval

Now your hands are moving in, either a sixth or a tenth apart. Focus on one hand at a time until you feel integration kick in. Your goal is to visualize both hands moving together.

Parallel sixths

Parallel tenths

Contrary Motion Away from the Center

Contrary motion can be easier than parallel because the hands are playing symmetrical patterns. Develop a habit of reading the music bottom to top, left hand before right. Keep your eyes on the music, visualize the synchronized movement, and trust your hands.

Scalewise motion away from the center

Chromatic motion away from the center

Listen to Track 109.

PLAY THIS!

Book V

Exercises: Practice, Practice, Practice

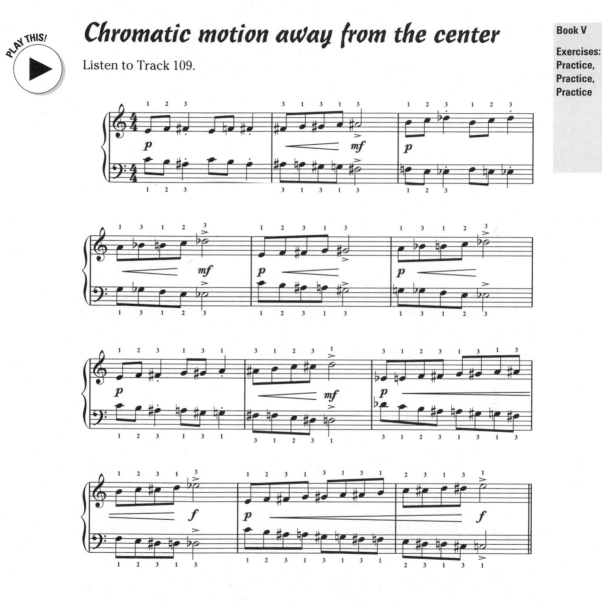

Contrary Motion Toward the Center

See the advice in the preceding section for tips on these exercises.

Scalewise motion toward the center

Patterns toward the center

Book V

Exercises:
Practice,
Practice,
Practice

Combination Movement Exercise

This exercise (Track 110) combines the different types of movement covered so far and provides a good fingering and coordination challenge. Look ahead to see what's coming in the next measure. Visualize the moves before you play them. Your fingers don't know where to go until directed with a clear image.

Performance Piece: "Turkey in the Straw"

Book V

**Exercises:
Practice,
Practice,
Practice**

The melody is paired with parallel motion harmony. Match the articulation and dynamics in both hands for the effect (listen to Track 111).

Using the Damper Pedal

The piano is essentially a percussion instrument. It produces a pitch that has a quick attack when you strike a key and the hammer strikes the strings. If you hold this key down, the pitch has a slow decay, because you're keeping the damper inside the piano off the string, allowing it to vibrate freely. But after you release the key, the damper returns to stop the string from vibrating, stopping the sound. Sustaining the sound is possible with the sustain pedal, which keeps the damper off the strings for you.

By using the pedal in a careful way, you gain a greater range of expression. It can help you to "sing" a melody, connect music in phrases, and create greater resonance and atmospheric illusions. Overuse of the pedal can have some big drawbacks — unintentional mixing of harmonies, blurring notes, and obscuring any articulation that should be clear. Your careful and attentive listening helps avoid these problems.

Pedaling Chords

The two most common pedaling indications are shown in the following figure. Press the pedal down at the "Ped." sign, and release (pedal up) at the asterisk or at the bracket ending the line. These indications are always shown below the bass staff.

The notch in the line in the following figure indicates where to change the pedal, quickly clearing any sustained sound (pedal up) and resetting the sustain (pedal down). Changing the pedal requires careful attention to clearing the harmony cleanly and completely.

Book V

Exercises: Practice, Practice, Practice

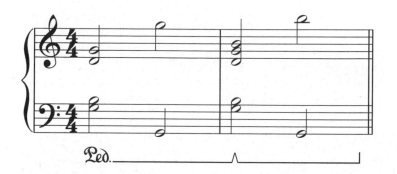

Good pedaling is a matter of timing and listening. Your goal is to train your ear to listen for a smooth transition and a clean change from note to note and chord to chord. You don't want to time your pedaling to match your hands, releasing and then pressing the pedal down as your fingers move from one chord to another; if you do, you'll hear a gap between chords. This is because you're lifting both the keys and the pedal together, so the dampers stop the sound when your fingers leave the keys. You need the sustain pedal down at this time. You have to wait to change the pedal so it happens simultaneously with playing the next chord.

Your heel should stay on the floor, and your toes can rest on the pedal. Some pedals require more weight and pressure, and foot size and power make a difference. You can use your longer toes plus some of the ball of your foot to press down the pedal, but as always go for comfort and ease. Your ankle is the hinge that allows your foot to move with the least amount of movement and effort. Pedaling shouldn't affect your general posture, so if you find that you have to shift around or adjust your balance to accommodate pedaling, you may not have started from a good position.

Broken-chord pedaling

In this exercise (Track 112), you change the pedal on a single note.

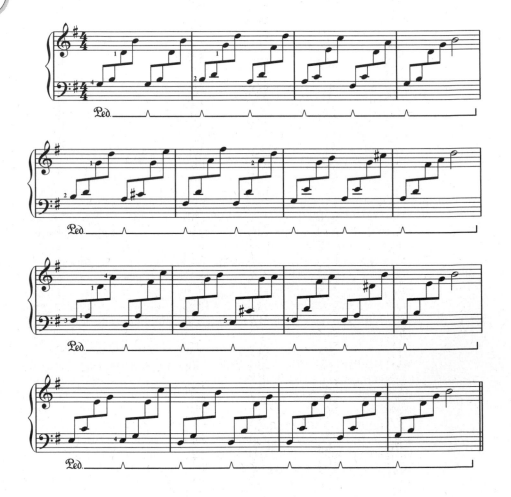

Block-chord pedaling

In this exercise you change going from chord to chord and on any moving lines within the harmony. Listen for smooth transitions!

Book V

**Exercises:
Practice,
Practice,
Practice**

Uniform Pedal Changes on One Line

Although changing the pedal with the change of harmony is a general rule, change it more frequently when you're also playing a melodic line. With a slow melody, you may change the pedal before the harmony changes so the melody doesn't get too blurry.

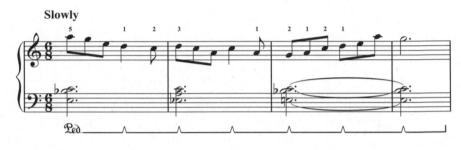

Varied Pedal Changes on One Line

Book V

**Exercises:
Practice,
Practice,
Practice**

You can enhance your legato phrasing by pedaling even more frequently along the melodic line, especially in melodic lines with a wide range that call for a singer's phrasing. Try it with the melody to Stephen Foster's "Jeanie with the Light Brown Hair."

Pedaling for Effect

Use the sustain pedal for *atmospheric effect* (sustaining for a blurred effect) or to sustain a note or chord over several measures. Here, the pedal helps sustain the long notes in one hand while smoothing the melodic movement in the other (Track 113).

Sustaining as the Hands Move

You can use the pedal to give notes their full value when you have to move your hands to a new position on the keyboard. This can be a plus musically, because you can exaggerate the rhythms and the differences between the long and short articulations (Track 114).

Performance Piece: "Simple Gifts"

The pedal is up when the melody is in the left hand, and down when the melody is in the upper register of the right hand. During the last three measures, you keep the pedal down to layer the G major chord over the full range of the piano (Track 115).

Chapter 4

Jumping Across the Keyboard

In This Chapter

▶ Jumping from note to note and chord to chord

▶ Discovering new accuracy skills

▶ Exercising with left-hand accompaniment patterns

▶ Playing a ragtime-style performance piece featuring hand jumps

▶ Access the audio tracks at www.dummies.com/go/pianokeyboardaio/

Covering the full territory of the 88 keys is certainly one of the enticing attributes of the piano. Jumping registers, from low to high or high to low, is a potent tool that few other instruments can match. The exercises in this chapter give you practice jumping from one note to another and from chord to chord, over both smaller and larger intervals. This practice will help your accuracy as you move across the keyboard, help develop your "feel" for where your hands go, and improve your sense of distance.

This chapter also gives you lots of practice with the most common left-hand patterns — a variety of bass-note-to-chord accompaniments essential to playing waltzes, rags, marches, and many other dance rhythms. The exercises warm you up for the lively performance piece at the end of the chapter.

Jumping and Landing Accuracy

The key to making good, accurate jumps is the same whether the jump is big or small: Maintain a comfortable, balanced hand position as you jump from the starting hand position across the keyboard to your landing destination. Jumping with an overextended pinky and your hand outstretched like the descent of a giant hawk upon its prey is very common. Instead, the image you want to keep in mind is of a frog jumping from lily pad to lily pad. A frog starts and lands with its body centered over the lily pad, contracting to the same closed, restful shape. Your hands are two frogs. As they jump from one position to another, they should look the same before and after the jump. You can practice this skill with every exercise.

Note-to-note jumps

In this first exercise (Track 116), you try jumping from note to note. Visualize each jump before you make the move. Include the relaxed, frog-like shape of your hand, the arc it traces, and the finger landing on its target key.

Note-to-chord jumps

Book V

**Exercises:
Practice,
Practice,
Practice**

Same principle — visualize and jump to an easy, relaxed position on the chord notes, and don't overextend your fingers or move with your hand stuck in an awkward hand position.

Chord-to-chord jumps

You want just enough muscle flexion to keep your position stable. Your hands should also have enough flexion to hold their position as they come down into the keys without collapsing in the joints. Flexibility in your wrists absorbs the weight as you play the chords.

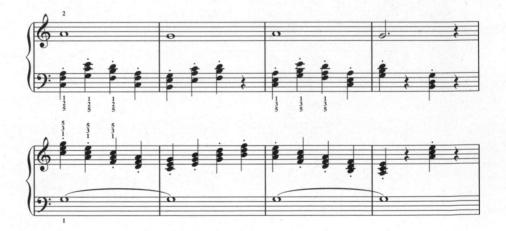

Accents on the downbeat

Book V

**Exercises:
Practice,
Practice,
Practice**

The next two exercises increase the challenge level with greater hand independence, varied articulation, and faster hand position changes. Here, your frogs get a springboard from the upbeat (on beat four) to the downbeat (on beat one). Practice with a light upbeat and a well-accented downbeat.

Accents on the upbeat

Now move the accent to the upbeat, with a light, springy downbeat.

Jumping with Both Hands Together

Synchronize jumps in both hands — matching movements in parallel motion and mirroring the jumps in contrary motion (the first exercise is Track 117).

Two-hand parallel motion jumps

Book V

Exercises:
Practice,
Practice,
Practice

Two-hand contrary motion jumps

Left-Hand Accompaniment Patterns

Jumps are common in left-hand accompaniments, while your right hand handles the melodic duties. Exercise this vital function in the next four exercises, first, with the sustain pedal for smooth accompaniment patterns.

Bass note-to-chord pattern in 4/4

Book V

**Exercises:
Practice,
Practice,
Practice**

PLAY THIS!

You'll find this left-hand pattern (Track 118) when you play marches and dance rhythms like the foxtrot. Lift the pedal on the upbeats.

Bass note-to-chord pattern in 3/4

This is a common pattern for a slow waltz, like Satie's well-known Gymnopédies. You get a smooth jump with the pedal down for each measure.

Ragtime and stride pattern

Book V

**Exercises:
Practice,
Practice,
Practice**

Practicing without the pedal is good for keeping an even rhythm, matching articulation, and smooth movement. Here's a pattern typical of a ragtime or basic stride piano style. Moving quickly off the bass note and rushing up to the chord is tempting, but that usually cuts the bass note short. Stay on the bass note a little longer to give the rhythm and harmony a solid foundation.

Waltz pattern

Let your right hand sing out the melody while the left hand accompanies it with a waltz pattern.

Performance Piece: "Lily Pad Rag"

Book V

**Exercises:
Practice,
Practice,
Practice**

The combination of a syncopated right-hand melody set over a steady 4-beat left-hand pattern gives ragtime its bouncy allure. As you work on this one (Track 119), develop a clear mental picture of when and where a melody note coincides with the left hand and when it is played between beats and held over, at the syncopation. Give extra emphasis to these syncopated notes.

Chapter 5

Exercising with Arpeggios and Alternating Hands

In This Chapter

▶ Improving finger accuracy and independence in open hand positions

▶ Practicing three- and four-note chord arpeggios and broken-chord patterns

▶ Crossing hands and making use of hand-to-hand scales and arpeggios

▶ Attempting strange and extreme keyboard positions

▶ Access the audio tracks at www.dummies.com/go/pianokeyboardaio/

*P*laying broken-chord patterns, or *arpeggios,* on the piano is very satisfying. In addition to the beauty and speed they can give your playing, they lend a bit of the style from the guitar and harp. In fact, *arpeggio* comes from the Italian word for harp, *arpa.*

Practicing arpeggio patterns is excellent for improving your accuracy while making short interval jumps from finger to finger, your crossover and pass-under technique as you practice multi-octave arpeggios, and your finger control and independence.

The alternating-hand techniques covered in the second half of this chapter are not only fun to play, but also useful in all kinds of keyboard music, from Scarlatti to Ravel, blues to Broadway.

Finger Jumps

In this section, you make a sequence of interval jumps from finger to finger. Your hand shape is open, with a wider span than five-finger position. The interval jumps are the same moves you make when you play arpeggios, but the

exercises give you practice with each interval separately, starting with thirds (Track 120) and on to fourths and fifths. The fingerings in each exercise will guide your hand position changes, so take time to map them out as you play.

Jumping thirds

Jumping fourths

Book V

**Exercises:
Practice,
Practice,
Practice**

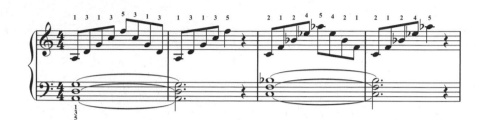

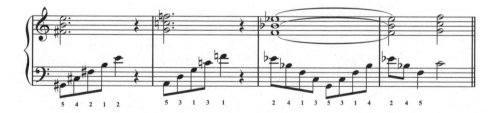

Jumping fifths

The Arpeggiator

The exercises in this section give you simple up-down patterns as well as nonsequential and inverted chord patterns. Practice these arpeggios with both staccato and legato articulation.

Triad arpeggio exercise #1

Book V

Exercises: Practice, Practice, Practice

Triad arpeggio exercise #2

Seventh-chord arpeggio exercise

Book V

**Exercises:
Practice,
Practice,
Practice**

Broken Chords

Broken-chord patterns are common in accompaniment figures. This section gives you four patterns found in a wide range of styles.

Alberti bass exercise

The Alberti bass is common in classical-style accompaniments. The pattern is a simple re-ordering of the chord notes in an arpeggio. This first piece is on Track 121.

Guitar-style broken chord exercise

Playing guitar-style arpeggio patterns often involves spreading the chord out over both hands. The next song is an arrangement of the classic "Careless Love" (Track 122), with the right hand playing the melody and completing the arpeggio pattern started in the left.

Blues-style broken chord exercise

Although you'll easily recognize the blues pattern in this piece, it's fun to realize it's simply an arpeggio set in a triplet rhythm. Try the pattern with the melody to W.C. Handy's "St. Louis Blues."

Octave, extended broken chord exercise

Book V

**Exercises:
Practice,
Practice,
Practice**

For a big, full piano sound, extend the arpeggio up to the octave and beyond. This extended pattern is a great exercise for the left hand. Keep the arpeggio smooth during "House of the Rising Sun." Alternate fingerings are in parentheses.

Performance Piece: "Harp Heaven"

For these arpeggios (Track 123) anticipate the change in harmony from measure to measure. Get the feel of the chord progression by practicing each chord shape in both your hands before you play.

Book V

**Exercises:
Practice,
Practice,
Practice**

Playing with Alternating Hands: Hand-to-Hand Scale Handoffs

A handoff is achieved by passing a melodic line from one hand to the other. Typically your left hand will hand off an ascending line to your right hand, and vice versa.

A hand crossover is for when you find it handy (and impressive) to cross one hand over the other to grab a note or a chord or two. Even if showing off isn't your thing, the exercises here help bring both hands to an equal level, because they're collaborating on the main musical part instead of one supporting the other.

As you hand off the scale from hand to hand, you want a smooth transition. Try to fool your ears; the handoff should be so smooth that you can't tell where one hand takes over from the other. And you should hear no noticeable change in dynamic or articulation.

Some of these techniques look complicated written on the grand staff! Unless marked with a "*R.H.*" or "*L.H.*" your right hand will play the notes on the top staff, and your left hand will play the notes on the bottom staff.

Scale handoff exercise #1

Prepare the hand position for both hands before you begin each phrase. Playing a smooth scale in one hand is easier if the other is waiting quietly in position to take over. Listen to Track 124.

Book V

**Exercises:
Practice,
Practice,
Practice**

Scale handoff exercise #2

Arpeggio handoff exercise #1

Book V

**Exercises:
Practice,
Practice,
Practice**

The same hand preparation from the previous section applies for hand-to-hand handoffs: Aim for a smooth line throughout.

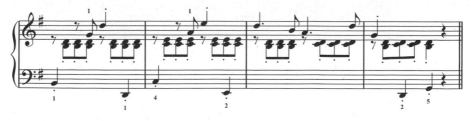

Arpeggio handoff exercise #2

Crossing over with the right hand

Give yourself room to cross over comfortably (Track 125).

Book V

**Exercises:
Practice,
Practice,
Practice**

Crossing over with the left hand

Chapter 6

Stepping Up to Octaves and Chord Progressions

* *

In This Chapter

▶ Gaining precision with octave jumps and practicing octave chords

▶ Getting an octave workout with Schumann's "Papillons"

▶ Trying seventh chord patterns and checking out chord progressions and chord cadences

▶ Access the audio tracks at www.dummies.com/go/pianokeyboardaio/

* *

Yes, octaves are hard. Everybody has to figure out how their own unique hands best meet the challenge. In this chapter, you'll find some new exercises designed to help you examine and improve your octave technique, and you may also find some tips here to make playing octaves easier. In octave practice, you use your entire hand as a single unit. Good octave technique combines an open (but not overextended) hand position with a confident, comfortable arm drop. Most of your attention is focused on the position of your pinky and thumb, which play most of the notes.

The second half of the chapter covers chord progressions. The fun and fascination of playing chord progressions comes in exploring their dual vertical and horizontal function. The vertical role is in each chord itself — how it's constructed from bottom to top. The horizontal role is in the way chords progress from one to another.

Opening Up to the Octave

There is no single, best way for you to play octaves; what works for one person may be different for others. A lot depends on the size and shape of your hands and fingers. Closely examine the thumb and pinky joints to see whether they are collapsed or whether you can modify their angle for more control. Look to maximize your advantages and minimize your disadvantages.

Octave scale exercise

This exercise (Track 126) begins with your hand in an easy, open fifth position. As you expand the intervals out to a sixth, seventh, and then to the octave, maintain a consistent shape, control, and touch.

Octave interval exercise

For this one, try to keep the octave shape as you move across the keyboard over a variety of close intervals. Don't tense your muscles into a locked grip. If your hands are big enough, use your 4th finger on the upper note.

Octave Jumps

Focus on your 5th finger — that's where most of the misses happen. You'll need more firmness in your pinky, with the thumb more relaxed and not grabbing. Aim down into the keys. Open your hand into a bigger arch for accuracy. Develop a clear mental image of where and how you're moving and practicing a comfortable, confident hand move.

Exercise with shorter jumps

PLAY THIS!

Exercise with longer jumps

Listen to Track 127.

Book V

**Exercises:
Practice,
Practice,
Practice**

Broken octave exercise with wrist rotation

Rotating your wrist transferring weight from pinky to thumb, and thumb to pinky, you can provide a tension-relief rhythm in your hand.

Broken octave exercise with hand contraction and expansion

PLAY THIS!

Listen to Track 128. Exaggerate the weight transfer when you cross your 2nd finger over. Allow your 5th finger to leave its note during this move.

Book V

Exercises: Practice, Practice, Practice

Octave Chords

Go for an even, comfortable position and a fluid movement. It's a tricky combination you're after: a firm hand shape with supple movement.

Adding one inner note

Adding two inner notes

Book V

**Exercises:
Practice,
Practice,
Practice**

Performance Piece: "Schumann's Octave Workout"

This piece (Track 129) is an adaptation of the first dance piece from Robert Schumann's "Papillons." It's an excellent workout for right-hand octaves.

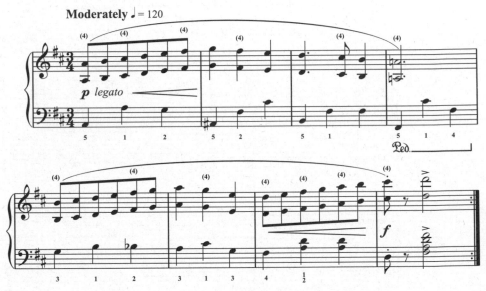

Seventh Chord Progressions

It's easy to hear — the tension caused by a dominant seventh chord tells you that the chord is unresolved.

Seventh chord progressions exercise #1

This exercise has dominant sevenths that resolve to the six major and minor triads in the diatonic scale. Try playing the eight-measure phrases randomly.

Book V

Exercises: Practice, Practice, Practice

Seventh chord progressions exercise #2

In the first half of this exercise, you cycle through all 12 dominant seventh chords by playing around the Circle of Fifths. On the second half, the chord sequence has minor seventh chords leading to dominant sevenths.

Chord Cadences, Familiar Patterns

This section shows you some chord patterns you find frequently in all types of music: cadences, turnarounds, and sequences. A *cadence* is a short progression, usually two or three chords, that establishes tonality and resolution. Here are common cadences in C major and A minor.

Book V

**Exercises:
Practice,
Practice,
Practice**

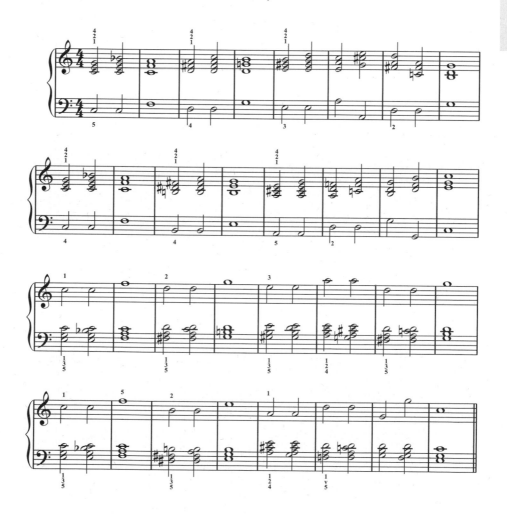

Turnarounds get you "turned around" to go back to the home key. This usually means getting to the V chord, which leads back to the I chord. Chord sequences are fundamental building blocks of chord progressions.

Extended Chord Progressions

Here are two pieces where the chord progressions are the defining feature. Both use diatonic chords, nondiatonic chords, sequences, and cadences.

Extended major-key chord progression

This exercise (Track 130) is adapted from Tchaikovsky's *Morning Prayer, Album for the Young, Opus 39.*

Extended minor-key chord progression

This exercise (Track 131) is from Chopin's *Prelude,* Opus 28, No. 20.

Book VI

Exploring Electronic Keyboard Technology

For some tips on getting yourself out and gigging with other musicians, check out a free online article at www.dummies.com/extras/pianokeyboardaio.

Contents at a Glance

Chapter 1: Choosing Sounds and Effects.........................481

First Things First: Understanding Some Important Terminology 482
Knowing and Using Effects 485
Meeting the Main Types of Effects...486
Choosing Effects for Each Type Of Sound 495

Chapter 2: Adding Accompaniment, Rhythm Patterns, and Arpeggiation 499

Getting Your Groove On: Working with Onboard Drum Rhythms 500
Playing with Accompaniment..506
Letting the Keyboard Make the Choices for You 514
Using Some Fancy Extras 516
Exploring Arpeggiation 517
Exploring More Arpeggiator Features...520
Trying Out Some Different Sounds: Matching Sounds and Arp Patterns..............522
Adding Fun Sound and Effects Tweaks 523

Chapter 3: Recording and Editing Your Sounds 525

Audio Recording versus MIDI Recording...526
Capturing What You Hear As It Happens: One-Pass Recording 530
Recording Multitrack MIDI 533
Refining Your MIDI Recordings...536
Trying Some Common Sound Edits 542
Getting Your Song out of the Keyboard and into the World 549

Chapter 4: Using Onboard Learning Systems 551

Working with Built-In Songs...551
Introducing Casio's Step-up Lesson System 555
Exploring Yamaha's Educational Suite Lesson System...............................562

Chapter 5: Playing Along with Recordings and Using Music Software..565

Exploring the Advantages of Playing Along 566
Connecting an Audio Device to Your Keyboard to Hear Both Together 567
Getting in Tune 570
Figuring Out a Song You Don't Know...571
The Computer Connection: Using Software to Enhance Your Music-Making.......575
Connecting Your Keyboard to Your Computer 578
Hooking Up to Your iPad 584
Exploring Popular Types of Music Software..585

Chapter 1

Choosing Sounds and Effects

In This Chapter

▶ Getting keyboard sound terminology straight and calling up sounds

▶ Understanding and recognizing various types of effects

▶ Identifying the basic parameters for each effect type

▶ Access the audio tracks at www.dummies.com/go/pianokeyboardaio/

This chapter aims to help you get a handle on how to get different sounds out of your keyboard. Have you ever watched a guitar player in concert step on some little box with his foot at different parts of the song? Or rock his foot forward and back on a pedal? He's using effects to enhance and change his sound, turning different ones on and off for each part of the song. You can do the same with a keyboard.

Effects add qualities to the sound that the basic tone production method doesn't include, so using them can change the character of any sound. Over time, well-established groups of effects have developed, most of which are explained in this chapter.

Your keyboard already has some effects configured with each sound, and you may or may not have much control over them. Working with the effects may be as simple as flipping an on/off switch or may go into greater detail. Developing the ability to hear and identify the various types of effects helps you recognize them being used in the music you listen to and reproduce those sounds for the songs you want to play.

A likely reason you've chosen to play an electronic keyboard is that it offers more than one sound. Having a variety of sound keeps you interested in playing longer. Can you imagine hearing Mozart played by Jimi Hendrix? Chuck Berry played with a flute? Nirvana played on a harpsichord? Having the right sounds for the type of music you like to play is essential. And that's why a keyboardist is the luckiest musician of all. Your keyboard can transform into any instrument you want at the push of a button. No other player has that power, so use it wisely!

First Things First: Understanding Some Important Terminology

One of the most confusing things about shopping for keyboards, talking about them with your friends, or just using them is the crazy array of names used to describe the choice of sounds available. Even the term *sound* may not be that simple. Is "a sound" the re-creation of a single known instrument such as the piano or a pipe organ? The combination of multiple instruments being played at the same time, such as a whole orchestra or a big-band sax section? Two instruments being played together such as a guitar and a flute or an electric piano and a bass guitar?

All these things are possible, but this variety means you need a name for the individual "thing" a keyboard can reproduce, the combination of multiple "things," and so on. To make matters worse, each company has its own name for each of these "things."

This section tries to clear up this confusion and introduce you to a few concepts about the Musical Instrument Digital Interface (MIDI for short), covered in greater detail in Book VI Chapter 3.

A sound by any other name: Recognizing the various terms

To keep things simple and clear, some refer to single "things" as *sounds*, and the combinations of "things" as *multipart sounds*. If only real life were so simple. Each manufacturer uses its own terms for these things, which creates a world of confusion. Take a look at Tables 1-1 and 1-2 to see what this means.

Table 1-1	Brand Names and Individual-Sound Terminology
Brand Name	*Terms for Individual Sounds*
Casio	Tone (all)
Hammond/ Suzuki	Voice (all)
Kawai	Internal Sound, Voice (all)
Korg	Program (synth, workstation), Sound (digital piano, arranger)

Brand Name	Terms for Individual Sounds
Kurzweil	Preset, Voice Preset (synth, stage piano), Preset Program, Sound Program (digital piano)
Moog	Preset, Patch (synth)
Nord	Program (all)
Roland	Patch (synth, workstation), Tone (digital piano, arranger), Registration (combo organ)
Yamaha	Voice, Sweet! Voice, Cool! Voice, Live! Voice, Mega Voice, Super Articulation Voice (all)

Table 1-2	**Brand Names and Multiple-Sound Terminology**
Brand Name	**Terms for Multiple Sounds**
Casio	Tone (all)
Kawai	User Setup (stage piano), Registration (digital pianos)
Korg	Combination (synth, workstation), Performance (arranger)
Kurzweil	MIDI Setup (synth, digital piano)
Roland	Performance (arranger, stage piano), Live Set (synth, workstation)
Yamaha	Performance (all)

Book VI

Exploring Electronic Keyboard Technology

Table 1-1 shows a list of brand names and the name(s) they use for single sounds in their various keyboards.

What a crazy and confusing list of terms all meaning the same thing. Can't we all just get along?

If that wasn't confusing enough, some of these words have other meanings in music tech terms.

Tone can also mean the brightness or bassy quality of a sound. Many home stereos, guitar amplifiers, and other audio devices have a control for tone that doesn't change to another instrument sound; it affects the EQ (brightness and bass amount) of the device (more about EQ toward the end of this chapter).

Voice is sometimes used when describing how many notes you can play at the same time, which is called *polyphony* (which means "many voices"). A guitar is six-note polyphonic (it has six strings), and an acoustic piano is 88-note polyphonic. As a side note, many instruments can only play one note at a time (woodwinds, brass, the human voice, some analog synthesizers), and they're called *monophonic.* So a spec sheet for a keyboard may use the term *100-voice polyphony,* meaning it can produce 100 notes at the same time.

Preset can also mean a memory location that can't be changed or overwritten. Products that use this term list a number of Preset and User locations to describe what can't and can be changed.

Moving on to the multipart sounds, Table 1-2 shows how different brands refer to these sounds in their keyboards.

Makes you wish you had a scorecard to follow, doesn't it?

MIDI: Defining GM/GM2

As you look at web pages, literature, keyboard manuals, and keyboard front panels and displays, you're going to come across General MIDI logos. *General MIDI* (GM) is a standard that defines a set of sounds, instrumental effects, and numerous standard features so MIDI-based music can be shared among various devices (keyboards, computers, web pages, and even cellphones) and always sound the same. GM defines a set of 128 sounds that cover the most basic and universal group of instruments. So when you select a sound in the GM bank or group of sounds, it will sound similar to that same sound in any other brand or type of keyboard you have.

MIDI stands for *Musical Instrument Digital Interface,* a technology standard developed in 1983 by a number of keyboard companies to allow keyboards to "talk" to each other — to trigger sounds from one keyboard (the *master*) and have other keyboards (the *slave*) sound at the same time. This setup enabled layering of sounds between different keyboards and brands for a fuller sound. It has evolved into a universally supported and wonderful capability to not only play keyboards connected together but also to connect keyboards to computers for recording, sound editing, musical notation, and other activities. (MIDI is covered in more detail in Book VI Chapter 3.)

General MIDI 2 (GM2) is an expanded set of sounds that adds more diversity and variety to the library, but the concept remains the same: guaranteed sound conformity so that songs and arrangements can be reproduced with consistency and accuracy no matter what the playback device.

These logos indicate that the product includes the complete General MIDI sound set and responds properly to sound selection commands via MIDI. Figure 1-1 shows an example of these logos.

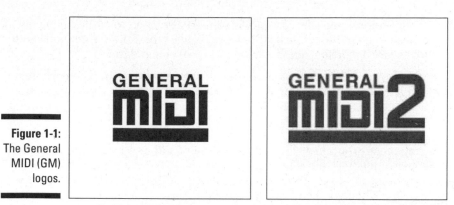

Figure 1-1:
The General
MIDI (GM)
logos.

The General MIDI logos are trademarks of MIDI Manufacturers Association (MMA) and used with permission.

Two other GM-like standards are brand specific. *GS* is a Roland standard that's similar to GM2, and *XG* is a Yamaha standard that goes even further than GM2. But the idea is the same (as far as sounds are concerned) — a pre-specified list of sounds that is always the same in products bearing the logo.

Knowing and Using Effects

Effects are used in electronic musical instruments, amplifiers, large sound systems in performance venues, and recording studios. Often, you don't think about them; they've become a natural part of the sound you associate with an instrument. Some are easy to identify because they add a signature color and quality to a sound, but others are seemingly invisible because they correct or enhance the basic tonal nature of a sound without adding anything noticeable.

Here are the most common groups of effects:

- ✔ **Tonal correction:** This effect is commonly called *EQ* for *equalizer* or *equalization*. It's like the basic treble and bass controls of a stereo but can be much fancier and more detailed.

- ✔ **Volume control:** *Volume* is often called *gain* in audio terms, but it means just what you think: the level of the sound. Effects such as a compressor, a limiter, and a preamp fall into this category.

- ✔ **Modulation:** *Modulation* is the broadest category of effects and the most obvious to hear. These effects add motion and color to your sound and can be subtle or wildly psychedelic. Popular effects include chorus, phase shifting, flanging, tremolo, and rotary speaker.

✔ **Tonal coloration:** This category is somewhat related to modulation but doesn't add motion. It just colors, or changes, the sound. Common candidates are distortion, amp models, and speaker simulators.

✔ **Ambience:** These effects simulate the characteristics of an environment such as a room, a large hall, a cathedral, or a canyon. Common effects are delay (distinct echoes) and reverb (a more indistinct wash of sound reflections).

Knowing these groupings, you can listen to a sound or a recording and start to define what you're hearing. If an acoustic piano sound seems to be very far away and has some subtle echoes, you should think reverb and perhaps some delay. When you hear a very "crunchy" clavinet (clav) sound with a thick, aggressive quality, you may rightfully assume it's being run through some distortion or perhaps an amp simulator (or a real guitar amp).

Meeting the Main Types of Effects

This book is about pianos and keyboards, not guitars or recording studios, so the following sections introduce you to only the most common effects you'll find and want to use in your instrument. This section covers onboard effects; you can buy additional boxes to run your keyboard through, but covering those would require a separate book.

Reverb

Reverb adds space around your notes and can make your sound seem farther away, even dreamy. It's short for *reverberation,* which describes the continuation of sound in a particular space after the original sound is produced and stops or decays away. Reverb produces a kind of hazy or blurred type of echo that's very pleasing to the ear and gives a sense of the space you're playing in.

The character of a reverb is defined by several factors, including the following:

✔ The overall size of the space you produce the sound in

✔ The number of surfaces the sound can bounce off of (how enclosed is the room, how high is the ceiling, and so on)

✔ The material of the walls (wood, concrete, glass, or whatever), which affects how much sound they absorb and how distinct the repetitions/reflections are

Put simply, various types of reverbs can make it sound like you're playing in all kinds of different spaces.

Keyboards typically give you a limited set of parameters you can use to adjust reverb. Here are the most common:

TIP

✔ **Mix or wet/dry mix:** *Mix* controls how much of your original, unaffected *(dry)* signal is passed on and how much of the reverberated *(wet)* signal is introduced. Often, just a little wet signal is good enough to produce a nice, not-too-sloppy sound. But sometimes a lot more of the wet signal is nice, giving your playing a spacious quality and majestic sound.

The more notes you play or the faster the tempo, the less reverb you want to use. This way, all your playing can be clearly heard without blurring together.

✔ **Type:** *Type* is an overall selection that sets the size of the space and other associated parameters, or even the method of producing the reflections. Common choices are room, hall, stage, cathedral, and so on. You may sometimes see *plate* or *spring,* which is a form of artificial reflection where a sound is played into a box that contains a metal plate or large spring, which vibrates from the incoming sound waves.

✔ **Size:** The *size* control defines the overall size of your chosen simulated space. So a small room may seem like a tiny hallway or closet, and a large room may be 10 feet by 20 feet or 40 feet by 40 feet. The idea of a small cathedral or canyon may seem funny, but remember that the type of room is defined not only by its floor space but also by characteristics like ceiling height and the materials the walls are made of.

✔ **Reverb time:** This control simulates how long the sound reflections take to die away or stop sounding. It's casually described as a length — a short reverb, a long reverb — and the reflections are sometimes called the *reverb tail.*

On many simple keyboards and digital pianos, mix and type may be your only control choices. More advanced reverbs that offer deeper programmability include parameters such as

✔ **EQ:** Shapes the tone of the sound a bit.

✔ **Damping:** Simulates how much of the sound is absorbed; higher values cause the reflections to come back darker or less bright.

✔ **Pre-delay:** Pushes back the whole reflective simulation, so your original dry sound can be heard before the reflections start. Adding some pre-delay (or raising its existing value) helps your sound be clearer and more distinct before being wrapped in the ambience of the effect.

PLAY THIS!

Track 132 plays examples of various reverb types.

Book VI

Exploring Electronic Keyboard Technology

Delay

Delay (sometimes called *echo*) is an ambience effect, adding the impression of space around your notes. But it works differently from reverb in that the reflections are distinct, clear echoes or repeats of the incoming notes. You've probably seen a cartoon where the character yells into the Grand Canyon and his exact words come back a few moments later. That's delay. Used very subtly, it adds some ambience to your playing; brought up more in the mix it becomes a highly rhythmic counterpoint to play against.

The most common delay parameters your keyboard will let you adjust are

- ✔ **Mix or wet/dry mix:** Determines how much of your dry signal is passed on and how much the distinct echoes *(wet sounds)* are introduced.

- ✔ **Delay time:** *Delay time* controls the timing of the repetitions — specifically, the interval of time between the original signal and each repeat. It's usually represented in milliseconds but can be set to note values or even rhythmic figures in more advanced instruments.

- ✔ **Feedback:** This parameter manipulates how many distinct repetitions will sound. At most settings, these repetitions decay in volume with each occurrence, so they seem to fade out.

   Be careful when adjusting this parameter! High feedback values can cause the repetitions to get louder and keep generating endlessly. Things can get very loud quickly and damage your speakers and/or hearing.

- ✔ **Damping:** *Damping* adjusts the brightness of each repetition to simulate the effect of sound absorption; each occurrence gets darker. Along with the level decay that may be built into feedback, damping helps keep your playing from sounding too cluttered.

Track 133 demonstrates delay.

Chorus/flanging/phase shifting

Chorus, flanging, and phase shifting are modulation effects that produce a warm, swirling sort of thickened sound. Each one sounds different, but they're all closely related in concept and use.

Listen to Track 134 to hear flanging, chorus, and phase shifting demonstrated and compared.

Chorus

Chorus is produced by constantly varying the pitch of a slightly delayed copy of your sound. When this variation is mixed back with the original signal, it produces a pleasing, rich result. The chorus effect was first designed to sound like a choir of voices singing together, with the slight imperfections in tuning and timing that produced an ensemble sound.

Common chorus parameters to adjust on your keyboard include

- ✔ **Mix or wet/dry mix:** Controls how much of your dry signal is passed on and how much of the original-plus-varied *(wet)* signal is introduced. Unlike reverb, mix sounds better at higher, or wetter, values for chorus.

- ✔ **Depth:** This parameter indicates how much pitch variation is produced.

- ✔ **Rate/frequency:** This control adjusts the speed of the pitch variations. Very slow to medium sounds good; too fast, and your sound takes on a wobbly, underwater quality. But maybe that's what you want.

Book VI

Exploring Electronic Keyboard Technology

More advanced choruses may have some built-in EQ to shape the tone of the sound and may offer a delay time parameter to determine the amount of time the signal is delayed. This parameter setting can be the critical difference between chorus and flanging (see the following section): Values between 1 and 15 milliseconds produce flanging, and chorus starts at 20 milliseconds.

Flanging

Flanging is less warm than chorus because flanging's closer delay time sounds more metallic and less like close copies of the original signal. Flanging adds one critical additional parameter: feedback.

Feedback routes some of the output back to the input, so the whole process starts again but on an already-affected sound. This accentuates the sweep and creates some resonant peaks in the harmonics, not unlike resonance or Q in a filter. At extreme feedback settings, flanging can produce a whoosh sort of sound resembling a jet takeoff.

Phase shifting

Phase shifting differs from chorus and flanging in that it doesn't use a delay-line shifted copy of the incoming signal, which has all frequencies shifted by the same amount. Rather, it mixes a copy of the sound that has been shifted slightly out-of-phase by an all-pass filter, which shifts different frequencies by different amounts. (Check out the later section "Filter" for details on this control.) This produces a very rich, warm sound with more tonal peaks than chorus, because it has a feedback loop in its design like the flanger does. And it sounds less metallic than flanging because of the differing frequency shifts.

EQ

EQ allows you to boost or cut the level of various frequency ranges within your sound. You can find EQ settings (with names like rock, jazz, concert hall, acoustic, dance, and so on) on your music players and electronics. They show multiple columns, each representing a frequency or pitch area. If the bar is tall, it's boosting that range; if it's low, it's cutting the range. Figure 1-2 shows a common representation of this setup.

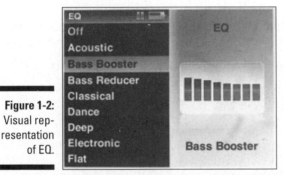

Figure 1-2: Visual representation of EQ.

Apple iPod equalizer screenshot courtesy of Jerry Kovarsky

Your keyboard's EQ function gives you control over various frequencies that you can shape to change the tonal nature of your sound. The frequency ranges are represented as numbers in hertz (Hz) and kilohertz (kHz or k), such as 100 Hz or 2.5 kHz (2,500 hertz). Low frequencies are called *bass,* or *lows,* middle frequencies are called *mids* (naturally), and upper frequencies are called *highs.* EQs come in a couple of common types:

- ✔ A *graphic EQ* (see Figure 1-3) offers 5 to 31 frequencies, called *bands,* which are fixed values that can be cut or boosted.

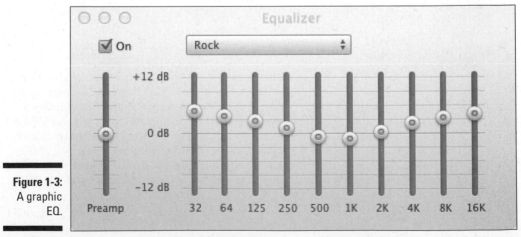

Figure 1-3: A graphic EQ.

Apple iTunes equalizer screenshot courtesy of Jerry Kovarsky

✔ A *hi-shelf EQ* cuts or boost frequencies above the value defined (like a brightness control).

✔ A *low-shelf EQ* cuts or boost frequencies below a defined value (like a bass control).

✔ A *parametric EQ* offers some number of bands (usually between two and four); you can freely select their frequencies, so you can use them to flexibly shape the sound any way you want, as shown in Figure 1-4.

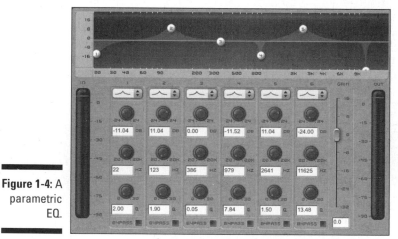

Figure 1-4: A parametric EQ.

Bias SuperFreq-6 EQ screenshot courtesy of Jerry Kovarsky

Some EQs combine these concepts, with a low-shelf band followed by one or two parametric bands and a hi-shelf band on top, for example. Or the outer bands can be changed from shelving to parametric as needed.

Keyboards commonly offer these parametric EQ parameters:

✔ **Frequency:** The pitch or frequency center for the band of EQ.

✔ **Q:** The width of frequencies that the cut or boost affects, sometimes called *bandwidth*. With a wide Q, you affect a broad range of your sound. You can use very narrow Q to reduce a harsh frequency or noise or add some extra emphasis to a specific noise or character of a sound.

✔ **Gain:** The amount that a band is boosted (a positive value) or cut (a negative value).

Many people think they need to boost a band to improve the sound, but cutting a band can often be more effective. Reducing a frequency that is already covered by another sound (cutting bass so you can hear the bass guitar and bass drum better) is a good approach.

You can hear demonstrations of shelving and parametric EQs in Track 135.

Distortion

Distortion adds a dirty, harsh quality to your sound. You're most familiar with this concept in rock guitar; the crunching rhythmic figures of classic riffs like "Smoke on the Water" by Deep Purple and "Satisfaction" by the Rolling Stones are well-known examples. Varying levels of distortion may be called *overdrive, fuzz,* or *gain booster.*

Distortion is created by overloading the input to an amplifier, causing the circuitry to produce internal clipping or errors. Nowadays, electronics and software code can readily imitate it without the need for an actual guitar amp.

Here are some common distortion controls you can adjust:

- ✔ **Mix or wet/dry mix:** This option controls how much dry signal is passed on, and how much of the distorted *(wet)* signal is introduced. Because distortion can be a very heavy effect, you get a better sound if you mix some dry signal in for clarity, especially for keyboard sounds. For emulating rock guitar, you can never have too much distortion!

- ✔ **Type or model:** Many distortion effects are emulating other famous devices, be they classic guitar amplifiers, pedal effects (often called *stomp boxes*), or combinations thereof. The *type* control is where you decide which you want to use.

- ✔ **Input gain:** *Input gain* is the parameter that you turn up to produce the overloaded tone. Low values produce a slightly thicker, warmer sound, and higher values get crunchier up into full-out fuzz bliss.

- ✔ **Output level:** Because turning up the input increases the volume, you use this control to bring the overall level back down so you don't blow the roof off your home!

- ✔ **EQ:** Many distortion effects include some type of tone controls to help tame or shape the sound further. This setup can range from a single tone knob or parameter to multiband graphic and parametric equalizers. (The preceding section has info on these types of equalizers.)

Listen to Track 136 to hear various types of distortion demonstrated.

Rotary speaker

The *rotary speaker* effect emulates the famous spinning speaker cabinet (called a *Leslie*) invented for use with the Hammond organ. It was named after its creator, Donald Leslie, who wanted to make the organ sound more like a pipe organ, with its pipes spread out in a large space. What resulted is a strange yet wonderful-sounding contraption that has two spinning speakers inside. They spin at different speeds, producing a rich, moving quality to the sound. They can be switched to spin slowly or very quickly — a dramatic effect that organists use to build excitement for various parts of a song.

The rotary speaker is an integral part of the tonewheel organ sound but has also been used by rock guitar players, on other electric keyboard sounds, and even on vocals (John Lennon famously sang through one on the song "Tomorrow Never Knows").

This speaker is a complex effect that may or may not have more parameters to adjust (you may only have the option to toggle the speed control from slow to fast). That said, common adjustable factors include the following:

- ✔ **Horn/rotor speed:** The upper horn can rotate at two different speeds, each of which may be adjusted. Similarly, the lower spinning drum (the rotor) has a two-speed control as well.

- ✔ **Horn/rotor acceleration and deceleration:** These control the time the horn and rotor each take to transition from slow to fast and back again.

- ✔ **Mode:** *Mode* chooses whether the speaker is stopped or spinning. Completely stopping the speakers from spinning is called *brake,* and some designs allow all three states — brake, slow, fast — to be used. (Early Leslies had two settings: no spinning and spinning fast.)

- ✔ **Horn/rotor balance:** Microphones are usually placed by the rotary speaker to further amplify it in concert or to record it in the studio. This control positions the mic to be closer to the high horn (producing a brighter, thinner sound) or lower by the spinning drum (producing a bassier, heavier sound). More advanced designs allow you to choose the position and distance for each microphone.

Listen to Track 137 to hear the rotary speaker effect.

Filter

A *filter* is a tone-modifying control that allows certain frequencies to pass through while blocking others. The point at which it gradually starts to remove the frequencies is called the *filter cutoff.* Book VI Chapter 3 talks more about filters.

Book VI

Exploring Electronic Keyboard Technology

Common tone parameters you can adjust on your keyboard are

- **Type:** The most common filter type is called a *low-pass,* which allows all frequencies below the cutoff to pass through, gradually removing everything above it. A *high-pass* filter does the opposite, only allowing frequencies above the cutoff to pass through.

- **Cutoff:** The point at which the filter gradually starts to remove frequencies by fading them out. Moving around this cutoff point (called *sweeping* the cutoff) produces a very cool sound, most often associated with synthesizer sounds.

- **Resonance or Q:** This parameter emphasizes frequencies close to either side of the cutoff, like a sharp, narrow band of EQ boost. It produces a nasal, piercing quality at high settings and sounds great when combined with the sweeping of the cutoff. A classic synth sound effect.

Check out Track 138 to hear demonstrations of various filters.

Wah-wah and auto-wah

The *wah-wah* is a filter placed into a rocking pedal to make it easy to sweep the cutoff with your foot while playing. Commonly used for guitar, it's also popular for keyboards, especially the clav.

The *auto-wah* (also called *envelope follow filter* or *envelope filter*) produces the sweep movement based on the incoming audio signal, so you don't need to move your foot. Each note or chord played triggers the sweep, letting you easily play highly rhythmic parts without wearing out your ankle. Common auto-wah parameters that keyboards let you adjust include the following:

- **Response/rate:** Controls the speed at which the filter opens up in reaction to the incoming signal.

- **Decay:** Sets the length of time the filter takes to close back down.

- **Range/manual/frequency:** Sets the frequency of the filter cutoff at the bottom and top of the sweep. This control is helpful to optimize the effect for the type of sound you're using it on (bass, type of keyboard sound, guitar).

  Note: This parameter is the only one that would be available for a wah-wah effect.

- **Sensitivity:** Adjusts the range of the sweep, based on the strength of the incoming signal. Low settings don't allow the range of the sweep to change much based on the incoming signal. At higher settings, soft levels produce very little sweep (a darker sound), and stronger signals produce a more full-range sweep.

Higher sensitivity helps produce the more expressive and dramatic auto-wah effect. But it needs to be adjusted to match your playing technique and how hard or soft your touch is. Adjust the setting up or down until it's easy to produce and control the range of sweep you like.

Track 139 plays examples of wah and auto-wah.

Choosing Effects for Each Type Of Sound

Book VI

Exploring Electronic Keyboard Technology

Certain instrument and effect combinations are matches made in rock-and-roll heaven! Some are commonly used based on musical genre (funk and wah-wah, for example), and others are associated with specific artists.

To help you get the sound you want for various songs, the following sections list the essential keyboard sounds and the effects commonly used and associated with them, often naming artists and songs as examples.

Note: Reverb is used on pretty much everything, so it's not highlighted here.

Piano-type and synth sounds

You can use keyboard effects with many common piano sounds:

- **Acoustic piano:** Sometimes a little EQ can help modify a piano for a specific song or style of music. Classical sounds good with a less bright, more mellow sound, and rock works with a much brighter piano to stand out when drums and guitars are playing. Some pop and rock music uses a little chorus on the piano (think of Journey's "Don't Stop Believin'"), and deeper chorus with more pitch variation (an increase of the depth parameter) helps make piano sound more honky-tonk.

- **Tine/Rhodes electric piano:** So many effects can work on this classic instrument:
    - **Phase shifting:** Use subtle phaser settings to get that Billy Joel "Just the Way You Are" sound, Steely Dan/Donald Fagen tunes (check out "Green Flower Street"), late 1980s Doobie Brothers ("Minute by Minute"), or the immortal sound of Richard Tee as featured on many Paul Simon, Grover Washington ("Just the Two of Us"), and Stuff recordings.
    - **Chorus:** Using a chorus helps to get the sound of Jamiroquai as well as the whole L.A. 1980s sound (think Al Jarreau, Toto, Quincy Jones, Chicago, and early Yellowjackets).

- **Distortion/wah-wah:** To sound like vintage/early 1970s jazz, fusion, and rock artists, don't use any modulation effect. Do use EQ if needed to darken the sound a little bit. However, a little distortion (not too much) helps to get the aggressive solo sound of fusion players like Jan Hammer (Mahavishnu Orchestra's "Inner Mounting Flame"), Chick Corea (early *Return to Forever*), and George Duke (solo and with Frank Zappa), who often played through guitar amps. Many artists also used wah-wah, still a good way to "funk-up" electric piano (both tine and reed versions).

- **Delay:** You can use delay to get the spacey sound of early electric Herbie Hancock ("Mwandishi" and "Headhunters"), Brian Auger ("Live Oblivion"), Ramsey Lewis ("Sun Goddess"), and many reggae and dub recordings.

✔ **Reed/Wurlitzer electric piano:** This electric piano wasn't processed with effects as much, but the number one application is putting a deep chorus on it to get that Supertramp sound ("Logical Song" and "Goodbye Stranger"). EQ and distortion can help to get a stronger rock sound.

Many people like putting electric piano through a rotary speaker.

✔ **Clavinet:** Clavinet through a wah-wah or auto-wah is one of the classic sounds of funk music. Listen to songs like Stevie Wonder ("Higher Ground" and "Maybe Your Baby"), Billy Preston ("Outa-Space"), Rufus ("Tell Me Something Good"), Herbie Hancock ("Chameleon"), and the funkiest non-funk tune ever recorded, The Band's "Up on Cripple Creek." It was also prominently featured in reggae, like in Bob Marley/ the Wailers "Burnin' and Lootin'" and "Get Up, Stand Up."

Distortion also sounds good on clav, which often was played through a guitar amp. You can hear this effect in varying degrees on the afore-mentioned Billy Preston songs, Stevie Wonder ("We Can Work It Out"), Led Zeppelin ("Trampled Under Foot"), Phish's "Tubes," and the always-amazing John Medeski (Medeski Martin & Wood).

✔ **Tonewheel organ:** A lot of famous organists have pretty specific and well-known sounds:

- Tonewheel organ and Leslie go hand in hand. Many jazz players are known for using only the brake and fast settings, whereas most rock, soul, and other players use the slow and fast speeds. Two prominent exceptions in rock/soul are Steve Winwood (solo and with Traffic and Blind Faith) and Booker T. (solo and with Booker T. & the MG's), who both favor brake and fast settings.

- Progressive rocker Keith Emerson ran his organ through both Leslies and guitar amps to get more overdrive in his sound. He also used a distortion pedal effect on the smaller L-100 he'd abuse nightly to get feedback from it (find live versions of "Rondo" to hear/see this in action). Hard-rock organist Jon Lord (Deep Purple) stopped using a rotary speaker altogether, favoring using guitar amps to crank up his sound to match the rest of the band ("Machine Head" and "Made in Japan"). Jazz/rock organist Brian Auger is another famous non-Leslie user.

- Tony Banks (Genesis) ran his tonewheel organ through a phase shifter and sometimes a chorus; listen to albums like *Wind and Wuthering, And Then There Were Three,* and *Duke.*

✔ **Synth sounds:** This group is a vast category, and basically, anything is possible. Have fun!

Book VI

Exploring Electronic Keyboard Technology

Guitar sounds

You really should add some effects to the guitar sounds coming out of your keyboard to make them more realistic and pleasing. Here are some ideas:

✔ **Guitar:** Guitar works well with a wide variety of effects. All the modulation effects can sound good, as do delay and reverb when you want to play more open, arpeggiated background parts. Andy Summers (The Police) and especially The Edge (U2) are famous for this. For stronger rock songs and solos, distortion and amp models become an important part of your needed sound. Wah-wah works well for some rock songs and certainly for funky tunes, and auto-wah is perfect for funk.

✔ **Bass guitar:** Bass is the one sound that doesn't want much reverb, if any. Keeping it dry helps to anchor the feel and clarity of a song's groove. Sometimes subtle chorus or flanging can work, especially on fretless bass. For heavier rock and metal music, distortion is appropriate. Auto-wah can work for some funk.

Other sounds

What to do with more-orchestral instruments? Less is more:

✔ **Wind/brass instruments:** These instruments rarely require anything more than a little reverb to taste.

✔ **Strings:** All acoustic instruments sound good with reverb. String parts in songs sometimes come from real strings or from electronic string synthesizers and such. Slight chorus or phasing adds animation and movement to these instruments.

Chapter 2

Adding Accompaniment, Rhythm Patterns, and Arpeggiation

• •

In This Chapter

▶ Manipulating drum patterns with variations, drum fills, intros, and endings

▶ Exploring auto-accompaniment and walking through how an arpeggiator works

▶ Checking out simple and more complex arps

▶ Choosing sounds that work best with arpeggiation

▶ Access the audio tracks at www.dummies.com/go/pianokeyboardaio/

• •

Drums and rhythm are the most primal aspect of music; all music fans have tapped on their legs/knees/steering wheels to their favorite songs. It's a natural reaction to a song with a good groove. If you don't know any drummers, onboard drum rhythms on keyboards can make a fine rhythmic partner for practicing and playing. Onboard drums are much more fun and inspiring rhythm-keepers than a metronome.

This chapter takes you through possibilities of using onboard drum machines and backing parts that feature drum and percussion rhythm. You discover how to use them as good practice and performance tools and how to vary the parts so things don't get boring. Later the chapter expands on this idea for full-band auto-accompaniment, adding some controls that help the drummer and the rest of the band keep things interesting.

For some people, the concept of automatic accompaniment brings up images of hokey one-finger mall organ demos and corny '80s ads. All too often, "serious" musicians looked down their noses at these products.

Well, the fact is, the sound realism and musical quality of the auto-accompaniment in today's keyboards are markedly improved and nothing to scoff at. They can provide a child, student, or casual player with tools to help him play better and enjoy his time making music, which is a wonderful thing. Across Europe, Asia, and the Middle East, accompaniment keyboards are *the* professional keyboard; very skilled players use them (in public!) with pride.

This chapter shows you how to get auto-accompaniment features started and how you can feed them the chords they need to generate their full backing band parts. It goes under the hood a little to better understand the musical parts that make up their patterns and shows you plenty of tips and tricks to keep the parts interesting and not canned-sounding.

If you're a fan of late-'70s and '80s pop, synth-pop and new wave music, or the club dance music since the turn of the 21st century (trance, electro, hardstyle, and so on), then you've heard an *arpeggiator* in action. Early synth artists and producers such as Jean Michel Jarre, Giorgio Moroder, Gary Numan, Thomas Dolby, Howard Jones, and Duran Duran used synths and arpeggiators in many of the pop and dance hits of their eras. Not sure what that means? Have you heard any of these songs?

✔ Donna Summer: "I Feel Love"

✔ Duran Duran: "Rio," "Save a Prayer," and "Hungry Like the Wolf"

✔ Eurythmics: "Here Comes the Rain Again"

✔ Talking Heads: "Once In a Lifetime" intro

✔ Irene Cara: "Flashdance (What a Feeling)"

✔ Cyndi Lauper: "All Through the Night"

✔ Alan Parsons Project: "Games People Play"

✔ Erasure: "Drama," "Chains of Love" intro

In each of these songs, you hear a repeated synth figure of some sort; up high in the background, for the bass line, or providing an outline of the chordal harmony. That's an arpeggiator — often abbreviated *arp* — in action, and for many people, that type of sound is the definition of the sound of a synthesizer in popular music. At the end of this chapter, you'll discover the basics of arpeggiation and some of the most common settings to tweak. Not all keyboards have this feature, but it's a cool tool to know about.

Getting Your Groove On: Working with Onboard Drum Rhythms

Playing in time is a fundamental part of a good performance. But keeping proper, even timing is only part of the process; the act of playing with a good feel is a more intangible but still critical element. Musicians use terms like *groove* and *in the pocket* to describe the act of playing with good feel. *Feel* relates to not only keeping steady time but also to subdividing the time with just the right nuance and perfectly in sync with the other musicians. You shouldn't *rush* (play slightly ahead of) or *drag* (play behind) the tempo too much or be generally unsteady (going back and forth between rushing and dragging).

Developing that sort of timing against a cold, impersonal metronome click is hard. But using preprogrammed drum rhythms can bring you much closer. Nowadays, the onboard drum patterns in a keyboard were likely played by a real drummer and have a highly nuanced and great feel.

So how do you know whether your keyboard has onboard drums?

- ✔ All arrangers and portable keyboards have onboard drums. Anything that has auto-accompaniment includes drums as part of its band.

- ✔ Many high-end home digital pianos include auto-accompaniment as well.

- ✔ Workstation keyboards all include drum programs, so you can write your own music with drums grooves.

- ✔ Some stage pianos include preset, play-along drum grooves.

- ✔ Workstations, pro synths, and stage pianos with terms such as Rhythm, Rhythm Set, Drum Track, and Drum Pattern likely have this function.

Some keyboards (workstations and synths) use an arpeggiator to produce drum patterns, so look there for this function (see later in this chapter).

Book VI

Exploring Electronic Keyboard Technology

Selecting a drum pattern

An instrument with drums always has a beat ready to go; you don't have to dig through a bunch of menu options or anything special to hear them. Locate and press the Start/Stop or Play button, and something will start playing. If it doesn't, try playing a key on the keyboard, and the drums may start with you.

Portable keyboards

Portable keyboards don't always have auto-accompaniment, but they often offer drum grooves. Casio calls them Rhythms; Yamaha calls them Styles.

To select a different drum pattern (my generic term), do the following:

1. Press the Style or Rhythm button.

Use the + and – buttons to move up or down to the next pattern or to scroll through the available patterns one at a time. Or use the *numeric keypad* (if available) to enter the number of a specific pattern you want.

On these low-end models, the pattern names may appear on the front panel, as shown in Figure 2-1. On other models, the names are displayed on the screen.

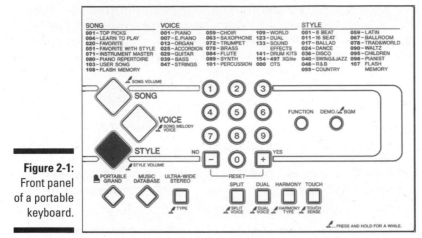

Figure 2-1:
Front panel
of a portable
keyboard.

Image courtesy of Yamaha Corporation of America

2. When you've selected the desired pattern, press Start/Stop.

Note that you can usually scroll or select another pattern while the drums are playing, and it will start on the next downbeat.

Arranger keyboards and high-end digital pianos

Full accompaniment is more than you're looking for right now. You just want to have drums playing along with your keyboard playing, so find the button that turns off the rest of the accompaniment (see Figure 2-2). This button may be labeled Chords On/Off, Accompaniment On/Off, ACMP On/Off, Arranger Mode, and so on. On some Roland arrangers, you need to turn off all the Backing Type elements (Style, Song, and USB) until only drums remain. With the accompaniment/chords turned off, you can freely select drum patterns without calling up a full backing band.

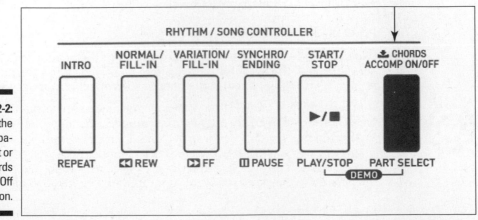

Figure 2-2:
Locate the
Accompa-
niment or
Chords
On/Off
button.

Image courtesy of Casio America, Inc.

To select a different drum pattern, press the Style or Rhythm button. You can use the + and – buttons or value dial to move up or down to the next pattern or to scroll through the list of available patterns one at a time. If available, you can use the numeric keypad to directly enter the number of a specific pattern you want. Then press Play.

Higher-end models may present the Styles/Rhythms on multiple buttons, with each button representing a category of styles arranged by musical genre: Rock, Ballroom, Waltz, World, Jazz/Big-Band, and so on, as shown in Figure 2-3. Press the button for the category you like and select the specific drum pattern you want from the choices shown on the keyboard's display and then press Play. Note that you can usually scroll or select another pattern while the drums are playing, and it will start on the next *downbeat,* or start of a measure.

Book VI

Exploring
Electronic
Keyboard
Technology

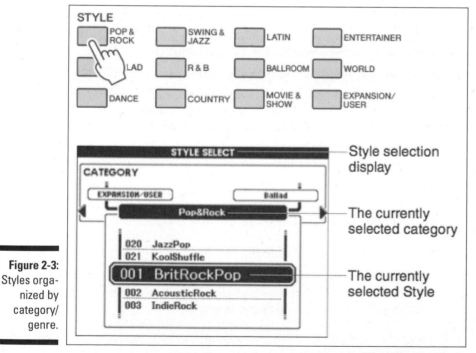

Figure 2-3: Styles organized by category/genre.

Images courtesy of Yamaha Corporation of America

Synths and workstations

Synths and workstations don't generally have full backing accompaniment but may have drum grooves set up behind their sounds. Depending on the product, the pattern is either created by a small phrase/pattern player or by an arpeggiator. Drums are usually incorporated in a multisound mode of some sort, be it a layer, a split, or a combination of both. Korg calls these Combinations, Kurzweil calls them Setups, Roland calls them Live Sets, and Yamaha calls them Performances.

Some Korg models have a feature called a *drum track,* which is a drum groove set up behind their single sounds (called *programs*). They always have a dedicated front panel button for starting these drum patterns.

Selecting a different drum pattern is a little more complicated in these situations than for the instruments in the preceding sections. Follow these steps:

1. **Go into Edit Mode for the multisound mode your product offers.**

    Note that some products have dedicated arpeggiator edit buttons or controls available right from the front panel, and you don't need to go into Edit Mode to adjust them.

2. **Find the page for the drum pattern (phrase) player or the arpeggiator.**

3. **Locate the Pattern/Arp number parameter; this number is the currently assigned drum groove for the sound.**

4. **Locate and select the pattern you want to use.**

    Use the + and − buttons, value dial, or data slider to move up or down to the next pattern or to scroll through the available patterns one at a time. Use the numeric keypad (if available) to directly enter the number of a specific drum/arp pattern you want.

5. **When you've selected the desired pattern, press Start/Stop or Arp On/Off.**

Starting the pattern playing

Generally you press a Start/Stop or Play button and your drums start playing right away. That works out well if you want a few bars of drum groove before you come in with your playing. But if you want to start playing at the same time, pressing the button and getting your hand back to the keyboard in time for that first downbeat can be nearly impossible.

Workstations and pro synths that use an arpeggiator to create drum patterns start only when you touch a key on the keyboard. This setup is necessary because an arpeggiator rearranges notes you play to create more complex patterns. So it needs some note trigger to do its thing even when it's used to create a background drum groove.

All keyboards with accompaniment offer a setting called *Synchro Start* or *Sync Start.* It waits for you to play the first note before it starts the drums or accompaniment. So pressing the Synchro Start button (see Figure 2-4) tells the drums to be ready to play but to wait for a key to be played to trigger the start of the groove. Perfect solution!

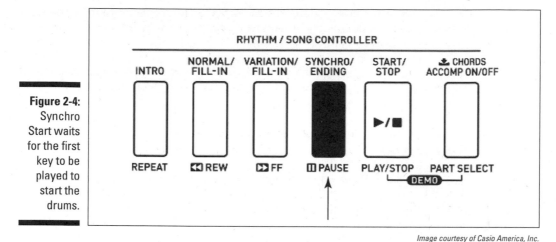

Figure 2-4:
Synchro
Start waits
for the first
key to be
played to
start the
drums.

Image courtesy of Casio America, Inc.

Many higher-end keyboards offer the ability to set up a footswitch to perform the start/stop function, freeing up your hands to stay on the keyboard. That's a convenient way to do things, but it does involve buying the footswitch (they're always an option). The Synchro Start feature is easier.

Every keyboard that offers rhythms, accompaniment, or arpeggiators has some type of tempo control on the front panel, whether that's up and down/ + and – buttons, a knob or dial, or a tempo parameter in the display.

Many keyboards offer a feature called *Tap Tempo*, which gives you the ability to tap on a button at the BPM you want and set the drum tempo to that input. Some keyboards have a dedicated button for this capability, but many use a combination of two buttons. When setting the tempo with Tap Tempo, you need to tap at least three times to give the keyboard a clear indication of the tempo you want. Watch the display; it will indicate when it has changed to the new tempo.

Digging into natural drum fills

Every arranger-type keyboard offers controls to select drum fills; some models have more than others. *Note:* Arrangers are specifically designed to offer these types of variations and fills to emulate the complete performance of a song. If you have a workstation, synth, or stage piano that has some drum grooves but no apparent fills, that's too bad — this is one of the differences in these types of instruments. Some of the drum patterns may have a fill preprogrammed at the end of the phrase, but you can't make it happen whenever you want, and you can't get rid of it.

Check out Track 140 to hear drum fills added to various patterns from a Casio keyboard.

On a fancier arranger keyboard, the drum fill button is separate from the variations, giving you complete control over what happens. And you may have more than one drum fill to select from.

Experiment with pressing the Fill button at different times within a measure to hear how the drum fill differs. The earlier in a bar you press it, the more drum fill you get.

Listen to Track 141 to hear various drum fills added to patterns from a Korg keyboard.

If you press the Fill button very close to the end of the bar, you may not hear a fill at all because the keyboard barely plays the fill before going back to the pattern. Press it too late, and you actually get a full measure (or more) of fill on the next bar.

Using fills to transition to a new variation is so common that most arrangers have a button called Auto-Fill that automatically adds a fill when you press a new Variation button. With that function turned on, you don't need to press as many buttons during performance.

Roland and Yamaha arrangers don't have dedicated fill-in buttons. Pressing the currently playing Variation button again produces a drum fill; pressing a different variation button produces a fill when Auto-Fill is turned on.

Incorporating intros

An *intro* is a beginning phrase that starts off a song and leads into the first section. With drums only, these patterns don't seem all that different from the main groove. They become important when you use the full accompaniment, providing some interesting parts for the chords you play.

Many arrangers offer a special type of intro called a *count-in.* This four-beat click sets up the tempo and gives you a reference for what it sounds and feels like. This feature is similar to what happens in an actual band when the drummer counts off by clicking her sticks to give everyone something to follow. Look for it in your keyboard; it may appear on the panel or be a dedicated Intro variation.

Playing with Accompaniment

The concept of using auto-accompaniment is simple: You play some notes on the lower range of your keyboard, and that tells the system to start playing some backing music in the key you gave it. You choose the style of music it plays from the choices presented on the front panel.

The result is the sound of a full band playing, giving you a professional backing track that you're in complete control over. You've moved up from being a solo pianist to being the leader of an ever-changing cast of musicians who can play any song in any style of music you need. All you need to do is pick the style of music and provide the band with some chords to follow.

Sound too good to be true? It's actually a marvel of technology; inside, your keyboard is doing some pretty amazing computational stuff, but as the player, your job couldn't be simpler. The following sections lay out what's really going on.

How auto-accompaniment works

Playing with accompaniment usually means you have a split keyboard, with the lower range (left hand) dedicated to playing notes/chords to trigger the accompaniment and the right hand having a live sound (or two) to play your melodies with. Some arrangers and digital pianos have a full-play mode, where you play acoustic piano with two hands and the keyboard uses your two-handed playing to determine the chords.

Accompaniment uses *styles* or *rhythms* — collections of MIDI-based music tracks that play various instrument sounds to produce the sound of a backing band. They've been played and recorded by skilled musicians to faithfully reproduce various musical styles. Some are written to sound generic so that you can play any song within that genre of music, and others are very specific re-creations of a famous song.

The unique thing about the accompaniment "engine" is that it can adapt these parts for any chord you give it, changing the notes within the pattern to fit the various root tones and chord qualities in music (major, minor, diminished, augmented, and so on). This adaptability is how auto-accompaniment differs from a prerecorded backing track, which rigidly plays back the exact notes you played to create the part. Accompaniment is interactive — able to change to any chord you play the instant you play it.

Starting a pattern playing

As mentioned earlier, the patterns that make up the accompaniment backing have various names: Casio and Roland call them *Rhythms*; Keytron, Korg, and Yamaha call them *Styles*.

Simple portable keyboards don't always have full auto-accompaniment, so look for a button labeled Chords, Accompaniment On/Off, ACMP On/Off, Arranger Mode, and so on. These options indicate that you have full accompaniment parts, not just drums.

Here's how to get a pattern playing:

1. **Press the Styles or Rhythm button.**

2. **Make sure the Chord/Accomp button is on.**

3. **Play a low C on the keyboard to start the pattern playing.**

   If you feel comfortable, try playing a C triad (C-E-G) instead. If the music doesn't start, press the Start/Stop or Play button while you play the note or chord.

Accompaniment needs you to play a chord to tell the players what key and what chord type you want them to play (C major, F minor, and so on). So if you just press Start/Stop or Play, the drums will start without the rest of the band.

4. **With the music playing, select some other patterns and listen to how the music and parts change.**

   No need to play another chord for now. Just hear how the parts sound for various selections. For simple models, you can use the + and – buttons to move up or down to the next pattern or to scroll through the available patterns one at a time. Or use the numeric keypad (if available) to directly enter the number of a specific pattern you want.

On low-end models, the pattern names may appear on the front panel. On other models, the names are displayed on the screen. Higher-end models present the Styles/Rhythms on multiple buttons, with each button representing a category of styles arranged by musical genre — Pop & Rock, Ballroom, World, Swing & Jazz, and so on.

Listen to Track 142 to hear various styles being played using a simple C triad.

Breaking down an accompaniment pattern

An accompaniment pattern usually has the following elements:

- **Drums:** Drums include the traditional drum kit, with bass drum, snare, hi-hat, cymbals, and so on, playing a beat.

- **Percussion:** This element includes things such as tambourine, cowbell, shakers, congas/timbales/bongos, triangle, and other hand percussion, providing extra color to the rhythm.

- **Bass:** Bass presents the low notes that play some sort of rhythmic, moving series of notes. It may be an electric, acoustic (upright), or synth bass sound, depending on the style of music.

- **Chordal part(s):** *Chordal parts* are often a keyboard sound (acoustic or electric piano, organ, clav, and so on.) and possibly some strummed guitar parts (acoustic or electric). Having a few tracks of this sort is common (just as a band may have multiple players).

✔ **Other sustained parts:** These options include string, vocal, and synth pad sounds — sustained chords for additional interest and sound variety.

✔ **Background melodic figures:** These can be string lines, brass and woodwind melodies, synth patterns and arpeggiations, and guitar licks.

Every part will not always be playing; parts may come in and out depending on a number of settings and factors, such as which variation you're using and the taste of the pattern programmer. In general, an arranger keyboard uses up to 12 parts for these patterns, plus the live sounds that you can play on the keyboard along with the accompaniment.

Track 143 illustrates a style broken down into its separate elements or tracks.

Book VI

Exploring Electronic Keyboard Technology

Feeding the band the chord changes: Chord triggering

You have to play chords to tell the accompaniment "engine" what to do. All arrangers and portable keyboards offer a couple of ways of playing chords, some simpler than others.

Part of the fun of auto-accompaniment is how it can help fill out your musical performance when your skills aren't as well developed. Each brand offers an easy method of chord triggering, which doesn't require you to know what specific notes make up a particular chord. The following sections break down two methods for this process: Casio's and everyone else's.

These easy chord methods don't support the ability to play diminished, augmented, or suspended chords. You have to use a fingered mode instead; see the later section "Playing the chords yourself" for details.

Casio

Here's how to trigger easy chords for Casio keyboards:

1. **Press and hold the Chords/Accomp On/Off button until CHORDS:Fingered or F1 shows up in the display.**

2. **Use the + or – button to change the value to CHORDS: CC (meaning Casio Chord).**

   Now whenever you play a single note in the lower part of the keyboard, you'll produce a major triad.

3. **To change the kind of chord, press the root tone and one or more higher keys.**

To play a minor triad, press the root tone you want (C, for example) and any other note (white or black) above it. Check out Figure 2-5 for an example. To play a dominant seventh or minor seventh chord, press your desired root tone and any two or three notes, respectively, above it.

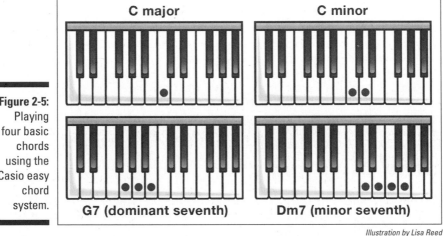

Figure 2-5: Playing four basic chords using the Casio easy chord system.

Illustration by Lisa Reed

Listen to Track 144 to hear these four chord qualities (major and minor triad, dominant and minor seventh) demonstrated.

Figure 2-6 shows how to play a simple chord progression by using the Casio chord method.

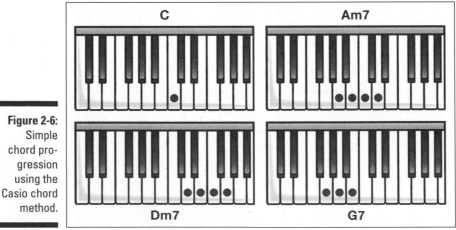

Figure 2-6: Simple chord progression using the Casio chord method.

Illustration by Lisa Reed

The other guys

Korg and Roland arrangers don't wake up with their easy chord method selected (Yamaha is ready to go!), so you need to turn that on before you continue. Here's how:

- Korg

    1. Press the Global mode button, followed by Mode Preferences.

    For most models, this sequence takes you where you need to go, but note that some models locate the easy chord function in the Style Play mode, Split Tab.

    2. Select the Style tab/page and choose the parameter Chord Recognition.

    3. Change the value to One Finger.

- Roland

    1. Press the Menu button, followed by Arranger Settings.

    2. Select the Type parameter.

    3. Change the value to Easy.

Now you're ready to trigger chords the easy way!

- **Major triad:** Play a single note in the lower part of the keyboard. Figure 2-7 shows an example.

Book VI

**Exploring
Electronic
Keyboard
Technology**

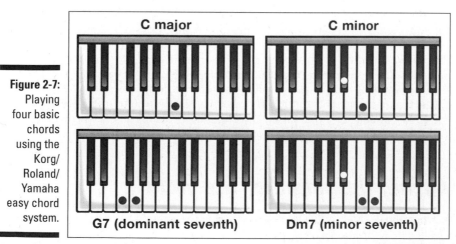

Figure 2-7: Playing four basic chords using the Korg/ Roland/ Yamaha easy chord system.

C major

C minor

G7 (dominant seventh)

Dm7 (minor seventh)

Illustration by Lisa Reed

- **Minor triad:** Press the root tone you want and any black note below it.
- **Dominant seventh chord:** Press the root tone you want and any white key below it.
- **Minor seventh chord:** Press the root tone you want and both a white and black key below it (three keys in total).

Figure 2-8 shows how to play the same chord progression shown in Figure 2-6 by using another brand's method.

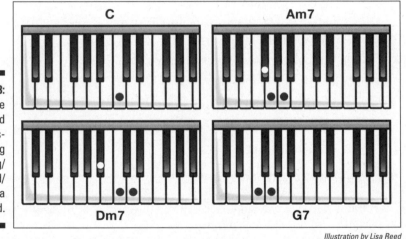

Figure 2-8: Simple chord progression using the Korg/ Roland/ Yamaha method.

Illustration by Lisa Reed

Listen to Track 145 to hear this simple chord progression in several styles.

The *fingered* method is self-explanatory: You play the full chords with your left hand and the system reads them and produces the backing parts. So you need to know how to play chords fairly well to use this method successfully. Depending on the manufacturer, this form of chord playing is referred to as Fingered (Casio and Korg), Multi Finger (Yamaha), and Standard (Roland) and is the default method for chord recognition for all keyboards when powered on.

Mixing the sound of the band

Mixing a musical recording involves adjusting the volume balance of each of the instruments, deciding which speaker they come out of (called *panning*), and possibly adjusting or changing the effects that are being used. Mid- and higher-priced arrangers give you access to these functions in addition to letting you decide which sound is being used for each part. Taking control of these aspects of your backing band allows you to make the sound exactly the way you want it.

How do you know whether your keyboard has this capability? Look for a feature/parameter called the Mixer; it may be a dedicated button or a page within the Style/Rhythm Play mode (look in your manual, on the front panel, or within the menus). Figure 2-9 shows some example screens of mixers as presented in a few arrangers.

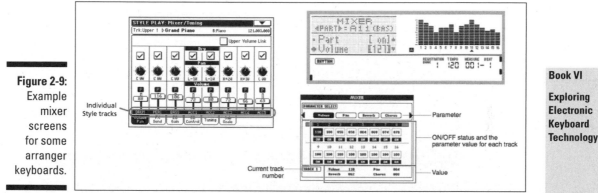

Figure 2-9: Example mixer screens for some arranger keyboards.

Images courtesy of Korg Italy; Casio America, Inc; and Yamaha Corporation of America

Book VI

Exploring Electronic Keyboard Technology

A skilled musician/producer has already volume-balanced all the styles and rhythms in your keyboard, so you probably don't need to make big changes. But two common scenarios require a little adjustment here and there:

✔ **Slightly increasing or decreasing the volume of a backing instrument:** Perhaps you're having a little problem hearing the bass part clearly enough, or the string lines stand out a little too much for your taste. These fixes are small; you're not trying to redo the whole band mix.

✔ **Turning off a part:** This process is called *muting* a part or channel.

To change the volume of a part (it may be called a Part or a Track), you select it, use the interface controls to increase or decrease the volume parameter value, and then resave the style/rhythm.

To turn off a part entirely, you may have two options. If your mixer design has a dedicated *Mute* parameter, you can use that parameter to turn off the part. If it doesn't have a Mute, simply turn the part volume all the way down to 00. Again, be sure to resave the Style/Rhythm.

Some parts play only during a specific variation in a style or rhythm. So be sure to check all the variations your keyboard offers to find and be able to hear them.

Letting the Keyboard Make the Choices for You

Arranger keyboards and high-end digital pianos are very advanced instruments; they're actually pretty complicated to even the average tech-minded electronic keyboardist. The front panel has so many buttons, and you seem to need an extra set of hands just to operate all the features. To counteract that, the instrument designers build in a variety of timesaving functions to automate these choices. They often set up a bunch of options for you so you can quickly make the sound and setting features you need, and they offer features that you can configure for yourself to do the same. The following sections give you a few to check out.

Taking advantage of one-touch settings

Most mid- and upper-end arrangers offer three or four sounds for live playing on the keyboard. Most are for the right hand part of the key range, with maybe one to layer with the left hand while triggering the chords for the accompaniment. These sounds aren't always all active at the same time; you usually choose between them to vary your melody playing at different parts of the song. For example, you may switch sounds (like starting a melody with a flute and changing to trumpet at the bridge) or layer a second sound on top of the first (like adding strings behind your piano).

To extend these possibilities even further, you can save and recall sets of these sounds as part of your accompaniment. Called Single Touch (Korg) or One Touch Settings (Roland and Yamaha), these buttons instantly recall all four sounds, with their volume, panning, effects, and key ranges all predecided, and some fancy extras thrown in. If your keyboard has this feature, try it out to see how easily it recalls a wide variety of sounds that have all been chosen to work with the current style or rhythm you're using.

Advanced models from Casio have an extended version of this function called a Registration. Along with saving the selection of live sounds, these one-touch settings can also recall the rhythm pattern, tempo, and some other cool extras. But they don't have to change any of the accompaniment parts when selecting a new rhythm; a Global Mode setting can disable that, so they only will recall the live part sounds and effects and so on just like the other brands offer.

Yamaha also has a Registration feature, which recalls sounds and other settings. It differs from the One Touch settings in that it has nothing to do with the accompaniment memories. So you may end up choosing some sounds that don't go well with the style of music you're playing.

Diving into the music database

As you develop a large repertoire of songs you can play, remembering what style or rhythm, tempo, and other settings to use for each song becomes confusing. Plus, setting all those things up takes time; no keyboardist wants to leave the audience waiting while he pokes around the front panel of his keyboard.

Professional arrangers take care of this problem with yet another type of memory, called a SongBook (Korg), Music Assistant/Performance List (Roland), or Music Finder (Yamaha). This feature stores all the needed settings for a specific song (sounds, accompaniment, tempo, effects), along with text reminders such as the key you like to play the song in, lyrics, other text notes, and more. It's a database, so you can search for songs by title, artist, genre, and many other tags much like you can in your computer media player. The keyboard comes with many songs already defined, and you can add more of your own and download and share entries with other users around the world. Figure 2-10 shows some example screens for this feature.

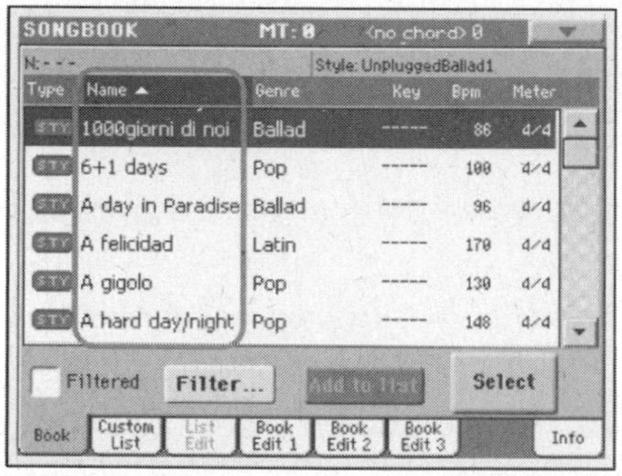

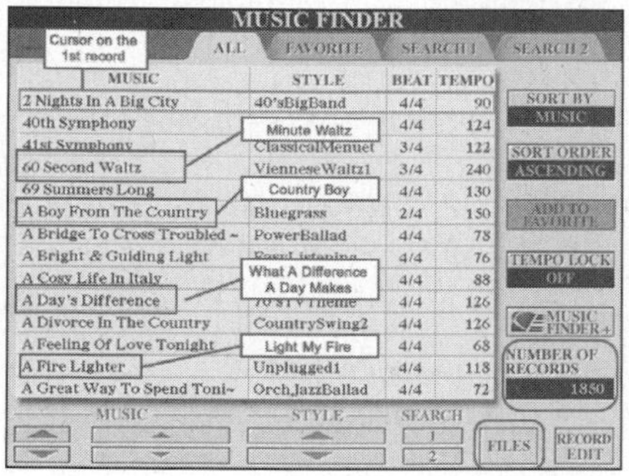

Book VI

Exploring
Electronic
Keyboard
Technology

Figure 2-10: The Korg and Yamaha music database main screens.

Images courtesy of Yamaha Corporation of America and Korg Italy

Using Some Fancy Extras

But wait, there's more! Modern arrangers have a number of other cool features that help your playing sound fuller and fancier without any extra work on your part.

Adding harmony to your melodies

Block chords is a style of playing right hand melodies where the melody is harmonized with additional notes below it to form full chord voicings, using smooth voice-leading. Organ players often use this technique, as did jazz pianist George Shearing, and it's popular in jazz and dance big-band arranging within their sax section writing.

And you can too; it's just a button-push away. Look on your front panel for a button labeled Ensemble (Korg), Harmony/Echo (Yamaha), or Melody Intelligence (Roland). Turn it on and then try the following:

1. **Set up your accompaniment to play.**

2. **Start the accompaniment with a simple C major chord.**

3. **Play a single note with your right hand; notice it's playing a whole chord.**

4. **Move around to some other notes while keeping the left hand chord the same and listen for how the sound changes.**

5. **Hold a C note with your right hand and change your left hand chord to an F major.**

   Notice how the melody (right hand) part changes; it's now adding harmony using notes that match an F chord.

6. **Change your left hand chord to an A minor and hear the change.**

Your keyboard may have different settings for the type of harmony it creates when using this feature. Read your owner's manual and explore all the possibilities.

Listen to Track 146 to hear examples of auto-harmony.

Hitting the chord pads

Some arrangers offer some buttons called *pads* or *multi pads* that you can use to tap out drum beats and trigger sound effects or even phrases of music. This setting is a fun way of adding more sounds and parts to your playing without having to worry about playing the right keys on the keyboard. These chord pads have various names and operate in a variety of ways:

✔ **Momentary/Hit:** Touch the pad and a sound triggers once. This option is good for playing a single drum sound or synth sound effect (such as a zap).

✔ **Once:** A musical phrase plays one time and then stops. You can use this method for something like a harp arpeggio or flamenco guitar strum flourish.

✔ **Looped:** A musical phrase or sound keeps playing endlessly (in time with your accompaniment parts) until you turn it off. This function can add an additional percussion groove or a cool synth arpeggiated phrase (or even trigger the sound of endless audience applause).

Book VI

Exploring Electronic Keyboard Technology

Each style and rhythm has its own saved settings for the pads, so take some time and explore them.

Track 147 demonstrates some chord pad applications.

Exploring Arpeggiation

The word *arpeggiate* means to play the notes of a chord in a broken fashion, one at a time. It comes from the Italian word *arpeggiare,* which means "to play on a harp," which was a common way of outlining the harmony or chords of a piece of music.

Practicing arpeggios is an essential part of serious piano study because it builds technique and the ability to cleanly go up and down the full range of the keyboard.

Listen to Track 148 to hear examples of arpeggiated chords played on the piano.

Not every person who ever wanted to play a keyboard develops that level of technique, though, so in the late '60s, organ manufacturers added a simple form of auto-accompaniment that took the held notes of a chord and played them one after another to produce arpeggios. Though your image of those big console home theater organs may be of hokey show tunes and cheesy drum grooves, this feature is how Pete Townsend created the keyboard part for the Who song "Eminence Front" on a Yamaha E-70 home organ.

The first synthesizer to include an arpeggiator was the Roland Jupiter 4, released in 1978. Many others followed, and arpeggiators were quite popular in instruments through the mid-'80s. After falling out of favor for a period of time, they came back with a vengeance, with many new features and capabilities. Many of today's synths, workstations, and software synthesizers include arpeggiators, as do computer software sequencers and digital audio workstations (DAWs).

Looking at some arp examples

In the most basic scenario, an arpeggiator takes the notes you hold on the keyboard and plays them one after the other, in a direction that you can choose (up, down, or up and down). Figure 2-11 (Track 149) shows a simple C major triad that produces various repeating patterns when held and driven by an arpeggiator.

Figure 2-11: A basic arp pattern.

Illustration by Jerry Kovarsky

In this example, holding down a three-note chord can produce these various patterns based on the three most common settings for the note direction, or *order*.

Which notes you play on the keyboard doesn't matter; the arpeggiator obediently plays them back for you over and over. A common use of this function in many of the songs mentioned earlier in the chapter is to just hold a single note or an octave to produce a pulsating rhythm or alternating bass line without sounding like a full chordal arpeggio.

Moving to a more complex example, playing a two-handed chord like the one shown in Figure 2-12 (Track 150) gets you a more complex arp pattern. A cool aspect of such a *running arp* pattern is that it doesn't have to repeat at the bar line of your music, so using an odd number of notes produces a less regular-sounding repeating pattern than using an even number of notes. Holding down a five-note chord creates the pattern in Figure 2-12.

Figure 2-12:
A two-handed arp pattern.

Illustration by Jerry Kovarsky

Of course, you don't have to hold down the same chord all the time. By changing chords, you make the arp pattern sound more interesting and less repetitive.

Another technique you hear in a lot of music is the player pressing notes down to trigger the arp for a little bit, letting go to introduce space or rests, and then playing some notes again.

Listen to Track 151 to hear various examples of changing chords and using space to make simple up/down arpeggiated patterns more interesting.

Early modular synths, many analog synths, and some modern keyboards have a function called a *step sequencer,* which many people confuse with an arpeggiator. A step sequencer allows you to define the pitch for each step of a pattern and then always plays back that pitch. The only interaction with the keyboard may be to allow you to transpose the whole pattern to another note or key from the keyboard. But the step sequencer is a pre-programmed riff, or pattern; it's not changing chord qualities or the span of the note intervals based on what you play on the keyboard, so the riff doesn't really change. The result may sound the same to your ears, but the step sequencer isn't as interactive as the arpeggiator. To its advantage, it can produce more complex patterns. A step sequencer was used for Pink Floyd's famous "On the Run" synth pattern, for example.

Exploring More Arpeggiator Features

If all an arpeggiator could do was play back the notes you hold on the keyboard, the effect would be cool but would get boring and predictable pretty quickly. And other than using them on different sounds, all arpeggiated parts would sound much the same. Thankfully, arpeggiators have gained many new features over time and grown to be very complex and creative. The following sections take you on a tour of the most common features of a modern arpeggiator.

Extending the range

In its most basic setting, an arpeggiator just repeats the exact notes you play, over and over again. A *range parameter* gives you a choice of how many octaves to repeat the pattern of notes, usually expressed as one, two, three, and sometimes even four octaves. By setting a range parameter, you can tell the arpeggiator to play the original notes and then to play those same notes again up an octave, and yet again up another octave, and so on.

Track 152 presents various patterns being played first at one octave and then expanded to two, three, and four octaves. The examples have some effects and filter sweeps included to sound more interesting — as they'd be used in a song.

Changing the timing/speed

Of course, any arp pattern is being played in some rhythm, and they usually are very simple timings — perhaps eighth notes against the tempo. All arpeggiators give you some choices for this timing resolution. As you increase the *resolution,* or subdivision, of the beat, the arp pattern plays back faster and sounds busier. But it's always in time with your music. Common timing options can range from a whole note per step down to sixteenth notes, various triplet timings, and even 32nd notes.

If all your sound is coming from one keyboard, this timing happens automatically. If you want to use multiple instruments or a hardware keyboard and sounds running from your computer, you need to connect them via MIDI and set the MIDI synchronization between the devices. One device will produce what is called the *Master Clock,* and all the other devices will be set to listen to this *external MIDI Clock.*

Check out Track 153 to hear a pattern being played along with a drum rhythm and then switched between various timing settings.

Getting into the swing of things

Swing is a way of playing a rhythm where the notes aren't equally timed; when you play two eighth notes, the first note is longer than the second, producing a pleasing, lopsided feel. You may have heard the term related to a style of jazz music played in the late '30s and '40s. In fact, the swing pulse of rhythm is a core component of jazz playing. But it's also used in boogie-woogie, country, blues and rock shuffles, and hip-hop music.

More modern arpeggiators offer swing as an adjustable parameter (sometimes called *shuffle*), so your pattern can go from a very even, straight feel to this cooler, more lopsided feel. Swing may be presented as a percentage or a strength value, but increasing it makes the relationship between each group of two notes more irregular, with the first note getting longer and the second getting shorter to make up the difference.

Book VI

Exploring Electronic Keyboard Technology

In general, swing rhythms have a *triplet* feel, where the quarter note is divided into three parts. The first note holds for the first two triplets and the third is the last triplet. In print music, the rhythm is still written as straight eighth notes and then just marked as "swing feel" or something similar. Writing everything as triplets would make the music difficult to read.

Track 154 features a pattern being played straight along with a swung drum rhythm (which sounds bad) and then gradually swung to feel better against the groove.

Higher swing strengths on arpeggio patterns work best with swing/jazz, shuffle, 6/8, 12/8, and hip-hop/R & B drum grooves.

Making the notes shorter/longer

Increasing and decreasing the duration of the notes being played is a very effective technique in making an arp pattern fit the music or vary as a part develops. This parameter may be called *length, duration,* or *gate time* in various arpeggiators. If you increase the duration to the maximum, the notes will play completely connected, or *legato.*

Hearing the notes being held along with the arp

Some arpeggiators can sound the notes being held down along with the generated notes from the pattern. This feature results in a kind of layered sound, where you can hear a chord sustaining while the arp bubbles up beneath it.

It's a great sound and works well as long as your keyboard has enough *polyphony* (ability to generate enough new notes or voices) to keep the chord sound sustaining while all the other notes are generated. This parameter is called different things by different companies: Often, it's just *keyboard* or *kybd,* but Yamaha calls it *direct,* for example.

Keeping the arp playing without holding the keys

If you want the arp pattern to keep repeating for a longer period of time, you don't always need to keep holding the keys. *Latch* (sometimes called *hold*) is a parameter that keeps the pattern playing based on the note(s) you played until you press another key or chord. So you can feed the arp a few notes, let go, and let it do its thing while you play another part of the keyboard range or another keyboard (or get your audience to clap along). To stop the pattern, you can either turn off the latch function or stop the arp.

Adding variety with different patterns

You don't have to use the same pattern for a whole song. Changing the pattern from section to section can be a great way to add variety to you music. If you're playing a song that has a more traditional form with verses, a chorus, a breakdown or solo section, and so on, you can try changing to a subtly different pattern for one of the sections and then returning to your original pattern later on. Or not. Feel free to experiment and find instances where adding some variety is just what you need to keep your music from getting too predictable.

Trying Out Some Different Sounds: Matching Sounds and Arp Patterns

No keyboard law defines what sounds you can and can't arpeggiate; feel free to experiment away! That said, here are some tips and practical advice for matching sounds and arp patterns:

> ✓ **Sounds with a fast attack work well at any tempo.** If a sound has a slower attack and you're playing at a fast tempo or using a fast timing subdivision (sixteenth notes, for example), the results can be kind of

sluggish and unclear. The sound just doesn't have enough time to speak before the next note is being triggered. In this case, you need to adjust the amp envelope attack to a faster value.

- ✔ **Sounds with long releases don't work as well.** You have to adjust the amp envelope release (see Book VI Chapter 3) to a shorter value. Soft string ensembles, spacey vocal pads, and other atmospheric sounds typically need this type of edit to work.

- ✔ **Most synth sounds are great to use.** People associate arpeggiators with synths, so this pairing is a match made in synthesizer heaven. However, swirly sound effects and evolving imaginative synth sounds may not work that well, especially at faster tempos/timing.

- ✔ **Plucked and short decay sounds are good choices.** Consider guitars; other plucked string instruments (including ethnic sounds); mallets and tuned percussion; and keyboard sounds such as piano, electric piano, clav, and harpsichord.

- ✔ **Short noises and non-pitched percussion work well.** Not everything has to be about chords and harmony; sometimes a unique arpeggiated sound effect adds a nice texture to a part.

Be sure to match the arp range to the sound used. Some sounds don't sound good at their extreme ranges (either at the top or the bottom), so be sure to pick your trigger note range carefully and consider how many octaves to set the range to. Judge where the sweet spot is for a given sound or arp pattern.

Adding Fun Sound and Effects Tweaks

Sometimes just finding the right arp pattern, sound, and chord(s) is enough for a song. Mix it well, and you'll be happy. But often arpeggiated parts get to sound a bit static and predictable when you just leave them running on their own. So varying any or all the parameters discussed earlier in this chapter will help your music greatly.

But wait, there's more! Here are a few cool tips to further enhance your arp-ing adventures:

- ✔ **Sweep the filter as the pattern plays.** This move is a classic. Many musicians and producers use a sound that has a low frequency oscillator (LFO) slowly modulating the filter cutoff, so this effect happens automatically. Book VI Chapter 3 talks about these parameters.

Book VI

Exploring Electronic Keyboard Technology

✔ **Pan the sound back and forth as the pattern plays.** Arpeggiated parts sound great when they move back and forth between the speakers. Try making the panning cycle different from the pattern length so it doesn't seem to repeat so regularly. A slow pan for a fast arp pattern sounds great, as does a faster pan on a slower part. Using an LFO to modulate amplifier pan position makes this task easy.

✔ **Put a delay effect on your sound.** Timed delays work wonderfully combined with an arp pattern. Slower arp patterns with shorter note durations leave space so you can hear the delays. Don't let the delay regenerate too many repeats because that can get in the way of your new notes. And be sure the delay is mixed back a little so it's supporting echoes, not just a sloppy wash of notes. Listen to The Edge, the guitarist from U2; he's a master of this effect, even though he (not an arpeggiator) is playing the parts.

✔ **Let go of your notes once in a while, especially when using delays.** Many arpeggiators have a latch or hold function, which keeps the notes playing even when you lift your hands off the keys. Turn that off so you can be in control of introducing rests and space into the pattern as you want. Going manual also lets you use delays with more repeats or longer repetition times. Feed the keyboard a chord, let a few notes arpeggiate, and then let go and just listen to the stream of echoes that follows. Repeat and enjoy.

Listen to Tracks 155 through 158 to hear filter sweeps, panning, and delays in action.

Chapter 3

Recording and Editing Your Sounds

In This Chapter

▶ Defining MIDI and audio recording

▶ Examining multitrack MIDI recording and editing

▶ Transferring your music from keyboard to computer and beyond

▶ Breaking down the various forms of synthesis

▶ Looking at editing parameters and edit scenarios

▶ Access the audio tracks at www.dummies.com/go/pianokeyboardaio/

Most of today's electronic keyboards offer some form of recording, so you can capture and then listen back to your playing, compose and create a complete musical production, and do all steps in between. It's pretty amazing to realize that what used to take tens of thousands of dollars of complicated and specialized equipment, a room designed for recording, and a group of musicians with expensive instruments is something you can now achieve within the humble keyboard that sits in front of you.

Look at your keyboard; you probably see the word(s) *recorder, sequencer, music recorder, song,* or something similar to indicate that it has some sort of recording function. Even easier: A button labeled Record or REC is a sure sign you have this capability.

In this chapter, you discover the basics of both audio and MIDI recording, how the techniques differ, and why you'd choose one form over the other. You get a basic overview of how to do these types of recording — at least enough to help you when it comes time to crack open the manual for your specific model. Plus you'll see how to get your music out of your keyboard and onto your computer and then how to share it with family, friends, and fans around the world.

This chapter also talks about editing your sounds. Most keyboards offer some ability to shape their sounds and even make new sounds of your own. Your keyboard may be called a digital piano or an arranger, but all electronic keyboards are actually a type of synthesizer at their roots. They generate tones called *waveforms,* which are molded and shaped to sound like the instruments you recognize (and some you don't!).

Some keyboards are preset synthesizers; they offer you no apparent control over the sounds they provide. Most others offer some degree of variability, from slight tweaks to make sounds brighter or darker to the ability to have the sound keep ringing when you take your finger off the key.

You'll see how sounds are made and how you can modify the sounds to meet your taste and needs. If the thought of editing sounds conjures visions of some mad scientist plugging wires into a large panel of jacks or a DJ surrounded by boxes with blinking lights, this chapter will show you that editing sounds can be much easier than you may think.

Audio Recording versus MIDI Recording

As an electronic keyboardist, you have two forms of recording technology available: audio recording and MIDI recording. They're very different from one another, each with certain advantages, covered in the following sections.

Recording with analog and digital audio

For most people, a recording is something you listen to — a record, a cassette (who remembers those?), a CD, or an MP3. These are all products of *audio recording,* the act of capturing the sound of singers, players, and instruments and storing them on a device capable of reproducing them whenever you want. Capturing the *sound* is the key distinction of audio recording — the actual sound as you hear it, frozen in time for all to hear and enjoy.

Audio recording comes in two flavors: analog and digital. Both use some type of device to convert the live sound waves produced by the player/instrument into a signal. The most common is a microphone (shown in Figure 3-1), though electronic instruments can hook up to the recorder directly, and a keyboard with recording capability can do its own recording.

Analog recording gear converts the sound into a voltage or electrical signal that can be routed through various devices and then usually stored onto magnetic tape. (Figure 3-2 shows a common analog studio recorder.) Analog recording was the only form of recording for decades and is still used in professional recording studios that favor its warmth and tonal qualities.

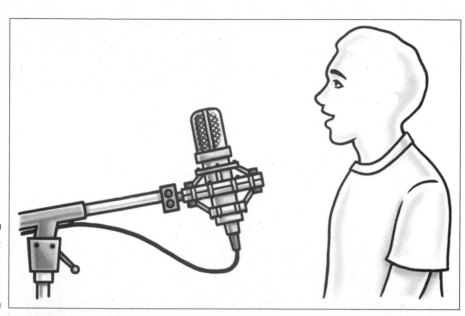

Figure 3-1:
Using a
microphone
to record.

Illustration by Lisa Reed

Figure 3-2:
A pro studio
analog tape
recorder.

Photograph courtesy of Roy Hendrickson

For the vast majority of users, the development of digital technology and computers has paved the way for digital recording. In *digital recording,* the sound is converted into 1s and 0s (a kind of electronic code) and can be stored onto a hard drive, digital storage media such as an SD card (the same kind your camera and smartphone use), and mobile devices. The sound can be run through other devices before being converted into the digital format or be manipulated later in the digital format to produce the same results. Most standalone recorders — either small handheld devices (see Figure 3-3), desktop-sized studios in a box, or larger systems — employ digital recording, as do all computer-based recording packages (commonly called digital audio workstations; see Figure 3-4).

Figure 3-3:
A common handheld digital recorder.

Photograph courtesy of TASCAM

Digital recording has many functional advantages over analog recording, mostly involving editing. To rearrange a song, for example, tape has to be cut and joined back together, which is a difficult task to do accurately. Digital data can easily and freely be copied, pasted, and manipulated.

Figure 3-4:
Audio-
recording
computer
software.

Image courtesy of PreSonus Audio Electronics, Inc., © 2013

Making sense of MIDI recording

MIDI (Musical Instrument Digital Interface) is a digital language that electronic instruments and devices use to speak to each other. It communicates information such as what key you've pressed on a keyboard, how hard you played it, how long you held it, and so on. Unlike audio recording, it captures only the gestures that produce the sound, *not* the sound itself. Therefore, you can't listen back to a MIDI performance without it being connected to and replaying a MIDI device live. That device may be a hardware instrument you can see or a software instrument running on your computer (or phone!), but it's being played in real time as you listen back.

The beauty of MIDI as a recording method is that it's infinitely editable. Figure 3-5 shows a screen shot of MIDI data in what's called an event edit list. You can select, edit, copy, or delete each MIDI event in this edit list as you want. Hit a bad note or don't like the sound you played? No problem; erase it or, better yet, change it to the right note/another sound! Didn't play with the best timing? You can fix that later. Can't play something fast enough? Record it slowly and then speed up the playback later; your recorder will now play the MIDI device at whatever tempo you set it to. These examples are just a taste of the things you can do with MIDI editing.

Position				Status	Ch	Num	Val	Length/Info
1	1	1	1	Control	1	7	127	Volume
1	1	1	1	Note	1	G1	39	. 3 3 237
1	1	1	1	Note	1	A#2	46	. 1 2 39
1	1	1	1	Note	1	D3	72	. 1 2 8
1	1	1	1	Note	1	E3	62	. 1 2 17
1	1	1	1	Note	1	A3	62	. 1 1 208
1	1	4	190	Control	1	64	127	Sustain
1	2	4	61	Note	1	A2	61	. 1 3 128
1	3	2	1	Note	1	A#2	55	. 1 1 158
1	3	3	214	Control	1	64	0	Sustain
1	3	4	1	Note	1	G3	71	. . 3 29
1	4	2	38	Control	1	64	127	Sustain
1	4	3	1	Note	1	D3	75	. . . 173
1	4	4	236	Control	1	64	0	Sustain
2	1	1	1	Note	1	D1	32	. 3 0 215
2	1	1	1	Note	1	D2	41	. 3 2 83
2	1	1	1	Note	1	A2	45	. 1 1 74
2	1	1	1	Note	1	A#2	49	. 1 1 88
2	1	1	1	Note	1	D3	76	. 1 1 77
2	1	1	1	Note	1	D#3	58	. 1 1 64
2	2	1	140	Control	1	64	127	Sustain
2	2	4	1	Note	1	A#2	58	. . . 72
2	2	4	1	Note	1	D#3	65	. . . 3
2	2	4	1	Note	1	A3	73	. . . 79
2	3	1	166	Control	1	64	0	Sustain
2	3	2	58	Control	1	64	127	Sustain
2	3	4	1	Note	1	D4	92	. . 2 122
2	4	1	1	PitchBd	1	48	66	= 304
2	4	1	23	PitchBd	1	96	67	= 480
2	4	1	43	PitchBd	1	16	69	= 656
2	4	1	63	PitchBd	1	112	70	= 880
2	4	1	83	PitchBd	1	64	72	= 1088
2	4	1	103	PitchBd	1	112	74	= 1392
2	4	3	123	PitchBd	1	64	77	= 1728

Figure 3-5: A MIDI event edit list.

Apple Logic Pro 9 screenshot courtesy of Jerry Kovarsky

MIDI sounds like the universal answer to all recording, right? Well, it's not. You can't capture your singing voice with MIDI, unless you're some sort of MIDI robot. So a live person or an acoustic instrument isn't going to be able to be MIDI-recorded. And eventually, you're going to want your MIDI recordings to be captured as audio so you can listen to them anywhere, away from your MIDI gear, and share them with your friends and the world.

Capturing What You Hear As It Happens: One-Pass Recording

The most basic form of recording is to capture a performance as it happens. Whether it's one person playing solo on a single instrument, a small group, the playback of your electronic keyboard that has drums and accompaniment, or a symphony orchestra doesn't matter. You set up the recording system as needed, press *record,* and it all happens at the same time — in one pass. The following sections help you set up one-pass recording for both the audio and MIDI approaches.

Tackling audio recording in one pass

The ability to record one complete audio performance from your keyboard is becoming a more common feature on many digital pianos, stage pianos, arrangers, and workstations. Basically, with this option, anything that can be produced by the keyboard all at once can be recorded.

Typically, the keyboard has a USB port that you can connect a memory stick or drive to; that's what the keyboard records the digital audio onto. (Note that some workstations and arrangers have an internal hard drive that can be used as the recording medium.) The recording is made as a stereo *wave* file (abbreviated as WAV or .wav), which is the most common digital audio format for use on computers. Without getting too technical, the settings for this wave file will be at the right resolution to be able to listen to on any device, to burn a CD from, and to share with anyone you want.

Book VI

Exploring Electronic Keyboard Technology

Recording a one-pass audio track doesn't require a complicated setup:

1. **Make sure your keyboard is in the right mode (single sound, multi-sound, accompaniment playback, or whatever).**

2. **Choose the audio recording feature.**

   This function may be a dedicated button, but you may have to select Record and then choose audio as the format. The method of choosing varies from product to product; read your owner's manual.

3. **Select where to record to: internal hard drive, USB stick or drive, and so on.**

   Your owner's manual will tell you what to do.

4. **Press Record or Start and begin playing (or sit back while the keyboards plays).**

5. **Press Stop when you've recorded what you want.**

   Your wave file is now on your memory stick or hard drive, ready to be listened to, shared, or brought into your computer.

One-pass audio recording is a great way to capture your practicing or playing so you can listen back to yourself. Hearing your recorded playing once in a while is a good idea because it lets you evaluate how you sound and how your practicing is progressing. You hear yourself differently this way compared to when you're involved in the act of playing. Plus, it's a fun way to share your music with friends and family or share your child's progress with others.

Grabbing a one pass MIDI recording

Being able to record one pass of MIDI is even more common than audio recording on today's keyboards. You often don't even know your recording function is MIDI recording; many digital pianos and stage pianos just call it a music recorder and don't bother to explain the technology. On most keyboards, though, the MIDI recorder is called a *sequencer*.

Recording a one pass MIDI track is straightforward and simple for live playing. Your keyboard may have a simple Record button and a Start/Stop button, or it may have a more complete set of buttons called *transport controls* as shown in Figure 3-6. These controls are copied from the buttons that were used to operate tape recorders and digital recorders.

Figure 3-6:
Recorder
transport
controls.

Image courtesy of M-Audio

Here's how to make a one pass MIDI recording:

1. **Select the sound you want to use.**

2. **Choose the recording feature.**

   This capability may be a dedicated button, or you may have to select Record and then choose MIDI as the format. It varies from product to product, so check out your owner's manual.

3. **Press Record or Start.**

   Note: Some products don't start recording the moment you press Record. They go into a record-ready state and usually start a click rhythm so you can listen to the current tempo to get ready to play. You typically must press Start or Play before it begins recording. (For some products, you start recording from this wait mode the moment you play a note.)

In general, MIDI recorders default to playing a click when recording so that the recorded data can be matched up to bars and beats for later editing. So you should set the tempo of the click/recording before you start. You can easily do so during the record-ready time by pressing Record and using the front panel tempo controls to set the speed.

4. **When you're ready, press the Start or Play button, or just play away!**

5. **Press Stop when you're finished.**

6. **Relocate to the beginning of the recording.**

   For some keyboards, you do so by pressing Stop twice. For others, you have to hold the Rewind button.

7. **Press Play to listen to your recording.**

   If you don't like what you played, you can just do it over by pressing Record (and perhaps Start or Play) and trying again. You can rerecord as many times as you want; each new recording erases the previous one.

Most workstations, higher-end portables, and mid-to-high-end arrangers have to be in sequencer mode to do any MIDI recording. For these products, you have to set up a sound on the first recording part or track and often have to copy it with its effects to sound like it did when you were just playing the sound. You may have a shortcut for this, or it may require a set of steps. Look to your owner's manual for more info and read the following section.

Book VI

Exploring
Electronic
Keyboard
Technology

Recording Multitrack MIDI

If you want to record more than one sound via MIDI (either at the same time or by building up parts one at a time), you need to use the full sequencer of your keyboard. Perhaps you want to record your keyboard playing along with an accompanying drum groove or record all the backing parts from the auto-accompaniment features of your digital piano or arranger. You may want to add more parts to your solo piano performance to make a full production from it. All these situations require you to create different parts, one for each distinct sound or part that is playing.

The design/layout and capabilities of each product's onboard sequencer (and computer-based sequencers/digital audio workstations (DAWs) is somewhat different, but the following sections explain the concepts; you can then go to your product's owner's manual and support documentation and videos for more specific help.

Setting up your session

The basic concept of any multitrack recorder/sequencer is that for each sound you want to record, you use a separate track. Think of each track as another instrument or player that's going to provide a part for your song. Each track is set to a different MIDI channel; this way, each instrument gets only the notes, controller information, and program change meant for it.

You choose a sound (such as piano, drums, bass, and so on) for each track and can adjust the volume and the *panning* for the track (which speaker it's coming out of, left or right). Note that you can adjust all these parameters again later, when you mix your song (discussed later in the chapter).

The most confusing part of setting up for recording in a sequencer has to do with assigning the effects used for each sound. When you play a sound by itself in single sound or multisound mode, that sound has already been programmed to use specific effects — certainly some reverb and quite possibly some coloration effect like chorus or phase shifting, with very specific settings for each effect. Guitars may have distortion and so on. When you first call up a sound on a track in a sequencer, though, it likely doesn't have any of these effects assigned, so it sounds very different and very plain. You must reassign, or reconfigure, the effects yourself with those exact settings to get the sound back to the way it is in the sound mode. To do so you need to understand the structure of your keyboard's effects system.

Some effects are commonly *global*, meaning every sound in the sequencer or song can share the same effect. These overarching effects are called *master effects* or *system effects;* they may be limited to certain choices (the two most common being some form of reverb and chorus), or you may be able to freely choose what effects go in these master locations. Each track or sound has a *send amount* parameter to run it into each master effect, so you can decide on a sound-by-sound basis how much effect to give. If your model always pre-assigns the master effects, the parameter may even say Reverb Amount and Chorus Amount.

Other effects are configured on a per-track or per-part basis. This design is called an *insert effect* or *insertion effect* because you place it in-line with a given track or part such that it's not available to all parts. This configuration usually applies to the more special, colorful types of effects such as deeper modulation effects, distortion, and rotary speaker. It doesn't have a send amount because you choose how much of the effect to hear with a wet/dry or mix parameter within the effect itself. (*Dry* is the unaffected sound; *wet* is the sound with effect added in.) **Note:** Each product is different, but keyboards usually have a limited number of these insert effects, so every track/sound can't have its own effect.

You don't always have to go to the hassle of figuring out what each sound's effects are and manually reprogramming them in the sequencer mode; many instruments have a Copy With Effects or Copy Effects From Sound menu command you can use when assigning a sound to a track. This may be a one-step process for all effects — master and insert — or you may have to do it separately for the master effects and the insert effects. Look for this type of helper to get your first sound/first track set up so it sounds the way it should.

Recording the first track

You've picked the sound you want to record first and you've copied back the effects it uses so it sounds good when you play the keyboard. Just follow these steps to record:

1. **Press Record or Rec.**

   For some keyboards, this function gives you a count-in of four clicks, and then you're recording. For other keyboards, you need to press Play or Start while in this record-ready mode to start actual recording.

   You're working with MIDI recording, so the tempo doesn't matter; you can always change it later. You may want to set it a little bit slower so you can concentrate and play cleanly for now.

2. **Press Stop when you're finished playing.**

3. **Relocate to the beginning of the recording.**

   The earlier section "Creating a one pass MIDI recording" talks about this.

4. **Press Play to listen to your recording.**

   Repeat Steps 1 through 3 to record over it if you don't like what you hear.

Adding more tracks

Your first track/part sounds great; time to move on to the next. Here's how to record subsequent tracks:

1. **On the interface for your sequencer, find how to select Track 2.**

   You didn't have to think about track selection to record the first track, but now you need to change to a different track so you don't record over your first part and lose that perfect performance!

2. **Choose a sound for this second part.**

   Remember that it will probably sound dry at first. *Don't* use one of the copy commands related to effects at this time. If you do, you'll likely change the effects that your first track uses.

3. **Go to Track 2's send parameters and dial in a little reverb and/or the other master effect to suit your needs.**

   Remember that you can always add to and improve this mix later. Just get the sound close enough so you feel comfortable playing it.

4. **If needed, reassign or copy the desired insert effect (which may be called Insert or DSP effect) for Track 2.**

If you want more than just the master effects, determine whether you can reassign an insert effect or copy only that effect from the program you selected to your second sound. Some products have up to five or six insert effects. Your sequencer likely has 16 tracks, but with multiple insert effects, you can decide which tracks really need the extra sonic help and which can get by with only using the master effects.

Play the keyboard; you'll hear this second sound and can judge whether you have the effects set up the way you want. As with the master effects, don't worry about getting the sound perfect at this stage. You'll be able to tweak these settings again later when you have all your parts recorded.

With your sound parameters set, practice your new part before recording it by pressing Play and playing along with the previous track(s). You don't need to record until you're comfortable and ready to go.

5. **Repeat Steps 1 and 2 in the preceding section to record the part.**

6. **Relocate to the beginning and press Play to listen to your two parts playing together.**

If you like what you hear, great. If you like your playing but not the sound you chose, keep the track and change the sound later through the wonders of MIDI. (You can read about how to do so in the next section.) If you hate the whole thing, rerecord the second part until you're happy.

Repeat the preceding steps, selecting a new track each time you want to record a new part. Pick your sound, adjust the effects as needed, and record!

Refining Your MIDI Recordings

As already mentioned, MIDI recording captures only the gestures you made, not the resulting sounds. MIDI technology gives you the freedom both to make tweaks and changes here and there to smooth out imperfections and to completely change aspects of what you originally played. The following sections discuss several of the most common adjustments.

Fixing small mistakes

Any keyboard that has a multipart MIDI sequencer is going to have an edit mode of some sort, and all recording software for computers has sophisticated edit modes. If you really don't like what you played, of course, you're better off to just try again with a new recording. But if your part is pretty good, with only a few small issues, editing the MIDI data is the way to go.

Adjusting the timing of your playing

If your rhythm was a little sloppy or you started to play ahead of or behind the beat, you can use an edit tool called *quantize* or *quantization*. This function lines up all your notes to the nearest subdivision of the beat that you select. Basically, any note in the track that doesn't play exactly on the subdivision you've selected gets moved forward or backward so it now appears in the right spot. The size of the subdivision (eighth note, sixteenth note, and so on) that you should use depends on the type of part you're playing. Long, sustained chords can be quantized to half notes or whole notes, for example.

You can almost always undo edits of this sort to revert the track back to its original state, so feel free to experiment with different timing resolutions (levels of subdivision). Try to use the finest or highest resolution (greatest level of subdivision) that still gives you a good result. You may start with thirty-second notes or sixteenth notes to see whether that level fixes the problems without changing the feel of the majority of the track. If you choose a resolution that messes with a lot of the notes you played, moving them around in ways you don't like, just undo the command and try another setting. The coarser the resolution you use (perhaps eighth notes or quarter notes), the more likely it is to adversely affect your recorded performance.

Book VI

Exploring Electronic Keyboard Technology

If only a few notes of your performance are off, you don't have to quantize the whole track. If your sequencer allows you to view an event edit list, you can find the bad note and edit the timing location it starts at to move it to the right place. This approach is certainly more detailed editing, but it may be safer than changing the feel of your whole track with a quantize command. Figure 3-7 shows a MIDI event list with a bad note highlighted so you can change the start time to fix it. The highlighted note was played a little late; by changing the 6 to a 1 you can move it back on time with the rest of the chord that was played.

Figure 3-7: Editing note timing in a MIDI event list.

Position				Status	Ch	Num	Val	Length/Info			
1	1	1	1	Note	1	A#2	46	.	1	2	39
1	1	1	1	Note	1	D3	72	.	1	2	8
1	1	1	1	Note	1	E3	62	.	1	2	17
1	1	1	1	Note	1	A3	62	.	1	1	208
1	1	1	6	Note	1	G1	39	.	3	3	237
1	1	4	190	Control	1	64	127	Sustain			
1	2	4	61	Note	1	A2	61	.	1	3	128
1	3	2	1	Note	1	A#2	55	.	1	1	158

BFly Rhodes2

Apple Logic Pro 9 screenshot courtesy of Jerry Kovarsky

Some sequencers offer another type of view of your data to use while making edits. A *piano roll* view (shown in Figure 3-8) displays notes as small dots or rectangles along a grid where the vertical axis represents the notes of a keyboard and the horizontal axis represents the time in your recording. You can scroll from the beginning (far left) to the end (far right), selecting, copying, deleting, and dragging notes to change their timing (left to right) or their pitches (top to bottom). In Figure 3-8, the highlighted note was played a little late; by dragging it slightly to the left, you can move it back on time with the rest of the chord that was played.

Correcting wrong notes

Everyone makes mistakes at times, including playing bum notes. If you've played a lot of them, record another pass. However, if your recording has only a few bad notes, go in and edit them in either event list or piano roll views. Listen to the song, pay attention to the measure and beat where the mistake occurs, and isolate and change the note to any other note you want. ***Remember:*** The note will still be played in the same place, at the same level, and for the same duration. The only change will be to the pitch.

A common mistake for all keyboard players is hitting two notes together when you meant to play only one. Your finger may slightly graze the side of the intended key and grab the adjacent note along with it. These small mistakes are easy to find in editing modes. Try piano roll view if possible because you can easily see the two notes next to each other.

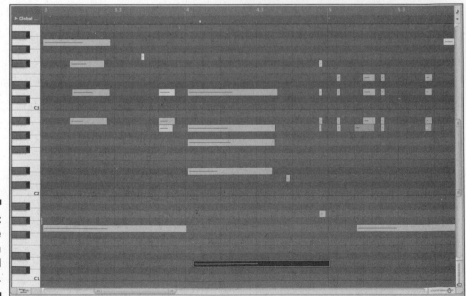

Figure 3-8:
Editing note timing in a piano roll view.

Apple Logic Pro 9 screenshot courtesy of Jerry Kovarsky

Here's a great pointer for finding those accidentally brushed notes: They'll always be much quieter than the main note (a characteristic easily seen in an event list) and will often be very short in duration (a characteristic easily seen in piano roll view). So when you see two notes occurring right next to each other at the exact same timing location, look for those two attributes. That will always be the bum note!

Changing the pitch of a note

You can also use the editing features of your sequencer to enhance your MIDI performance without losing that perfect take. If you're writing a song, you can always go into edit mode and change a note or two in your melody to try out new melodic ideas. Here are other ways to use this capability:

Book VI

Exploring
Electronic
Keyboard
Technology

- ✔ **Try alternate bass notes.** If you always play the root for each chord, you can make your part more interesting by changing some of the notes to the fifth or creating more of a walking bass line.

- ✔ **Add more notes to your chords.** Playing large chords can be difficult. No problem: Take a given note in the chord, copy, it, and then change its pitch. This way, you make a three-note chord a four-note chord, adding a seventh or other fancier tone. If you find it hard to reach octaves while playing other notes in between, just build them up after the fact.

- ✔ **Change your left-hand part.** If you played single notes, you can turn them into octaves by copying each note and then changing the pitch of the copied note to an octave higher or lower. You can also do the reverse to make octaves gentler: Delete each octave note, turning it into single notes in the left hand.

- ✔ **Try out different drum sounds.** The various drum sounds in a drum program are arranged across the keyboard so that you can easily play a normal drum part within a two-octave range (MIDI notes C2 through C4). That leaves a lot of other sounds that are assigned to the rest of the key range. Many are percussion sounds such as congas, triangle, shakers, and the all-important cowbell, but you usually also find alternate bass and snare drums as well as different cymbals. For your recorded drum part, you can try out these variations by using the note shift/change function.

  Say your snare drum is E2. Locate another snare drum sound — perhaps A1. When you find a possible replacement, in edit mode select all the E2 notes (consult your owner's manual for specific instructions). After you've selected all the E2s, you can change them to the new note, A1.

If you change all the notes, you put the song into another key. This process is called *transposing,* and it's commonly a separate function or edit choice. Common reasons for transposing include helping a singer be in a comfortable range for his or her voice — men and women rarely sing in the same keys — and letting guitar players use more open strings (which sounds good when strumming chords and playing strong, distorted parts) Piano players like to play in C major, for example, because it uses all the white notes. But guitars sound really good in E major because so many of the open strings work well for that key. No problem; transpose to the rescue!

Editing notes played too softly or too loudly

Sometimes as you play, a note's volume comes out a little too loud or soft relative to the other notes around it. You can easily fix this discrepancy by editing the velocity of the note. Make these changes in event edit view if at all possible because you can clearly see and highlight the MIDI velocity value that you want to change. Remember that you can always undo an edit and try again until you find the value that best matches the music.

Some sequencers let you *scale* the velocity of a given track or range of notes. You encounter two interpretations of this concept:

- ✔ **Scale to create crescendos or decrescendos:** This option takes the range of notes that you select and alters their velocity to *crescendo,* where each subsequent note is slightly louder than the one before it, or *decrescendo,* where each subsequent note is slightly softer than the one before it. You can usually set the start velocity and the end velocity to achieve the most natural gradation in *dynamics* (changes in volume).

- ✔ **Scale all the velocities relative to their current values:** This approach keeps all the relative dynamic values between notes the same but can increase or decrease them all by a chosen amount. Whether you think of it as adding or subtracting some value from each level or multiplying each level by some value, the result should be clear: Your whole part gets softer or louder but still sounds the same dynamically.

You may be thinking, "Why not just use the mixer to change the level of the track?" Good question! You can use touch to change a lot of aspects of a sound, such as switching multisample layers or the velocity routed to the filter. When you scale the velocity of the MIDI data, you interact with these settings in ways that changing the volume of the track doesn't. You might use this type of command on parts where the switching of velocity layers in a performance isn't feeling just right or where you simply didn't play a part as softly or loudly as you wanted.

Mixing your MIDI song

After you've recorded all the parts you want and are happy with the performances, it's time to mix your song. *Mixing* is the act of adjusting the blend of sounds and parts in a song to make them all sound good (volume, panning, and effects), blend together without clashing (EQ), and ensure each part can be heard without overpowering each other (volume). If you hear nothing but drums (or everything but drums) or your piano left hand, the guitar chords and bass guitar are creating a muddy mess, and that's no good.

Your sequencer or recorder menu has a page that may be labeled something like Mixer or may just be the main track view page. It has controls for the level of each track, a pan knob, and perhaps some control over effects.

EQ (equalization) may be available as its own set of parameters or may be part of the effects. It's an important tool in the mixing process, so be sure to find out where it's available in your keyboard.

To first experiment with mixing, try the following approach:

1. **Pick a single track and note its current volume level.**

   Good choices to start with are the drums or the bass if your song has these parts. (If it doesn't, try a supporting part behind your keyboard sound such as strings or a synth pad part.)

2. **Bring its level all the way down to 0 and notice how that change affects your perception of the whole song.**

3. **Bring the level up slowly and listen to the results.**

   Don't look at the value; use your ears.

4. **When it sounds good to you, look at what value you ended up at.**

   There are no wrong choices; it's just personal taste.

5. **Repeat Steps 1 through 4 with other parts, always taking note of the starting level.**

You can certainly bring all the volume sliders down to 0 and then try to build up the mix from scratch, but try to only do so only after you've gotten used to the sound of a good mix.

There's no one rule or magic formula for making a song sound good. Here are a few suggestions to help you achieve a good balance in your mix:

- ✔ **Don't allow the melody to get buried or lost within the other instruments.** No matter what type of music or instruments you use, the melody of your song is the most important thing.

- ✔ **If you're having trouble getting your melody loud enough, try lowering the levels of the other parts instead.**

- ✔ **Consider starting by getting the drums' and bass's balance right (if your music has those sounds).** Bring the drums up first and then add the bass, raising its level until it sounds strong and tightly connected to the drums — especially the bass drum. Then start adding other tracks without overpowering those first two sounds.

Book VI

Exploring Electronic Keyboard Technology

- **The main parts of your music (melody, drums, and bass) should be panned center.** Other parts can be panned slightly to the left or right to add aural interest to your music. Having everything come from the center or equally from both speakers sounds a little plain.

- **Don't overdo the reverb levels.** If you increase the reverb send for every part, your song will sound sloppy and become a wash of echoes. A safe starting point is to put only medium reverb at most on your drums, use no reverb for your bass, and add reverb to other parts carefully.

  Here's a good basic concept: Adding reverb to a part makes it sound farther away. You want your important melodic parts to be close, so don't overdo their reverb. To move back in the mix, you can lower its volume, but you can also add reverb to move it farther away.

- **If you find that parts are getting too thick or muddy sounding, use EQ to help make each track work in the combined mix.** Try cutting the levels of some frequencies to help parts sound distinct. Your bass drum and bass are the most important low frequency sounds, so try cutting the lows from other parts to let the bass part stand out clearly. (Do this cut on the other parts first, before just boosting the lows on the bass/ bass drum.)

  Too many high frequencies may fight with your melody, so try cutting them on some other parts if they're getting in the way. If you want a part to stand out a little bit more, boosting some higher EQ can really help. Pick your parts carefully — you can't just boost the EQ on everything.

- **You can make some parts more colorful and interesting by adding some specialized effects treatment to them.** If you have any available insert effects left unused, experiment with them. You can also consider using the insert effects to put a different type of reverb on a part or two.

If you're interested in discovering more about this topic, search out Jeff Strong's *Home Recording For Musicians For Dummies* (Wiley, 2011). It's a great book on the complete art of recording and mixing, and you can apply many of the concepts there to using a keyboard recorder or sequencer.

Trying Some Common Sound Edits

Sometimes you play a sound and you like most of what you hear and how it responds to your playing, but you wish you could change some small characteristic. Maybe the sound is a little too dark or too bright, or it rings on too long after you release the key. In most keyboards, you can fix that without becoming an expert in synth terms and tools or creating a sound from scratch. Just follow the suggestions in the following sections, and you can start to personalize your sounds and achieve the results you want.

Varying the basic timbre (waveform)

The fastest way to create a new sound is to simply change the waveform of an existing sound.

1. **Go into the sound or program edit mode of your keyboard.**
2. **Find the oscillator parameter or page.**
3. **Select a new waveform or multisample.**
4. **Save the new sound.**

    Don't forget to give it a new name and save location; otherwise, you'll lose your first sound!

The sections that follow have some common applications for making this type of edit.

Trying a slight variation of the current sound type

Many sample-playback keyboards offer more than one multisample or wave-form of a given type of sound. But the sound they offer for each one has been greatly changed to present you with the most sonic variation. So you may have two electric piano sounds, but the second one has completely different effects, is more distorted (for a heavier rock sound), and is less dynamic to your touch. That's a lot of things to try to edit to make the sound you want, right? No worries; just edit the first sound (which you liked) to use the second electric piano multisample, and then save it to a new location.

Here are a few other ideas:

✔ Take an electric bass sound and replace the waveform with a synth waveform. Voilà! Instant synth bass.

✔ You can make more synth lead sounds from the onboard waveform selection. Find a lead synth sound you like, go into edit mode, and try out many of the different synth waveforms. Very few keyboards deliver so many closely related lead sounds, but often all you need is a different waveform to add more lead sounds to your arsenal.

✔ When you have a sound that's a *layer* (two sounds on top of each other — say, acoustic piano with strings), you can make some cool variations by changing the waveform for the layered part (the strings). Many times, going to a mellow synth or vocal multisample yields another great sound without much effort.

Track 159 demonstrates some slight variation edit concepts.

Using similar amp characteristics to make a different sound

If a sound plays right (meaning it attacks, sustains, and decays a certain way), you can change it to another type of sound by swapping the multisample. Figure 3-9 shows some common envelope generator (EG) amp shapes.

Try some of these possibilities:

- ✔ Change a bass guitar sound to a synth wave and then raise the pitch an octave or two. Now you have a new lead synth sound.

- ✔ Take a sound that attacks quickly but also decays quickly, like a marimba, xylophone, or plucked string. Change the waveform, and you have all sorts of new short sounds that work well for percussive parts or for arpeggiated patterns.

- ✔ Change the waveform of an organ sound to make a good fast synth sound for playing choppy chord parts.

- ✔ Swap out multisamples to make nice synth pad sounds from sustaining string and vocal sounds.

Track 160 offers examples of making new sounds using EG shape concepts.

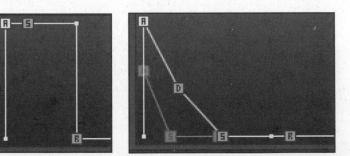

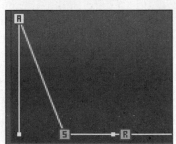

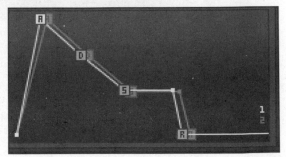

Figure 3-9:
Common
amp EG
waveform
shapes.

Illustration courtesy of Jerry Kovarsky

Changing the brightness (filter)

This common sound tweak is sometimes just a small adjustment to darken or brighten a sound; that can be all you need to go from "not quite" to "perfect." For example, this edit is the first thing many players like to do to acoustic piano sounds. What sounds good playing alone at home (warm and darker) doesn't end up cutting through the sound of a full band when you play in a club, at church, or wherever. So brighten up the sound a little! The easiest way to change the brightness one way or the other is to simply alter the level of the filter cutoff. If you don't see a front-panel control labeled Filter or Filter Cutoff, do the following:

1. **Go into the sound or program edit mode of your keyboard.**

2. **Find the filter parameters or page and locate the filter cutoff parameter.**

3. **Raise or lower the value to change the sound.**

   To darken the sound, lower the value; to brighten it, raise the value.

4. **Save your new sound.**

   Be sure to give it a new name and save it to a different location so that you don't lose your first sound!

TIP

Many keyboards have a front panel knob dedicated to controlling the filter cutoff as you play, which means you don't have to go into edit mode to sweep the cutoff (a popular thing to do, especially for synth sounds). Some synths have a ribbon controller with the filter cutoff assigned to it. And many small performance synths that don't have this dedicated knob assign filter cutoff to the mod wheel for easy filter sweeps.

You may not be able to darken the sound by this simple edit if the sound is using an envelope generator to vary the filter cutoff over time. An easy clue you're in this scenario: The filter cutoff is very low, yet you still find the sound is bright. In this case, you need to lessen the effect the envelope has on the attack section of the shape in order to darken the filter. Look for the envelope depth parameter (it may be called Filter EG) or for an envelope being used as a modulator assigned to filter cutoff and lower the modulation amount.

If your keyboard doesn't have a Filter EG parameter but has the more advanced rate and level envelope generator, lower the attack level value. Doing so causes the envelope to not go as high before moving to the decay stage, which darkens your sound.

Book VI

Exploring Electronic Keyboard Technology

Finally, some sounds use velocity to modulate the filter cutoff or how much the filter EG affects the cutoff. When you play this type of sound, a very soft touch produces a dark sound, and harder hits produce a brighter sound. If you reduce the velocity control over the filter EG or velocity modulation amount routed to the filter cutoff, you can darken the sound. Yes, it will still get brighter the harder you play, but not as bright. (Note that the softer touch will now be even darker, but often that difference isn't an issue. If it does bother you, raise the filter cutoff just a few numbers.)

Don't forget that EQ is also a type of filter control; you can lower the high EQ level to darken your sound some and raise it to brighten it.

Adjusting the amp parameters (volume over time)

Changing the attack and release of a sound is another common, very effective tweak to make. Many good sounds that have some release after you let go of the key can sound sloppy when you're playing faster phrases.

To fix this issue, just follow these steps:

1. **Go into the sound or program edit mode of your keyboard.**

2. **Find the amp parameters or page, locate the amp envelope generator, and lower the release or release rate/time parameter.**

   This step lessens or tightens up the ringing after you let go of a key.

   Note: Most synthesizers have dedicated front panel knobs for the amplifier envelope (likely labeled ADSR), so you can make this change without looking through menus or pages.

3. **Save your new sound.**

   Give it a new name and save location so you avoid losing your first sound.

Likewise, a too-slow attack makes a sound hard to play quickly. To adjust the attack, repeat Steps 2 and 3 in the preceding list, substituting the attack rate parameter for the release parameter in Step 2. To speed up the attack, lower the value.

A quick tip is to take a quick on/quick off sound such as an organ and slightly slow up the attack and lengthen the release. This process turns the sound into a different type of pad sound, great for dreamier background chords in a slow song.

Tweaking the filter envelope

When changing attack/release significantly on a sound, you may expose the filter envelope movement because it's now different from your amp envelope shape. Say you speed up the attack of the amp and now hear the filter slowly opening up at the start of each new note, or you lengthen the release of the amp and now hear the filter closing too quickly while your sound is fading away. The filter envelope used to match or follow the amp envelope shape closely, but now it stands out. In these cases, you want to go to the filter envelope and make similar edits to its attack and release times as those explained in the preceding section "Adjusting the amp parameters (volume over time)." Some synths even offer the ability to tweak the filter and amp envelopes at the same time, presented as a single/grouped parameter in a quick edit or performance edit page.

Some more advanced envelope designs offer a start level and then a second stage for the attack level and rate. To get a quicker attack, check to see whether the start level is very low or very high. If it's quite low, try raising that level to the same level as the attack in the second stage. To slow down an attack, a high start level may get in your way. If so, lower the start level back to 00 before working on the attack time.

Personalizing the touch response of a sound

A common issue among owners of keyboards is liking a sound though it still doesn't "feel" right to them. It gets loud too easily or is too hard to control when playing quietly. Playing harder and softer does switch between waveforms, but getting the hardest velocity layer to sound consistently is difficult. The following sections present a few easy edits to make to correct this problem. These types of edits are easy to do and can often be the most satisfying fix to make.

Customizing a sound's dynamics

Dynamics refer to how loudly or softly you play a note and are usually controlled by your touch on the key. All keyboards offer a touch curve or touch setting that affects dynamics. This parameter translates your playing force into instructions for how a sound will respond. If a sound isn't feeling quite right, go to the touch curve or velocity curve parameter first. You most often find it in the global or settings mode of a keyboard.

You can also manipulate how your touch affects the dynamics by routing velocity to the amp output. Increasing this amount of modulation makes your soft touch produce an even quieter sound, so you'll need more force to get the sound louder. Often velocity will be routed to modulate the amp envelope amount so you need to locate that parameter and increase its value as well.

If your sound gets too quiet and then too easily gets way loud, you need to reduce the amount of velocity modulation of the amp or amp envelope output. Your sound will get louder overall, so you'll need to lower the amp output to compensate. Be sure to check whether any velocity is routed to filter modulation; if so, you want to lessen that as well.

Not all keyboards allow you to do this level of editing. Certainly, synths and workstations, advanced arrangers, and perhaps a more advanced stage piano do, but otherwise, you may be limited to the touch curve method.

Another cool way to make a sound seem more dynamic is to add or increase the amount of velocity controlling the filter cutoff. When you do so, your soft touch causes the filter to be darker, which makes a sound seem quieter. If you're first adding this amount, you need to lower the filter cutoff to give the velocity some room to move. Try starting with the filter cutoff all the way down to 00 and then adjusting the velocity modulation amount and the cutoff until it feels right.

This change should be subtle; you're looking to get a sense of volume change, not a drastic filter sweep. If a sound is already using velocity to modulate the amount of filter envelope control, increase this modulation amount and work with it and the filter cutoff value until it feels right. If you find that your sound gets too bright with more forceful playing, you're modulating it too much.

Matching velocity switch points to your touch

Sample-playback keyboards often use different multisamples of a keyboard, recorded at softer and harder touches, to make a sound more realistic and expressive. All the better sampled acoustic and electric piano sounds do, for sure. Although this method is a great approach to re-creating these sounds, the programmed velocity values for when to switch to the next multisample may not match your touch. Basically, what you perceive as a touch to dynamics or brightness problem may actually be a problem with when the keyboard switches to a different multisample. If you have a synth, workstation, or more advanced stage piano or arranger, you may be able to access the multisample switching to see whether it's the issue before you go to the amp and filter parameters. Here's how:

1. **Go into sound/program edit mode.**

2. **Find the oscillator page(s) and look to see whether multiple waveforms or multisamples are arranged to be switched by velocity values.**

   On some instruments, this info is all presented on one oscillator page, but on others it's another part, tone, or layer that is a complete sound element set to be triggered by a certain velocity range.

3. **Check the velocity values.**

   Look at the velocity values used for each multisample or part. MIDI velocity ranges from 001 to 127, so you'll encounter several subranges for an oscillator or multisample — maybe 001 to 32, 033 to 070, 071 to 100, and 101 to 127. Notice that the numbers all run consecutively, with no range overlapping.

4. **Adjust the value of the appropriate layer(s).**

If the top layer is coming in too easily for you or producing too bright a sound, you want to move its start value to a higher velocity number, making it take even more force to trigger it. Set the range to 112 to 127 and see whether that feels better. Remember, though, that you can't leave a hole between two layers. With your change, nothing is sounding from 100 to 111, so you have to go back to layer three and raise the top threshold so that the range covers 071 to 111. Now the full range of values will produce sound.

To make a sound more dynamic and softer at low velocity levels, increase the range of values that the lower layers occupy, only bringing in the upper layers at the highest values. To make a sound brighter and more aggressive, increase the range that the upper layers use, spreading them across the majority of the range and only using the lower layers for the lowest numbers.

 If you want to get to hear the character of each multisample, you can go to an initialized sound location in your keyboard (if it has one) and assign this multisample to that "raw" sound. It won't sound perfect, but you can hear the true character of the recording and can better judge what each waveform sounds like.

Book VI

Exploring Electronic Keyboard Technology

Getting Your Song out of the Keyboard and into the World

After your MIDI-based song is mixed, you need to capture the sound of it to allow others to hear it away from your keyboard. Translation: You need to make an audio recording of the song. If your keyboard can record both MIDI and audio, it will have some sort of command, often called Bouncing or Bouncing Down to record the whole song to audio. Follow the instructions from your owner's manual.

If your keyboard can only do MIDI recording, you need an external audio recorder or computer software and audio interface for your computer to make the recording. You connect the main audio outputs of your keyboard to the audio inputs of the recorder or audio interface, and then you can capture/record the song.

When you use audio recording, however, you're already saving your work to some form of media as you record. And most products record in the industry standard wave file format, so sharing it with others is simple.

With the file you want visible, move or copy it to your hard drive. Make a folder on your computer for saving your personal recording files to. After the file is on your computer, you can play it, import it into your music library, and share it with your friends. Here are some common ways to share:

✔ **E-mail it.** Because you're using wave files, the file size may be too large. (Some e-mail systems can't accept files larger than 8 to 10MB, for example.) First, compress the file (the most common form is .zip) and see how much smaller it gets. Compressing is a good first step because it doesn't degrade the quality of your music file; it just packs it smaller to send it. If it becomes small enough to send, great. When your recipient unzips the file, it will be back to its full size and pristine audio quality.

✔ **Use a file transfer service.** If the file is still very large after compressing, you can consider using one of the many online options for sending bigger files, such as Dropbox. You upload your file to a service's website; the service stores it and sends your recipient a link so he can download the file privately through his web browser, avoiding the e-mail size limits. Many services offer free transfers up to 2 GB and paid options for larger files.

✔ **Upload it to a music-sharing site.** Many sites allow you to share, stream, and offer your music for free or paid download. These sites often perform the file compression for you; you upload your wave file, and they take care of the rest. Popular sites include Soundcloud (`www.soundcloud.com`), Reverb Nation (`www.reverbnation.com`), and YouTube (`www.youtube.com` — yes, you can share just audio files there). When the music is uploaded, you can post a link to your social media accounts to share it with anyone with an Internet connection. Remember, these sites may be visible to the population at large, so consider just how public you want to make your performance.

Converting to MP3 and other compressed formats

If your compressed file is still too big to send, another choice is to convert your wave file to another audio format that makes it smaller. MP3 is the most widely used format and is fine for casual use, but note that it degrades the sound quality of your music to some degree. Your computer music player application (such as Apple iTunes or Windows Media Player) can probably perform this conversion. If you go this route, check the settings to be sure you're using the highest-quality conversion. Often such programs convert to 128 Kbps (kilobits per second) format, which is too low and compromises audio quality. Use the highest setting: 320 Kbps.

Other formats for compressing music sound better, such as Apple's Apple Lossless Audio Codec or ALAC format, MP4 (shown as either .mp4 or .m4a), Ogg Vorbis (.ogg), and FLAC. Keep in mind that not all your recipients may know about or have the right playback applications for these file types, so check in advance before sending them. Depending on the size, you may now be able to e-mail it or stay within a file-sharing service's free limits.

Chapter 4

Using Onboard Learning Systems

In This Chapter

▶ Getting familiar with your keyboard's built-in songs

▶ Walking through the lessons features of Casio and Yamaha

▶ Playing with some fun instructional features

▶ Access the audio track at www.dummies.com/go/pianokeyboardaio/

*P*laying an instrument is a wonderful activity, and being able to express yourself through music is both satisfying and actually good for your long-term health and well being. Learning to read music and develop your technique involves hard work; there are no magic shortcuts to developing your skills, no matter what those Internet ads and online courses may promise.

However, many portable keyboards today offer some great features to help you get started, guide you through proper practice routines, and make the study of music into a fun game for kids of all ages.

This chapter takes you through the educational features and helpers built into many of the Casio and Yamaha keyboards. People often find the included manuals a bit cryptic — the intent here is to explain both how and *why* you want to do things. Even if you don't own one of these keyboards, you'll find this chapter interesting and helpful when shopping for a new keyboard.

Working with Built-In Songs

Most electronic keyboards have some built-in demo songs, which the store uses to show off the instrument's sounds and sonic capabilities. But this class of portable keyboards, along with many digital pianos, usually also has a library of simple folk songs, holiday favorites, popular classical selections, and instructional songs to help you in your studies. Look on the front panel for a button labeled Song (Yamaha) or Song Bank (Casio) to confirm that your keyboard has actual songs built in, not just a few in-store demos.

Some of these tunes are simple two-handed piano playing, others use the onboard auto-accompaniment, and some are orchestrated to sound like a full production. No matter what the style, you can listen and learn from them.

Selecting a song

First, you need to choose a song. On most low-end models the song names, or at least the categories, appear on the front panel, as shown in Figure 4-1.

🎹 **110 SONG BANK** _____

001~045 WORLD	046~050 EVENT	053 JE TE VEUX	091~110 EXERCISE
001 TWINKLE TWINKLE LITTLE STAR	046 SILENT NIGHT	067 ODE TO JOY	EXERCISE I
007 AMAZING GRACE	051~090 PIANO/CLASSICS	071 RÊVERIE	EXERCISE II
020 GREENSLEEVES	051 MARY HAD A LITTLE LAMB	074 FÜR ELISE	

Figure 4-1:
Front panel
song list.

Illustration courtesy of Casio America, Inc.

1. **To select a built-in song, press the Song or Song Bank mode button.**

   You'll also see the word *Demos* on the front panel; usually, it means you have to hold down two buttons to bring up a special playback mode of all the built-in songs. That's not what you're looking for in this step; that function plays through all the songs like a jukebox gone mad. You need to be able to select one specific song of your choosing for this process.

2. **Use any of the data entry controls (+/–, up/down, numeric keypad, value wheel/slider, or whatever applies) to select the song you want to listen to.**

3. **Press Play or Start/Stop to listen to the song.**

4. **While the song is playing, press the Pause button (see Figure 4-2) to stop the song but keep it at the current location.**

   To resume play from where you left off, press Pause again. If you press Stop, you stop the song and relocate to the beginning.

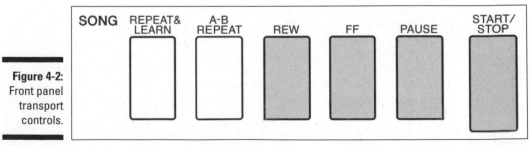

Figure 4-2:
Front panel
transport
controls.

Illustration courtesy of Yamaha Corporation of America

5. **Press the Fast Forward (FF) button to move ahead through the song while it's playing and the Rewind (REW) button to scroll back to an earlier section of the song.**

On many keyboards, if you press FF or REW once, the song moves one measure in the chosen direction. Holding down the button causes the keyboard to speed through the song until you let go. Then it resumes playing.

Note: A couple of other buttons — Repeat & Learn and A-B Repeat — also appear in Figure 4-2. These buttons come into play in the later section "Repeating small sections."

Book VI

Exploring
Electronic
Keyboard
Technology

Slowing down the tempo

You've found a song you like, and now you want to attempt to play it for yourself. Your keyboard may come with printed music for the included songs as part of the manual, or you may want to figure it out by ear. Whatever method you choose, the first step should be slowing down the song so you can hear it at a slower tempo, good for learning and playing along with. Learning a song at a comfortable (meaning slow) tempo before attempting to play it at the final, correct tempo is important. Work slowly and gradually increase the speed as you get comfortable.

Your keyboard has two buttons labeled Tempo — an Up control and a Down control (as shown in Figure 4-3) — or a Tempo knob or slider. You can use these to adjust the tempo as desired.

Figure 4-3: Front panel tempo controls.

Illustration courtesy of Yamaha Corporation of America

Use the Tap Tempo feature if it's available; refer to Figure 4-3. This function lets you tap on a marked button at the speed/timing you want to set the tempo to. When setting the tempo with Tap Tempo, you need to tap at least three times to give the keyboard a clear indication of the tempo you want.

Turning off one of the parts (RH or LH)

Many keyboards that offer piano pieces as part of their learning systems have a feature for turning off one of the hands or parts. This functionality is a good way to be able to listen to and focus on one part at a time without being distracted by the other part. After you've learned one of the parts, you can turn it off, turn on the other part, and play a duet with the system, each playing one hand.

Look on the front panel of your keyboard for a button labeled Part Select or buttons labeled Part 1 and Part 2 or RH/R (right hand) and LH/L (left hand). Figure 4-4 shows some examples. These buttons turn off a selected part, toggling it on and off with each press. Look at your display for visual feedback of what you're doing with each button press.

You may need to be in Lesson mode to turn off parts on some models. Lesson modes are discussed later in the chapter.

Repeating small sections

As you start to learn a song, you want to limit the playback to small sections at a time. Dividing a piece into small phrases is an essential part of practicing that allows you to concentrate on each section and work on it over and over again. Plus, working on small phrases helps when you're trying to figure out a song by ear.

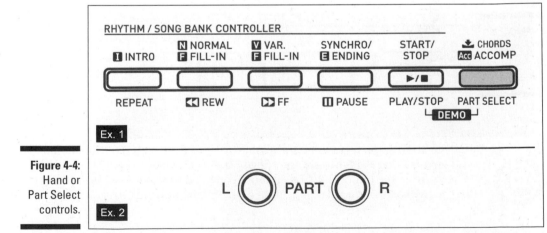

Figure 4-4:
Hand or
Part Select
controls.

Illustrations courtesy of Casio America, Inc, and Yamaha Corporation of America

The easiest way to create these smaller phrases is to press a button to mark the start and end locations you want while the song is playing. On Casio keyboards, this button is labeled Repeat; on Yamaha, it's often A-B Repeat (refer to Figure 4-2). On both brands, setting up these repeats is easy to do:

1. **Select and start the song playing.**

2. **As you come to the measure you want to start repeating from, simply press the Repeat or A-B Repeat button to set the start marker.**

3. **When you reach the end of the phrase you want to use, press the same button again to set the end marker.**

TIP

If you're having trouble setting the right measures, try slowing down the tempo while you set the markers. Then you can raise it back to the speed you want. If you miss the bar you wanted, you can just press the REW button to move back one measure with each tap.

Now when you play the song, it will start with a count-in to get you ready and then play the same selected range of measures over and over. While it's playing, you can still use the FF, REW, and Pause buttons and adjust the tempo.

4. **To turn off these repeat markers, simply press the Repeat or A-B Repeat button again.**

Doing so clears those markers so that your song plays fully from beginning to end.

Introducing Casio's Step-up Lesson System

You're not on your own to learn the onboard songs; a patient electronic teacher is waiting to help! Each system is a little different; the following sections get you up to speed on the Casio version.

Following the steps: Listen, watch, and remember

The Casio teacher takes you through three levels of learning and practice:

✔ **Listen:** Sit back, let the song play, and get familiar with it. The song plays in small phrase sections, and the display shows you what notes to play and what fingers to use.

✔ **Watch:** Now the system guides you, requiring you to play the notes your-self. The display shows you the notes and fingering. On certain models, the keys even light up to show you the way. Some models talk to you, with the teacher telling you what finger to use. Follow the guides and play through the phrase; timing/tempo isn't important at this stage, only the right notes. If you make a mistake, the system will wait for you and guide you with the right answer.

✔ **Remember:** Now the helpers are turned off, and hopefully you've learned what to do. But not to worry; the helpers come back when you get stuck! Play the song in time, still in the smaller phrase context.

You can play each phrase section as many times as you want and at any tempo, so you can master them all no matter how easy or difficult you find each one. You can stay on each of the teaching modes for as long as you like.

When first learning a song you should work each phrase through the system (Listen, Watch, and Remember) instead of trying to absorb too many phrases in a row.

Getting started: Picking what to work on

Your first step is to choose a song you want to work with. Consider a song you've heard before if this is the first time you're trying this feature. Here's how it works:

1. **To select a built-in song, press the Song Bank mode button.**

2. **Use any of the data entry controls (+/–, up/down, numeric keypad, or whatever) to select the song you want to learn.**

3. **Choose where to start.**

   If you're just starting out with a new song, you want to begin at the beginning. But if you want to work on a different phrase, press the Next button to advance through them. Watch the screen to find the phrase number you want.

   You can also use the FF and REW buttons to move back and forth through the phrases.

You can (and should!) work on new songs one hand at a time. To select which hand to work on, press the button labeled Part Select. (The label appears under the button; above the button is the label for Chord/Accomp On/Off.)

Each press of the button toggles from one hand to the other to both hands on to both off. As Figure 4-5 shows, the selected hand/part has a faint shadow around it.

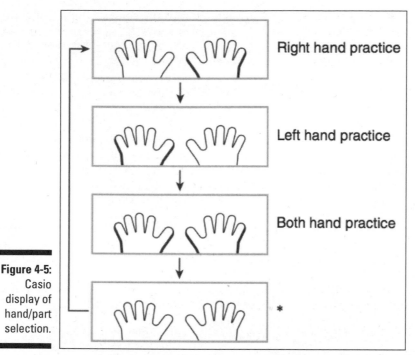

Figure 4-5:
Casio display of hand/part selection.

Illustration courtesy of Casio America, Inc.

Book VI

Exploring Electronic Keyboard Technology

Lesson 1: Listening and letting the teacher show you how

The first step in learning a new song is to listen and let the teacher demonstrate what to do. You've already selected your song and the hand/part to work on, so all you need to do is press the Listen button. (Figure 4-6 illustrates all the Casio lesson controls.)

Figure 4-6:
Casio lesson controls.

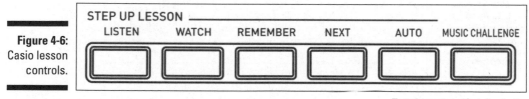

Illustration courtesy of Casio America, Inc.

After a short count-in, the song starts playing. If the song has an introduction before your melody comes in, the display will show "Wait" and then "Next" as it moves into the first phrase you need to learn. When the phrase starts, the display shows you two things (as shown in Figure 4-7):

- ✔ The keyboard graphic indicates the proper note.
- ✔ The hand graphic indicates the correct finger.

The phrase will keep repeating over and over. Listen to get familiar with the music, first for the rhythm of the notes — when do they play, and for how long? Then pay attention to the screen to see the notes and fingerings. Try to memorize both the notes and the fingerings; you might play "air keys" just above the notes to start to get a feel for what will happen when you play for real.

Note you'll hear the parts for both hands, not just the one you selected. Your part selection determines only what the keyboard displays, so be sure to listen closely to the hand you've chosen to work on.

When you feel comfortable with this step, press Listen again to stop the phrase play. You're ready to move on to Lesson 2 (described in the following section).

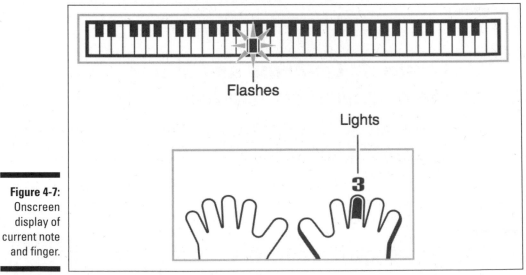

Flashes

Lights

3

Figure 4-7: Onscreen display of current note and finger.

Illustration courtesy of Casio America, Inc.

Lesson 2: Playing and watching the display for guidance

When you have the phrase in your ears and the notes and fingerings somewhat memorized, you can move on to trying to play the phrase:

1. **Press the Watch button (refer to Figure 4-6); you get a count-in, and then the phrase starts to play.**

2. **Follow the instructions and play along.**

   The display shows you each note to play as it comes up, blinking the note until it's time to play it, at which point it turns solid. The display indicates which finger to use by highlighting it on the hand graphic. If you pause, the teacher's voice will tell you which finger to use.

   Listen to Track 161 to hear an example of the onboard teacher.

   The phrase will keep repeating over and over; at first, you should concentrate on playing the right note with the right finger. You don't have to worry about your timing for now, although it's good to try to be in rhythm. If you make a mistake don't worry, the music will sit and wait for you until you play the right note. If you play the right note quickly, the music will advance to match what you do. As you get comfortable, work on playing the notes with the right rhythm/timing.

3. **When you're finished, press Watch again to stop the phrase play.**

   You can also use the Stop button to turn off the phrase play.

Lesson 3: Progressing from watch to remember

The third mode, Remember, is the way of testing whether you've really learned Lessons 1 and 2. The music plays with no guidance from the teacher, and you must play the right notes in the right timing to succeed.

1. **Press Remember (refer to Figure 4-6); the system gives you a count-in to get ready.**

2. **Start to play, being sure to play with good timing.**

Book VI

Exploring Electronic Keyboard Technology

If you get stuck or play a wrong note, the helpers will come back to point you back on track. The note will sound and show on the display, and the teacher will tell you the correct finger. After you've played the right note, you're back on your own until you have a problem.

When you've played through the whole phrase, the system will give you a reaction like "Do it again" or "Bravo!" Either way, the lesson will repeat over and over until you press Remember or Stop.

When you've mastered the chosen phrase, you can go back, pick another phrase (as outlined in the earlier section "Getting started: Picking what to work on"), and start the process again!

As you get comfortable with a song, you can use the Auto-Lesson mode (refer to Figure 4-6), which steps you through each phrase for the currently selected hand. Each lesson type is demonstrated once (watch) and then the remember phase is repeated three times. Then you have to play from the beginning, so the farther you get into the phrases, the more of the song you have to play. This mode is best when you've already worked through the phrases individually; it makes for a great practice routine after learning a song.

Turning off some of the helpers

You don't have to use all the helpers all the time; you can turn each one off if desired. Here are a few suggestions:

- ✔ **Press the Auto button (refer to Figure 4-6) to turn off the phrase repeats.** Now each section only plays once and then goes to the next. This option is best for when you've gotten comfortable with each phrase.

- ✔ **You can turn off the voice that guides you for the fingerings.** Here's how the process works for some models:

    1. **Keep pressing the Function button until you get to Speak = On.**

    2. **Press – on the numeric keypad to turn it off. Press + to turn it back on.**

    For other models

    1. **Press the Function button.**

    2. **Scroll using the right arrow button (6 on the numeric keypad) or left arrow button (4 on the numeric keypad) until you get to Lesson.**

    3. Press Enter (the 9 button).

    4. Scroll until the display shows Speak; press – on the numeric keypad to turn it off and + to turn it back on.

✔ **You can turn off the note guide that sounds the note when you get stuck.** Some models use the following process:

    1. **Keep pressing the Function button until you get to NoteGuid=On.**

    2. **Press – on the numeric keypad to turn it off; press + to turn it back on.**

For other models

    1. **Press the Function button.**

    2. **Scroll using the right arrow button or left arrow button until you get to Lesson.**

    3. **Press Enter.**

    4. **Scroll until the display shows NoteGuid; press – on the numeric keypad to turn it off and + to turn it back on.**

✔ **You can go through any lesson level without the song being divided into smaller phrases.** This exercise is good when you think you've mastered the whole song but still want some guidance. For some models, you

    1. **Keep pressing the Function button until you get to Phrase Ln=PrE (preset).**

    2. **Press – on the numeric keypad to turn it off and + to turn it back on.**

For other models

    1. **Press the Function button.**

    2. **Scroll using the right arrow button or left arrow button until you get to Phrase Ln.**

    3. **Press Enter.**

    4. **Scroll until the display shows Phrase Ln; press – on the numeric keypad to turn it off and + to turn it back on.**

Book VI

Exploring Electronic Keyboard Technology

Playing the whole song yourself

When you've mastered all the lessons, you can play the song from beginning to end with no helpers and no pauses. This approach works best for songs that have some additional backing; it's not helpful for a solo piano piece. Do the following:

1. **Press the Part Select button (see Figure 4-4, Ex.2) until both hands are shadowed in the display.**

   This move stops the keyboard from playing the parts; it's all up to you!

2. **Press Start to begin the song playing.**

   It will play from beginning to end with no reaction to what you play. The display still shows you the notes and fingerings if you want to use the guide, but it doesn't wait for you or say anything.

You can have some fun with this level of playback because you can add some extra notes or even improvise over the backing. Have a good time and be creative!

Exploring Yamaha's Educational Suite Lesson System

Yamaha calls its lesson system the Yamaha Educational Suite (Y.E.S. for short). It has various implementations, meaning some keyboards offer more and deeper educational features than others. This section goes over the basic aspects that are common to all of them in the following sections.

To select which hand to work on, press one of the buttons labeled L or R (refer to Figure 4-4, Ex.2 earlier in the chapter) near the Lesson section of the front panel. Pressing both buttons lets you choose two-hand playing.

If you need to, use the REW button to move back a few measures to try a part again. Even better, Yamaha has a dedicated Repeat & Learn button (see Figure 4-8) that moves you back four measures and then keeps repeating that phrase over and over until you press the button again. If you want to keep practicing a specific phrase within the song, you can use the A-B Repeat button to set the start and end of the phrase. Then the phrase will play, stop, count-in and then play again, over and over. You can change the number of bars it jumps back by pressing a number on the keypad (1 through 9) just after pressing the Repeat & Learn button. This function works in any of the lesson modes. In any lesson mode, you can also always stop the song by pressing Start/Stop.

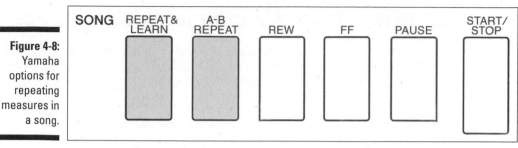

Figure 4-8:
Yamaha options for repeating measures in a song.

Illustration courtesy of Yamaha Corporation of America

Following the steps: Listening, waiting, your tempo, and minus one

The Yamaha teacher takes you through three levels of learning and practice — Waiting, Your Tempo, and Minus One — but these instructions add a fourth (Listening):

- ✔ **Listening:** You start the song and listen as it plays to get familiar with it. The keyboard displays the note(s) being played, both on a music staff (notation) and with an indicator over the graphic of the keys. You're on your own for fingering.

   Most of the Y.E.S.-based keyboards don't show this mode (Listening) from the front panel, but you can easily get them to play their songs with the visual guidance. Just select a song and press Start/Stop.

- ✔ **Waiting:** The keyboard displays the note you need to play the same as it does for the Listening step. It waits until you play the correct note to move on to the next. As with the Listening phase, it doesn't show you fingering.

- ✔ **Your Tempo:** In this level, the song keeps playing, and it's up to you to play the right notes with the right timing. If you make mistakes or miss the timing, the backing band slows down and makes things easier for you.

- ✔ **Minus One:** Now you're on your own. You choose which hand(s) to play yourself, and you play the part while the band accompanies you. The display still shows you the notes to play (both on a staff and on the graphic of the keys) but the keyboard doesn't wait or slow down or anything. Use this mode when you think you've got the song down.

As technologies progress, sometimes terminology changes too. The preceding is how Yamaha termed things as of this book's printing, but the company may well have changed some things since then.

Starting off by deciding what to work on

The Yamaha keyboards have a number of songs built in, and not all are good for the lesson function. The manual covers this topic, but basically you want to use the Piano Solo, Piano Ensemble, Piano Accompaniment, Classical, and Traditional Melodies for the lessons.

1. **To select a built-in song, press the Song mode button.**

2. **Use any of the data entry controls (+/–, up/down, numeric keypad, or whatever) to select the song you want to learn.**

A very cool feature of most Yamaha Y.E.S.-equipped keyboards is the ability to load in songs downloaded from the Internet or shared among friends in the Standard MIDI File (SMF) format. Yamaha has a large library of popular songs, classics, and more available to use with its lesson system. Visit www.yamahamusicsoft.com to see all the offerings.

Chapter 5

Playing Along with Recordings and Using Music Software

In This Chapter

▶ Hooking your music player up to your keyboard

▶ Breaking down the track into easy-to-figure-out elements

▶ Understanding how MIDI works

▶ Linking your keyboard with your computer or Apple iPad

▶ Enhancing your sound with music software

*P*erhaps, like many people, you've decided to play keyboard because a performer, a group, or a song caught your attention and made you wish you could do that. So you get an instrument and the first thing you want to do is play that song to relive that initial dream. But you find out that to learn an instrument, you first have to do all this other stuff: Develop technique through exercises, learn to read music, read a *For Dummies* book to figure out how to . . . hey, wait a minute!

You should have the chance to get what you want from playing music. Learning to play by ear and figuring out music from recordings is the way to learn those all-important first-influence songs and is an important part of good musicianship. Every good musician masters these skills along with technique, reading, and style studies.

This chapter discusses playing with recordings and working out your favorite songs from them. It helps you get your music player and keyboard connected so you can hear both from the same headphone or speakers. It provides a lot of the methods and tips that the pros use to break down a song and easily play all the elements of it. And it acquaints you with some computer-based tools that make figuring out a song easier than it used to be.

Computers, as you surely know, play an ever-increasing role in daily life. And so it is with music; you can integrate a computer or tablet device into your musical study, performance, and enjoyment in innumerable ways. The last section of this chapter goes over how MIDI works, helps you to connect your keyboard to your computer or iPad, and exposes you to the many types of software that you can use to enrich your music making, learning, and fun.

Exploring the Advantages of Playing Along

No doubt about it: Playing an instrument by yourself at home can be a bit lonely at times. Sure, it feels good to express yourself, to celebrate when you feel happy, or to cheer yourself up when you don't. But after a while everyone craves the company of others. At first, you may not feel good enough to play in front of people. And your early learning steps can sound kind of plain and often lack the full punch that a band or ensemble of musicians can provide.

An easy answer to this dilemma for the beginning musician is to play along with your favorite artists through their recordings. You don't need to play a lot because you're not replacing any member of the band (just yet!). You can add your part to the recording, whether that's playing along with the melody, finding your own simple countermelodies, or just holding down some simple chords. Being part of that wonderful noise that is your favorite band or backing band will feel good.

Playing along with recordings has other, tangible benefits:

- **It helps your time-keeping and feel.** Being able to keep a steady beat is an important part of making music sound and feel good. You can learn how to count and you can play with a metronome, but to really get the feel of a piece or style of music, nothing beats playing along with musicians who are experts at it.

- **It's easier for a beginner.** If you don't read music especially well, just poking around while a recording is playing can help you start to learn a song.

- **It helps your musical ear.** Musicians study something in school called *ear training,* which is the ability to hear notes, *intervals* (the distance between two notes), and *chord qualities* (major, minor, and so on) by ear. And the best practice for ear training is (wait for it) figuring out songs by playing along with recordings.

✔ **It gives you a more complete version of the song.** Printed music is often a simplified reduction of a song. Notating the actual feel of the rhythm would make it unnecessarily complicated, and parts are often simplified to make a songbook version easy to follow. Listening to and playing with the original recording can help fill in those instructions so you can feel and understand the music better. True story: A very famous jazz pianist was once presented with a detailed transcription of his playing, and he reacted by saying, "I can't play this stuff; it looks too hard!" Yet it was something he had performed with ease by ear, experience, and feeling.

✔ **It's fun!** If it's a song or band that you love, why wouldn't you want to be a part of it? You only need to play a little bit; let the original artist do the heavy lifting, and you'll sound great and have a blast. Part of your music-making should always be having fun!

Book VI

Exploring Electronic Keyboard Technology

Connecting an Audio Device to Your Keyboard to Hear Both Together

To play keyboard alongside your favorite song, of course, that song has to be playing on something. Many electronic keyboards have inputs for plugging another device (such as another instrument, a microphone, or a music player or iPod or phone) into them. This setup simplifies your cabling and connections and lets you listen to both devices at the same time through headphones. This section helps you figure out how to hook up your music player of choice (or another audio device) to your keyboard so you can jam with the greats.

 Get some good headphones. You want to be able to listen to the song very intently, and that's best done with headphones on. If you're going to be figuring out a song, you'll be repeating sections of it over and over (and over), which can get pretty annoying to other members of your household who can't help but hear what you're doing.

Finding a line input and getting connected

Take a look at the back panel of your keyboard for jacks labeled Line In, Audio In, Aux In, and so on. If your instrument has this kind of jack arrangement, then connecting an audio player to it is no problem. If it doesn't have the appropriate jack(s), skip to the next section.

With the jack located, you need to determine the right type of cable to use. Most portable CD players and all MP3 players have a stereo 1/8-inch (actually mini 3.5-millimeter) jack for the output. If your keyboard has a single jack labeled for input, you need a cable with a stereo 1/8-inch (3.5 millimeter) male plug on each end. This size plug is the most common one found on mobile phones, media players, and most earbud headphones. It's available in mono and stereo versions, so be sure you have the stereo version, indicated by dual black rings near the tip of the plug.

The 3.5 millimeter plug makes a good connection, but can be a bit fragile. Always be careful not to tug on the cable or put pressure on this connection.

If your keyboard has dual inputs, they likely use 1/4-inch phone plugs (shown in Figure 5-1).

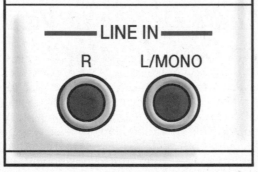

Figure 5-1: Dual inputs for 1/4-inch mono phone plugs.

Illustration by Lisa Reed

At most stereo, music, and electronics stores, you can find cheap adapters that let you convert 1/8-inch connectors into 1/4-inch connectors and vice versa. So if you have the wrong connectors for what you're trying to do, go get an adapter.

1/4-inch size is the most common plug used in musical instruments, mixing boards, and instrument amplifiers. It's the largest plug used and makes a great connection because of its long shaft. It's available in mono and stereo versions, so be sure you have the mono versions, indicated by single black rings near the tip of the plug.

To connect this kind of jack to your device, you need a cable that has a male 1/8-inch stereo plug on one end and splits out into dual mono 1/4-inch male plugs on the other. You can find this *Y cable* in some electronic stores and online. Or use the adapter mentioned earlier.

Finally, if your keyboard has dual RCA inputs — round inputs with a raised ring with a deep hole in the middle — you'll need a cable with a male 1/8-inch stereo plug on one end and dual RCA male plugs on the other. The RCA plug is commonly used in home stereo and home theatre audio/video products. It makes a great connection because its metal ring/shield fits securely over the jack on the device you're plugging into.

With the music player connected, you should check your owner's manual for instructions on setting the levels for the inputs and test out your connection by listening to some music through your keyboard (ideally on headphones).

No input? No worries: Moving forward with a mixer

If your keyboard doesn't have dedicated inputs to connect your music player to, you need to use a device called a *line mixer* or *mixer.* A mixer combines multiple sources of audio and allows you to hear them all from a single set of outputs, such as headphones. Your music player likely has a stereo 1/8-inch (3.5-millimeter) output that needs to connect to the mixer; the keyboard probably has dual 1/4-inch or RCA outputs. Or you can use the single stereo headphone output (either 1/8-inch or 1/4-inch) to connect the keyboard to the mixer.

Mixers have inputs called *channels,* and these are usually mono. Because your device and keyboard have stereo outputs, your mixer needs two channels to connect your music player and another two channels for your keyboard. Therefore, you need a four-channel mixer. Some mixers have stereo channels (two inputs for one channel) or have stereo tape or aux inputs, so you can get by with fewer channels in these cases. Some two-channel micro mixers have a stereo 1/8-inch input for one channel and dual RCA inputs for the other channel, which would also covers your needs.

Bottom line: You have some options when it comes to mixer setup. As of this writing, there are models costing less than $60 that work with most standard keyboards and music players. Just be sure that the mixer has a headphone output (1/8-inch or 1/4-inch stereo jack; it may not specifically be labeled "headphones"). Figure 5-2 shows a small audio mixer that can be used to connect both a keyboard and an audio player device.

Figure 5-2:
Audio mixer for connecting both a keyboard and an audio player device.

Photograph courtesy of Alto Professional

The cables you use to connect your keyboard and audio player to the mixer have male plugs on both ends, though what kinds of plugs those are depends on your specific equipment.

Getting in Tune

You may not realize it, but not every song is going to be perfectly in tune with your keyboard. Some older recordings were recorded a little bit slow or fast, and sometimes artists intentionally change the speed of a recording because they like how it makes their voice(s) sound. Fans of the Beatles are well aware of this fact; the band often played with playback speed intended to make its voices sound younger, deeper, or just different.

When you first pick a song to play along to, you may find that your keyboard sounds a little off. That's a sure sign you need to adjust the tuning, which is almost always a small adjustment.

Look for a parameter called Master Tune or Fine Tune. You can find this setting in the Global (Korg), System (some Roland), Setting (some Casio), Function (Casio, Kurzweil, Roland, and Yamaha), or Utility (some Yamaha) mode depending on your brand and model. This function allows you to slightly adjust the tuning of your keyboard up or down in very small increments. The tuning always defaults to A = 440.0 Hertz, which is the agreed-upon tuning standard in most parts of the world. It means that the A note above middle C is pitched to 440 Hertz frequency. You can raise it to 440.1, 440.2, and so on, or lower it to 439.9, 439.8 — you get the idea. You should find a note that you know is correct in the song and then repeat it over and over as you change this value until things sound better.

Don't forget to reset this value back to 440.0 when you're done playing along with that particular recording!

Book VI

Exploring Electronic Keyboard Technology

Figuring Out a Song You Don't Know

For some people, playing a new song is an easy process. They can sit at a keyboard, hunt and peck around for a bit, and quickly find the notes of a melody. Some even have *perfect pitch,* where they just know what note a pitch is and can find it effortlessly. They recognize whether something is in perfect tune (and are greatly bothered when it isn't).

Good for them. This section is for everyone else. Hearing pitches and chords and figuring out songs by ear is a skill, which means those not naturally inclined to it can still pick it up through practice. Of course, the more you know about scales, chords, and music theory (covered elsewhere in this book), the easier this process becomes, but the following sections help you get started without much of that knowledge.

Training your ear by trial and error

A good exercise to start developing your skills is to pick out simple nursery rhymes, holiday songs, and well-known melodies by ear. Just start at middle C on the keyboard and try to find the notes of some tune you know the sound of. Play the C and then figure out whether the next note of the song goes up or down from there or stays the same. If it moves, does it seem to be very close or very far? When you've figured one tune out, move to another starting note — say, the G above middle C — and try the same song again. Same melody, different keys on the keyboard.

Ready to move on to recordings? Pick really simple songs in the beginning. You need to develop some skills and gain confidence, so don't start with tunes that are very long and complicated or require a level of technique that you're not ready for. You need a lot of small victories during your development; this positive reinforcement feels good and motivates you to move forward.

When you've picked out a song you want to learn, first listen to it over and over and immerse yourself in it. Listen without touching the keyboard or trying too hard to analyze the song. Get familiar with it so you can hum/sing the melody, tap out the groove on your steering wheel or desk, and recognize and anticipate the various section changes.

Next, just let it play a few times while you hunt and peck around the keys. Try to find a note or two that sound good for the beginning of the song. This step can help you to figure out what key it's in and what scale fits the best. When you've found a note or two that sound good, try playing a major triad based on that note and then a minor triad from it. Which sounds more right? Major keys often sound happy, and minor keys sound sadder; do you get either feeling from the music?

Listening to a phrase to learn it

After you get a basic sense of the key or tonality of the song, your best bet is to break it into smaller chunks so you can focus on it in greater detail.

All music can be divided up into *phrases,* which are complete musical "thoughts" that have a beginning and end. These phrases can be easy to hear and feel; in vocal music, just follow the lyrics. Perhaps each sentence is a phrase, or you hear a couple of sentences and then a pause. The goal here is to work on these smaller segments one at a time.

Work on only a few bars of the tune at a time — certainly no more than eight.

As you play the short phrase over and over, you need to listen to one aspect of the music at a time. The main choices are as follows:

- **Rhythm:** This aspect can be the rhythm of the chords, the melody, or even the drums. You're not worried about any notes yet; you just want to pay attention to how the notes/chords move around. How many chords occur per bar? Do the chords change only every few bars? How *busy* is the melody (how many notes per bar does it have)? What you're doing is identifying targets that you're going to figure out while playing, and you want to know how many you have and when they happen.

- **Bass notes:** Working out the bass notes is a good first step when it comes to notes. Finding the low notes, usually played by bass guitar or a pianist's left hand, creates the building blocks of everything that comes later. In most music, the bass notes are the *roots,* or names of the chords being used, so finding them exposes a lot about the song. If you prefer starting with the melody, that's perfectly fine, too.

A really good tip is to sing the note you're looking for. Sing the bass note along with the recording and stop the music right after the note while you keep singing the tone. Then search on the keyboard for the note you're singing. You don't have to be able to sing well — just well enough to match the pitch from your recording. Just remember that your headphones may contain the music from your keyboard and recording, but anyone within earshot will hear your singing.

✔ **Basic chords:** After you know the bass notes, try playing them as triad chords. Listen to hear whether a major or minor triad is the right choice. Some songs use a note other than the root of the chord in the bass, so if the root-based triad doesn't sound right, think of the bass note as the fifth of a triad and try that. Still not right? Try it as the third of a chord.

If major or minor doesn't sound right, check out the fancier chords in Book III Chapter 6, like the diminished and augmented chords.

Try to find one note that sounds good, like it's part of the chord. Then look for another and then another until you build up the chord one note at a time.

✔ **Melody:** Because the melody is the most memorable part of a song, many people like to start with it. After all, most people can sing along with a song without knowing anything about chords and bass lines. Just sing the first note, find it at the keyboard, and you're off and running!

Another thing that may help you break down phrases is to find other versions of the same song. If you have the album/studio version, go look for a live version; it may have some of the parts more exposed because it has less studio production. Maybe you can find cover versions of the song by other artists. They may change parts of the song to make it their own, but a cover can be a good reference to better understand the song.

After you've figured out one phrase, move on to the next. When you've picked up all the phrases that make up the first part of the song, try to play them all together. Then start working on the chorus or main hook of the song. Keep working in these small sections until you've progressed through the whole song.

You may need to step away from a song after working for a while and refresh your ears and your brain. Don't force it. Put it away for a day or a few days and then come back to it. You'll often find that you hear something more clearly and can finish a section that had been causing you endless frustration.

Using your computer to help

Playing the music file on a computer rather than a CD player or MP3 player is easy and has some real advantages. Simply hook up the audio output of your computer to the inputs of your keyboard or to a mixer as mentioned in the earlier section "Connecting an Audio Device to Your Keyboard to Hear Both Together." It's no different than using those other devices, so you can still work with headphones. Here's where computers have the upper hand:

- ✔ **Repeatedly relocating to a section:** Whatever music player application you use, it will have better controls for relocating to a specific spot in the tune than a physical player does. Computer applications that have a timeline/progress bar make moving your mouse to a visual location easy to do.

- ✔ **Emphasizing a frequency range with EQ:** Most music player apps have some form of equalization built in, and you can use it to help hear parts more clearly. Boost the low frequencies when you're figuring out the bass notes; you can even bring down the levels on the high notes to help further remove them from your attention. When you're figuring out chords, you can boost some mid-range frequency to help you hear the harmony better. Try one EQ band at a time to find the one that helps emphasize the chords the most.

Many times what you want to do is get the drums out of your way, so lowering some frequency bands can help. Lower highs to remove cymbal noise, lessen the lows to remove a strong bass drum, and so on.

- ✔ **Using special audio applications:** *Audio applications* are programs for recording or editing speech and music. They often let you *loop,* or repeat a section of the song over and over. You can set when to start and when to loop back, so you can play however many bars you need to work on over and over without have to manually reset the player every time. Audio applications often can set several of these markers, so you can set up loops for the verse, the chorus, the bridge, the solo section, and so on.

Some audio applications allow you to slow down the speed of a piece of music without changing the pitch. This is called *time-stretching,* and it can be the best tool you ever invest in for learning songs. It's like asking the band or your teacher to play the song for you very slowly so you can watch and listen to what she's doing. Slowing down a song by around 25 percent or so sounds pretty good; any further than that and it starts to sound funny (though you can still tell the pitch of the notes). Time-stretching is invaluable in helping you to figure out fast passages and riffs in the music — check out later in this chapter for some options.

Finally, some applications are specifically designed for learning songs from recordings. This process is called *transcribing,* which is the act of committing a live performance or recording to musical notation. These applications offer a simple interface for playing music files and include time-stretching capabilities, EQ, and easy-to-use location markers (more details later in this chapter). They're well worth the small cost for all they bring to this activity.

Another way you can use your computer to help: Search for videos of people teaching the song on the Internet. With resources such as YouTube, you can often find other musicians teaching how to play popular songs. It may be a guitar lesson, but the player will still name the chords and talk about the melody. It's not cheating to get some help. Everybody learns from others — even, or perhaps especially, the greats.

The Computer Connection: Using Software to Enhance Your Music-Making

Book VI

Exploring Electronic Keyboard Technology

Every keyboard made since the mid-'80s has a connection on the back called MIDI, which stands for Musical Instrument Digital Interface. This round jack with five pin connections revolutionized keyboard playing and music making by providing a way for all keyboards to "talk" to each other. First developed as a way of layering keyboards together, the MIDI language sent messages between the connected devices, so when you played one keyboard the same notes and performance gestures were sent to another keyboard for instant triggering.

From this humble beginning, MIDI grew into a more detailed language that enabled musicians to use computers for storing the settings for sounds from their keyboard, editing those sounds by using a larger graphic interface, recording and editing the MIDI-based performances, mixing music, controlling stage lighting, and many other activities. MIDI forever changed the way music is made, and its inventors received a Technical Grammy Award in 2013 for their achievement. Every company making electronic musical instruments uses MIDI in some way; when you see MIDI listed as a feature on a product, you can be guaranteed that it will work with other MIDI devices and with various types of music software.

How MIDI works: Explaining common MIDI messages

MIDI sends various messages that describe what you're doing at the keyboard. Play a note, and it transmits which note you play, how hard you play it, how long you hold it, whether you use the sustain pedal to hold the note, whether you move any other controllers on the keyboard (the mod wheel, a slider, a switch), and more. Without getting too technical, here are the main types of messages that MIDI represents:

- **Note Number:** *Note Number* is the pitch or note you're playing. MIDI allows for 128 possible notes — many more than are even found on a piano keyboard! Each octave of a keyboard has a number, so notes are represented like C4, F3, A0, E♭5, and so on. The range goes from C1 to C9.

- ✔ **Note On/Note Off:** These two commands indicate when you start a note and when you let go of the key. Taken together, they define the length of time you hold the note for.

  Just like on a piano, a note can keep ringing after you let go of a key if you're holding down a sustain pedal. MIDI accounts for this situation as well, so a sustain pedal message will override a Note Off command when necessary, keeping the note ringing until you let go of the sustain pedal.

- ✔ **Velocity:** *Velocity* indicates how hard you play the note. It's called velocity and not force (for example) because it measures the time the key takes to leave its top point of contact and reach the bottom point of contact. That speed or timing translates into a dynamic because playing more forcefully moves the key to the bottom more quickly than playing more softly does.

- ✔ **Control Change:** *Control Change* is a broad selection of messages that define some other modifying action. These controllers can represent a continually moving motion (like moving a wheel, knob, or slider) or a single status, like the toggling of a switch on or off. A number of these messages are strictly defined; for example, Control Change (CC) #7 always represents volume, such as the volume knob or slider on an audio device or mixer. *Note:* Pitch Bend and aftertouch are considered special messages and aren't within the Control Change range of messages.

- ✔ **MIDI channel:** MIDI offers 16 channels of communication, so a single output can send different messages to different devices at the same time. Only the keyboard(s) set to listen to a given channel respond to those messages, so multipart music can easily be transmitted and reproduced. A keyboard that can listen to multiple MIDI channels at once is called *multitimbral.*

- ✔ **MIDI port:** To further increase the size of the MIDI network or group, a keyboard can have more than one MIDI port to communicate on. Each port adds another 16 channels to communicate on. These can be physical inputs and outputs on a device or software ports all available over the same USB port. They're usually named A, B, and so on.

- ✔ **Program Change:** This message is used to call up a specific sound on a keyboard or module. It simply represents a memory location in the device; any sound may be stored there. There are 128 possible Program Change values.

- ✔ **Bank Select:** To expand the number of programs that can be called up, a group of 128 programs is considered a *bank,* and products can have up to 128 banks. 128 possible banks × 128 program locations = 16,384 sounds.

(Hopefully, that's enough for you.) You select a new sound in a different bank from the current one by sending the Bank Select message followed by a Program Change number.

✔ **System Exclusive:** Keyboards have many things that aren't common and can't be standardized by a specification such as MIDI. These items are most often the parameters of the type of synthesis and other special features. *System Exclusive* messages are defined by each manufacturer to manipulate and store all these individual things. This type of message can only be heard and responded to by that specific brand and model of keyboard. They are most often used for the editing and storage of sounds for a given keyboard.

All these messages are how keyboards and other sound-producing devices, like drum machines and sound modules, talk to each other. MIDI grew into a recording technology as well, so messages also exist for tempo; start, stop, and continue controls for operating a recorder; and many other functions. You can read more about MIDI recording in Book VI Chapter 3.

Book VI

Exploring Electronic Keyboard Technology

Examining MIDI ports

MIDI connectors on a keyboard are usually *DIN connectors* You have separate in and out connections; one device transmits via an Out, and another device listens or receives the messages via an In (see Figure 5-3). The hardware looks the same, so be careful when connecting devices. (You won't harm your keyboard if you connect them wrong; it simply won't pass the MIDI signal.)

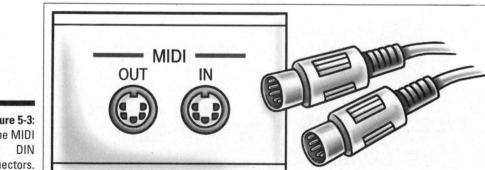

Figure 5-3: The MIDI DIN connectors.

Illustration by Lisa Reed

You may see a third MIDI port labeled Thru; this port just passes on whatever signal comes to the In. This option is a way of connecting multiple devices in a chain, passing the signal from the first to the second to the third and so on.

More and more modern keyboards are transmitting MIDI over a USB port and may or may not have the traditional DIN ports as well. The USB port is *bidirectional;* it can send and receive messages over the same cable. The port is likely not labeled MIDI; it just says USB and possibly To Host as shown in Figure 5-4. Study up on your keyboard to find out whether it supports MIDI USB functionality.

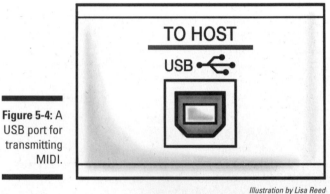

Figure 5-4: A USB port for transmitting MIDI.

Illustration by Lisa Reed

The most common misconception about MIDI is that it passes the audio signal between devices. People often connect two devices together via MIDI and then are confused when they can't hear them. MIDI only sends control-type messages between the devices; you have to connect the device to a speaker, mixer, or even headphones to hear the sound. It's like the devices are being played in real time, so they need to be monitored the same as if you were playing the keys.

Connecting Your Keyboard to Your Computer

You can hook up a MIDI keyboard to any type of computer: tower or laptop, Mac or PC. The main consideration is what type of MIDI jacks your keyboard has. If they are the round DIN connectors, you need to use a MIDI interface; if they're USB, you need only the correct cable. (See the preceding section for more on connector types.)

If you're trying to connect to a computer that doesn't offer USB, get a new computer! USB became popular in the late '90s, which is considered the Stone Age for computer technology. You won't find any MIDI/music software that's supported on such an old system, so getting connected will only be the beginning of your troubles.

Using a direct USB connection

This setup is the simplest situation; all you need is a common *USB device cable,* as pictured in Figure 5-5. (It's the standard connection cable most USB devices use.) It has the USB Type B square connector on one end, which gets plugged into your keyboard, and the small, rectangular USB Type A connector on the other end, which connects to your computer.

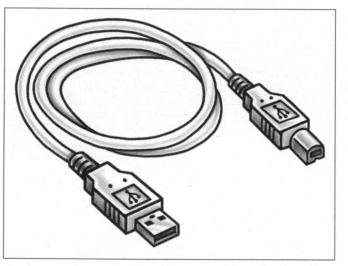

Figure 5-5:
A common
USB device
cable.

Illustration by Lisa Reed

Utilizing a MIDI interface

If your keyboard only has traditional DIN jacks, then you need some sort of MIDI interface. A *MIDI interface* is a box that offers a USB port to connect to your computer (the USB Type B/To Host connector, so you can use a USB device cable) and some number of DIN-based MIDI In and Out ports. The simplest MIDI interface is actually a cable that has DIN-based MIDI In and Out plugs on one end and a USB Type A plug on the other, as shown in Figure 5-6. This setup is fine to use if you have only one keyboard to connect to your computer. Just be sure to measure how far away the keyboard is from the computer because these cables are usually only available in 6-foot to 10-foot lengths.

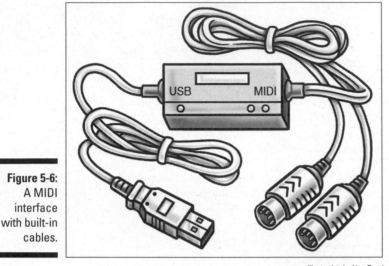

Figure 5-6:
A MIDI interface with built-in cables.

Illustration by Lisa Reed

If you have more than one keyboard (or device) or you think you'll be adding more later, buying a MIDI interface with more than one set of In and Out ports makes sense. Smaller interfaces may offer two In ports and two Out ports (such as the one in Figure 5-7), and larger ones commonly supply more outputs than inputs — for example two In and eight Out. Unless you're planning a large home studio with a lot of hardware synths and keyboards, you probably can get by with a two-In, two-Out interface.

Some MIDI interfaces get their power through the USB connection on your computer, which is fine if you don't have a lot of USB devices (printer, mouse, QWERTY keyboard, webcam, and so on). However, if you do rack up a lot of USB usage, consider getting an interface that has its own power adapter, especially if you use a laptop. Another option is to get a powered USB hub. Simple USB hubs can give you a few more ports to connect devices to, but they still rely on the computer to power them all, and often it can't. A powered hub is the only solution.

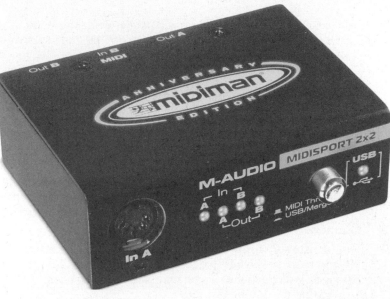

Figure 5-7: A basic MIDI interface with two Ins and two Outs.

Photograph courtesy of M-Audio

Book VI

Exploring Electronic Keyboard Technology

Many *USB audio interfaces* (used for recording audio into your computer, as discussed in Book VI Chapter 3) also include MIDI ports, so if you're planning to add one of those as well, you can save money and clutter/hassle by getting these two functions in one box.

After you have your MIDI interface, the cable connections are simple:

- ✔ USB device cable between interface and computer
- ✔ MIDI Out of your keyboard to MIDI In of the interface
- ✔ The matching MIDI Out of the interface back to the MIDI In of your keyboard.

So that's three cables needed, one USB and two MIDI.

Working with drivers and plug-and-play

It would be nice if, after you connected cables and devices, things just worked. But life, especially technology, just doesn't work that way. You need to take a few steps to finish configuring your system before you can start using music software and having fun. It's different for each operating system, as you may expect.

TIP

Here are a couple of hints that apply to both Mac and PC hookups:

✔ Go to the manufacturer's website and look for the latest driver there. Often the materials packed in the box are old and usually don't get revised until the company runs out of the pressed CDs. So the version in the box may be very old indeed. The newest drivers are always free for download.

✔ To test whether the interface you've installed is working, try online utilities. On a Mac, try the free utility called *MIDI Monitor;* for a PC, try the free utility *MIDI-OX.* (They may be free, but please consider donating some money to the authors for their hard work.) Search for these programs on the web; they're easy to install and show you whatever MIDI messages are coming into the computer and what is going out. They're perfect for quickly confirming that things are working without running a music application and are great for learning what messages your keyboard is transmitting.

On a Mac

If you're using an Apple computer, you likely don't need any other special software to make the interface work. But check the technical documents that came with your keyboard; some companies do have special MIDI drivers for the Mac that need to be installed.

Next, you need to run a utility that comes as part of OSX called *Audio MIDI Setup.* Look for it under Applications > Utilities. If you have everything connected and powered on when you run this application, it will scan your system and locate and identify all the devices connected. Figure 5-8 shows my setup in the application, with both a dedicated audio/MIDI interface with nothing currently connected to it (AudioBox 22VSL) and a Casio stage piano connected directly via USB. With a direct USB device you don't need to do anything else; after the system scans and finds it, your keyboard will be available to work with any application you run.

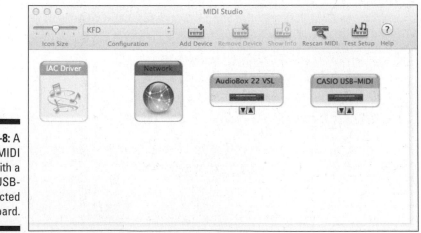

Figure 5-8: A simple MIDI setup with a direct USB-connected keyboard.

Apple Audio MIDI Setup screenshot courtesy of Jerry Kovarsky

If you're using a MIDI interface, the scan will show it. If a keyboard is connected to it via regular MIDI cables, it will likely work but won't show up as an icon and won't be fully configured. If you do nothing else, things will work, but your MIDI software won't show your keyboard by name when choosing a new track to record, for example. You can click on the Add Device icon at the top of the screen and manually configure your keyboard to fix this issue. Double-click on the *new external device* icon that was created, give it a name, and see whether it's already supported in the drop-down lists for Manufacturer and Model. Then connect the keyboard icon to the interface icon by dragging from the arrows to create virtual cables (as shown in Figure 5-9) and you're set.

On a PC

If you're using a PC/Windows-based computer, you need to install drivers. A few things to keep in mind:

✔ **Don't believe it when your computer just tells you it "installed" the device after you plug it in.** This function is the so-called plug-and-play that products promote, but it never works for MIDI interfaces or keyboards. Read the documentation that came with your keyboard about installing the software drivers and follow the steps carefully.

Book VI

Exploring Electronic Keyboard Technology

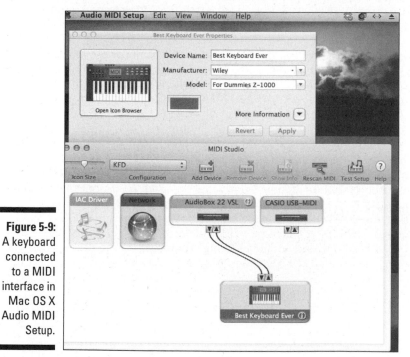

Figure 5-9:
A keyboard connected to a MIDI interface in Mac OS X Audio MIDI Setup.

Apple Audio MIDI Setup screen shot courtesy of Jerry Kovarsky

✔ **Don't connect the MIDI interface before installing the drivers.** The installation process will prompt you when to connect it; read and follow the instructions carefully.

✔ **Always put the MIDI interface on the same USB port you used when installing the drivers.** Thousands of hours of customer support and customer confusion have been caused by this little-known fact: Any device drivers installed on a PC work only for the port used during the installation. So if you unplug the device and later plug it into a different port, the device won't work.

Hooking Up to Your iPad

The Apple iPad has a growing number of music applications available and is becoming a favorite tool and toy for musicians around the world. To connect your MIDI keyboard to it, you have a few choices.

As with most technology, a new edition of the iPad seems to come out every five minutes, so you may be working with one of several versions. If you have the original or second or third generation iPad, you have a 30-pin connector on the bottom edge of the device. You need an Apple Camera Connection Kit, which plugs into that port and provides a USB jack. Plug in and you're ready to go.

If you have the fourth generation iPad or the iPad Mini (or even newer models), you have what is called a *Lightning connector*. These models already come with a cable in the box to connect USB devices to the Lightning jack, so you're all set.

If your keyboard has only DIN connectors, you need a MIDI interface to use your iPad. (Flip to the earlier sections "Examining MIDI ports" and "Utilizing a MIDI interface" for details on DIN connectors and general purpose MIDI interfaces, respectively.) But for the iPad, you need a special MIDI interface that supports the unique connectors the tablet uses. A number of companies make dedicated iPad interface cables that support the 30-pin connector of the older models, with MIDI In and Out plugs on the other end of the cable. For the newer, Lightning-based models, you can buy an adapter cable with the 30-pin jack on one end and a Lightning connector on the other. Then you can use any of the available iOS interfaces. (iOS is Apple's mobile operating system.)

You can find a smaller adapter that converts the Lightning jack to a 30-pin jack, but this option leaves you with two bulky connectors hanging off your iPad. That setup is risky, both in terms of coming disconnected and of straining or even breaking the connector on your expensive toy. Better to get the cable instead.

No drivers or other setup software is required to use MIDI keyboards and music apps on the iPad. Plug in your keyboard and start up an app, and you're ready to play and have fun.

Exploring Popular Types of Music Software

Music software has been commercially available since the mid-'80s and provides all sorts of cool things to enhance your music making. The following sections divide these options into easy-to-understand groups to give you a brief peek into the wonderful possibilities that await you.

Sequencer/MIDI recorder

This category, commonly called a *digital audio workstation* (DAW), is a recording studio in a box. MIDI is the language you'll likely be using to play into these applications, but they all actually record audio and cover editing, mixing, and outputting final files that you can make CDs from, post files to the web, and share for fun or profit.

They come in many different designs. Some DAWs are designed to emulate the linear tape concept, with tracks that you record from beginning to end. Others take a more modular or chunk-style approach to music making, where you create small sections, or patterns, and then arrange them in any order you like. This method is often used in a live performance like when a DJ cues up different songs. Some DAWs combine these two approaches.

Many DAWs include software instruments and sounds, so you can get new sounds, often using technologies that your keyboard may not offer. Getting a DAW is like buying additional keyboards along with your recording studio. Some companies offer entry-level versions of their programs, which you can later upgrade up to the fuller-featured versions when you're ready for more. If your keyboard offers no recording function or only limited features, this category is a great one to consider and explore.

Popular DAWs include these:

✔ Ableton *Live* (Mac and Windows)

✔ Apple *GarageBand* (Mac only) — good for beginners as well!

✔ Apple *Logic Pro* (Mac only)

✔ Avid *Pro Tools* (Mac and Windows)

✔ Cakewalk *Sonar* (Windows only)

✔ Cockos *Reaper* (Mac and Windows)

✔ Image-Line *FL Studio* (Windows only)

✔ MOTU *Digital Performer* (Mac and Windows)

✔ PreSonus *Studio One* (Mac and Windows)

✔ Propellerhead *Reason* (Mac and Windows)

✔ Steinberg *Cubase* (Mac and Windows)

✔ Steinberg *Sequel* (Mac and Windows) — good for beginners as well!

Popular iPad DAWs include the following:

✔ Apple *GarageBand* — good for beginners as well!

✔ Beepstreet *iSequence*

✔ *FL Studio Mobile*

✔ 4Pockets *Meteor*

✔ Intua *Beatmaker*

✔ Steinberg *Cubasis*

✔ Xewton Music Studio

✔ Yamaha Mobile Music Sequencer

Another type of software is *play along* or *backing tracks,* where you give the software a chord progression and it generates backing parts (drums, bass, chords, and so on) so you can play along with it. Some DAWs have this type of functionality. The most popular software with this capability is PG Music's *Band-In-A-Box* (Mac and Windows).

Educational/learning software

A number of software titles can teach you how to play piano/keyboards (or even guitar or drums). You can study reading music, learn music theory, work on your ear training, study the works of famous composers, and much more.

The beauty this kind of software is that it's always ready to go when you are and is infinitely patient; you can move at your own speed. Working with a human certainly has its benefits, but educational software can be a great companion to traditional studies and lessons. The market has too many titles to list here, but look for software from the following companies and programs as a start:

- ✔ Computer:
    - Adventus
    - Alfred Publishing
    - Ars Nova
    - Harmonic Vision
    - Piano Marvel
    - Playground Sessions
    - Sibelius
- ✔ iPad/iPhone:
    - Electric Peel *Note-A-Lator*
    - Karajan *Beginner*, *Pro Music,* and *Ear Trainer*
    - Musictheory.net *Theory Lessons* and *Tenuto*
    - *My Rhythm HD*
    - Nitrovery *Rhythm*
    - *Polyrhythm*
    - *Rhythm Sight Reading Trainer*

Book VI

Exploring
Electronic
Keyboard
Technology

You can find a number of metronome apps that run on the iPad or your smartphone — very handy! *Metronome Plus* is very full-featured for a free app. The Pro (paid) version of *ProMetronome* is really great.

As mentioned earlier, computer software tools for transcribing songs you want to play along to are handy because they can slow down the speed of the music without changing the pitch, repeat sections you choose, and make many markers in the song file for easy location of your favorite parts. Examples include Roni Music's *Amazing Slow Downer* (Mac, Windows, and iPad) and

Seventh String Software's *Transcribe!* (Mac and Windows). A newer website, `http://jammit.com`, offers real backing tracks, which you can isolate or remove to learn how to play songs from the site's ever-growing library.

Music notation software

Gone are the days when a composer dipped his quill pen into ink and wrote out his music on manuscript paper. Well, okay, quill pens were gone by the early 1900s, but with the advent of the computer, preparing a musical score or a simple pop tune has never been easier. Just as the computer took over printing and publishing, it has become the de facto standard for music engraving.

Many music notation programs can record MIDI and instantly convert it to notation; though not perfect, this process can be much faster than placing notes one at a time onto a staff. After you enter notes, you can edit and manipulate them with the same flexibility that you do letters within a word processor. Notation software often has sounds built-in so you can hear your music played back from the computer with no other instruments connected. Many of the available packages are designed for the serious composer and arranger and may seem far too deep at first glance for the casual player. But even those programs have "lite" versions or offer easy templates to work from. The main notation computer titles are as follows:

- Avid *Sibelius* (Mac and Windows)
- Avid *Sibelius First* (Mac and Windows)
- DG Software *MagicScore Maestro* (Windows)
- DoReMIR *ScoreCleaner* (Mac and Windows)
- Lugert Verlag *Forte* (Windows)
- Make Music *Finale* and *Finale Notepad* (Mac and Windows)
- Make Music *Print Music* (Mac and Windows)
- *MuseScore* (free; Mac and Linux)
- Notion Music *Notion* (Mac and Windows)

Popular iPad titles include Gargant Studios *Reflow* and Notion Music *Notion*.

Digital sheet music

Digital sheet music is a subset of notation software; these programs are for viewing music scores or buying sheet music/songbooks, not creating them. You can just view scores as graphic files (like a JPEG, TIFF, or PDF), but a dedicated program can offer easier viewing (better page turning, for example) and more features. This activity is well covered by the music notation programs on the computer (see the preceding section), but it's a growing field for the iPad and tablet computers. Popular iPad titles include the following:

- Avid *Scorch* (only works with Sibelius and PDF files)
- Deep Dish Designs *DeepDish GigBook*
- Leoné *MusicReader PDF* (also available as Mac and PC software)
- Make Music *Finale Songbook* (free; only works with Finale files)
- MGS Development *forScore*
- UnReal Book

Additional instruments/sounds

This field is huge in both computer and iPad development. Software synthesizers are at the forefront of synthesis development and technologies, offering both models of classic synths from years gone by and new, powerful designs. Software sample-players have the largest memory (often reading the samples off the drive in real time, virtually eliminating the need to worry about memory size), and the most advanced feature sets and designs. Most of the major advancements in sample-playback technology happen in software instruments, and many companies create sounds libraries for these players.

Most major DAWs include some software synthesizers and often a sample-player engine. The main software sample-players for computers are as follows; all are compatible with both Mac and Windows unless otherwise noted:

- Ableton *Sampler*
- Apple Logic's *EXS24* (included in Logic Pro – Mac)

- Avid Pro Tool's *Structure*
- IK Multimedia *SampleTank*
- MOTU *MachFive*
- Native Instrument's *Kontakt* and *Battery*
- Propellerhead Reason's *NN-XT* (included in Reason – Mac and Windows)
- Steinberg *Halion*

Some of the companies that make sound libraries offer their own player engines, but these players are usually only able to play sounds from that company. Examples include East West's *Play* engine, Garritan's *Aria* player, and Best Service's *ENGINE*.

On iPad, the choices are more limited because memory is much smaller. Top titles include the following:

- Akai *iMPC*
- Bismark *bs-16i*
- IK Multimedia *SampleTank*
- *Samplr*

Software instruments are commonly called *virtual instruments* or *VIs*. You can divide software instruments into a few general categories:

- **Re-creations of classic synths:** These VIs are accurate emulations of famous synths, often analog legends from the '70s and '80s. Most are modeled, but some are digital synthesis, and some are based on sample-playback technology.

- **Models/emulations of well-known acoustic and electro-mechanical instruments:** This category includes most sampled pianos; modeled tonewheel organs; clavs and electric pianos; and modeled guitars, brass, and woodwinds.

- **Imaginative new synths:** This broad area includes fuller-featured versions based on classic analog synthesis, as well as hybrid technologies and completely new and fresh forms of synthesis.

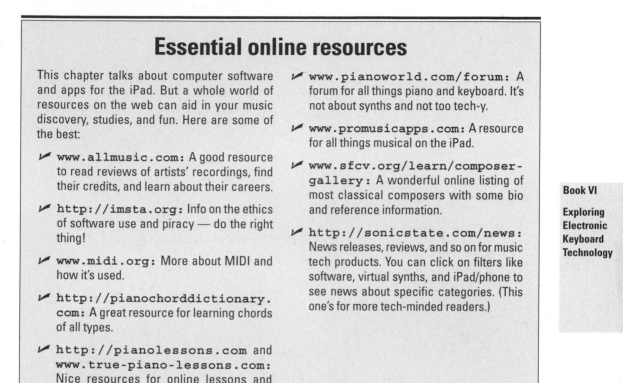

Essential online resources

This chapter talks about computer software and apps for the iPad. But a whole world of resources on the web can aid in your music discovery, studies, and fun. Here are some of the best:

✔ www.allmusic.com: A good resource to read reviews of artists' recordings, find their credits, and learn about their careers.

✔ http://imsta.org: Info on the ethics of software use and piracy — do the right thing!

✔ www.midi.org: More about MIDI and how it's used.

✔ http://pianochorddictionary.com: A great resource for learning chords of all types.

✔ http://pianolessons.com and www.true-piano-lessons.com: Nice resources for online lessons and study.

✔ www.pianoworld.com/forum: A forum for all things piano and keyboard. It's not about synths and not too tech-y.

✔ www.promusicapps.com: A resource for all things musical on the iPad.

✔ www.sfcv.org/learn/composer-gallery: A wonderful online listing of most classical composers with some bio and reference information.

✔ http://sonicstate.com/news: News releases, reviews, and so on for music tech products. You can click on filters like software, virtual synths, and iPad/phone to see news about specific categories. (This one's for more tech-minded readers.)

Book VI

Exploring Electronic Keyboard Technology

Appendix

Accessing the Audio Tracks

• •

Sometimes, reading about a concept and trying to practice it just doesn't cut it — you need to hear it, too. Wherever you see the "PlayThis!" icon in this book, you'll find references to audio tracks that demonstrate various musical pieces, audio effects, instrument samples, and more. Several of the audio tracks play a tune for your reference, so you can see the printed music and hear it at the same time. This appendix provides you with a handy list of all the audio tracks referenced throughout the book.

So, where *are* these audio tracks and how do you get them? They're on the Internet, at www.dummies.com/go/pianokeyboardaio/.

(If you don't have Internet access, call 877-762-2974 within the U.S. or 317-572-3993 outside the U.S.)

Discovering What's on the Audio Tracks

Table A-1 lists all the audio tracks that accompany each chapter, along with any figure numbers if applicable. You also find several backing and play-along tracks to help you with your practice.

Table A-1		Audio Tracks
Track Number	**Chapter**	**Description**
1	Book I Chapter 1	Sound of an acoustic piano
2	Book I Chapter 2	Vox combo organ sound example
3	Book I Chapter 2	Farfisa combo organ sound example
4	Book I Chapter 2	Moog synthesizer sound examples
5	Book II Chapter 3	Mixing up all the notes
6	Book II Chapter 3	"A Hot Time in the Old Town Tonight"

(continued)

Table A-1 *(continued)*

Track Number	Chapter	Description
7	Book II Chapter 3	"The Beautiful Blue Danube"
8	Book II Chapter 3	"Can Can"
9	Book II Chapter 3	"Lavender Blue" in 6/8 meter
10	Book II Chapter 5	Pick-up measure ("When the Saints Go Marching In")
11	Book II Chapter 5	Pick-up measure ("Oh, Susannah")
12	Book II Chapter 5	Ties that bind notes of the same pitch
13	Book II Chapter 5	Counting triplets
14	Book II Chapter 5	Swing those eighths
15	Book II Chapter 5	"After You've Gone"
16	Book II Chapter 5	"When the Saints Go Marching In"
17	Book II Chapter 5	"Oh, Susannah"
18	Book II Chapter 5	*Scheherazade*
19	Book II Chapter 5	"Swanee River"
20	Book II Chapter 5	"By the Light of the Silvery Moon"
21	Book II Chapter 5	"I've Been Working on the Railroad"
22	Book II Chapter 5	"Limehouse Blues"
23	Book III Chapter 1	Melody of "Frere Jacques"
24	Book III Chapter 1	"Skip to My Lou"
25	Book III Chapter 1	"Chiapanecas"
26	Book III Chapter 1	"Ode to Joy"
27	Book III Chapter 1	"Autumn"
28	Book III Chapter 1	"Oranges and Lemons"
29	Book III Chapter 1	"Simple Melody"
30	Book III Chapter 2	"Danny Boy"
31	Book III Chapter 2	"House of the Rising Sun"
32	Book III Chapter 2	"Greensleeves"
33	Book III Chapter 3	"Swing Low, Sweet Chariot"
34	Book III Chapter 3	"Little Brown Jug"
35	Book III Chapter 3	"When Johnny Comes Marching Home"
36	Book III Chapter 3	"A Musical Joke"

Track Number	Chapter	Description
37	Book III Chapter 3	"On Top of Old Smoky"
38	Book III Chapter 3	"The Sidewalks of New York"
39	Book III Chapter 3	"Stars and Stripes Forever"
40	Book III Chapter 4	"I'm Called Little Buttercup"
41	Book III Chapter 4	"Marianne"
42	Book III Chapter 4	"Aura Lee"
43	Book III Chapter 4	"Shenandoah"
44	Book III Chapter 4	"Auld Lang Syne"
45	Book III Chapter 5	"Good Night, Ladies" in C major
46	Book III Chapter 5	"Good Night, Ladies" in F major
47	Book III Chapter 5	A portion of "After the Ball"
48	Book III Chapter 5	"Worried Man Blues"
49	Book III Chapter 5	"After the Ball"
50	Book III Chapter 6	A little suspension tension
51	Book III Chapter 6	"Bingo"
52	Book III Chapter 6	Major scale tone triads
53	Book III Chapter 6	Blues chord progression
54	Book III Chapter 6	Doo-wop chord progression
55	Book III Chapter 6	Chord inversions
56	Book III Chapter 6	Blues progression using inversions
57	Book III Chapter 6	Left hand blues figures
58	Book III Chapter 6	Left hand doo-wop figures
59	Book III Chapter 6	Two hand blues chord playing
60	Book III Chapter 6	Two hand doo-wop chord playing
61	Book III Chapter 6	"Down by the Station"
62	Book III Chapter 6	"Sometimes I Feel Like a Motherless Child"
63	Book III Chapter 6	"Lullaby"
64	Book III Chapter 6	"Scarborough Fair"
65	Book III Chapter 6	"Red River Valley"
66	Book IV Chapter 1	"Pop! Goes the Weasel"
67	Book IV Chapter 1	"Polovtsian Dance"
68	Book IV Chapter 1	"Camptown Races"

(continued)

Table A-1 *(continued)*

Track Number	Chapter	Description
69	Book IV Chapter 1	"Trumpet Voluntary"
70	Book IV Chapter 1	"Also Sprach Zarathustra"
71	Book IV Chapter 1	"Quiet Sunset"
72	Book IV Chapter 2	Left-hand chords in varied rhythm patterns
73	Book IV Chapter 2	Root-fifth-octave patterns
74	Book IV Chapter 2	"Picking and Grinning"
75	Book IV Chapter 2	"Octaves in the Left"
76	Book IV Chapter 2	"Jumping Octaves"
77	Book IV Chapter 2	"Rockin' Intervals"
78	Book IV Chapter 2	"Berry-Style Blues"
79	Book IV Chapter 2	"Bum-ba-di-da" bass pattern
80	Book IV Chapter 2	"Boogie-woogie" bass line
81	Book IV Chapter 2	Intro #1
82	Book IV Chapter 2	Intro #2
83	Book IV Chapter 2	Intro #3
84	Book IV Chapter 2	Intro #4
85	Book IV Chapter 2	Intro #5
86	Book IV Chapter 2	Finale #1
87	Book IV Chapter 2	Finale #2
88	Book IV Chapter 2	Finale #3
89	Book IV Chapter 2	Finale #4
90	Book IV Chapter 2	"Country Riffin'"
91	Book IV Chapter 2	"Love Me Like You Used To"
92	Book IV Chapter 2	12-bar blues progression
93	Book IV Chapter 2	Rockin' bass line
94	Book IV Chapter 2	"Yankee Doodle" swings
95	Book IV Chapter 2	Motown syncopation
96	Book V Chapter 1	One under two, two over one
97	Book V Chapter 1	One under three, three over one
98	Book V Chapter 1	B flat and F major scale passages

Track Number	Chapter	Description
99	Book V Chapter 1	Aria from La Cenerentola
100	Book V Chapter 1	Finger combination: Two and three
101	Book V Chapter 1	Finger combinations: One and four, two and five, one and five
102	Book V Chapter 1	Exercise in fifths, sixths, and sevenths
103	Book V Chapter 1	"Take Me Out to the Ballgame"
104	Book V Chapter 2	C major, C harmonic minor, C melodic minor
105	Book V Chapter 2	Varied articulation
106	Book V Chapter 2	Varied rhythmic groupings
107	Book V Chapter 2	Variation VII from "Variations on 'Twinkle, Twinkle, Little Star'"
108	Book V Chapter 3	Parallel octave exercise #1
109	Book V Chapter 3	Chromatic motion away from the center
110	Book V Chapter 3	Combination movement exercise
111	Book V Chapter 3	"Turkey in the Straw"
112	Book V Chapter 3	Broken-chord pedaling
113	Book V Chapter 3	Blurred lines and long sustains
114	Book V Chapter 3	Sustaining as the hands leave the keyboard
115	Book V Chapter 3	"Simple Gifts"
116	Book V Chapter 4	Note-to-note jumps
117	Book V Chapter 4	Two-hand parallel motion jumps
118	Book V Chapter 4	Bass-note-to-chord pattern in 4/4
119	Book V Chapter 4	"Lily Pad Rag"
120	Book V Chapter 5	Jumping thirds
121	Book V Chapter 5	Alberti bass exercise
122	Book V Chapter 5	Guitar-style broken chord exercise
123	Book V Chapter 5	"Harp Heaven"
124	Book V Chapter 5	Scale handoff exercise #1
125	Book V Chapter 5	Crossing over with the right hand
126	Book V Chapter 6	Octave scale exercise

(continued)

Table A-1 *(continued)*

Track Number	Chapter	Description
127	Book V Chapter 6	Exercise with longer jumps
128	Book V Chapter 6	Exercise with hand contraction and expansion
129	Book V Chapter 6	"Schumann's Octave Workout"
130	Book V Chapter 6	Extended major-key chord progression
131	Book V Chapter 6	Extended minor-key chord progression
132	Book VI Chapter 1	Reverb effect demonstration
133	Book VI Chapter 1	Delay effect demonstration
134	Book VI Chapter 1	Chorus, flanging, and phase shifting effects demonstrations
135	Book VI Chapter 1	EQ effect demonstration
136	Book VI Chapter 1	Distortion effect demonstration
137	Book VI Chapter 1	Rotary speaker effect demonstration
138	Book VI Chapter 1	Filter effect demonstration
139	Book VI Chapter 1	Wah-wah and auto-wah effect demonstration
140	Book VI Chapter 2	Casio drum fills
141	Book VI Chapter 2	Korg multiple drum fill variations
142	Book VI Chapter 2	Various styles being played using a simple C triad
143	Book VI Chapter 2	A demonstration of each element within a style/rhythm
144	Book VI Chapter 2	An accompaniment pattern played with different chord types
145	Book VI Chapter 2	A simple chord progression with accompaniment
146	Book VI Chapter 2	Demonstrating right hand ensemble/harmony settings
147	Book VI Chapter 2	Demonstrating the pad feature
148	Book VI Chapter 2	Chords played in an arpeggiated fashion on the piano

Track Number	Chapter	Description
149	Book VI Chapter 2	Figure 2-11 demonstrated
150	Book VI Chapter 2	Figure 2-12 demonstrated
151	Book VI Chapter 2	Demonstration of changing chords and using space to vary a simple arp pattern
152	Book VI Chapter 2	Varying the octave range of an arp pattern
153	Book VI Chapter 2	An arp pattern played against a drum rhythm
154	Book VI Chapter 2	Demonstration of swing timing feel
155	Book VI Chapter 2	Filter sweeps while an arp plays
156	Book VI Chapter 2	Sound panning while an arp plays
157	Book VI Chapter 2	Delay effect used with an arp pattern
158	Book VI Chapter 2	Leaving space while using delay with an arpeggiator
159	Book VI Chapter 3	Demonstrating slight edit concepts to produce new sounds
160	Book VI Chapter 3	Demonstrating varying the waveforms in similar amp envelope shaped sounds to produce new sounds
161	Book VI Chapter 4	Listen as the onboard teacher tells you what fingers to use

Customer Care

If you have trouble downloading the companion files, please call Wiley Product Technical Support at 800-762-2974. Outside the United States, call 317-572-3994. You can also contact Wiley Product Technical Support at `http://support.wiley.com`. Wiley Publishing will provide technical support only for downloading and other general quality control items.

To place additional orders or to request information about other Wiley products, please call 877-762-2974.

Index

• *Numbers* •

2/4 meter, 121–122
3/4 meter, 120–121
4/4 meter
  example, 119–120
  explained, 118
6/8 time, 122–123
7 symbol, using with chords, 264
8-bar blues, 339
8va abbreviation, 129
12/8 time signature, 273
12-bar blues, 338–339, 342–343
16-bar blues, 339–340
24-bar blues, 340
32-bar blues, 340–341

• *A* •

A
  blues scale, 403
  harmonic minor left-hand scale, 193
  harmonic minor scale, 180
  melodic minor left-hand scale, 193
  melodic minor scales, 181
  minor scale, 179
  natural minor left-hand scales, 193
  natural minor scale, 180
  one-part form, 227
A flat blues scale, 404
AB (binary form), 227
ABA (three-part form), 227–228
ABCBA (arch form), 228
accelerando tempo indication, 289
accents articulation symbol, 287
accidentals
  changing pitch with, 133–135
  explained, 131
  flats, 134
  naturals, 135
  sharps, 133–134

accompaniment. *See also* arrangers; auto-accompaniment; LH accompaniment patterns
  chord triggering, 509–512
  mixing sound of band, 512–513
accompaniment patterns
  background melody, 509
  bass, 508
  chordal part(s), 508
  drums, 508
  percussion, 508
  sustained parts, 509
acoustic instruments, 15
acoustic keyboards, pros and cons, 42–43
acoustic pianos
  avoiding scams, 50
  choosing, 49–51
  considering locations, 49–50
  demo models, 50
  versus digital keyboards, 11
  versus electric pianos, 22
  grand, 22
  hammers, 24–25
  keys, 24–25
  lids, 24
  pedals, 50
  string layout, 24
  strings, 24–25
  upright, 23
adagio tempo indication, 116
"After the Ball," 253, 255
Airplane Sonata, 298
Alesis Studio Electronics website, 57
allegro tempo indication, 116
"Also Sprach Zarathustra," 299, 303
alternating hands. *See also* hand techniques
  arpeggio handoff, 459
  LH cross-over, 462
  RH cross-over, 461
  scale handoff, 456–458

ambience, 486
"America, the Beautiful," 223–224
amplifiers, connecting to, 74–76
analog electronics, 29
analog recording, 526–529
andante tempo indication, 116
Antheil, George, 298
arch contour, 210–211
arch form (ABCBA), 228
aria from *La Cenerentola*, 366
arp patterns, matching with sounds,
    522–523
arpeggiation
  examples, 518–519
  explained, 18, 517–518
arpeggiator
  exercises, 446–449
  extending ranges, 520
  hearing notes held, 521–522
  keeping playing, 522
  note lengths, 521
  range parameter, 520
  shuffle, 521
  swing, 521
  timing/speed, 520
  variety with patterns, 522
arpeggios
  left-hand, 198
  playing, 443
arranger keyboards
  music database, 515
  one-touch settings, 514
arrangers. *See also* accompaniment
  described, 17
  evaluating, 53
  features of, 32–33
  manufacturers, 57
articulation symbols
  accents, 287
  staccato, 287
  tenuto, 287
articulations
  adding to music, 287
  defined, 286
  importance of, 288
  slurs versus ties, 287
  using with melodies, 288

Asus chords, 262
attacks. *See* articulations
audio connectors, using, 73
audio devices, connecting to keyboards,
    567–570
audio recording. *See also* sounds
  explained, 19
  in one pass, 531
  versus MIDI recording, 526–530
aug interval, 214
augmentation dot, 106
augmented chords, 261–262
augmented interval, defined, 214
"Auld Lang Syne," 228, 233
"Aura Lee," 221–222, 228, 231
"Aus meines Herzens Grunde," 328
auto-accompaniment. *See also*
    accompaniment
  explained, 18
  playing patterns, 507–508
  rhythms, 507
  styles, 507
  using with arrangers, 32–33
"Autumn," 166, 168

• *B* •

B
  blues scale, 403
  flat major key signature, 249–250, 252
  flat natural minor key signature, 251
  natural minor key signature, 247
B flat blues scale, 405
Bach, J.S.
  "Aus meines Herzens Grunde," 328
  Fugue in C Major, 333
  musical style, 15
backbeats, 119. *See also* beats
Baldwin Piano & Organ Company
    website, 51
bands, playing in, 49
The Banshee, 298
bar lines
  double, 136
  end repeat, 136
  explained, 107
  final, 136

single, 136
start repeat, 136
using, 136
bars
    dividing music into, 136
    explained, 117
    mixing notes into, 118
    number of beats in, 117
bass clef
    explained, 14, 127
    lines, 135
    lower notes in, 190
    notes of, 127
    phrase line in, 225
    playing notes in, 189
    reading notes in, 189
    spaces, 135
    staff, 126
bass lines
    melodic style of, 313–315
    pop and rock music, 346
bass pattern, creating, 311
bass-guitar effect, 497
beats. *See also* backbeats; downbeats;
        upbeats
    defined, 100
    following, 100
    grouping into measures, 116–118
    hearing, 100
    practicing with notes, 113–114
    practicing with rests, 113–114
    practicing working with, 101
    rhythm sticks, 100
"The Beautiful Blue Danube," 121
Beethoven
    Fifth Symphony, 215–216
    Sonata in C Minor Opus 13, 329
benches versus chairs, 86–89
Berry, Chuck, 312
"Berry-Style Blues," 312–313
binary form (AB), 227
black keys, flats and sharps, 84–85
Blake's E-Z Key Finder. *See also* keys
    black keys, 84–85
    chopsticks and forks, 83
    white keys, 82–83
block chords, using, 516
blue notes, using, 183

blues
    8-bar, 339
    12-bar, 338–339, 342–343
    16-bar, 339–340
    24-bar, 340
    32-bar, 340–341
    chord progression, 269, 271
    chord substitutions, 343–344
    composer, 15
    explained, 337
    playing, 341
    playing in 4/4 time, 338
    song form, 338
    ternary form, 338
blues scales. *See also* scales
    example, 183
    features of, 183
    step pattern, 183
boogie-woogie pattern, 315
brass/wind instruments effect, 497
broken chords, 306–308
broken-chord patterns. *See also* chords
    Alberti bass, 450
    blues-style, 452
    guitar-style, 451
    octave, extended, 453
built-in songs. *See also* learning software;
        songs
    repeating sections, 554–555
    selecting, 552–553
    slowing down tempo, 553
    turning off LH part, 554
    turning off RH part, 554
"By the Light of the Silvery
        Moon," 147, 151

• *C* •

C
    blues scale, 402
    chord symbol, type and ingredients, 266
    key of, 236
    major key signature, 246
    major left-hand scale, 192
    natural minor key signature, 252
    "Ode to Joy," 158
    relative minor of, 179

C flat major key signature, 249–250

C major scale
explained, 172
illustrated, 174
intervals on, 213
numbering notes of, 212
practicing, 177

C position
assuming with left hand, 188
"Chiapanecas," 160
explained, 157
extending to B, 158–159
fingerings, 158
"Frere Jacques," 158
getting into, 157
stretching to limits, 160

C scales, major and minor, 178

C(sharp 5) chord symbol, type and ingredients, 266

C sharp major key signature, 251

C sharp natural minor key signature, 248–249

C+ chord symbol, type and ingredients, 266

C6 chord symbol, type and ingredients, 267

C7 chord symbol, type and ingredients, 267

C7 sharp 5 chord symbol, type and ingredients, 267

C7+ chord symbol, type and ingredients, 267

C7 flat 5 chord symbol, type and ingredients, 267

C7sus4 chord symbol, type and ingredients, 267

C(add*) chord symbols, type and ingredients, 267

"Camptown Races," 299, 301

Can Can, practicing, 121–122

carpal tunnel syndrome (CTS), avoiding, 92

Casio
sound terminology, 482–483
website, 57

Casio's Step-up Learning System. *See also* learning software; Yamaha's Educational Suite
choosing songs, 556–557
levels, 555–556
listening, 557–558
playing and watching, 559
playing songs, 562
turning off helpers, 560–561
watching to remembering, 559–560

Caug chord symbol, type and ingredients, 266

Cdim chord symbol, type and ingredients, 267

Cdim7 chord symbol, type and ingredients, 267

chairs versus benches, 86–89

"Chiapanecas," 160

chopsticks and forks, finding on keyboards, 83

chord cadences, 475–476

chord charts, writing, 269

chord inversions
three notes in LH (left hand), 272–273
three triads, 270–272
two-handed, 273–274

chord pads
Looped option, 517
Momentary/Hit option, 517
Once option, 517

chord picking, 308

chord progressions
blues, 269, 271
doo-wop, 270, 272–274
extended, 477
pop, 270

chord relaxation, 382–384

chord root, identifying, 265

chord symbols
explained, 12
playing songs with, 266
reading, 265–267
transforming into notes, 266

chord tones, 268–269

chord type, identifying, 265

chords. *See also* broken-chord patterns; notes; voicing chords
augmented, 261–262
broken, 306–308
building, 258–259
constructing, 266–267
diminished, 261–262

explained, 257
fixed chords, 306–308
four-note, 264–265
major, 259
minor, 260
pedaling, 420–421
playing songs with, 274–280
playing without tension, 382–385
root note, 258
suspended, 262–263
as triads, 258
chorus effect, 489
chromatic scale, 401. *See also* scales
Circle of Fifths. *See also* key signatures
explained, 240–241
finding minor keys in, 245
CLAP, 104
CLAP exercises
beats with notes, 113–114
beats with rests, 113–114
mixing notes, 108
classical music
"*Aus meines Herzens Grunde*," 328
Beethoven's *Sonata in C Minor Opus 13*, 329
concertos, 334
counterpoint, 327–328
duets, 335
etudes, 335
fantasias, 335
fugues, 332–333
performing with others, 48
pianists, 327
Piano Concerto, 325–326
rolling chords, 326–327
rondos, 331–332
Sonata in C, 326
sonatas, 328–331
symphonies, 333–334
clavinet sound effect, 496
cleaning keys and cases, 78
clefs
bass, 14, 127
explained, 126
treble, 14, 126

Cm(add*) chord symbol, type and ingredients, 267
Cm chord symbol, type and ingredients, 266
Cm6 chord symbol, type and ingredients, 267
CM7 chord symbol, type and ingredients, 267
Cm7 flat 5 chord symbol, type and ingredients, 267
Cmaj7 chord symbol, type and ingredients, 267
Cmaj7 flat 5 chord symbol, type and ingredients, 267
Cm(flat 5) chord symbol, type and ingredients, 267
Cmin chord symbol, type and ingredients, 266
C-minor scales
harmonic, 182
melodic minor, 182
natural, 182
Cm(maj7) chord symbol, type and ingredients, 267
combo organs, 28
composers
Bach, J.S., 15
Handy, W.C., 15
Joplin, Scott, 15
Satie, Erik, 15
compressed formats, converting to, 550
computers, playing music files on, 573–575
concertos, 334
connecting
audio devices, 567–570
keyboards to computers, 578–584
contour of pitch, 210
contrary motion
away from center, 414–416
toward center, 416–417
contrast form, 226
controller keyboards, features of, 33
controllers, 17
counterpoint, use in classical music, 327–328

country music
  keyboarders, 349
  styles, 348–349
"Country Riffin'," 322–323
Cowell, Henry, 298
crescendo, 286
crotchet, 99
Csus* chord symbols, type and
    ingredients, 267
CTS (carpal tunnel syndrome), avoiding, 92

• D •

D
  blues scale, 402
  damper pedal, using, 290–291, 420
  key of, 240
  major key signature, 247
  minor scale, 179
  natural minor key signature, 253
  natural minor left-hand scale, 193
D flat natural minor key signature, 251
"Danny Boy," 184
Dave Smith Instruments website, 57
DAW (digital audio workstation), 585
delay effect, 488
demo models, buying, 50
digital audio workstation (DAW), 585
digital features
  audio recording, 19
  MIDI recording, 19
digital keyboards. *See also* electrical-
    mechanical keyboards; electronic
    keyboards; hybrid keyboards
  versus acoustic pianos, 11
  adding memory, 54
  arrangers, 55
  avoiding obsolescence, 54
  buying, 58–59
  cables, 65
  digital synthesis, 34
  editing, 55
  electrical connection, 72
  finding place for, 65–66
  headphones, 73–74
  keeping clean, 66–67

libraries, 54
manufacturers, 54
MIDI capability, 55
modulation, 55
multi-note polyphony, 55
multi-timbral, 55
octave groupings, 85
operation guide, 64
owner's manual, 64
pedals, 94–95
performing onstage, 55
physical modeling, 34–35
piano action, 55
piano sound, 55
pitch bend, 55
power cable, 64
power supply, 64
price negotiation, 58–59
problems, 69–70
pros and cons, 43–44
quality considerations, 52–57
recording, 55
recording options, 60
registration cards, 69
sample-playback, 34
selecting, 52
selecting features, 55–56
sequencing, 55
setting up, 71
shopping online, 59
sound capabilities, 34–35
sound cards, 54
sound editing, 55
sound effects, 56
speakers, 55
standard sizes, 52
starting up, 72–73
sustain/damper pedal, 65
taking care of, 69
technical support, 69
testing before buying, 57–58
transporting, 78–79
transpose function, 47–48
upgrading, 54
virtual analog, 35
warranty card, 64

digital organs, types of, 53. *See also* organs
digital pianos. *See also* pianos
  explained, 16
  types of, 53
digital recording, 528
digital sheet music, 589
digital synthesis, 34
dim interval, 214
diminished chords
  explained, 261–262
  symbol, 265
diminished interval, defined, 214
diminished scales. *See also* scales
  starting on C, 400
  starting on D, 400
  starting on D flat, 400
distortion effect, 492
dominant note, 176
doo-wop chord progression, 270,
    272–273
dots, using, 106, 139–141
dotted
  eighth notes, 141
  half notes, 140
  quarter notes, 140
  rests, 113
double flat, 134
double sharp, 134
"Down by the Station," 274, 276
downbeats, 145. *See also* beats
drum fills, 505–506
drum patterns
  selecting, 501–504
  starting playing, 504–505
  Synchro Start setting, 505–506
  Tap Tempo feature, 505
drum rhythms
  availability of, 501
  explained, 18
duets, 335
dynamic markings
  forte, 285
  fortissimo, 285
  fortississimo, 285
  hairpin, 286
  mezzo forte, 285
  mezzo piano, 285

  pianissimo, 285
  pianississimo, 285
  piano, 285
dynamics
  customizing for sounds, 547–548
  explained, 283–284
  forte, 284–285
  piano, 284–285

• *E* •

E
  blues scale, 403
  to E flat, 134
  to E sharp, 134
  flat major key signature, 252
  flat natural minor key signature, 250
  major key signature, 248–249
  minor scale, 179
  natural minor key signature, 246–247
  natural minor left-hand scale, 193
E flat blues scale, 405
ear, training, 13, 571–572
educational software, 587–588
effects
  adding, 523–524
  ambience, 486
  auto-wah, 494
  availability on keyboards, 18
  choosing for sounds, 495–497
  chorus, 489
  delay, 488
  distortion, 492
  EQ, 490–492
  filter, 493–495
  flanging, 489
  guitar sounds, 497
  modulation, 485
  phase shifting, 489
  reverb, 486–487
  rotary speaker, 493
  strings, 497
  tonal coloration, 486
  tonal correction, 485
  volume control, 485
  wah-wah, 494–495
  wind/brass instruments, 497

eighth notes
  counting out, 105–106
  dotted, 141
  illustrated, 102
  rest for, 110
  value of, 105
electric versus acoustic pianos, 22
electrical-mechanical keyboards. *See also*
     digital keyboards; keyboards
  Hammond organ, 25, 27
  Hohner Clavinet, 25, 27
  Hohner Planet, 25
  Rhodes, 25–26
  types, 25–27
  Wurlitzer, 25–26
  Yamaha CP-70/80, 25
electro-mechanical instruments, 16
electronic instruments, 16
electronic keyboards. *See also* digital
     keyboards; hybrid keyboards;
     keyboards
  arrangers, 32–33
  choosing, 45–46
  combo organs, 28
  controller keyboards, 33
  overview, 15–17
  portable, 31
  versus synthesizers, 29
  synthesizers, 29–31
  workstations, 32
Emerson, Keith, 29–30
E-Mu Systems Incorporated website, 57
enharmonic, 175
EQ effect, 490–492
etudes, 335
E-Z Key Finder technique. *See also* keys
  black keys, 84–85
  chopsticks and forks, 83
  white keys, 82–83

• F •

F
  blues scale, 405
  key of, 237
  key signature, 239
    major key signature, 253
    major left-hand scale, 192
    major scale, B flat in, 174
    natural minor key signature, 251–252
    sharp key signature, 250
    sharp natural minor key signature, 248
    staff position, 130
F sharp blues scale, 404
fake book, 198
fantasias, 335
"The Farmer in the Dell," 175
fermata tempo indication, 289
fifth melodic interval, 217–219
Fifth Symphony, 215–216
fifths, finger combinations, 378–380
filter effect, 493–495
filter envelope, tweaking, 547
finales
  adjusting for keys, 316
  applying, 316
  "I Loved You, You Left Me," 320
  "Last Call," 321
  "Let's Load Up the Bus," 320
  "Shave and a Haircut," 321
finger coordination. *See also* parallel
     movement
  chromatic motion, 415
  combination movement, 418
  contrary motion, 414–418
  improving, 409
finger crossing
  explained, 163
  over thumb, 164
finger jumps, 443–446
fingerings
  C position, 158
  explained, 91
fingers
  arching, 90–91
  referring to, 155–156
The Firm Soundtrack, 298
first position
  assuming with left hand, 188
  "Chiapanecas," 160
  explained, 157
  extending to B, 158–159

fingerings, 158
"Frere Jacques," 158
getting into, 157
stretching to limits, 160
fixed chords, 306–308
flag of note, 101
flanging effect, 489
flat major, A key signatures, 251–252
flats
  canceling, 135
  key signatures with, 242–243
  major scales, 174–175
  versus sharps, 134
flatted notes, 131–132
footwork, improving, 409. *See also* parallel
    movement
form. *See* song form
forte dynamic, 284–285
forte dynamic marking, 285
fortissimo dynamic marking, 285
fortississimo dynamic marking, 285
four-note chords, adding seventh for,
    264–265
fourth melodic interval, 217–219
fourths, finger combinations, 376–377
"Frere Jacques," 158
Fugue in C Major, 333
fugues, 332–333
"Für Elise," 215

• *G* •

G
  blues scale, 402
  key signature, 239–240
  major key signature, 246–247
  major left-hand scale, 192
  major scale, F sharp in, 174
  natural minor key signature, 252
  staff position of, 130
G clef
  explained, 14
  lines, 135
  notes of, 126
  spaces, 135
  staff, 126

G flat major key signature, 250
G position
  getting into, 161
  "Little Bo-Peep," 162
  "This Old Man," 162
G sharp/A flat minor key signature, 249–250
"Get Ready, Here We Go" intro, 317
glissando
  beginning songs, 297
  ending songs, 297
  explained, 295
  hand positions, 295–296
  playing, 296–297
"Good Night, Ladies," 237
grace notes, using, 292–293. *See also* notes
grand pianos, 11, 22. *See also* pianos
grand staff
  explained, 127–128
  ledger lines, 127–128
  notes on, 129
"Greensleeves," 186
Grieg's *Piano Concerto*, 325–326
Grusin, Dave, 298
guitar sounds effect, 497

• *H* •

H (half), 173
hairpin symbol, 286
half notes
  counting out, 104
  dotted, 140
  dotting, 106
  explained, 104
  illustrated, 105
  rest for, 110–112
half steps
  explained, 131–132
  illustrated, 172–173
  lowering notes by, 134
  versus whole-steps, 133
hammers, 24–25
Hammond organ electrical-mechanical
    keyboards, 25
Hammond/Suzuki sound terminology,
    482–483

hand positions. *See also* positions
  shifting while playing, 163
  using, 157
hand techniques. *See also* alternating
      hands
  aria from *La Cenerentola*, 366
  chord relaxation, 382–384
  crossing under, 359–366
  passing over, 359–366
  playing fifths, 378–380
  playing fourths, 376–377
  playing seconds, 367–371
  playing sevenths, 378–380
  playing sixths, 378–380
  playing thirds, 372–375
  "Take Me Out to the Ballgame," 381
  voicing chords, 384
hands. *See also* two-handed chords
  arching, 90–91
  avoiding CTS (carpal tunnel
      syndrome), 92
  resting, 92
  switching, 189
hands-together
  playing songs, 198–202
  sharing melodies, 199
Handy, W.C., 15
harmonic intervals
  adding to melodies, 221–222
  combining notes for, 220–224
  with LH (left hand), 223–224
  playing notes together, 221
harmonic minor scales, 180
harmony. *See also* song form
  adding to melodies, 516
  playing songs with, 228–233
head of note, 101
headphones, using, 73–74
Hohner Clavinet electrical-mechanical
      keyboards, 25, 27
Hohner Planet electrical-mechanical
      keyboards, 25
home key. *See also* keys
  leaving, 243–244
  returning to, 243–244
home note, 236
horizontal music, 13

"A Hot Time in the Old Town Tonight," 120
"House of the Rising Sun," 185
hybrid keyboards, considering, 44. *See
      also* digital keyboards; electronic
      keyboards
hybrid piano, 11

• I •

"I Loved You, You Left Me" finale, 320
"I'm Called Little Buttercup," 228–229
instruments, availability of, 589–590
      See also keyboard instruments
intervals. *See* melodic intervals
intros
  adjusting for keys, 316
  applying, 316
  "Get Ready, Here We Go," 317
  "Killing Time" intro, 319
  "Rockin' Jam," 317–318
  "Saloon Salutations" intro, 319
  "Sweet Ballad," 317–318
inverted arch contour, 210–211
iPad, hooking up to, 584–585
"I've Been Working on the Railroad,"
      147, 152

• J •

jamming, 48–49
jazz
  improvising with, 350–351
  pianists, 352
  substituting chords, 352–353
jazz band, jamming in, 48–49
Joplin, Scott, 15
"Joy to the World"
  in C minor, 179
  descending C major scale, 175
jumping and landing. *See also* keyboards
  accents on downbeat, 433
  accents on upbeat, 434
  with both hands together, 434–436
  chord-to-chord, 432
  LH accompaniment patterns, 436–440
  note-chord, 431

note-to-note, 430
ragtime and stride pattern, 439
waltz pattern for left hand, 440
"Jumping Octaves," 310–311

• K •

Kawai
    sound terminology, 482–483
    website, 51, 56
key feel and response
    key weight, 37
    touch sensitivity, 35–37
key of C
    explained, 236
    "Good Night, Ladies," 237
key of D, playing melodies in, 240
key of F
    "Good Night, Ladies," 237
    key signature, 243
key signatures. *See also* Circle of Fifths
    A flat major, 251–252
    A major, 248
    A natural minor, 246
    A sharp natural minor, 251
    B flat major, 249–250, 252
    B flat natural minor, 251
    B natural minor, 247
    C flat major, 249–250
    C major, 246
    C natural minor, 252
    C sharp major, 251
    C sharp natural minor, 248–249
    D, 240
    D flat natural minor, 251
    D major, 247
    D natural minor, 253
    E flat major, 252
    E flat natural minor, 250
    E major, 248–249
    E natural minor, 246–247
    for each hand, 239
    explained, 238
    F, 239
    F major, 253
    F natural minor, 251–252

F sharp, 250
F sharp natural minor, 248
finding for keys, 243
with flats, 242–243
G, 239
G flat major, 250
G major, 246–247
G natural minor, 252
G sharp/A flat minor, 249–250
minor, 244–245
playing melodies with, 239
playing songs with, 253–255
reading, 238–240
relative minor, 244–245
with sharps, 241–242
key weights
    explained, 16
    fully weighted, 37
    non-weighted, 37
    semi-weighted, 37
    weighted, 37
keyboard brands. *See also* piano brands
    Kawai America Corporation, 56
    Korg USA, 56
    Nord Keyboards, 56
    Roland Corporation, 56
    Yamaha, 56
keyboard connection
    direct USB, 579
    drivers, 581–584
    MIDI interface, 579–581
    plug-and-play, 581–584
keyboard cover, using, 77–78
keyboard designs
    acoustic instruments, 15
    electro-mechanical instruments, 16
    electronic instruments, 16
keyboard instruments, 15–17. *See also*
        instruments
keyboard performance, solo, 47
keyboards. *See also* electrical-mechanical
        keyboards; jumping and landing
    acoustic pianos, 22–25
    arpeggiation, 18
    arrangers, 17
    auto-accompaniment, 18

keyboards *(continued)*
  automatic features, 18
  connecting audio devices, 567–570
  controllers, 17
  digital, 16
  drum rhythms, 18
  effects, 18
  electro-mechanical, 25–27
  electronic, 28–33
  Fine Tune parameter, 570
  Master Tune parameter, 570
  organs, 17
  portable, 17
  programming, 19
  sounds, 17
  stage, 16
  synthesizers, 17
  using multiple, 49
  workstations, 17
keys. *See also* Blake's E-Z Key Finder; home
      key; piano keys
  cleaning, 78
  explained, 236, 238
  playing, 156
  using to play music, 238
"Killing Time" intro, 319
Korg
  sound terminology, 482–483
  website, 56–57
"Kumbaya," 159
Korg Krome synthesizer, 31
Kurzweil
  sound terminology, 483
  website, 57

● *L* ●

L. Bösendorfer Klavier website, 51
La Cenerentola, aria from, 366
Lang Lang, 334
largo tempo indication, 116
"Last Call" finale, 321
leading tone note, 176
learning software, 587–588. *See also* built-in
      songs; Casio's Step-up Learning
      System; Yamaha's Educational Suite

ledger lines, using with grand staff, 127–128
left hand (LH). *See* LH (left hand)
left-hand grooves, 322–324
left-hand melodies
  "Little Brown Jug," 191
  plus one note, 200
  plus three-note accompaniment, 200–201
  "Swing Low, Sweet Chariot," 191
  in unison octaves, 201–202
left-hand scales. *See also* scales
  A harmonic minor, 193
  A melodic minor, 193
  A natural minor, 193
  accompaniment patterns, 194–198
  arpeggio patterns, 198
  C major, 192
  D natural minor, 193
  E natural minor, 193
  F major, 192
  fake book, 198
  four-note patterns, 196–198
  G major, 192
  patterns in eighth notes, 195–198
  patterns in quarter notes, 195–197
  root-fifth-top patterns, 194
  three-note patterns, 194–196
"Let's Load Up the Bus" finale, 320
Lewis, Jerry Lee, 346
LH (left hand)
  abbreviation, 155–156
  adding to RH (right hand), 198–202
  harmonizing with, 223–224
  moving into position, 188
  "Old Smoky," 201
  practicing use of, 188–190
  three-note chords, 272–273
LH accompaniment patterns. *See also*
      accompaniment
  arpeggiated, 307
  bass lines, 313–315
  broken chords, 306–308
  chord picking, 308
  examples, 436–440
  fixed chords, 306–308
  octave hammering, 308–310
  rock patterns, 310–313

"Lily Pad Rag," 441
"Limehouse Blues," 147, 152
line inputs, finding, 567–569
"Little Bo-Peep," 162
"Little Brown Jug," 191
"London Bridge," 215
loudness, determining, 283–284
"Love Me Like You Used To," 322, 324
"Lullaby," 275, 278

• *M* •

M interval, 214
m interval, 214
major, A key signatures, 248
major chords
  explained, 259
  for LH (left hand), 259
  making, 259
major interval, defined, 213
major scales. *See also* scales
  ascending step pattern, 173
  C, 174
  chord tones, 268–269
  degrees, 176
  F, 175
  flats, 174–175
  G, 174
  practicing, 177
  sharps, 174–175
  using, 181
major-key chord progression, 477
major-scale notes
  dominant, 176
  leading tone, 176
  mediant, 176
  subdominant, 176
  submediant, 176
  supertonic, 176
  tonic, 176
march time, 121–122
"Marianne," 228, 230
Mason & Hamlin website, 51
measures
  dividing music into, 136
  explained, 117

mixing notes into, 118
number of beats in, 117
mediant note, 176
melodic contours
  arch, 210–211
  inverted arch, 210–211
  pivotal, 210–212
  wave, 210–211
melodic intervals. *See also* song form
  abbreviations, 214
  augmented, 214
  diminished, 214
  fifths, 217–219
  fourths, 217–219
  "Für Elise," 215
  "London Bridge," 215
  major, 213
  measuring, 212
  minor, 213
  octaves, 219–220
  perfect, 214
  seconds, 214–215
  sevenths, 219–220
  sixths, 219–220
  thirds, 215–216
melodic minor scales, 180–181
melodies. *See also* song form
  adding harmony to, 516
  LH (left hand), 190–191
  notes of major scale, 175
  playing, 155
  playing in right hand, 166–167
  sharing in both hands, 199
  using articulations with, 288
metronome, using, 46
mezzo forte dynamic marking, 285
mezzo piano dynamic marking, 285
middle C
  significance of, 130
  writing with ledger lines, 128
middle pedal, using, 292
MIDI (Musical Instrument Digital
    Interface)
  GM/GM2, 484–485
  overview, 60–61
MIDI messages, 575–577

MIDI ports, 577–578
MIDI recorders, using, 585–586
MIDI recordings
  adjusting timing, 537–538
  versus audio recording, 526–530
  changing pitch of notes, 539–540
  correcting notes, 538–539
  editing notes, 540
  event edit list, 530
  explained, 19, 529–530
  multitrack, 533–536
  one-pass, 532–533
MIDI songs, mixing, 540–542
MIDI-based songs, sharing, 549–550
minor chords
  explained, 260
  making, 260
minor interval, defined, 213
minor key signatures, finding, 244–245
minor scales. *See also* scales
  A, 179
  D, 179
  E, 179
  harmonic, 180
  melodic, 180–181
  natural, 178–179
  playing, 179
  practicing, 181–182
  using, 181
minor-key chord progression, 478
minor-scale notes
  dominant, 178
  mediant, 178
  subdominant, 178
  submediant, 178
  subtonic, 178
  supertonic, 178
  tonic, 178
"Minuet," 164–165
mnemonics
  using with keys, 243
  using with notes, 135
modulation, 485
Moog
  sound terminology, 483
  synthesizer, 29
  website, 57

Motown sounds, 354–355
Mozart
  Rondo Alla Turca, 332
  Sonata in C, 326
MP3, converting to, 550
music. *See also* playing music; reading
    music
  developing ear for, 13
  horizontal, 13
  learning on piano, 8
  vertical, 13
music databases, accessing, 515
music files, playing on computers, 573–575.
    See also songs
music notation software, 588
music rack, using, 46
music software. *See also* software
  digital sheet music, 589
  educational/learning, 587–588
  instruments/sounds, 589–590
  notation, 588
  sequencer/MIDI recorder, 585–586
musical forms. *See also* song form
  contrast, 226
  creating, 226–228
  explained, 13
  ongoing, 226
musical ornaments, 13, 299–304
musical parts
  arch form (ABCBA), 228
  binary form (AB), 227
  linking to create
      forms, 226–228
  one-part (A), 227
  three-part form
      (ABA), 227–228
musical phrases
  bass notes, 572–573
  chords, 573
  explained, 225
  listening to, 572–573
  melody, 573
  rhythm, 572
musical staff
  explained, 127–128
  ledger lines, 127–128
  notes on, 129

musical styles
  baroque, 15
  blues, 15
  explained, 13
  identifying, 15
  ragtime, 15
  rhythm, 13
  waltzes, 15
"My Bonnie Lies Over the Ocean," 219

• *N* •

natural minor
  A key signatures, 246
  scales, 178–179
natural notes, 130
naturals, 135
Nord
  sound terminology, 483
  website, 56–57
note components
  flag, 101
  head, 101
  stem, 101, 104
note names
  recognizing, 14
  for white keys, 82–83
note values
  counting, 104
  defined, 100
  increasing, 106
  mixing together, 107
  tree of notes, 103
Notebook for Anna Magdelena Bach, 164–165
notes. *See also* chords; grace notes; pickup
    notes; root note
  adding time to, 138–141
  adding together with ties, 107
  defined, 100
  eighth, 102, 105–106
  extending, 106
  extending using dots, 139–141
  flatted, 131
  on grand staff, 129
  half, 104, 106
  linking using ties, 139
  mixing into measures, 118

  mnemonics, 135
  natural, 130
  playing in bass clef, 189
  playing together, 221
  playing with different hands, 128
  practicing beats with, 113–114
  quarter, 104–106
  reading in bass clef, 189
  remembering, 135
  sharped, 131
  sixteenth, 102, 106
  thirty-second, 102, 106
  voice leading, 271
  whole, 103–104, 106
notes with flags, connecting, 101
Novation website, 57

• *O* •

octave chords, 470–471
octave groupings, 85
octave hammering, 308–310
octave jumps, 466–469
octave lines, 129–130
octaves
  half steps, 130
  interval exercise, 465
  "Over the Rainbow," 220
  scale exercise, 464
  semitones, 130
  tones, 130
"Ode to Joy," 158, 166–167
offbeat rhythms, playing, 142–146. *See also*
    rhythm
Offenbach, Jacques, 121
"Oh, Susannah," 147–148
"Old Smoky," 201
one-man band, 47
one-part form (A), 227
one-pass recording, 530–533
ongoing form, 226
"Oranges and Lemons," 166, 169
organs. *See also* digital organs
  combo, 28
  described, 17
ornaments, 13, 299–304
"Over the Rainbow," 220

• P •

P interval, 214
parallel movement. *See also* finger coordination; footwork
  at interval, 412–413
  at octave, 409–411
Pärt, Arvo, 298
parts. *See* musical parts
patterns, recognizing in scales, 176
Pearl River website, 51
pedal changes, 424–425
pedal indications, 290
pedaling
  block-chord, 423
  broken-chord, 422
  chords, 420–421
  for effect, 426
  sustaining, 427
pedals
  considering, 50
  damper, 93, 290–291, 420
  digital keyboards, 94–95
  middle, 93–94, 292
  practice, 292
  soft, 93–94, 291–292
  sostenuto, 292
  sustain, 426
pentatonic scale, 14
perfect interval, defined, 214
performance pieces. *See also* songs
  "Harp Heaven," 454–455
  "Lily Pad Rag," 441
  "Schumann's Octave Workout," 472
  "Simple Gifts," 428
  "Turkey in the Straw," 419
periods, using with musical phrases, 225–226
Perlman, Itzhak, 334
phase shifting effect, 489
phrases. *See* musical phrases
physical modeling, 34–35
pianissimo dynamic marking, 285
pianississimo dynamic marking, 285
pianist, solo, 47

piano brands. *See also* keyboard brands
  Baldwin Piano & Organ Company, 51
  Kawai America Corporation, 51
  L. Bösendorfer Klavier, 51
  Mason & Hamlin, 51
  Pearl River, 51
  Steinway & Sons, 51
  Story & Clark, 51
  Yamaha, 51
Piano Concerto, 325–326
piano dynamic, 284–285
piano keyboards. *See* digital keyboards; electronic keyboards; keyboards
piano keys. *See also* keys
  non-weighted vs. weighted, 16
  synth-action, 16
piano playing
  as art, 9
  as challenge, 10
  characteristics, 8
  clefs, 14
  frustrations, 10
  learning, 9–10
  mind-body coordination, 12
  note names, 14
  pentatonic scale, 14
  reasons for quitting, 9–10
  re-creating compositions, 10
  re-creating songs, 10
  self-criticism, 10
  as skill, 9
  styles, 10
  time commitment, 10
  while reading music, 12
piano sounds, altering, 298
piano styles, 23
piano technicians, working with, 68
pianos. *See also* digital keyboards; digital pianos; grand pianos; stage pianos; upright pianos
  as accompaniment, 8
  acoustic, 11
  getting moved, 70
  getting tuned, 68
  hybrid, 11

learning music on, 8
number of keys on, 15
popularity, 11
as solo instrument, 8
piano-type sounds, 495–497
"Picking and Grinning," 309
pickup measure, example of, 138
pickup notes, 137. *See also* notes
pitch, changing with accidentals, 133–135
pitch bend, 100
pivotal contour, 210–212
playing
along with recordings, 566–567
blues, 341
keys, 156
minor scales, 179
pop and rock music, 346
pop ballads, 347
songs hands-together, 198–202
songs with both hands, 203–207
three-note chords, 270–271
playing intervals
fifths, 378–380
fourths, 376–377
seconds, 367–371
sevenths, 378–380
sixths, 378–380
thirds, 372–375
playing music, best practices, 14.
See also music
playing piano as art, 9
as challenge, 10
characteristics, 8
clefs, 14
frustrations, 10
learning, 9–10
mind-body coordination, 12
note names, 14
pentatonic scale, 14
reasons for quitting, 9–10
re-creating compositions, 10
re-creating songs, 10
self-criticism, 10
as skill, 9
styles, 10
time commitment, 10
while reading music, 12

"Polovtsian Dance," 299–300
polyphony
defined, 8, 483–484
overview, 38–39
pop and rock music
32-bar, 345
bass line, 346
compound AABA form, 345
playing, 346
song structure, 345
verse-chorus structure, 345
pop ballads
personalities, 347
picks, 347
playing, 347
sixth interval tone, 348
pop band, jamming in, 48–49
pop chord progression, 270
"Pop! Goes the Weasel," 293
portable keyboards
described, 17
features of, 31
positions. *See also* hand positions
C, 157–160
explained, 156
G, 161–162
posture, sitting versus standing, 85–90
practice pedal, using, 292
practicing
beats with notes, 113–114
beats with rests, 113–114
"The Beautiful Blue Danube," 121
blues scales, 183
C major scale, 177
dotted notes, 141
"A Hot Time in the Old Town Tonight," 120
left-hand scales, 192–193
minor scales, 181–182
mixing notes, 108
scales, 176–177
songs made of scales, 184–186
triplets, 143
use of LH (left hand), 188–190
preset, definitions of, 484
print music
chord symbols, 12
fake book, 12

• Q •

quarter notes
  counting out, 104, 106
  versus crotchets, 99
  dotted, 140
  explained, 104–105
  illustrated, 105
  rest for, 110–112
  tying, 107
quarter tone, 131
"Quiet Sunset," 299, 304

• R •

racks and stands, 89–90
ragtime and stride pattern, 439
reading music. *See also* music
  elements, 12
  while playing piano, 12
recording
  with analog and digital audio, 526–529
  audio, 19
  audio versus MIDI, 526–530
  MIDI, 19
  multitrack MIDI, 533–536
  one-pass, 530–533
recordings. *See also* songs
  Airplane Sonata, 298
  The Banshee, 298
  The Firm Soundtrack, 298
  piano styles, 23
  playing along with, 566–567
  Tabula rasa, 298
"Red River Valley," 275, 280
Reed/Wurlitzer electric piano, 496
relative minors, finding, 244–245
rests
  dotted, 113
  for eighth notes, 110
  explained, 109
  for half notes, 110–112
  practicing beats with, 113–114
  for quarter notes, 110–112
  for sixteenth notes, 110
  tree of, 110
  for whole notes, 110–111

reverb effect, 486–487
Reverb Nation website, 550
RH (right hand)
  abbreviation, 155–156
  adding LH (left hand) to, 198–202
  playing melodies in, 166–167
Rhodes electrical-mechanical keyboards, 25–26
rhythm. *See also* offbeat rhythms
  keeping with metronome, 46
  of melody, 123
  in musical style, 13
rhythm sticks, defined, 100
right hand (RH). *See* RH (right hand)
ritardando tempo indication, 289
rock and pop music
  32-bar, 345
  bass line, 346
  compound AABA form, 345
  playing, 346
  song structure, 345
  verse-chorus structure, 345
rock band, jamming in, 48–49
rock patterns, 310–313
rock pianists, 346
"Rockin' Intervals," 312
"Rockin' Jam" intro, 317–318
Roland
  sound terminology, 483
  website, 56–57
Rondo Alla Turca, 332
rondos, 331–332
root note, 258. *See also* notes
rotary speaker effect, 493
"Row, Row, Row Your Boat," 165–166

• S •

"Saloon Salutations" intro, 319
sample-playback, 34
Satie, Erik, 15
scale extensions
  A flat major/harmonic/melodic minor, 396
  A major/harmonic/melodic minor, 391
  B flat major/harmonic/melodic minor, 398
  B major/harmonic/melodic minor, 393
  C major/harmonic/melodic minor, 388

C sharp harmonic/melodic minor, 395
D flat major, 395
D major/harmonic/melodic minor, 390
E flat major/harmonic/melodic minor, 397
E major/harmonic/melodic minor, 392
F major/harmonic/melodic minor, 399
F sharp major/harmonic/melodic
    minor, 394
G major/harmonic/melodic minor, 389
scale triads, 268–269
scales. *See also* blues scales; chromatic
    scale; diminished scales; left-hand
    scales; major scales; minor scales;
    songs made of scales
C major, 172
defined, 172
extending with crossovers, 363–365
extending with pass-unders, 363–365
mastering, 176–177
recognizing patterns, 176–177
"Twinkle, Twinkle Little Star," 408
varied articulation, 406
varied rhythmic groupings, 407
"Scarborough Fair," 275, 279
Scheherazade, 147, 149
Schubert's *Unfinished Symphony*, 217
"Schumann's Octave Workout," 472
second interval, 214–215
seconds, finger combinations, 367–371
sequencers, using, 60, 585–586
seventh chord progressions, 473–474
seventh melodic interval, 219–220
sevenths
    adding for four-note chords, 264–265
    finger combinations, 378–380
sharing MIDI-based songs, 549–550
sharp natural minor, A key signatures, 251
sharped notes, 131–132
sharps
    canceling, 135
    in key signatures, 243
    key signatures with, 241–242
    major scales, 174–175
    placing before notes, 133–134
"Shave and a Haircut" finale, 321
"Shenandoah," 228, 232

shuffle feel, 145
"The Sidewalks of New York," 203–205
"Simple Gifts," 428
"Simple Melody," 166, 170
sitting versus standing, 85–90
sixteenth notes
    counting out, 106
    illustrated, 102
    rest for, 110
sixth melodic interval, 219–220
sixths, finger combinations, 378–380
"Skip to My Lou," 159
slurs versus ties, 107, 139, 287
soft pedal, using, 291–292
software. *See also* music software
    MIDI messages, 575–577
    MIDI ports, 577–578
solo pianist, 47
"Sometimes I Feel Like a Motherless Child,"
    275, 277
Sonata in C, 326
Sonata in C Minor Opus 13, 329
sonatas
    development, 329–330
    example, 330–331
    explained, 328
    exposition, 328–329
    movements, 328–329
    recapitulation, 330–331
song form, 210–212. *See also* harmony;
    melodic intervals; melodies; musical
    forms
songs. *See also* built-in songs; music files;
    performance pieces; recordings
"After the Ball," 253, 255
"Also Sprach Zarathustra," 299, 303
"America, the Beautiful," 223–224
"Auld Lang Syne," 228, 233
"Aura Lee," 221–222, 228, 231
"Autumn," 166, 168
"The Beautiful Blue Danube," 121
"Berry-Style Blues," 312–313
"Camptown Races," 299, 301
"Chiapanecas," 160
"Country Riffin'," 322–323
"Down by the Station," 274, 276

songs *(continued)*
  "The Farmer in the Dell," 175
  figuring out unknown, 571–575
  "Frere Jacques," 158
  "Für Elise," 215
  getting in tune with, 570–571
  "A Hot Time in the Old Town Tonight," 120
  "I'm Called Little Buttercup," 228–229
  increasing harmony, 228–233
  "I've Been Working on the Railroad," 147
  "Joy to the World," 175, 179
  "Jumping Octaves," 310–311
  "Kumbaya," 159
  "By the Light of the Silvery Moon," 147
  "Limehouse Blues," 147
  "Little Bo-Peep," 162
  "Little Brown Jug," 191
  "London Bridge," 215
  "Love Me Like You Used To," 322, 324
  "Lullaby," 275, 278
  "Marianne," 228, 230
  "Minuet," 164–165
  "My Bonnie Lies Over the Ocean," 219
  "Octaves in the Left," 310
  "Ode to Joy," 158, 166–167
  "Oh, Susannah," 147–148
  "Old Smoky," 201
  "Oranges and Lemons," 166, 169
  "Picking and Grinning," 309
  playing with both hands, 203–207
  playing with chord symbols, 266
  "Polovtsian Dance," 299–300
  "Pop! Goes the Weasel," 293
  "Quiet Sunset," 299, 304
  "Red River Valley," 275, 280
  "Rockin' Intervals," 312
  "Row, Row, Row Your Boat," 165–166
  "Scarborough Fair," 275, 279
  Scheherazade, 147
  "Shenandoah," 228, 232
  "The Sidewalks of New York," 203–205
  "Simple Melody," 166, 170
  "Skip to My Lou," 159
  "Sometimes I Feel Like a Motherless
    Child," 275, 277
  "Stars and Stripes Forever," 203, 206–207
  "Swanee River," 147
  "Swing Low, Sweet Chariot," 191
  "This Old Man," 162
  "Trumpet Voluntary," 299, 302
  "Twinkle, Twinkle Little Star," 217–218
  "When the Saints Go Marching In," 147–
    148
  "Worried Man Blues," 253–254
  "Yankee Doodle," 222
songs made of scales. *See also* scales
  "Danny Boy," 184
  "Greensleeves," 186
  "House of the Rising Sun," 185
sostenuto pedal, 292
soul music
  funky patterns, 356
  Motown sounds, 354–355
  rhythmic concepts, 354
sound design, 19
sound edits
  amp parameters, 546–547
  changing brightness, 545–546
  changing waveforms, 543–544
  Filter control, 545–546
  filter envelope, 547
  varying base timbre, 543–544
  volume over time, 546–547
sound terminology, 482–483
Soundcloud website, 550
sounds. *See also* audio recording
  adding, 523–524
  availability of, 589–590
  availability on keyboards, 17
  choosing effects for, 495–497
  customizing dynamics, 547–548
  matching with arp patterns, 522–523
  transitioning between, 48
  velocity switch and touch, 548–549
speakers, connecting to, 74–76
staccato articulation symbol, 287
staff. *See* musical staff
stage pianos. *See also* pianos
  evaluating, 53
  explained, 16
standing versus sitting, 85–90
stands and racks, 89–90

"Stars and Stripes Forever," 203, 206–207
staves
  bass clef, 126
  explained, 125
  treble clef, 126
Steinway & Sons website, 51
stem of note, 101
stems
  pointing down, 104
  pointing up, 104
steps
  half-, 172–173
  moving on piano, 131
  whole-, 172–173
Story & Clark website, 51
strings, 24–25
strings effect, 497
styles of music. *See* musical styles
subdominant note, 176
submediant note, 176
supertonic note, 176
suspended chords, 262–263
sustain pedal, using, 426
"Swanee River," 147, 150
"Sweet Ballad" intro, 317–318
swing beat, 144
"Swing Low, Sweet Chariot," 191
symphonies
  defined, 333
  experimentation, 334
  explained, 333–334
  movements, 333–334
syncopation
  downbeats, 145
  example, 146
  upbeats, 145
synth sounds, 495–497
synth-action keys, 16
synthesizers
  amplifier, 30
  considering, 54
  described, 17
  versus electronic keyboards, 29
  envelope generator, 30
  filter, 30

Korg Krome, 31
manufacturers, 57
Moog, 29
number of keys on, 29
oscillator, 30
sound creation, 29

● **T** ●

Tabula rasa, 298
"Take Me Out to the Ballgame," 381
technical problems, solving, 79–80
temperature extremes, avoiding, 77
tempo, controlling, 288–289
tempo indications
  accelerando, 289
  adagio, 116
  allegro, 116
  andante, 116
  fermata, 289
  largo, 116
  presto, 116
  ritardando, 289
  vivace, 116
tempos
  BPM (beats per minute), 116
  defined, 100
  explained, 116
tenuto articulation symbol, 287
third melodic interval, 215–216
thirds, finger combinations, 372–375
thirty-second notes
  counting out, 106
  illustrated, 102
"This Old Man," 162
three-note chords, playing, 270–271
three-part form (ABA), 227–228
thumb
  crossing over, 164
  passing under, 165–166
ties
  adding notes with, 107
  versus slurs, 107, 139, 287
  using to link notes, 139
timbre, varying, 543–544

time signatures
  2/4 meter, 121–122
  3/4 meter, 120–121
  4/4 meter, 118–120
  6/8 time, 122–123
  12/8, 273
  checking before playing, 161
  examples, 119
  explained, 118
  march time, 121–122
  waltzes, 120–121
tonal coloration, 486
tonal correction, 485
tone, definitions of, 483
tonewheel-organ effect, 496
tonic note, 176, 178
touch sensitivity
  dynamic, 35–36
  non-dynamic, 35–36
  velocity-sensitivity, 35–37
tracks. *See* songs
transpose function, using, 47–48
transposing, 539
treble clef
  explained, 14
  lines, 135
  notes of, 126
  spaces, 135
  staff, 126
tree of notes, 103
tremolos
  chords, 298–299
  notation, 298
  playing, 297
triads
  chords as, 258
  for scales, 268–269
trills
  adding, 295
  explained, 294
  sound of, 294
triplets
  counting, 143
  explained, 142–143
  practicing with, 143
troubleshooting problems, 79–80
"Trumpet Voluntary," 299, 302

tuning options, 570–571
"Turkey in the Straw," 419
"Twinkle, Twinkle Little Star," 217–218, 408
two-handed chords, 273–274. *See also* hands

• *U* •

Unfinished Symphony, 217
upbeats, 145. *See also* beats
upright pianos, 11, 23. *See also* pianos

• *V* •

velocity-sensitive key, 35–37
vertical music, 13
virtual analog, 35
vivace tempo indication, 116
vocalists, accompanying, 47–48
voice, definitions of, 483
voice leading, 271
voicing chords, 384–385. *See also* chords
volume control, 485
volume levels
  changing gradually, 285–286
  crescendo, 286
  determining, 284–285
Vox Continental combo organ, 28

• *W* •

W (whole), 173
wah-wah effect, 494–495
waltz time, 121
waltzes
  composer, 15
  pattern for left hand, 440
wave contour, 210–211
waveforms, changing, 543–544
websites
  Alesis Studio Electronics, 57
  Baldwin Piano & Organ Company, 51
  Casio Incorporated, 57
  Dave Smith Instruments, 57
  E-Mu Systems Incorporated, 57
  Kawai America Corporation, 51, 56
  Korg USA, 56–57

Kurzweil Music Systems, 57
L. Bösendorfer Klavier, 51
Mason & Hamlin, 51
Moog Music Incorporated, 57
Nord Keyboards, 56–57
Novation, 57
online resources, 591
Pearl River, 51
Reverb Nation, 550
Roland Corporation, 56–57
Soundcloud, 550
Steinway & Sons, 51
Story & Clark, 51
Yamaha, 51, 56–57
Yamaha library, 564
YouTube, 550
weighted keys, 16
"When the Saints Go Marching
    In," 147–148
white keys, note names, 82–83
whole notes
    dotting, 106
    explained, 103–104
    illustrated, 105
    rest for, 110–111
whole-steps
    explained, 132–133
    versus half steps, 133
    illustrated, 172–173

wind/brass instruments effect, 497
workstations
    considering, 54
    described, 17
    features of, 32
    manufacturers, 57
"Worried Man Blues," 253–254
Wurlitzer electrical-mechanical keyboards,
    25–26

• 𝒴 •

Yamaha
    CP-70/80 electrical-mechanical
        keyboards, 25
    sound terminology, 483
    website, 56–57
Yamaha's Educational Suite. See also
        Casio's Step-up Learning System;
        learning software
    choosing songs, 564
    library, 564
    listening, 563
    minus one, 563
    tempo, 563
    waiting, 563
"Yankee Doodle," 222
YouTube website, 550

Notes

About the Authors

Holly Day is a writing instructor at the Open Book Writing Collective in Minneapolis. She, along with Michael Pilhofer, is the coauthor of *Music Theory For Dummies* and, with Scott Jarrett, she is the coauthor of *Music Composition For Dummies*. She has also written about music for numerous publications, including *Guitar One*, *Music Alive!*, *Computer Music Journal*, *The Oxford American*, and *Mixdown* magazine.

Jerry Kovarsky is the author of *Keyboard For Dummies*. After studying music at Manhattan School of Music, University of Miami, and William Paterson College, he hit the road playing music of every shape and style. He has worked for Casio, Ensoniq, and Korg as a product developer, brand manager, and marketing director. He writes for *Keyboard* magazine.

Blake Neely is the author of *Piano For Dummies*, 2nd Edition. Upon graduation from the University of Texas in 1991, he moved to Los Angeles to experience the music business. An award-winning composer and author, he has written symphonies, a piano concerto, and numerous orchestral and chamber works. He is coauthor of the acclaimed *FastTrack* series, published by Hal Leonard Corporation.

David Pearl is the author of *Piano Exercises For Dummies*. He also wrote *The Art of Steely Dan* and *Color Your Chords* (Cherry Lane), a survey of the harmonic styles of 25 top jazz, blues, and rock pianists. He recently completed *The Jazz Piano Collection* (Amsco Publications), twenty-two jazz standards arranged for solo piano, and *The Art of Billy Strayhorn* (Cherry Lane), an in-depth exploration of five songs by one of jazz's greatest composers. He performs and records regularly.

Michael Pilhofer is the coauthor of *Music Theory For Dummies* (with Holly Day). He teaches music theory and percussion at McNally Smith College of Music in St. Paul, Minnesota. He has worked as a professional musician for more than 20 years and has toured and recorded with Joe Lovano, Marian McPartland, Kenny Wheeler, Dave Holland, Bill Holman, Wycliffe Gordon, Peter Erskine, and Gene Bertoncini.

Publisher's Acknowledgments

Acquisitions Editor: David Lutton

Editor: Corbin Collins

Technical Editor: Brian Noble

Art Coordinator: Alicia B. South

Project Coordinator: Rebekah Brownson

Special thanks to W. R. Music Service for some of the music engraving

Cover Image: ©iStockphoto.com/Daniel_M

Apple & Mac

iPad For Dummies,
5th Edition
978-1-118-49823-1

iPhone 5 For Dummies,
6th Edition
978-1-118-35201-4

MacBook For Dummies,
4th Edition
978-1-118-20920-2

OS X Mountain Lion
For Dummies
978-1-118-39418-2

Blogging & Social Media

Facebook For Dummies,
4th Edition
978-1-118-09562-1

Mom Blogging
For Dummies
978-1-118-03843-7

Pinterest For Dummies
978-1-118-32800-2

WordPress For Dummies,
5th Edition
978-1-118-38318-6

Business

Commodities For Dummies,
2nd Edition
978-1-118-01687-9

Investing For Dummies,
6th Edition
978-0-470-90545-6

Personal Finance
For Dummies,
7th Edition
978-1-118-11785-9

QuickBooks 2013
For Dummies
978-1-118-35641-8

Small Business Marketing Kit
For Dummies,
3rd Edition
978-1-118-31183-7

Careers

Job Interviews
For Dummies,
4th Edition
978-1-118-11290-8

Job Searching with
Social Media
For Dummies
978-0-470-93072-4

Personal Branding
For Dummies
978-1-118-11792-7

Resumes For Dummies,
6th Edition
978-0-470-87361-8

Success as a Mediator
For Dummies
978-1-118-07862-4

Diet & Nutrition

Belly Fat Diet For Dummies
978-1-118-34585-6

Eating Clean For Dummies
978-1-118-00013-7

Nutrition For Dummies,
5th Edition
978-0-470-93231-5

Digital Photography

Digital Photography
For Dummies,
7th Edition
978-1-118-09203-3

Digital SLR Cameras &
Photography For Dummies,
4th Edition
978-1-118-14489-3

Photoshop Elements 11
For Dummies
978-1-118-40821-6

Gardening

Herb Gardening
For Dummies,
2nd Edition
978-0-470-61778-6

Vegetable Gardening
For Dummies,
2nd Edition
978-0-470-49870-5

Health

Anti-Inflammation Diet
For Dummies
978-1-118-02381-5

Diabetes For Dummies,
3rd Edition
978-0-470-27086-8

Living Paleo For Dummies
978-1-118-29405-5

Hobbies

Beekeeping
For Dummies
978-0-470-43065-1

eBay For Dummies,
7th Edition
978-1-118-09806-6

Raising Chickens
For Dummies
978-0-470-46544-8

Wine For Dummies,
5th Edition
978-1-118-28872-6

Writing Young Adult Fiction
For Dummies
978-0-470-94954-2

Language &
Foreign Language

500 Spanish Verbs
For Dummies
978-1-118-02382-2

English Grammar
For Dummies,
2nd Edition
978-0-470-54664-2

French All-in One
For Dummies
978-1-118-22815-9

German Essentials
For Dummies
978-1-118-18422-6

Italian For Dummies
2nd Edition
978-1-118-00465-4

e **Available in print and e-book formats.**

Math & Science

Algebra I For Dummies,
2nd Edition
978-0-470-55964-2

Anatomy and Physiology
For Dummies,
2nd Edition
978-0-470-92326-9

Astronomy For Dummies,
3rd Edition
978-1-118-37697-3

Biology For Dummies,
2nd Edition
978-0-470-59875-7

Chemistry For Dummies,
2nd Edition
978-1-1180-0730-3

Pre-Algebra Essentials
For Dummies
978-0-470-61838-7

Microsoft Office

Excel 2013 For Dummies
978-1-118-51012-4

Office 2013 All-in-One
For Dummies
978-1-118-51636-2

PowerPoint 2013
For Dummies
978-1-118-50253-2

Word 2013 For Dummies
978-1-118-49123-2

Music

Blues Harmonica
For Dummies
978-1-118-25269-7

Guitar For Dummies,
3rd Edition
978-1-118-11554-1

iPod & iTunes
For Dummies,
10th Edition
978-1-118-50864-0

Programming

Android Application
Development For
Dummies, 2nd Edition
978-1-118-38710-8

iOS 6 Application
Development For Dummies
978-1-118-50880-0

Java For Dummies,
5th Edition
978-0-470-37173-2

Religion & Inspiration

The Bible For Dummies
978-0-7645-5296-0

Buddhism For Dummies,
2nd Edition
978-1-118-02379-2

Catholicism For Dummies,
2nd Edition
978-1-118-07778-8

Self-Help & Relationships

Bipolar Disorder
For Dummies,
2nd Edition
978-1-118-33882-7

Meditation For Dummies,
3rd Edition
978-1-118-29144-3

Seniors

Computers For Seniors
For Dummies,
3rd Edition
978-1-118-11553-4

iPad For Seniors
For Dummies,
5th Edition
978-1-118-49708-1

Social Security
For Dummies
978-1-118-20573-0

Smartphones & Tablets

Android Phones
For Dummies
978-1-118-16952-0

Kindle Fire HD
For Dummies
978-1-118-42223-6

NOOK HD For Dummies,
Portable Edition
978-1-118-39498-4

Surface For Dummies
978-1-118-49634-3

Test Prep

ACT For Dummies,
5th Edition
978-1-118-01259-8

ASVAB For Dummies,
3rd Edition
978-0-470-63760-9

GRE For Dummies,
7th Edition
978-0-470-88921-3

Officer Candidate Tests,
For Dummies
978-0-470-59876-4

Physician's Assistant Exam
For Dummies
978-1-118-11556-5

Series 7 Exam
For Dummies
978-0-470-09932-2

Windows 8

Windows 8 For Dummies
978-1-118-13461-0

Windows 8 For Dummies,
Book + DVD Bundle
978-1-118-27167-4

Windows 8 All-in-One
For Dummies
978-1-118-11920-4

Available in print and e-book formats.